Images of the

First World War

a photographic anthology

- B -

Edited by

Balaguier Publications

cover photograph: Highlanders returning from the trenches, Longeuval, Somme, France, July 1916

First published in Great Britain in 2003 by Balaguier Publications

A CIP catalogue record for this book is available from the British Library.

ISBN 0-9544532-0-4

Printed in England by The Stationery Office Limited

Cover design: Tempo Graphic Design *text origination:* Celeritas - www.officialdtp.com

Balaguier Publications, 2 Fore Street, HA5 2HY

sales enquiries - e.mail: sales@balaguier.com

Images of the First World War

a photographic anthology

LIVES, WORDS – millions of each have been expended on the First World War. This book does not pass judgement, but draws on original photographs and illustrations from that period. Although not in its infancy, photography had nowhere near reached the sophisticated levels achieved today – in fact, the bravery of the photographers themselves frequently warrants credit.

This selection, in chronological order of publication, reflects life in Europe in the early years of the twentieth century from the allied perspective. Over sixty nations took part in the conflict but the involvement of a number of these is often overlooked. This anthology includes participants from across the globe, thereby providing a salient reminder.

This volume is insufficient to chronicle the whole of the conflict, but it does represent a significant part of the allied battles. The photographs are taken from contemporary publications of their day, enhanced where possible and retaining actual, or near translations, of the original texts and weekly News Reports, detailing stories that appeared in the European press. These, on a weekly basis, precede photographs that were published during the respective period.

Progress by troops may appear slow and numbers unbelievable by today's standards. Taking and retaking ground, simultaneous battles across Europe and other areas of the World - this was life then, with no rapid end in sight.

- NEWS REPORTS -

Tuesday August 18th, 1914

The Germans have moved back from Landen, in Belgium, on the line from Liege to Brussels. The Belgians wait patiently, anticipating a major attack.

A detailed report from General Joffre, chief-of-staff of the French army, in Vitry-Le-François (Champagne region) - holding the valley of the Vosges and a good part of the Lorraine; the Germans are retreating to the south of Sarrebourg.

Wednesday August 19th, 1914

In Belgium, the Germans are bombing Tirlemont, between Liege and Brussels and moving towards the north-east, causing the frightened population to flee towards Brussels and Antwerp. The German army appears to have turned east, approaching the outskirts of Antwerp.

The Germans have reached the river Meuse. The French cavalry has had some success in Florenville, Luxembourg. In Lorraine, allied soldiers hold a line between Seille, Chateaux-Salins, Dieuze, Delme and Morhange - important because it commands the route from Sarrebourg to Metz.

There is documented evidence proving that Germany is responsible for atrocities in Belgium and the French Lorraine showing that they ordered the burning of villages and deaths of civilians, etc.

Thursday August 20th, 1914

Cordial telegrams have been exchanged between King George V. and Mr. Poincaré, president of France.

The Germans reached the Dînant-Neufchateau line, in Belgium, east of the river Meuse. A German cavalry division has occupied Brussels. In Lorraine, allied troops have withdrawn to the line of the Marne-Rhine, forming a solid defence. Russian troops have toppled the Germans at Eydtkuhnen, taking the important city of Gumbinnen in Prussia.

Friday August 21st, 1914

Britain announces that a million soldiers are now under arms, with many due to embark for the continent.

In Belgium, the Belgian army has established trenches around Antwerp with the German cavalry fast approaching. Germans are also gathering near Namur and moving towards the French border.

The Serbians have just inflicted a new defeat on the Austrians. The battle was important, since 300,000 men took part - 150,000 on each side.

Saturday August 22nd, 1914

The withdrawal of allied troops has become more urgent in Lorraine. There have been serious losses, but the enemy equally underwent losses. The German advance has been stopped to the north of Lunéville in Lorraine. This is of secondary importance though, as all the interest is on Belgium where they are fighting the British army.

News from the High Alsace is good, with the Vosges held by French troops. The success of the Serbians and Russians has been confirmed. The Czar's troops have now landed in Galicia. In Prussia, they are past Gumbinnen. Japan is ready to attack Kiao-Tcheou in China.

Sunday August 23rd, 1914

The Germans 12th and 14th army corps, are moving from Liege and Arlon, through Brussels, toward the river Sambre. The British and French troops are carrying out an offensive on the whole front in this region. In Lorraine, withdrawal has become necessary again. Luneville has been occupied by the enemy. A Zeppelin has been shot down, close to Mallonviller. The Belgian army, entrenched at Antwerp with 250,000 men, is fighting with the Germans.

The Russians are pursuing the German army at Gumbinnen and are now entering Insterburg where 350,000 inhabitants desperately need supplies and munitions. Insterburg is 62 kilometres (38 miles) inside Prussian territory. The German troops in this region seem to be scattering and at least 8,000 prisoners have been taken. The daily progress of the Russians is significant. Commanded by Grand Duke General Nicolas, the Russian army in Prussia is seven times larger than the German. The Slavs in the north are moving successfully against the Slavs (the Serbians) of the south. The Montenegrins have advanced, again, against Hercegovina.

Monday August 24th, 1914

The battle continues in Belgium. With a new Russian thrust, the Czar's armies are now moving out of Poland, some 180 kilometres (110 miles) to the west of Insterburg, and now threaten the front at Dantzig. The Serbians have inflicted new and serious defeats on the Austrians.

The illness of François Joseph, the King of Albania, has been denied. The hostilities have begun between Japan and Germany as the Germans refused to evacuate Kiao-Tcheou. It will not be long before Japan takes this city.

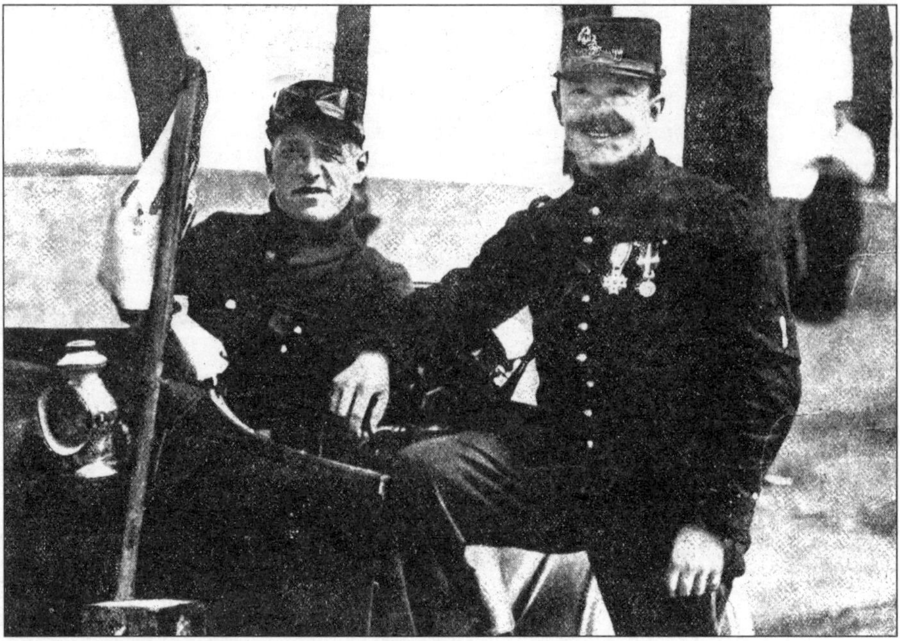

French aviator Pégoud who bombed and destroyed two German convoys

Pégoud, already famous for destroying the German convoys, with his assistant Monternier, on the way to Paris to collect another plane. The last having been riddled with bullets.

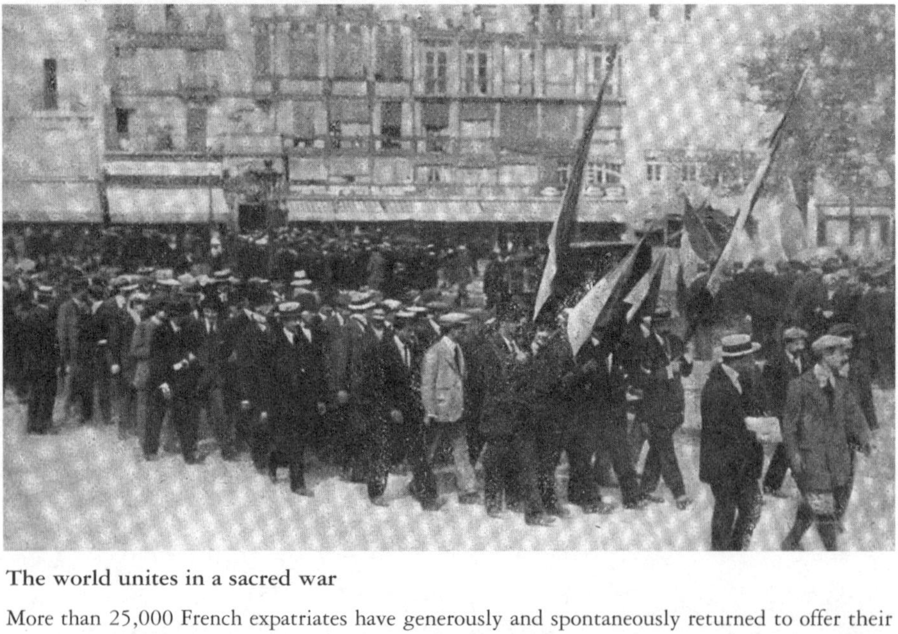

The world unites in a sacred war

More than 25,000 French expatriates have generously and spontaneously returned to offer their support and courage to France, their second homeland. Those include people from Italy, Greece, Switzerland, The Alsace (Lorraine), England, America, all have returned and are enthusiastically enrolling. Here, cheered on by the Parisian population while parading.

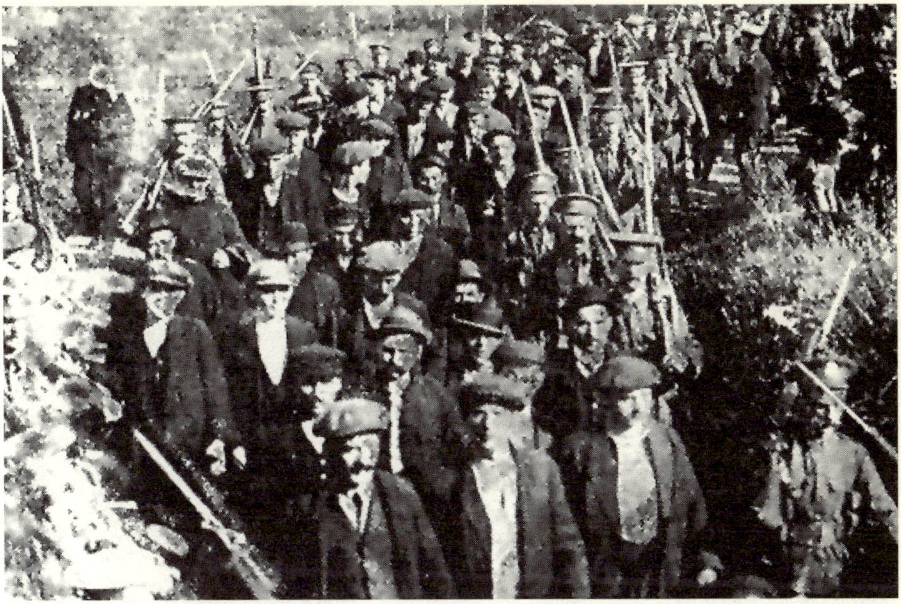

German subjects under internment

In England, Germans have been marched toward the cities of the north-east under armed escort. Similar events are happening in France where German residents from Paris have been moved to the west, away from the battles.

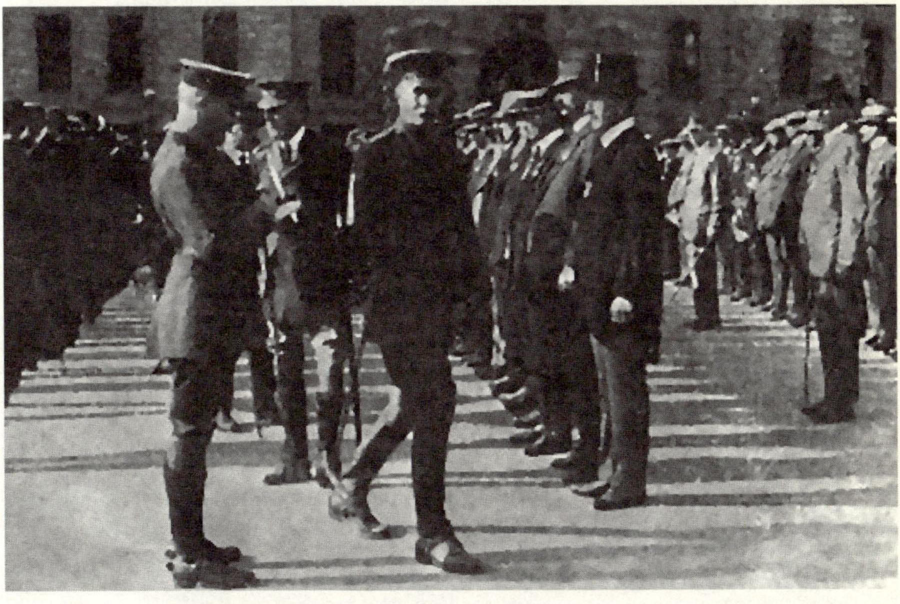

General Bethune inspecting the volunteers

In England, former civil servants and colonial soldiers have formed a special regiment that will soon be ready to fight. The sight of these gentlemen and former troopers, some tanned under the African sun, shows their determination.

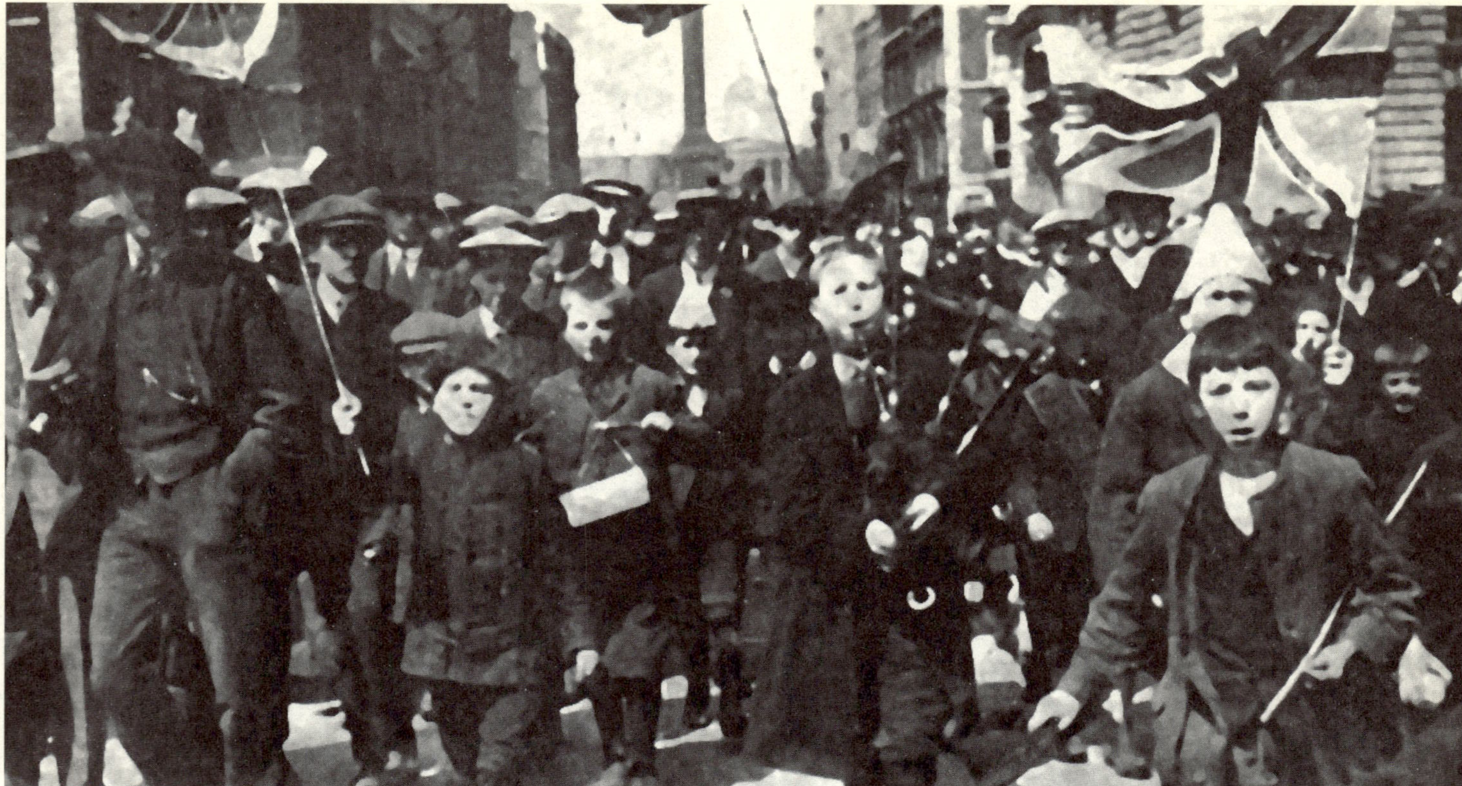

Passionate demonstrations in England in front of the War Office

The British stiff upper lip is sometimes dropped. This photograph proves the point that war is popular on both sides of the Channel, with flag waving children going to cheer departing soldiers at the station.

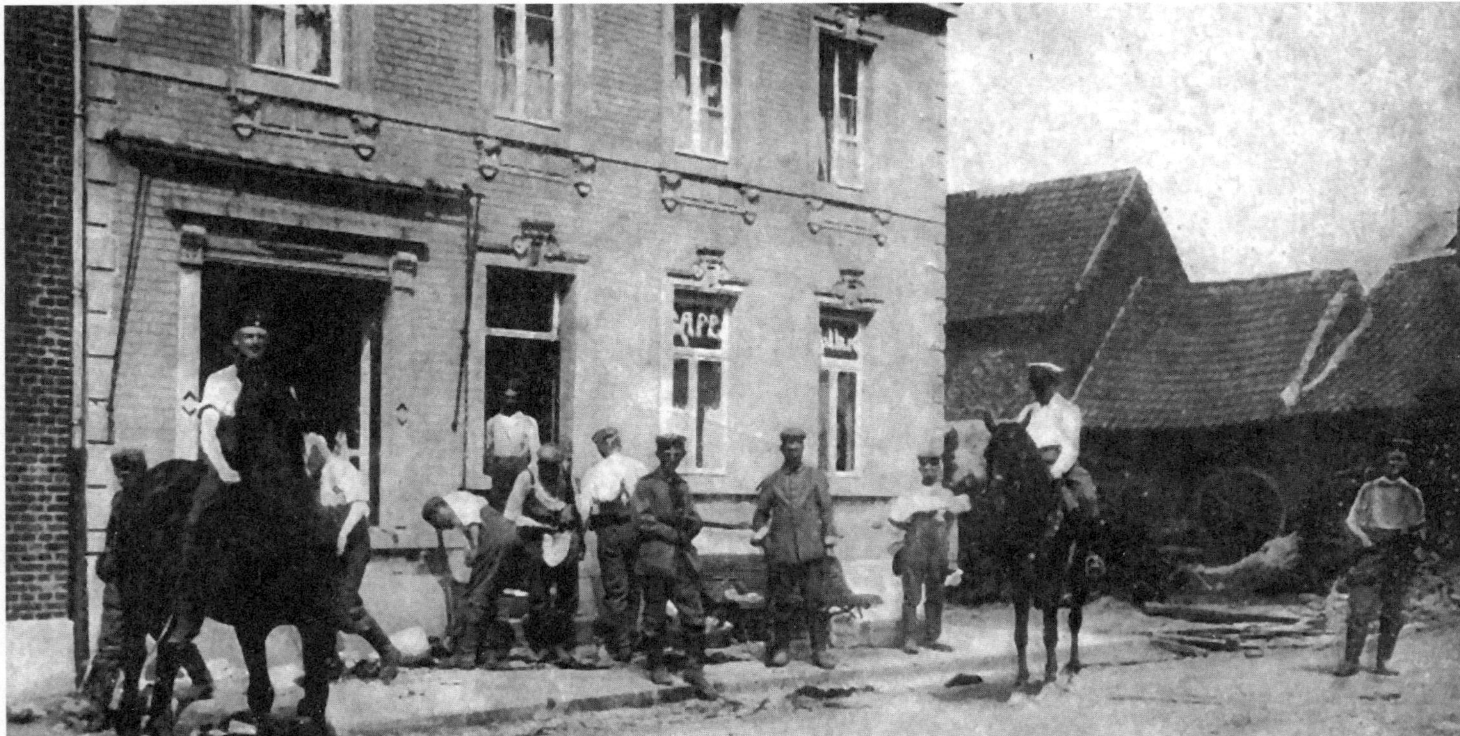

German hordes ravage Belgium

The small village of Mouland, situated on the Dutch-Belgian border, ten kilometres south of Maëstricht, and fifteen from Liege, has been devastated by the Germans, despite the inhabitants offering no resistance. They have systematically robbed, burnt the houses and brutalised the country folk. Here they are photographed raiding an inn - although they don't seem to appreciate the wines and strong liqueurs. All of the inhabitants have fled.

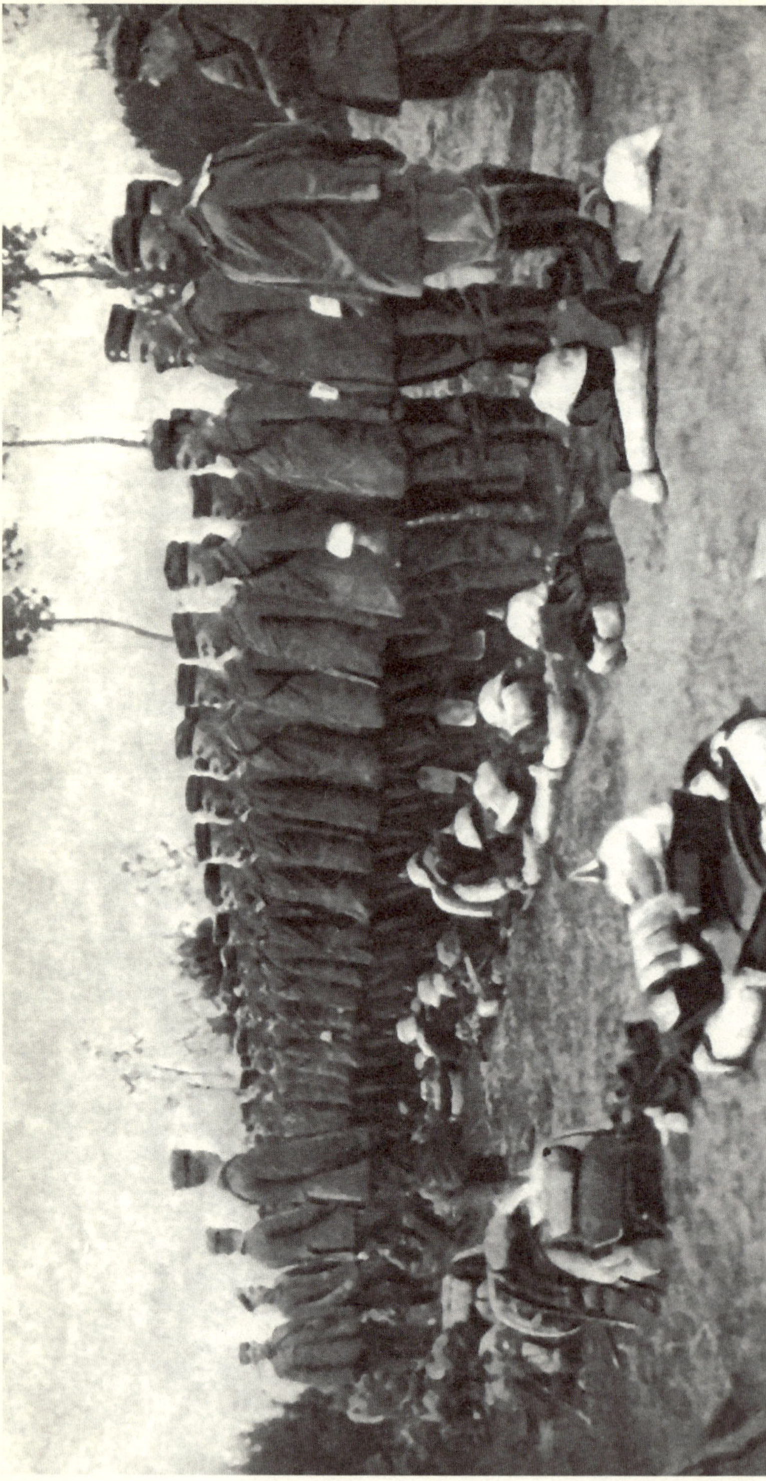

German troops after the battle and subsequent fires at the village of Mouland

The German officers, far from stopping their men from acting illegally (contrary to the laws of the war), actually encouraged acts of barbarism. Irrefutable documents, found on prisoners, establish that the German commanders oversaw these actions before setting fire to the houses.

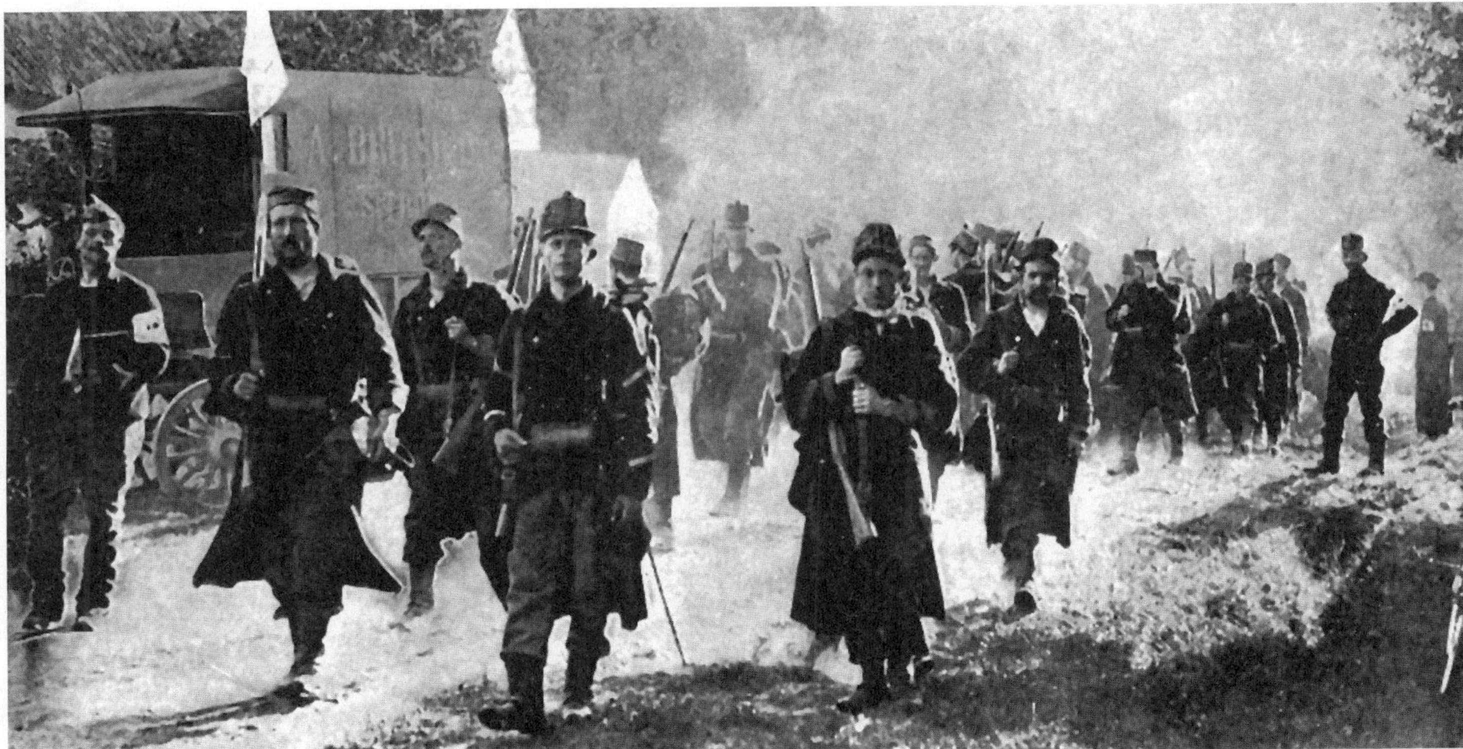

The Belgian army pulls back into Antwerp

After having heroically defended the first attack, the Belgians - who had allowed the French and English troops to concentrate behind their lines, folded back toward the northeast, following a plan established well in advance. The national army retreated into the trenches at Antwerp taking a dangerous flank position against the German troops. Here we see infantry soldiers walking back after a battle.

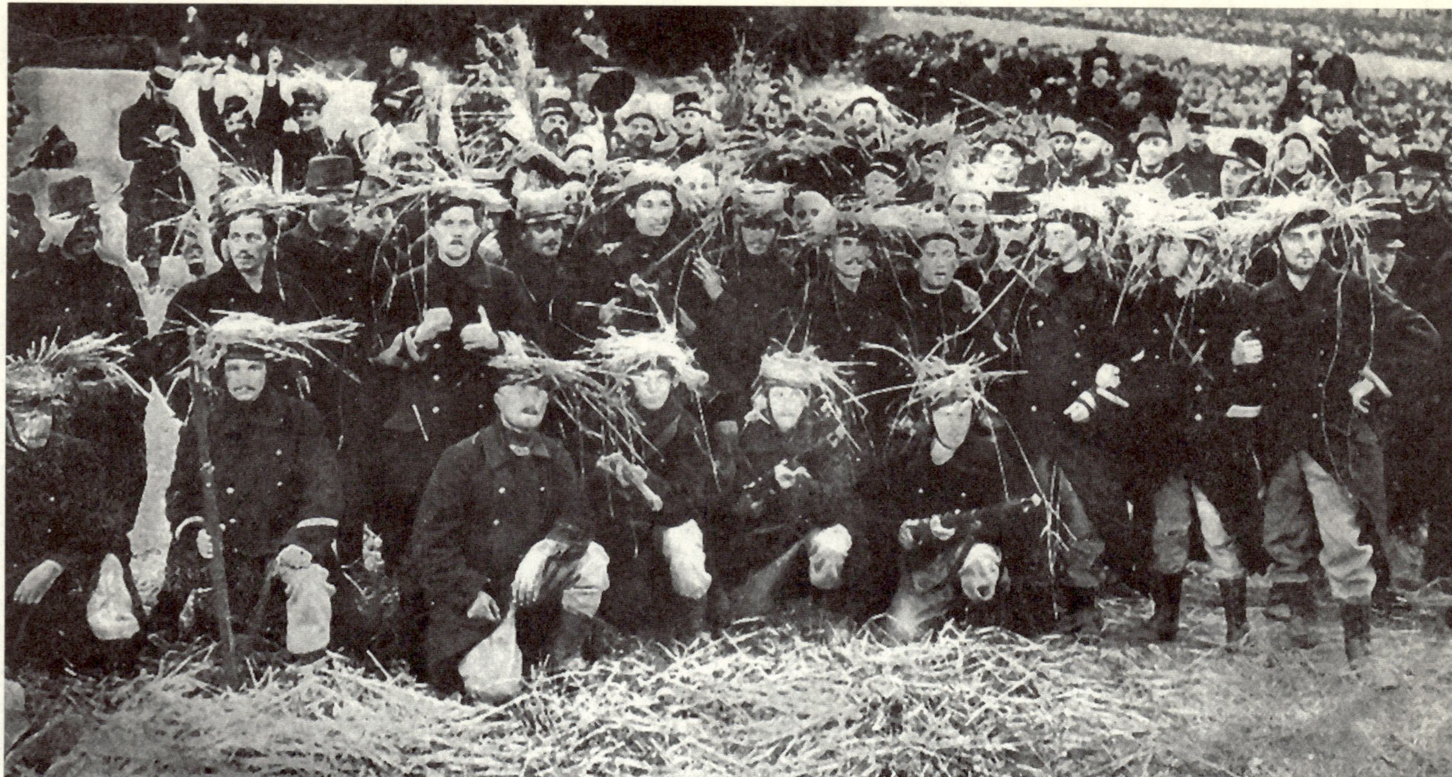

Belgians camouflage themselves with straw in the fields

Moving rapidly, the soldiers often hide in the fields amongst the crops - out of sight of the enemy, sometimes covering themselves in straw.

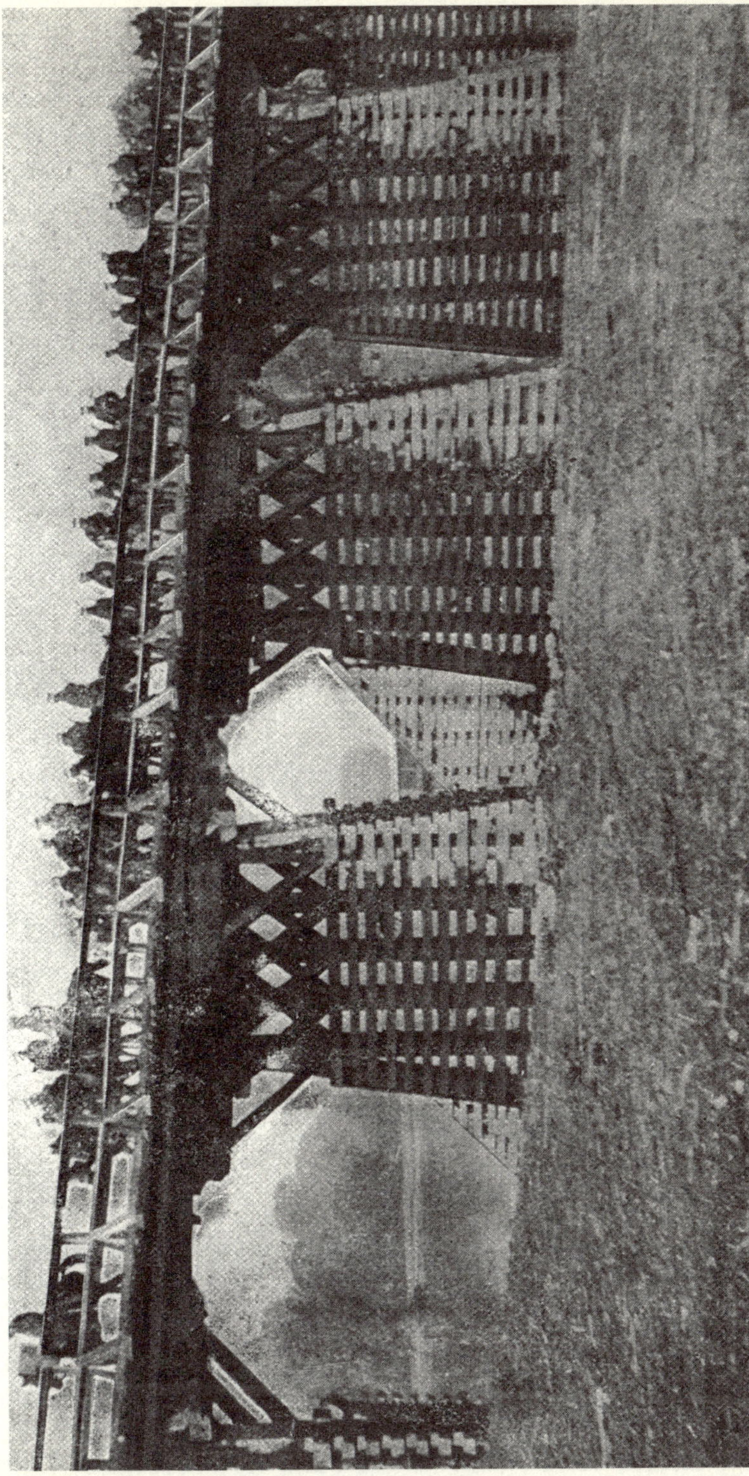

The heroic Serbian cavalry crosses the Drina en mass

The Serbian Army commanded by the French, has just pushed back the Tzar in Bosnia, entering Louzita and Ledmitz - a crushing victory against the Austrians that has cost the lives of 150,000 men. Although fighting six against one, the Serbians took 10,000 prisoners, attacking batteries of artillery. The Serbians are the new masters of the area surrounding the Drina.

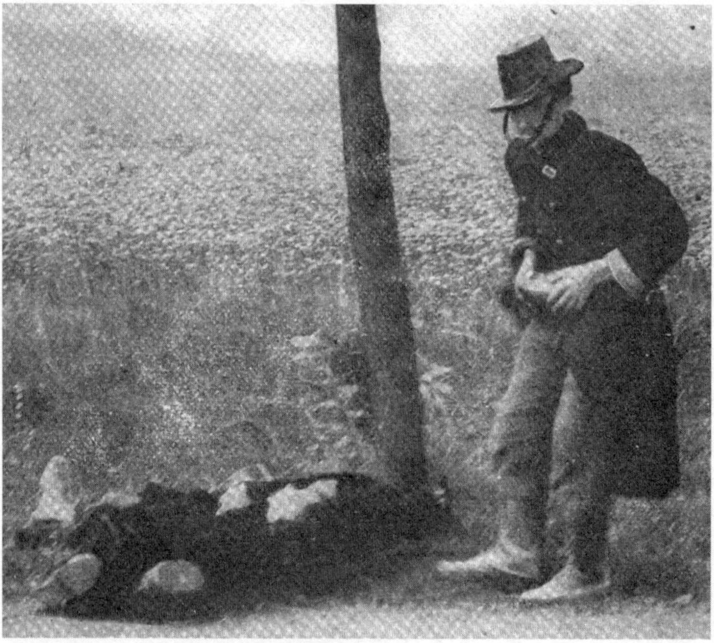

Police officer helps his wounded friend

The task of the reporters and photographers is especially difficult and sometimes compromising. At the side of the road, close to Namur, a Belgian police officer has just found a severely wounded friend.

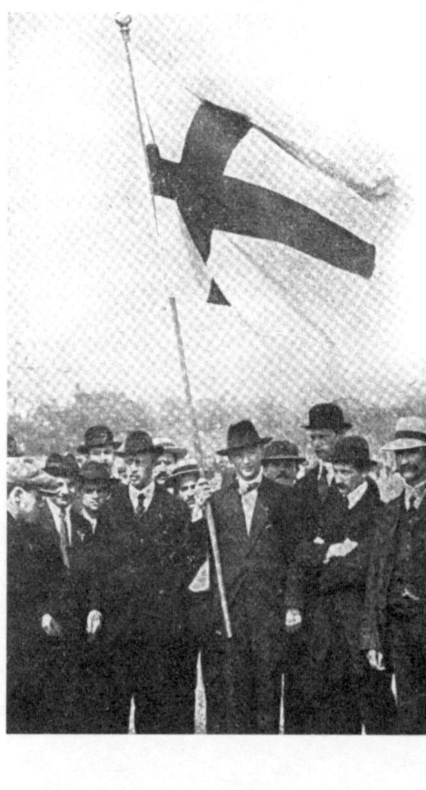

The Swedish volunteers

The generous Swedes have provided a legion of volunteers. A very important contingent, here they are assembling after their journey to France.

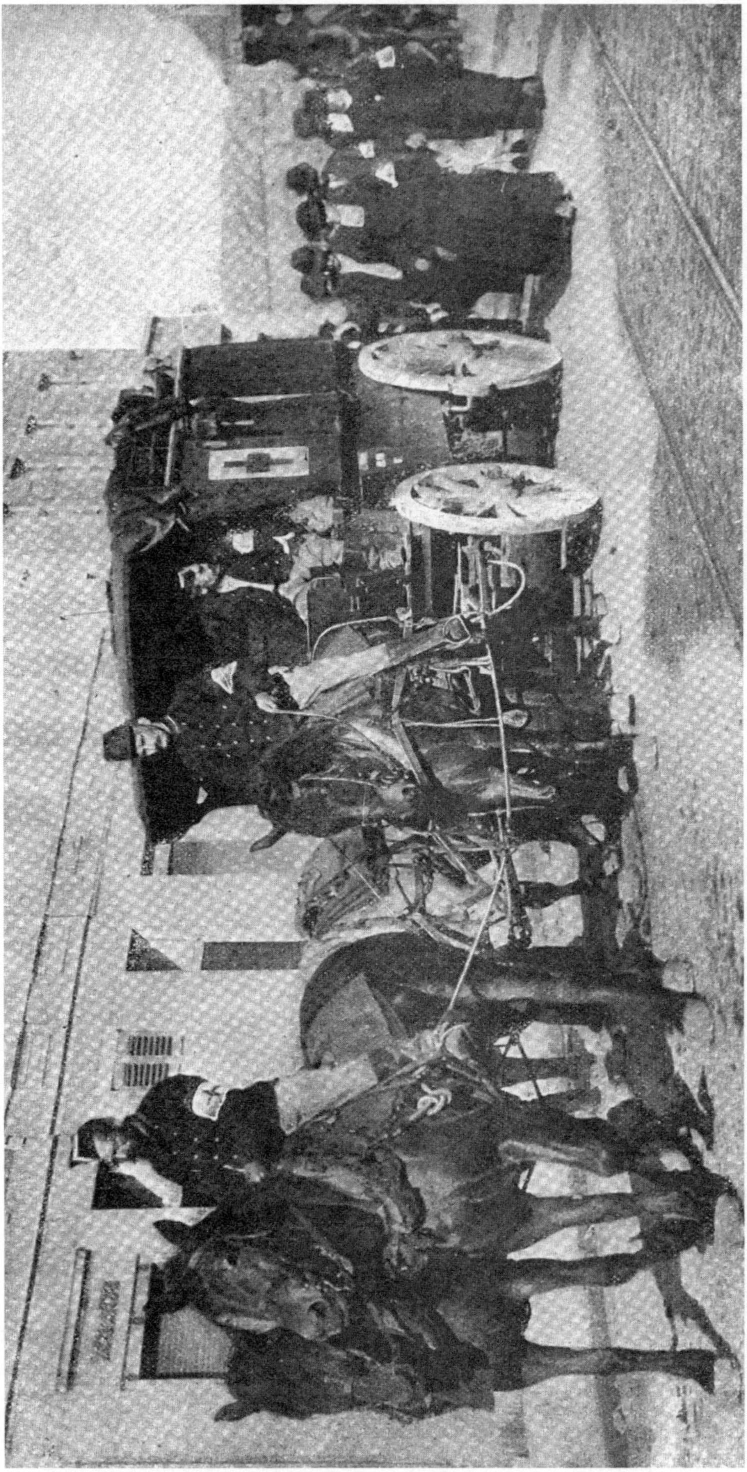

A convoy of wounded being evacuated

As the German hordes continue to invade Belgium, the wounded have to be evacuated over greater distances. This is how several convoys were moving in the north of France. The heroic soldiers, wounded near Liege, accept their sufferings and show unbelievable patience. This is a convoy of the Red Cross escorted by military chaplains.

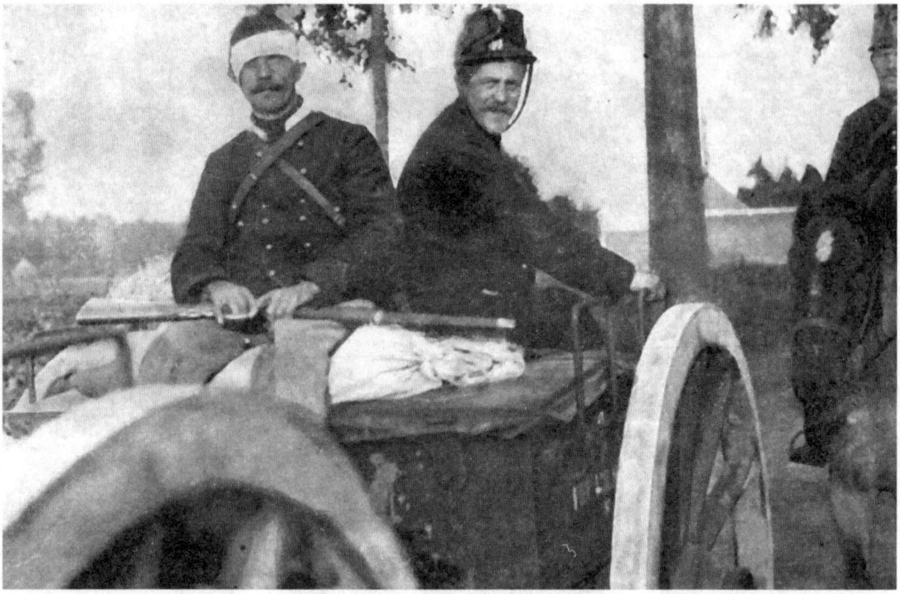

A wounded gunner determined to fight on

The state of mind of the wounded men is excellent. The soldiers in the ambulances often complain, not of their injuries, but of not being able to continue fighting! Here is one of thousands, a magnificent example of courage. The Belgian gunner seen here seated on a gun carriage had been severely injured on the front at the battle of Hoelen. He should have withdrawn to Antwerp, but he refused to leave.

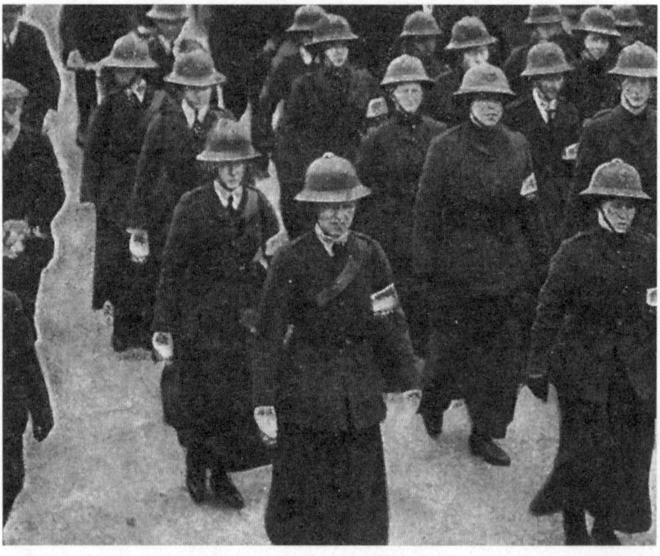

The British ambulance women marching like troopers

The English suffragettes, feminists of yesterday, are the women at the front today. As the ambulance women of the Red Cross, the Nursing Yeomanry proves their worth. Organized militarily, these ladies are now in the service of their country.

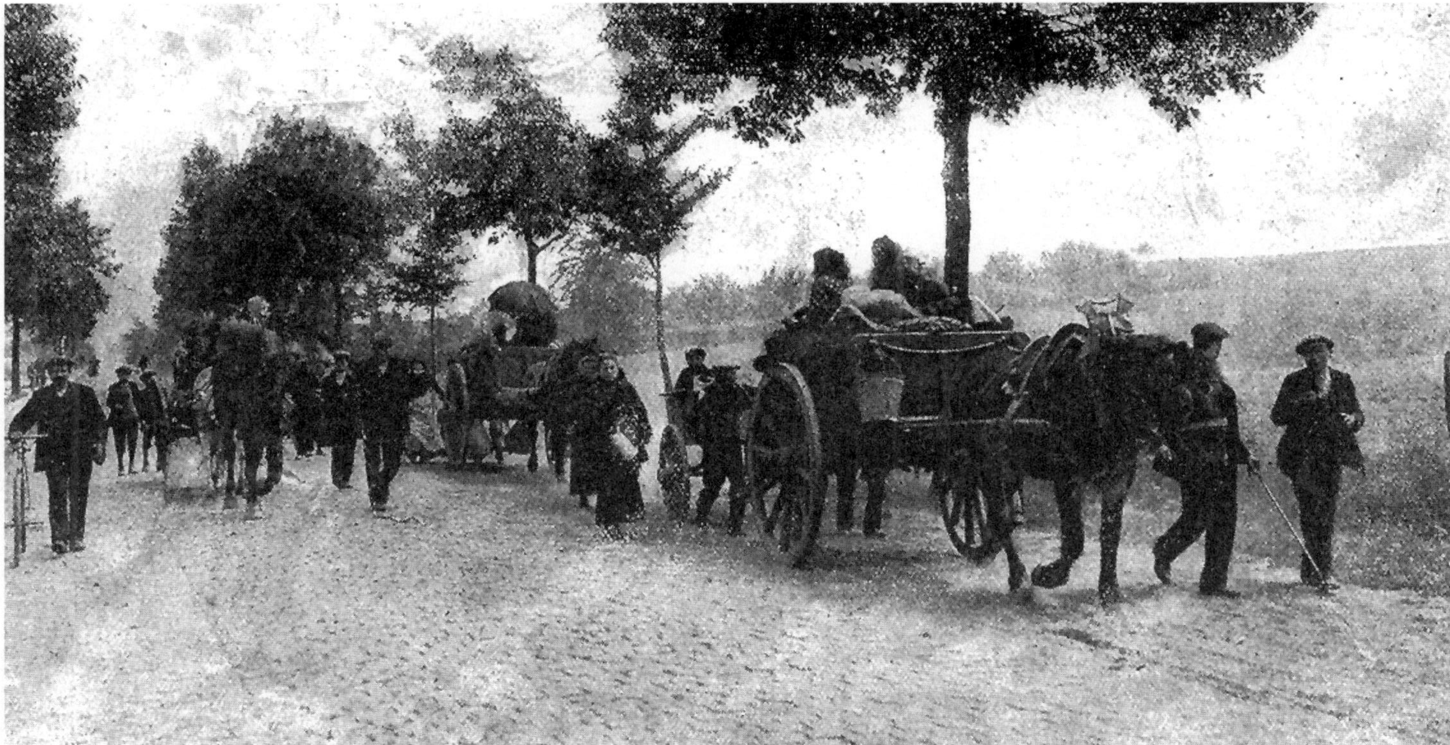

The exodus of Belgian country folk - the inhabitants move hastily before Germans arrive

Aware of the advance of the German barbarians towards their village, the Belgians abandon their houses quickly and flee in large numbers. Heaping their precious possessions in carts, many hand drawn, they move north. Many also cram into trains to reach the French border. All of these poor people remain strangely quiet in their misfortune and prayers.

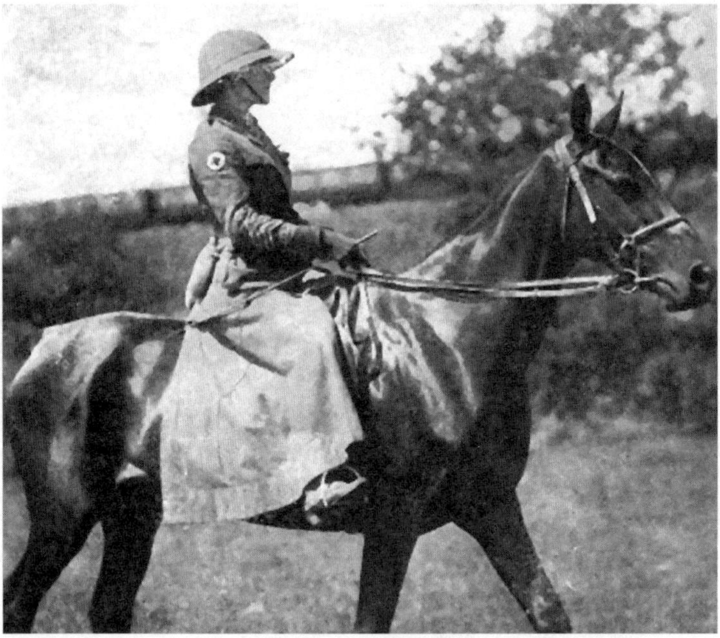

An ambulance women on horseback

The chiefs of the "Nursing Yeomanry" can inspect their staff quickly on horseback, out of the line of fire and moving easily around the cities and countryside.

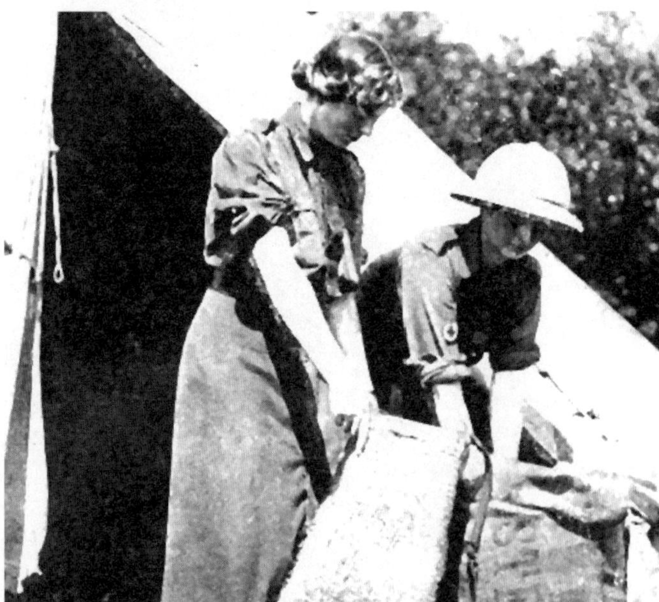

The nurses take care of the provisions

The ambulance women don't have to resort to men for help - even if their work is very laborious. They live in tents, feed and attend to the horses and also manage the kitchens.

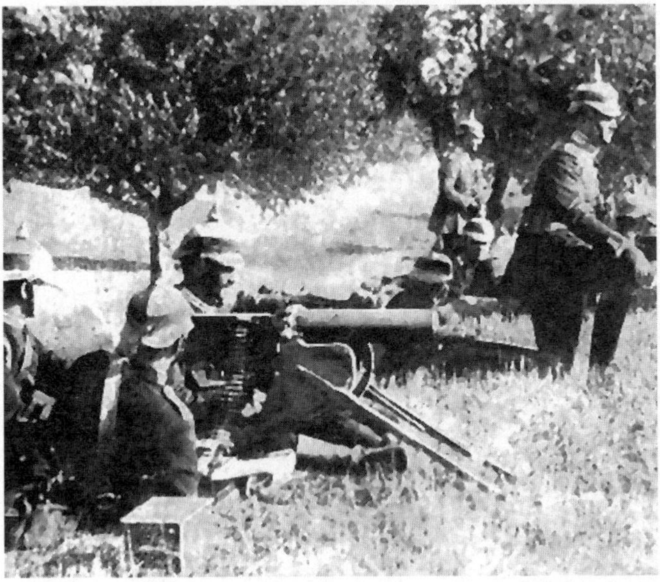

German machine guns in action

If the artillery of the enemy is distinctly less efficient than that of the allies, we must recognize that their machine guns are excellent and that they know how to make good use of them. However, this machine gunner didn't succeed in worrying the allied troops too much!

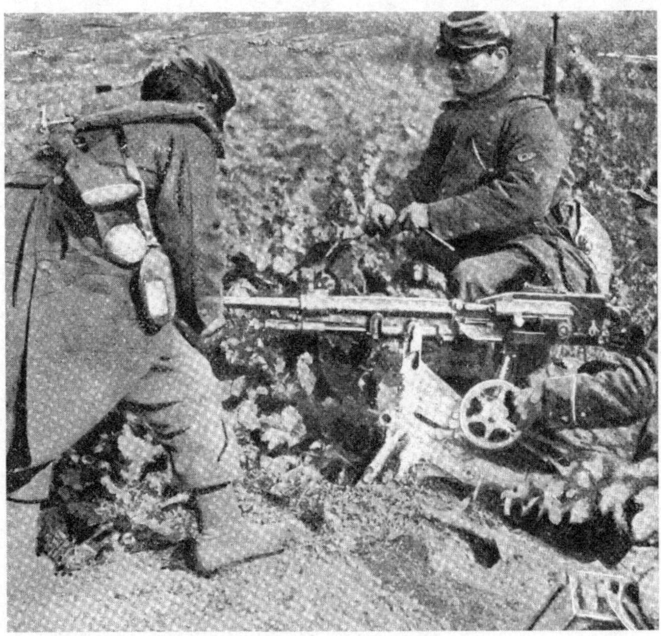

A French machine gun in action

The lightness of the French gun permits rapid dismantling and movement although it is a particularly dangerous weapon. Its speed of manoeuvre is of great benefit to the infantry.

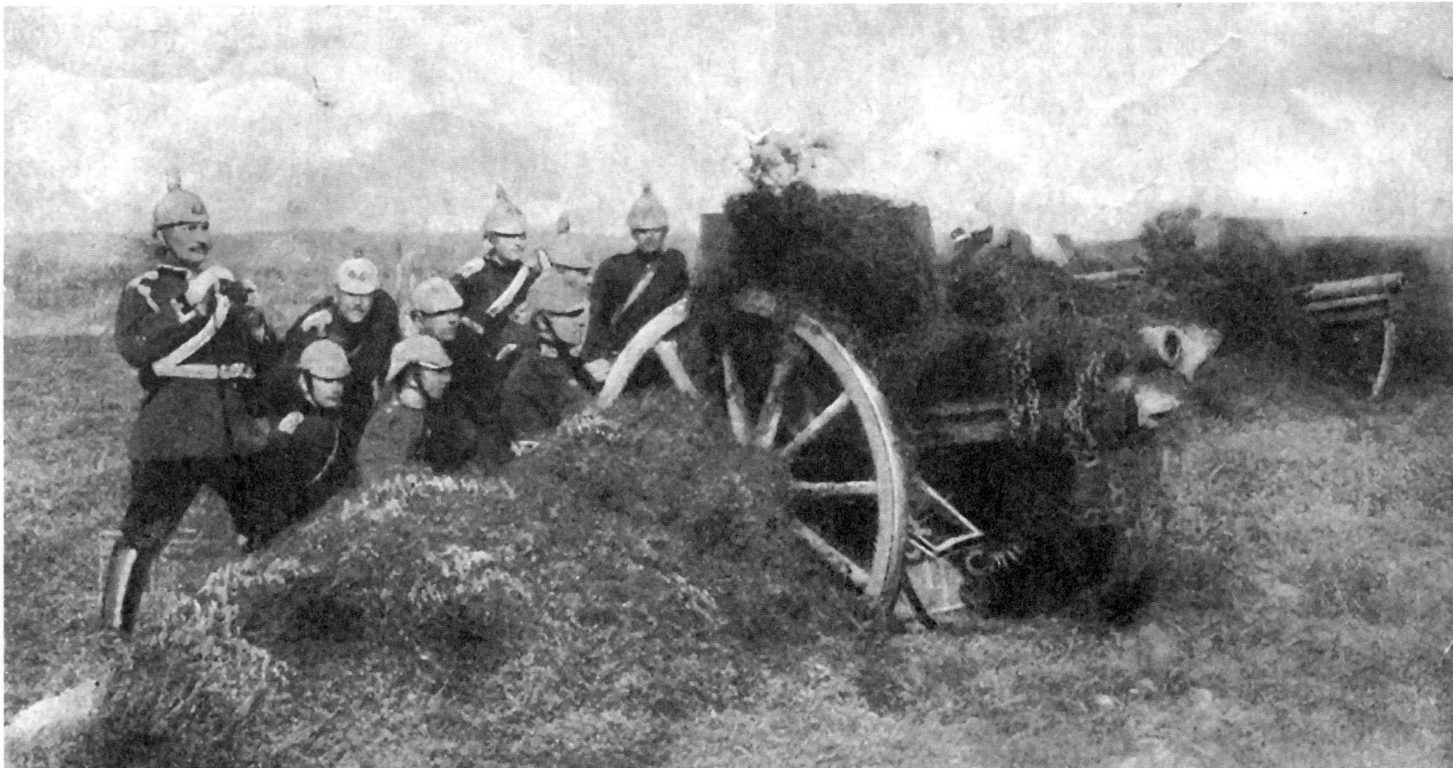

A battery of German light artillery trying to conceal themselves in a field of clover

Of similar calibre to allied 3" guns, this German light artillery is not very effective. It's carriage moves haphazardly after every firing, requiring realignment for every shot - a significant waste of time. The German gunners, too, are very mediocre and their shooting lacks accuracy. Additionally, a large majority of German shells don't explode properly, causing only petty damage.

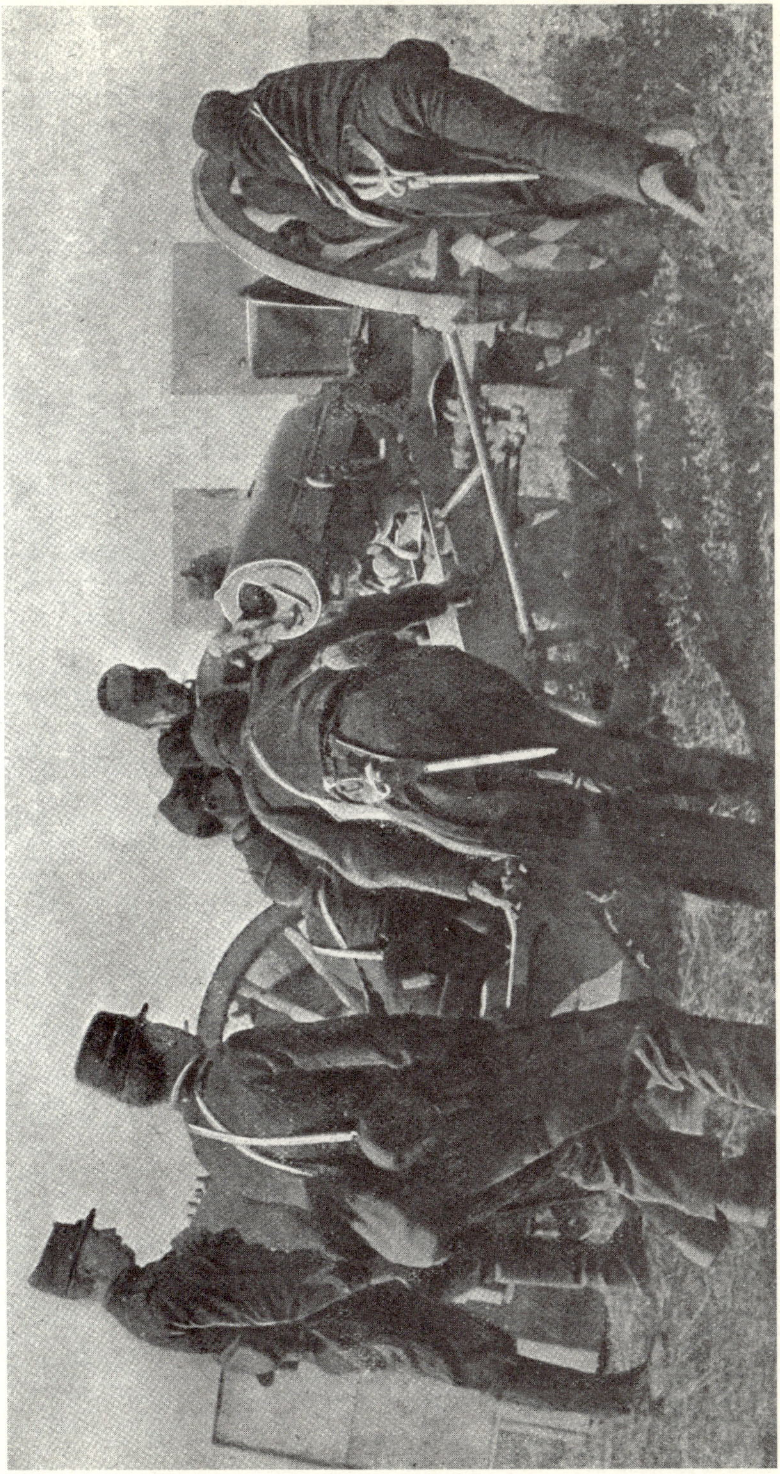

Serbian gunners positioning a 3" gun

Speed of loading is essential during major conflicts. These Serbians are involved in an artillery attack.

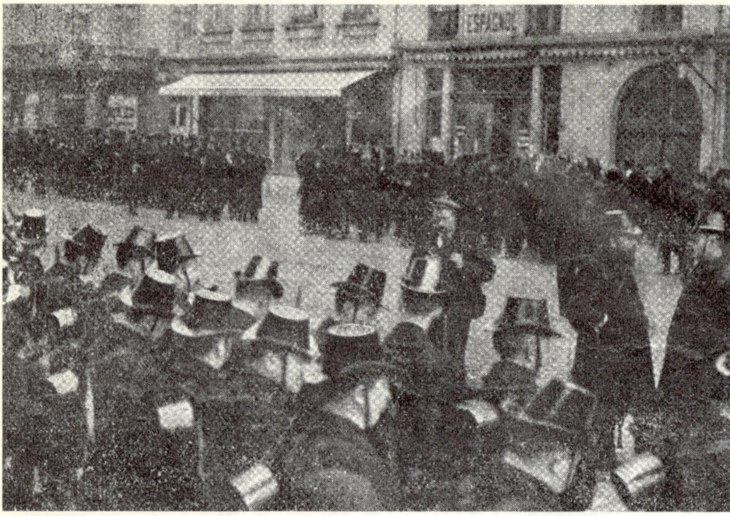

Belgium during the German invasion: Antwerp: Rue de Anvers

Since the government and the Belgian armies have retreated to Antwerp, the city has remained curiously active, despite the situation.

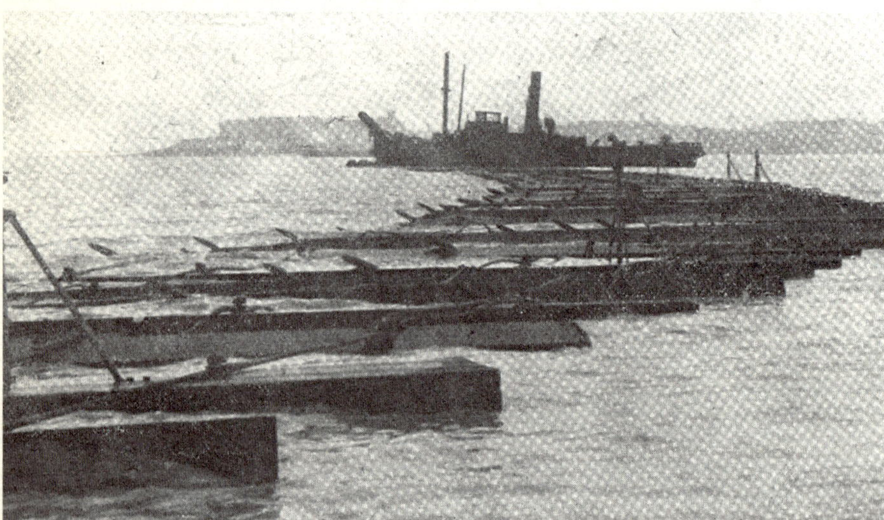

The Thames defence barrage

The Thames is blocked by a string of rafts, making a very dangerous gateway for any German destroyers that try to approach southern England.

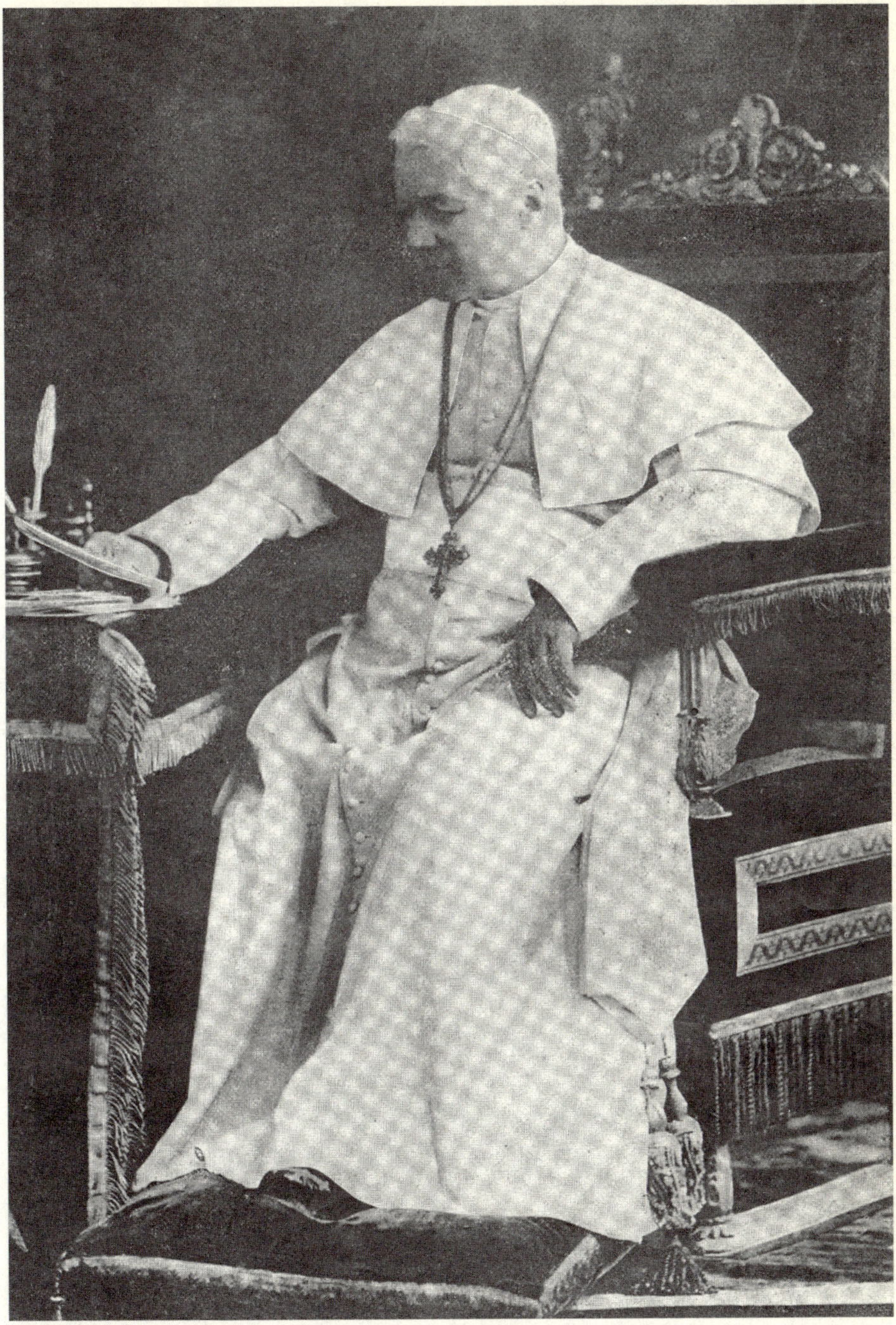

Death of the sixty-fourth Pope

A photograph of the Pope at work in the Vatican. Pope Pie X died on August 20th in Rome. From Riese, in the province of Trevise, he became patriarch of Venice in 1892. In August 9, 1903, he succeeded Léon XIII on the throne of Saint Peter's; Pie X leaves a brother and three sisters who were with him as he died.

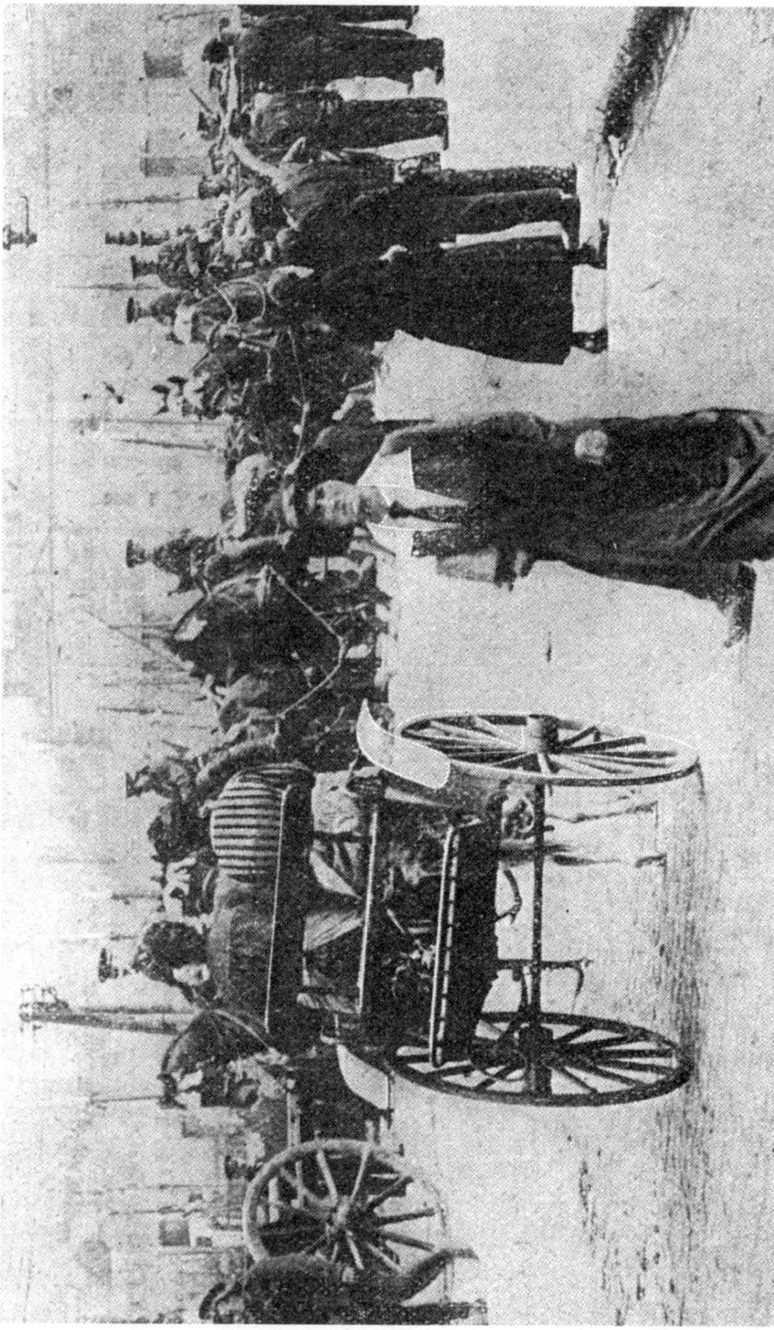

British artillery regiments disembark at Boulogne

British infantry, cavalry and artillery regiments disembark non-stop in both France and in Belgium. There are already 200,000 men at the front and more keep arriving.

- NEWS REPORTS -

Tuesday October 12th, 1914

Official bulletins suggest that the situation remains satisfactory, the enemy has not progressed and allied forces have won some new ground. The Germans only managed to take the outskirts of the city of Antwerp. The Russian troops took Vistule, and engaged the German army near Warsaw.

The Austro-Hungarian government, probably at the request of the German headquarters, has decided to change five of its army commanders. A confession of defeat, highlighted now that the Russian army has penetrated into Transylvania.

The Italian Foreign Minister, Mr. San Giuliano is seriously ill.

Wednesday October 14th, 1914

Considerable allied progress between Albert and Arras; to the east of Reims in the Argonne and in the High Meuse.

French cavalry took offensive action in the regions of Hazebrouck and Béthune against reinforced enemy detachments. A German army battalion has occupied Lille, which was previously defended by a territorial detachment. A German submarine has collided with the Russian cruiser Pallada, 7,800 tons, in the Baltic.

The fighting is getting heavier between the Russians and Austro-Germans near Warsaw. Prince Oleg, son of Grand Duke Constantine of Russia, wounded on the battlefield in Oriental Prussia, has died. The Montenegrins have inflicted serious injuries on the Austrians near Sarajevo. The Belgian government has temporarily moved to Le Havre.

Thursday October 15th, 1914

French and British planes have bombed Carlsruhe in south-western Germany, near the river Rhine. In the Spanish newspapers, a report that in Essen, Germany they are taking precautions against the possibility of British air raids. Serious losses around Ghent, Belgium - the German troops having entered the city, while the British forces have taken Ypres, after heavy fighting. German communiqués are endeavouring to sweeten the situation with their cavalry in the north, and their attacks on Verdun, but they have not actually recorded any success!

German troops are advancing towards the river Vistule, in Poland, but Russian troops have them strongly pressed down and have taken a number of prisoners. Two of the German submarines that had attacked and sunk, the cruiser Pallada in the Baltic have collided. The Cossacks have captured a Zeppelin near Warsaw. They brought it down intact with its crew, in the Polish capital.

In Italy, the foreign minister, Mr. San Giuliano will cede responsibility to the President, Mr. Salandra. The Serbians have attacked Austrians who tried to clear a route near the river Save. The hunt for the murderers of the heir of Austria, François-Ferdinand, has begun in Sarajevo.

Friday October 16th, 1914

The enemy has pulled back to the left of Lys and allied troops have advanced between Arras and Albert. Several kilometres have been won back surrounding Reims. Progress also in Woëvre and the High Meuse. In Belgium, German troops moved west from Antwerp, reaching Bruges. The Belgian government has expressed its appreciation of Holland assuring shelter to the Belgians being evacuated from Antwerp.

The Russians beat the Austrians and took many prisoners to the south of Przemysl, near the eastern border of Poland - contrary to the wording of the official bulletins issued by the government in Berlin. Warsaw will now become the focus of Russian action and is heavily defended. The military correspondents of the Berlin newspapers, finally, now recognise the difficulties of their country against Russia. The Montenegrins have inflicted a new defeat on the Austro-Hungarian troops in the fields of Sarajevo.

Japan has just agreed a humanitarian approach with Germany, deciding that the bombardment of Tsing-Tao, in China, would only begin once the civil population have evacuated the city.

Boer, Colonel Maritz, has rebelled against the government of the South-African union, as he is loath to organize the defence of the north-east border against the Germans from the neighbouring colony. He has taken command of the Germanic supporters in the region and Martial Law has been proclaimed in the Cape colony, despite the Boers showing sincere loyalty.

Saturday October 17, 1914

The cruiser British Hawke 7,300 tons, with 420 crew, was sunk by German submarine number 49, in the North Sea. A combined British, Belgian and French force have engaged the enemy near the Belgian border at Dunkerque and are understood to have occupied the whole area between Ypres and the sea, keeping back the enemy towards the direction of Lille. The number of Belgians sheltering in England has grown considerably and may now be 200,000.

The Russians continue to advance along the Vistule, towards Warsaw and the shelling of Przemysl has been non-stop, despite world-wide news reports transmitted by German radio stations.

The Serbo-Montenegrins announced that they took 150,000 Austrians on the approaches to Sarajevo. Mr. di San Giuliano, Italian Foreign Minister, has died following a heart attack. Mr. Salandra, president, has interim control of his ministry. There is talk of an overhaul of the whole Italian cabinet. Mr. Jagow, German foreign minister, has given an interview to the Italian press suggesting Russia take responsibility for the war, but the Italian press vigorously refutes this.

The Goeben and the Breslau, German cruisers that were taking refuge in Constantinople since the beginning of hostilities, have now moved into the Black Sea with the Russian fleet in pursuit.

Sunday October 18, 1914

The British have taken the town of Fronielles, to the southwest of Lille. A British flotilla, composed of one light cruiser Undaunted, and four destroyers has sunk four German destroyers off Holland. The Anglo-French naval squadron, operating in the Adriatic, sunk an Austrian torpedo boat.

The bombardment of Cattaro continues (near the border of Italy and Herzegovinia). The Russian navy, following the German example, has placed a number of mines in the Baltic Sea. Austria and its ally Germany, have taken control of the supply of cereals, vegetables and flour. The Japanese took Kiao-Tcheou, the hill that dominates Tsin-Tao in China. A party of Boer soldiers that was rebelling in the Cape, under colonel Maritz, was captured.

Monday October 19, 1914

Armentières has been reoccupied by the French and they also advanced to the north of Arras, acquiring a much stronger position. Each time the Germans attacked, they were vigorously driven back.

In the neutral countries, including Switzerland, it is noticeable that the press ironically comments that Germany no longer announces progress in France. Still no news from Petrograd - another phase of this long battle in Poland. We know that the Austrians have been driven back in Galicia, and that the Russians have captured many prisoners to the south of Przemysl.

The Belgian chancellor, Bethmann-Hollweg, went to make a report to Guillaume II (Kaiser Wilhelm II) on the situation. Several neutral states, Sweden and Norway especially, have just reinforced their laws against any possible war contraband. They do not want their impartiality compromised.

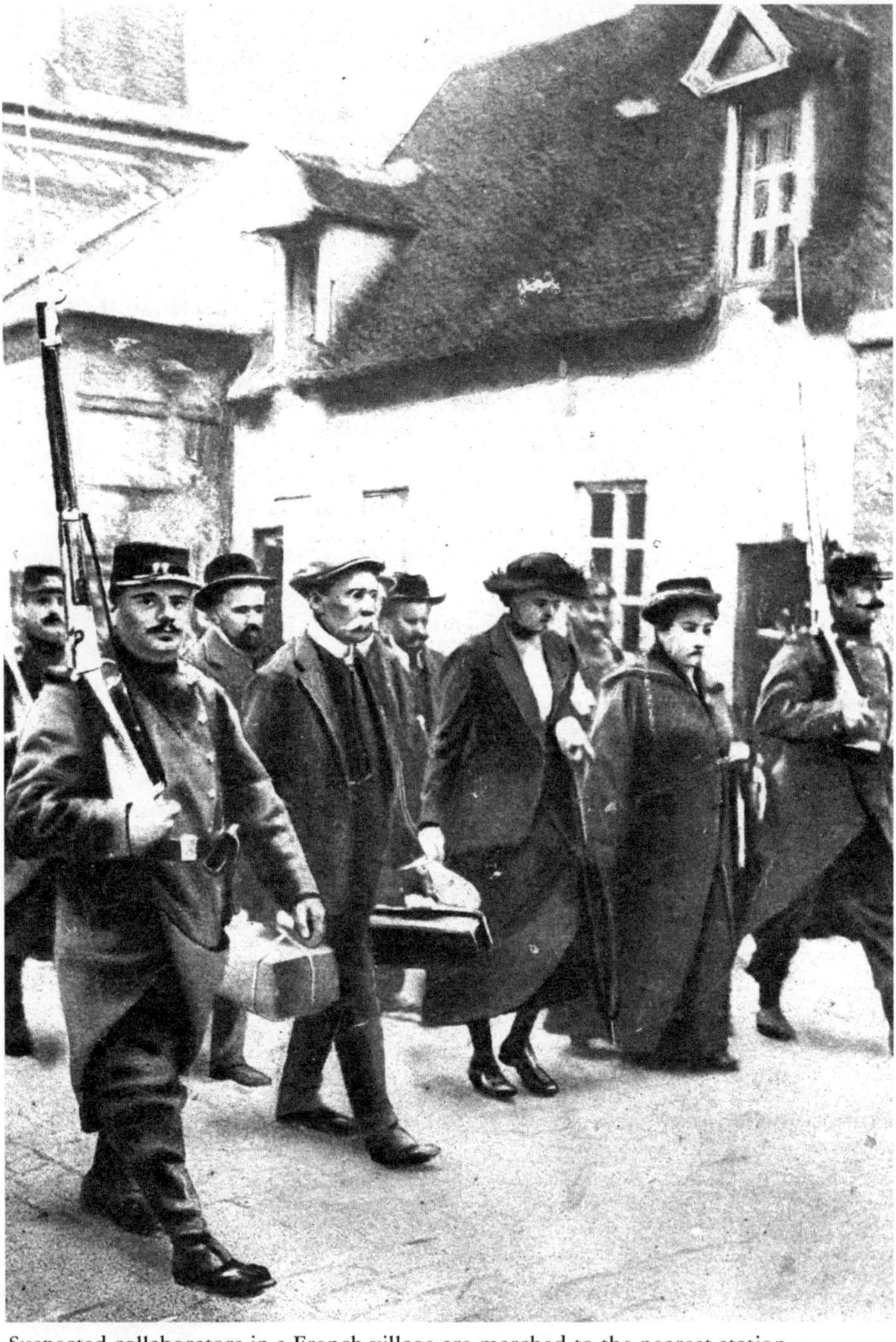

Suspected collaborators in a French village are marched to the nearest station

Since the beginning of the war, collaborators in England, France and Belgium have been traced. As soon as possible, they are rounded up and escorted away, where they can do no harm.

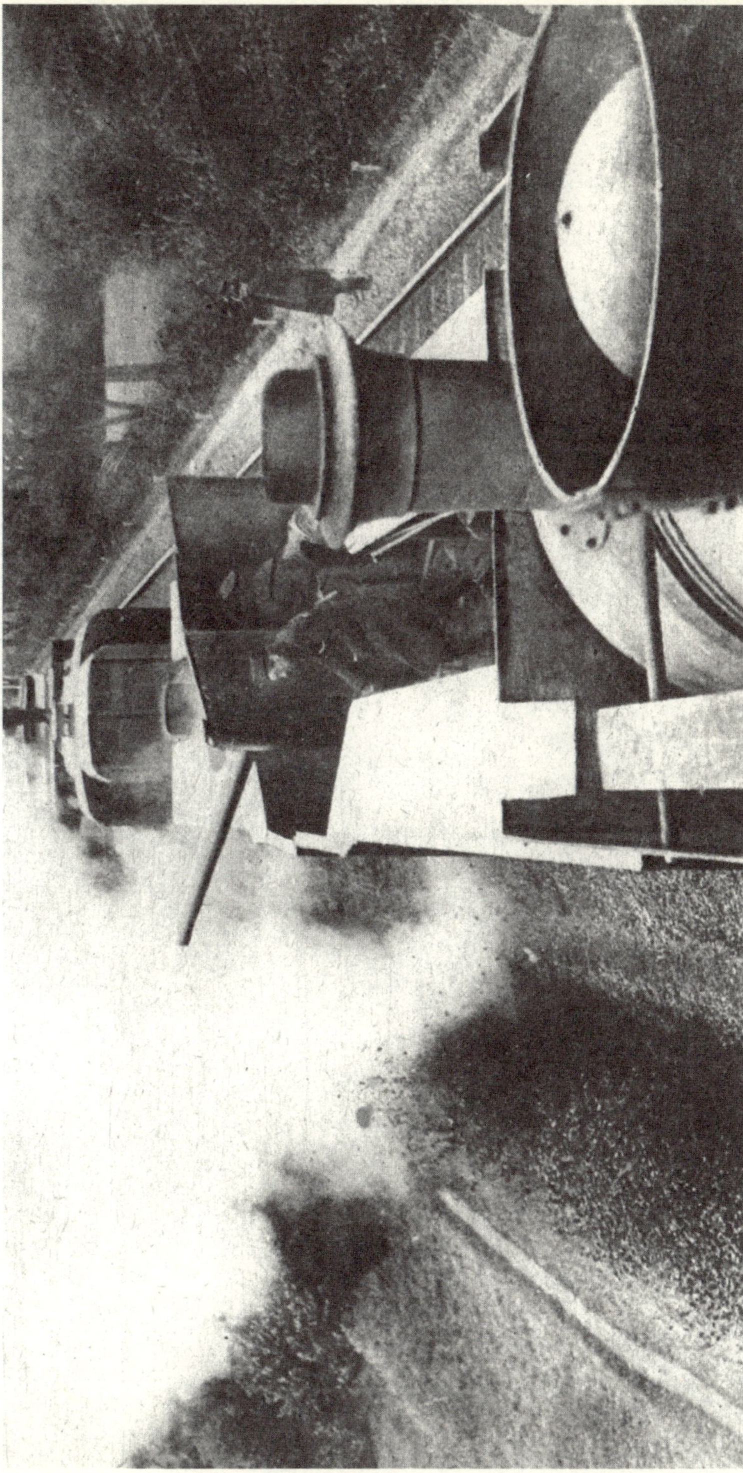

In full battle: an armoured train stops to fire its guns

Here is a photograph that testifies to the foolhardiness of newspaper photographers. Having stopped near hostile lines, the convoy has just fired its guns on the German trenches. The attack was as sudden as unforeseen. With bullers still flying, the train, unscathed, moves rapidly to a new position.

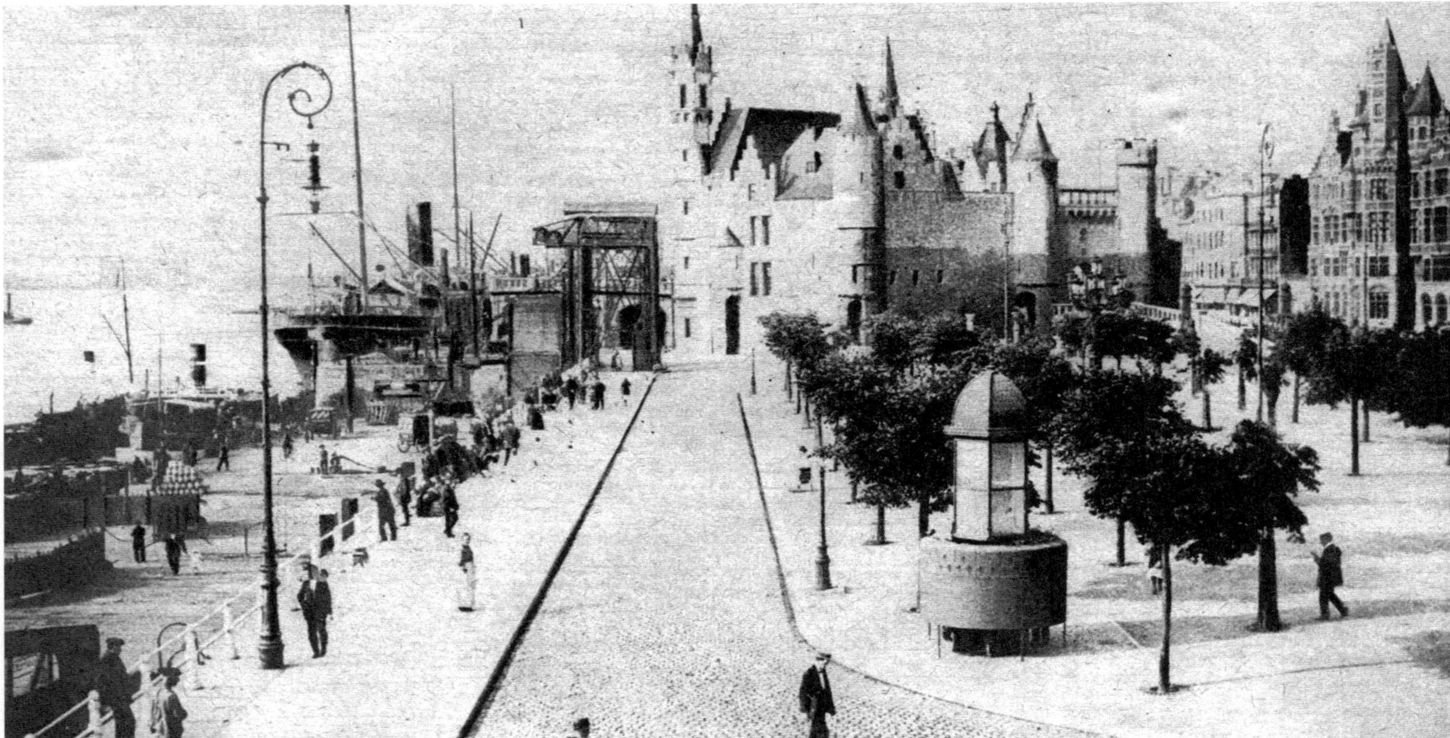

One of the embankments very close to of Antwerp

This embankment in Antwerp was constructed in 1877 and extended between 1899 and 1901, with docks some 5,500 metres long. It is frequented by a cosmopolitan mix of sailors and emigrants. The big ships are ready to leave, bound for Africa or America together with the sail boats. Because Antwerp is situated at the mouth of the river Escaut, the Germans cannot use it as a harbour without breaking the neutrality of Holland.

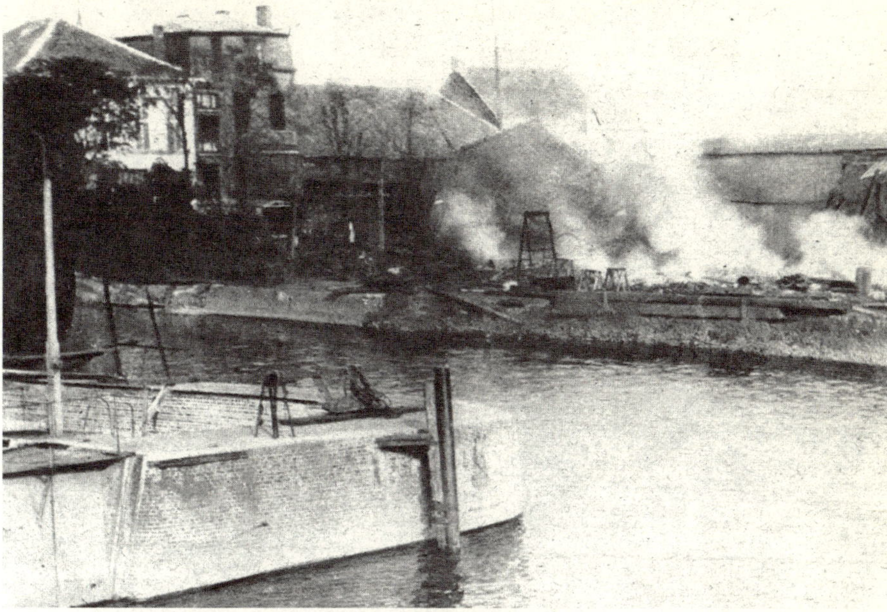

The first German shells fall on the outskirts of Antwerp

The first enemy attack on Antwerp was from the south-east. The photographer took this photograph on the bridge under a hail of fire from German shells. One can distinguish, on the bank opposite, smoke produced by the bursting shells. From this moment shells followed each other without interruption, a continual deluge of fire.

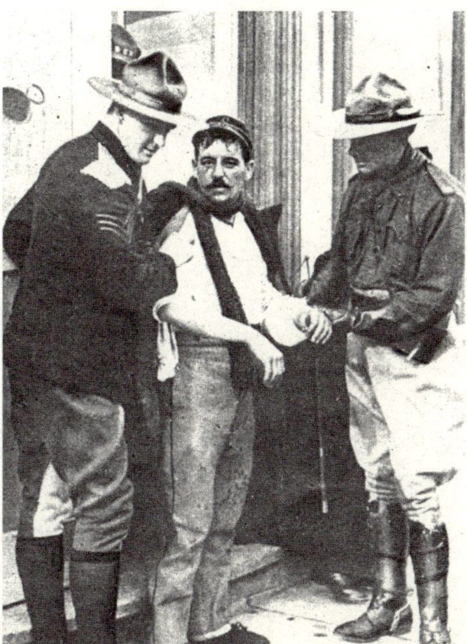

Canadians help the wounded

Valiant allies from Canada, many of French origin, are devoting themselves to help the unhappy Belgian soldiers during their retreat from Antwerp.

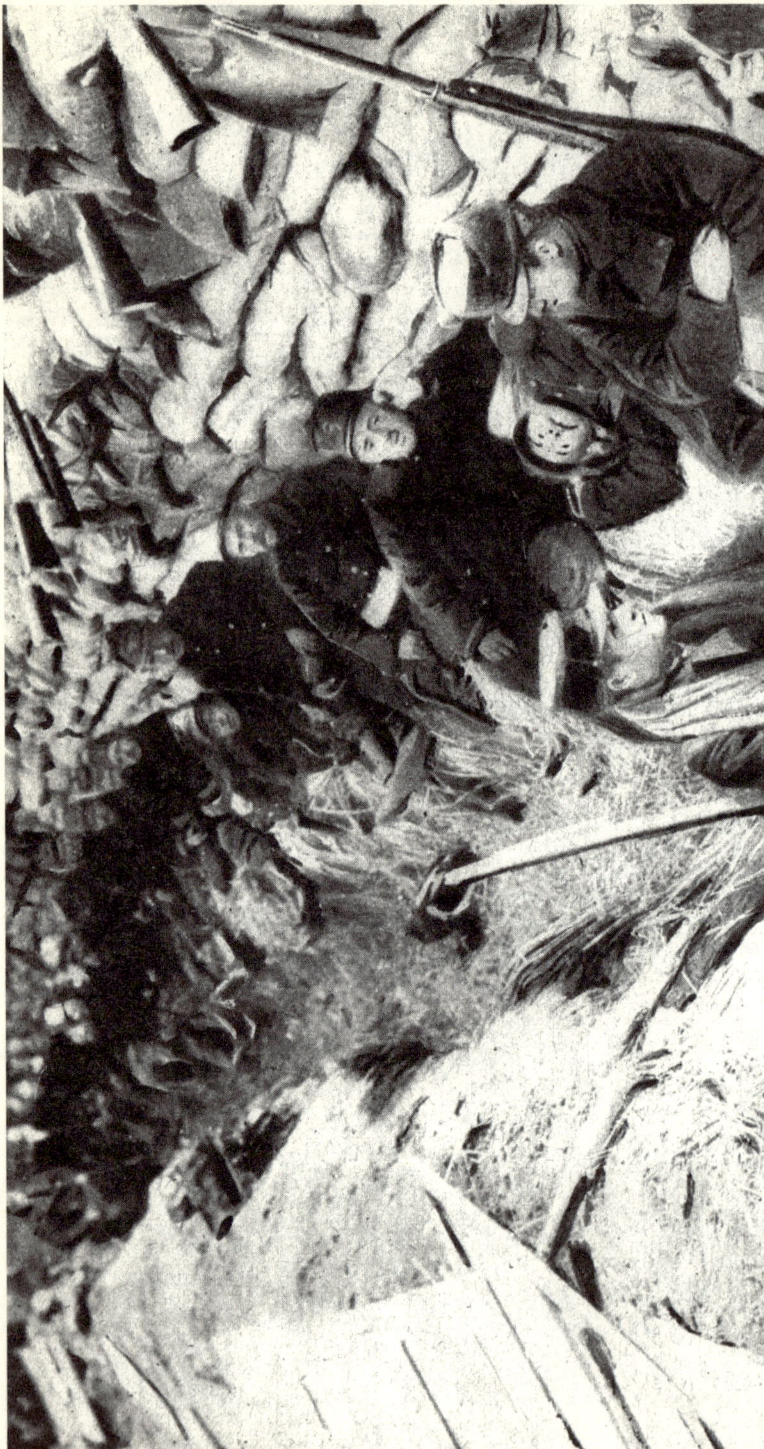

The Belgians wait in trenches for the attack by the Boches

Sheltered well to the bottom of a trench, behind a thick slope reinforced by bags of earth, branches and boxes, some Belgian soldiers await the Boches' attempt to force their line. This photograph was taken just before the German mortars attacked and troops advanced. One can appreciate the heroism of King Albert's troops in defending these trenches, inflicting losses of 45,000 enemy killed and wounded.

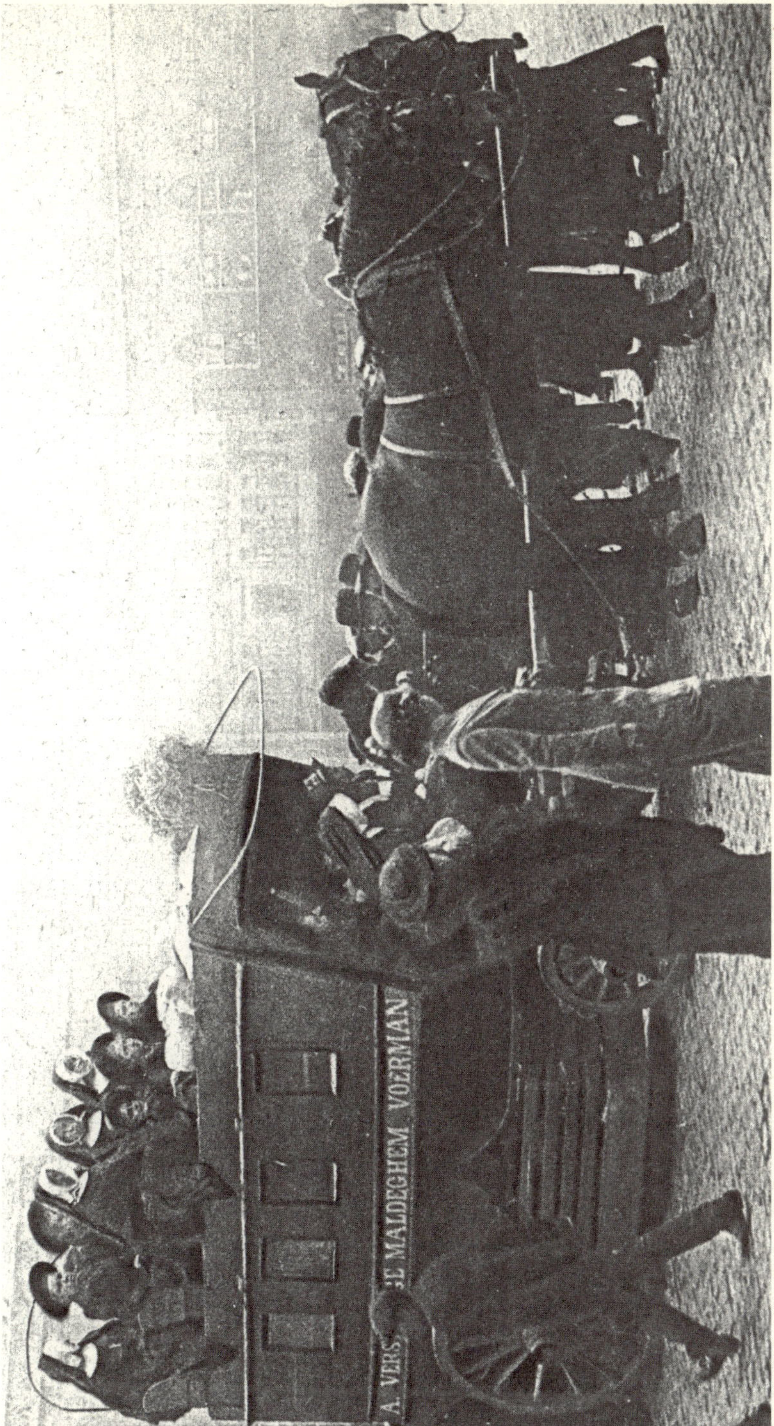

The residents of a convent hastily leave the city

Knowing the humiliation in Brussels, inhabitants of Antwerp left their city en mass following an announcement of the bombardment. Some will embark at Ostend for England, others going to the French border or to take refuge with their Dutch neighbours.

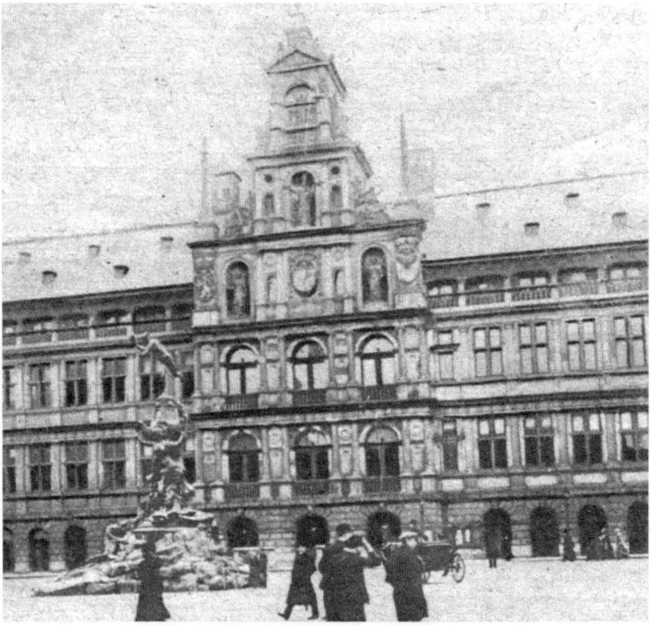

The city hall of Antwerp

Constructed in 1561 in the renaissance style, the city hall of Antwerp was rebuilt in 1581, having been destroyed by the Spanish. It is a vast, doric style building on a red marble base. Germans have now made it their headquarters.

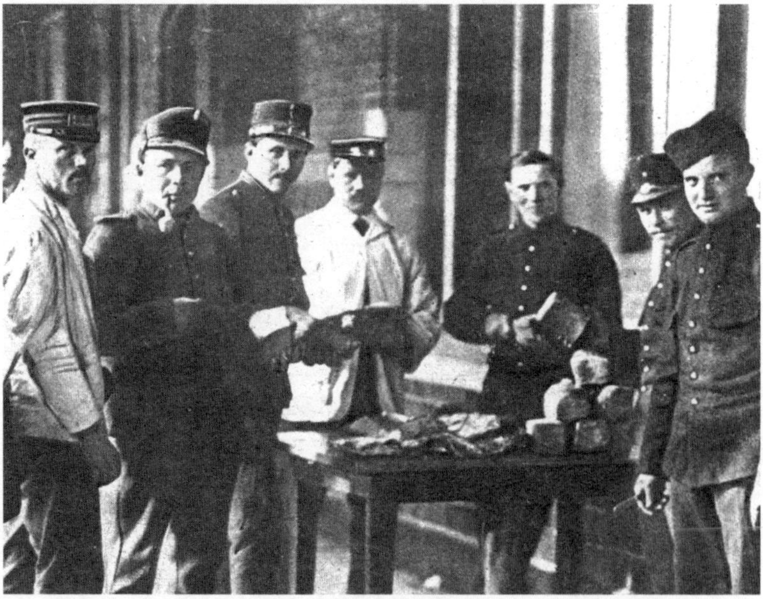

Dutchmen distributing supplies to refugees

Charitable Dutchmen, observing strict and fair neutrality, welcome the needy inhabitants of Antwerp, many of whom left their homes in absolute destitution. This is Rosendael, the first Dutch city after the border, where supplies are being distributed.

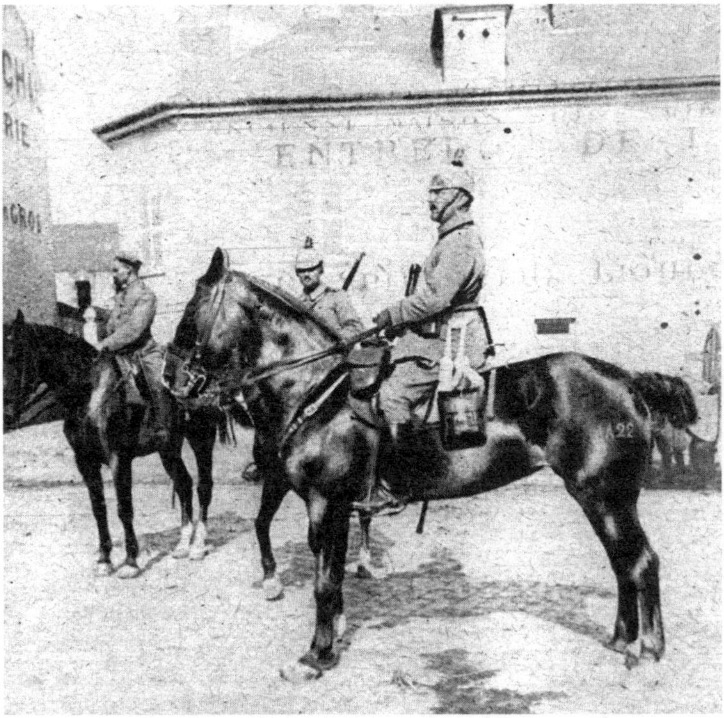

The first German cavalry riders arrive

It is always cavalry patrols that signal the German arrival. They have sometimes taken prisoners from thirty miles in advance of hostile lines.

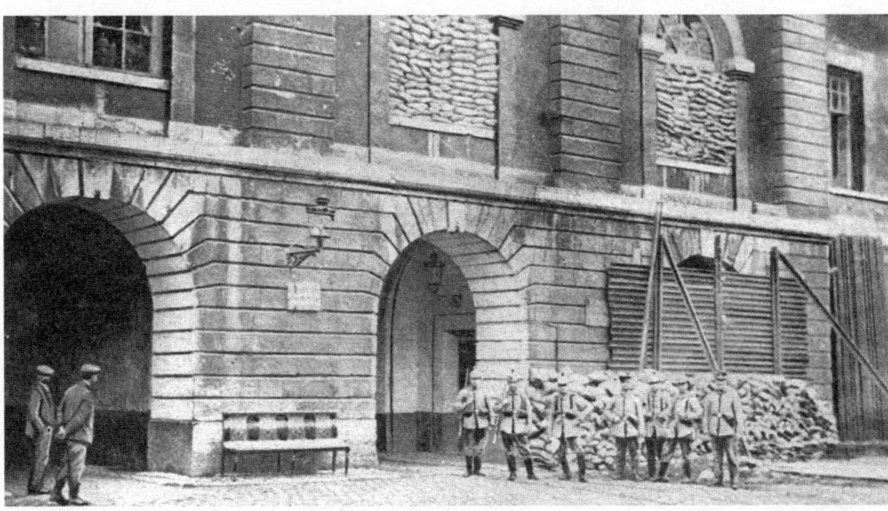

Germans don't feel safe in their conquered cities

This photo, taken in a city in Northern France, reveals that Germans were not totally confident of their position until they had also taken Paris. They have fortified themselves in many of the occupied cities. Here, a building situated between two barracks has been put in state of defence, indicating their wariness.

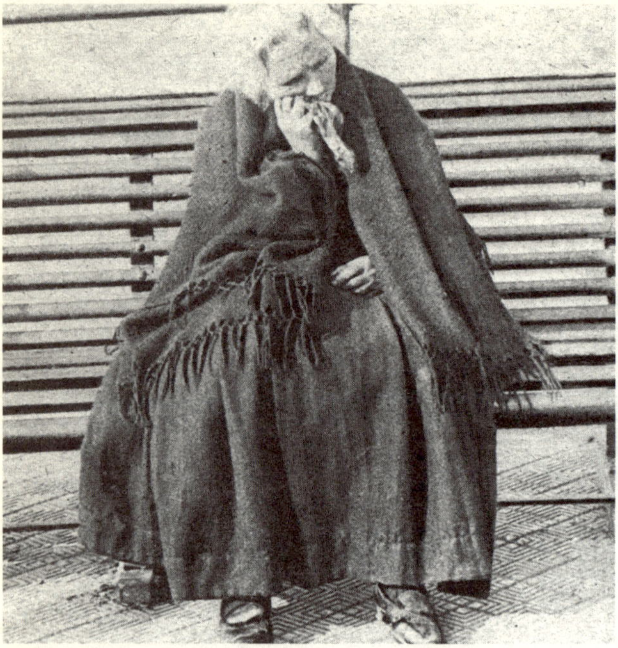

On the quay at Ostend harbour

What picture could show a nation's pain better than this simple photograph? It shows a typical Belgian, a poor old woman waiting on a quay at Ostend moments before she embarked for England.

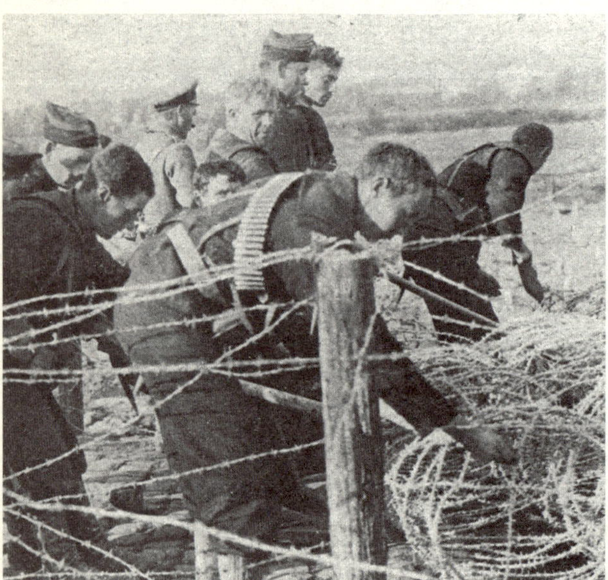

Belgians laying barbed wire

Since September 25th Antwerp has been a major centre of activity. As new trenches were dug, the Belgians put up barriers of barbed wire everywhere to delay the enemy advance.

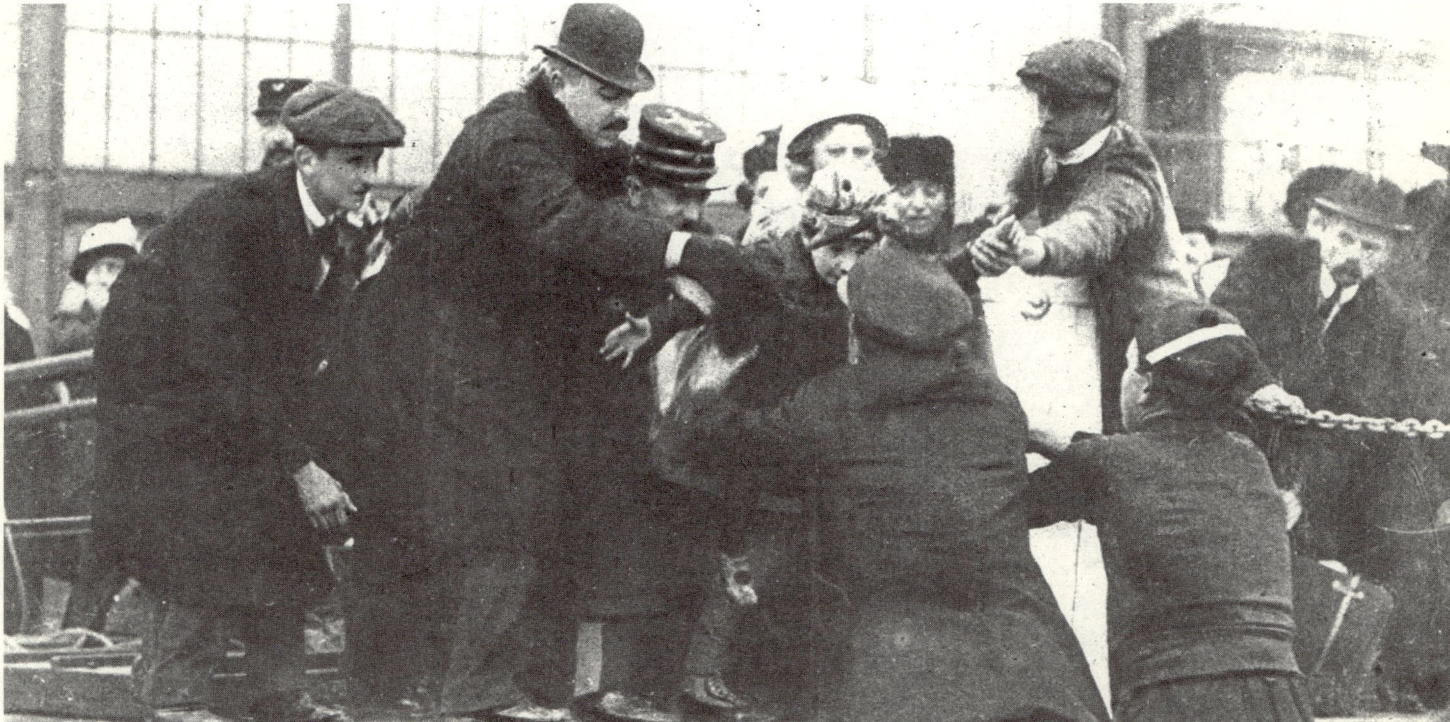

Belgians refugees embarking at Antwerp for England

When inhabitants of Antwerp began to flee, the river Escaut was filled with crafts of all types. Sometimes whole families were seen on rafts, others were seen in the water on buoys. At that moment, hundreds of shells fell and the city burnt. After three hours there were more than two thousand people on some steamers. From this photograph, one can judge the determination of these poor people driven by an understandable fear.

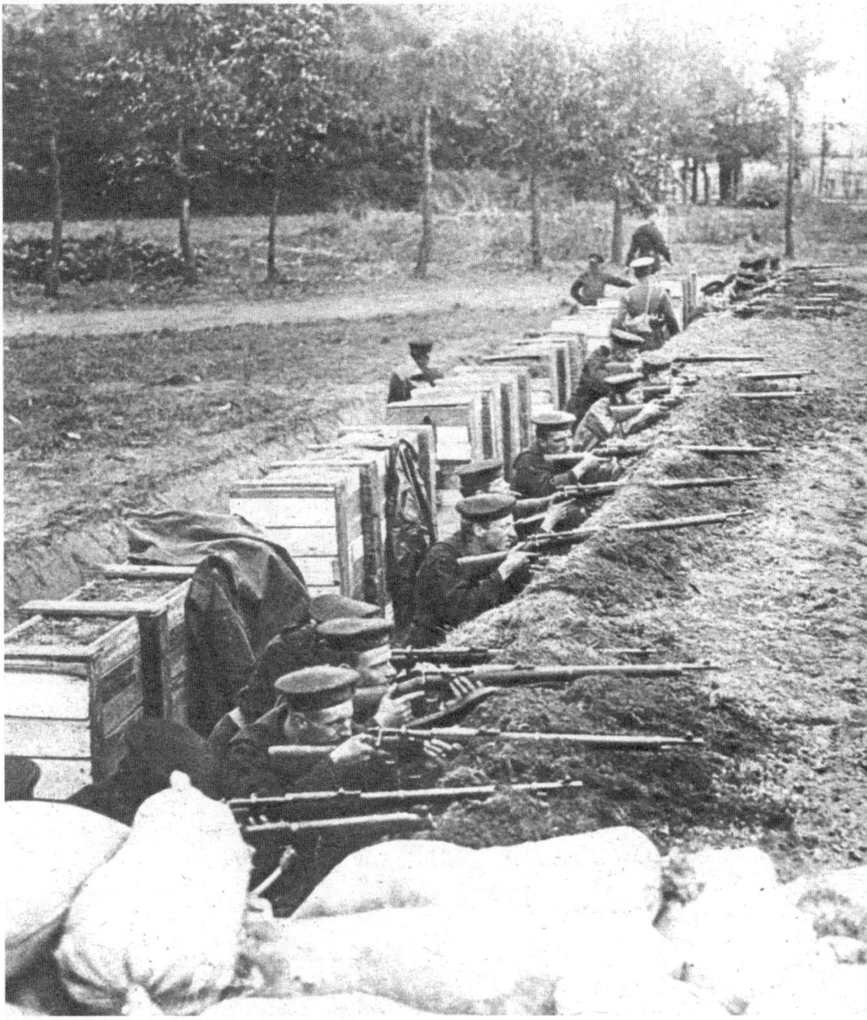

British sailors in the trenches at Lierre

A corps of Royal Marines occupies trenches near Lierre, very close to the Netherlands border. Obliged to pull back before the advancing enemy, these British sailors heroically held out for many hours, inflicting enormous losses on the enemy.

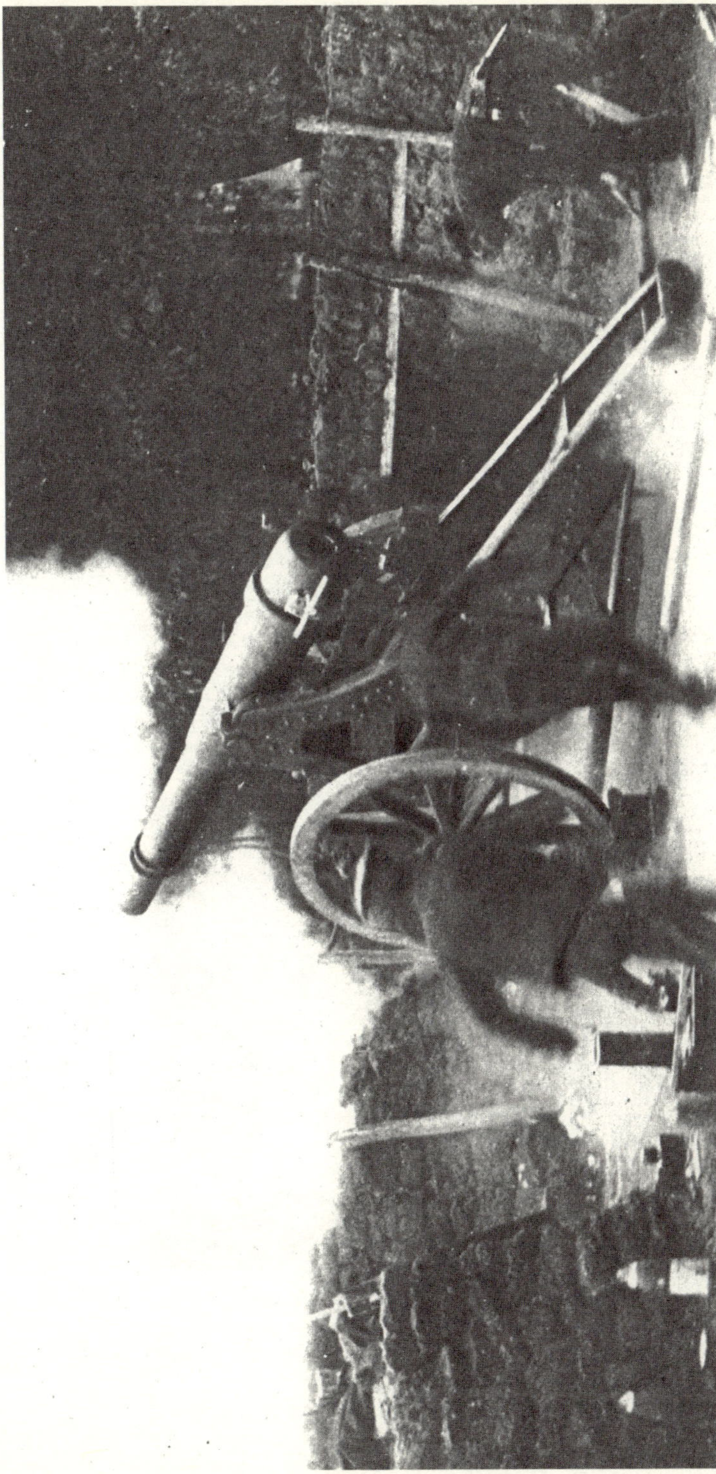

British artillery at a fort in Antwerp

Taken in the height of action, close to one of the batteries where the English troops help the Belgians to defend Antwerp. Words cannot describe as much as this simple photograph. It gives a good impression of the gunners' activity during the shelling.

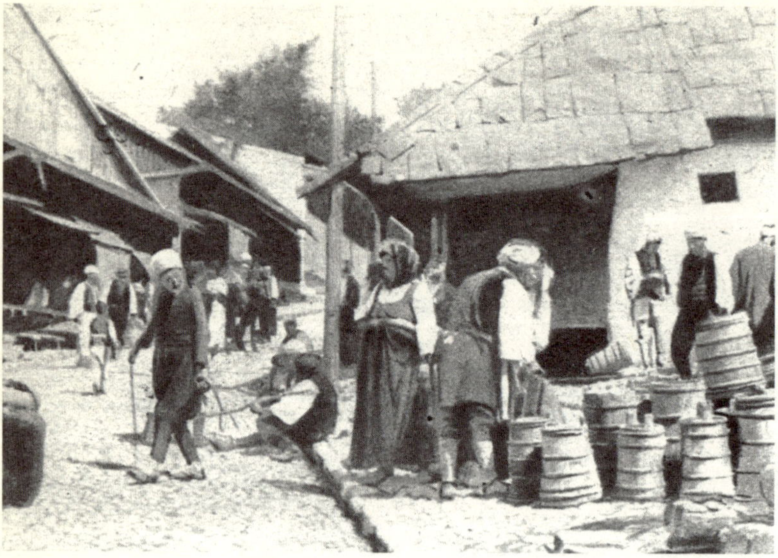

A street in old Sarajevo

Compared to the modern city with a distinctly European character, the old district is infinitely curious and very Oriental.

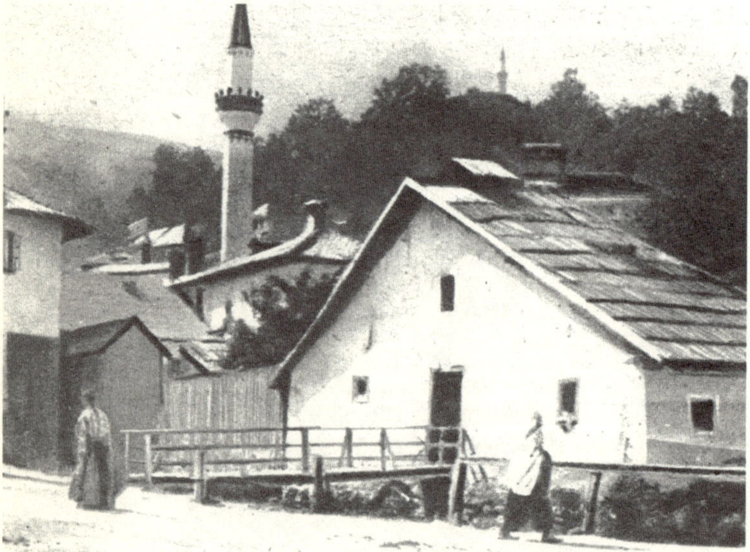

A Turkish district in the corner of Sarajevo

The 'city' Seraglio justifies its name with its wives veiled, following the Moslem tradition.

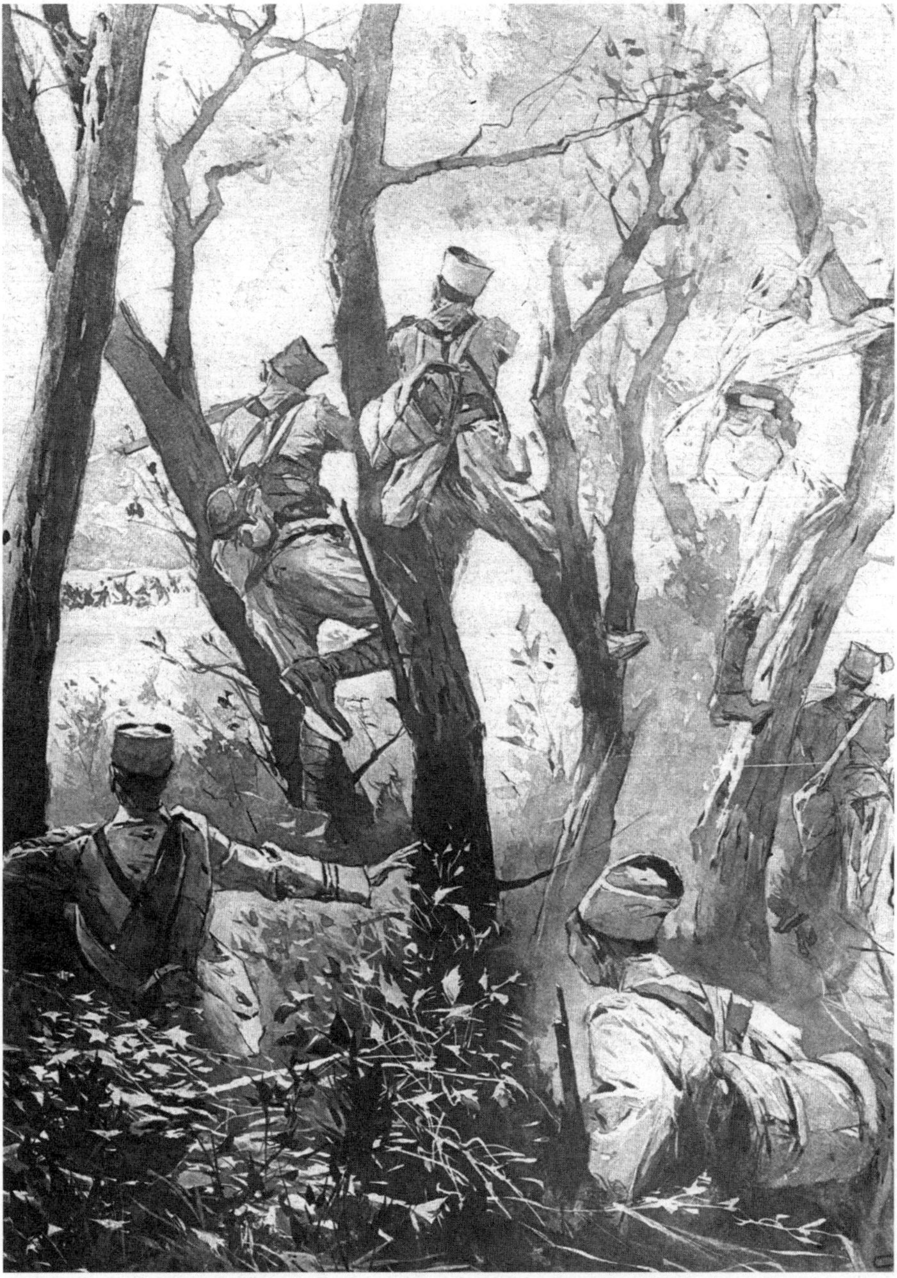

An artists impression of Senegalese troops lodged in trees to fire on the enemy

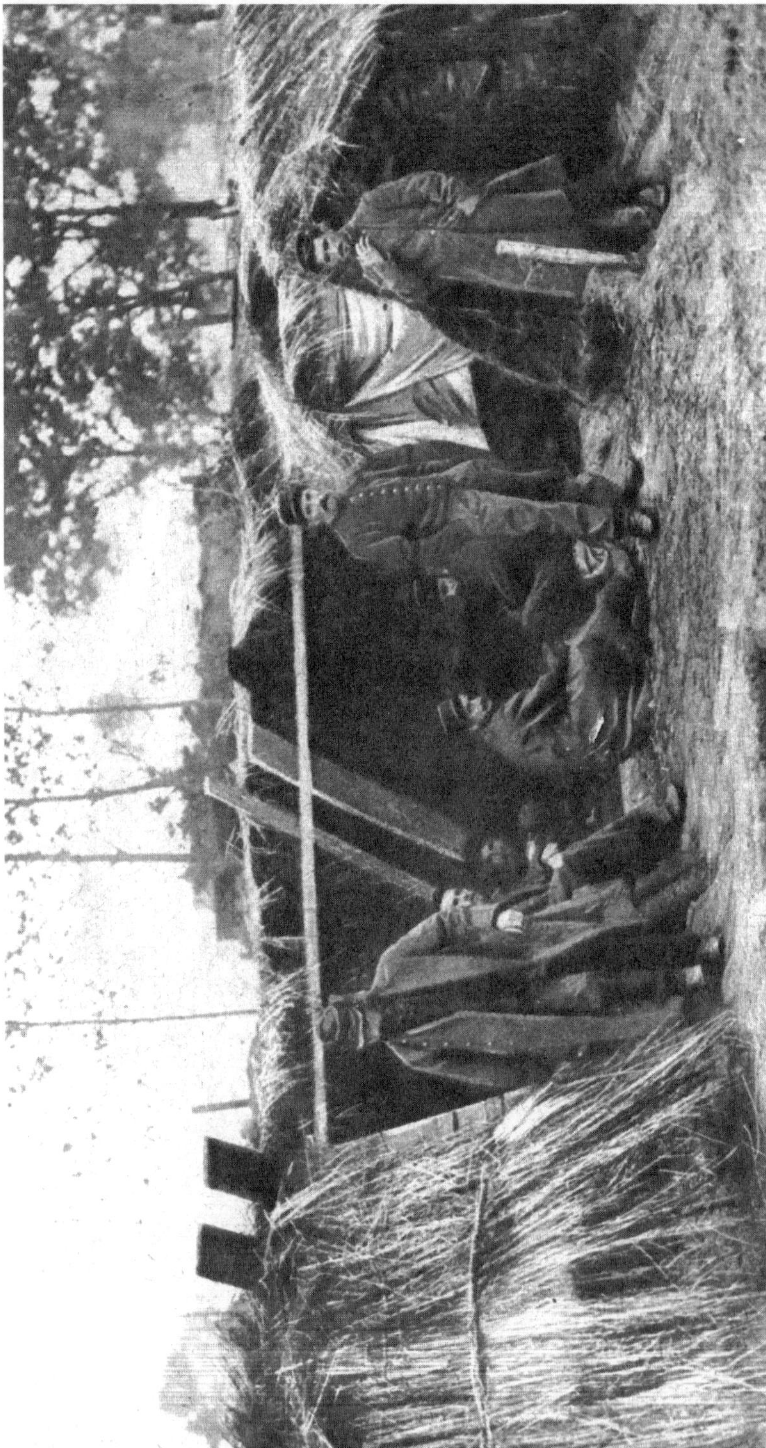

French soldiers under guard in a camp in Westphalia

Thanks to the international Red Cross agency in Geneva, we have begun to get information and photographs of prisoners. It is impossible to indicate the exact place where this has been taken.

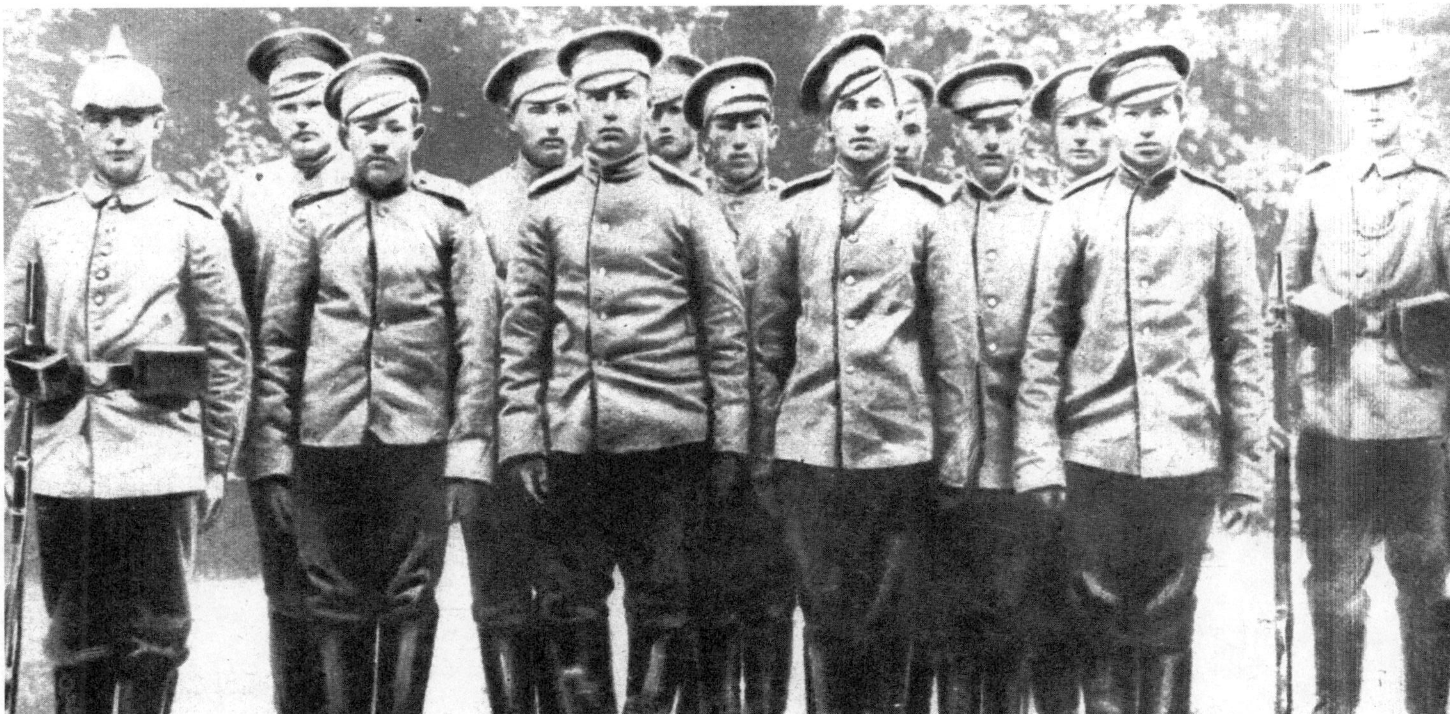

Russian soldiers captured in Bavaria

A party of Russian prisoners captured by the Germans in Bavaria. Nearly 6,000 French, English and Belgian prisoners are at Nieder-Zwehren, close to Cassel. Less is known about the Russians, but one supposes that they are also guarded in the west of Germany.

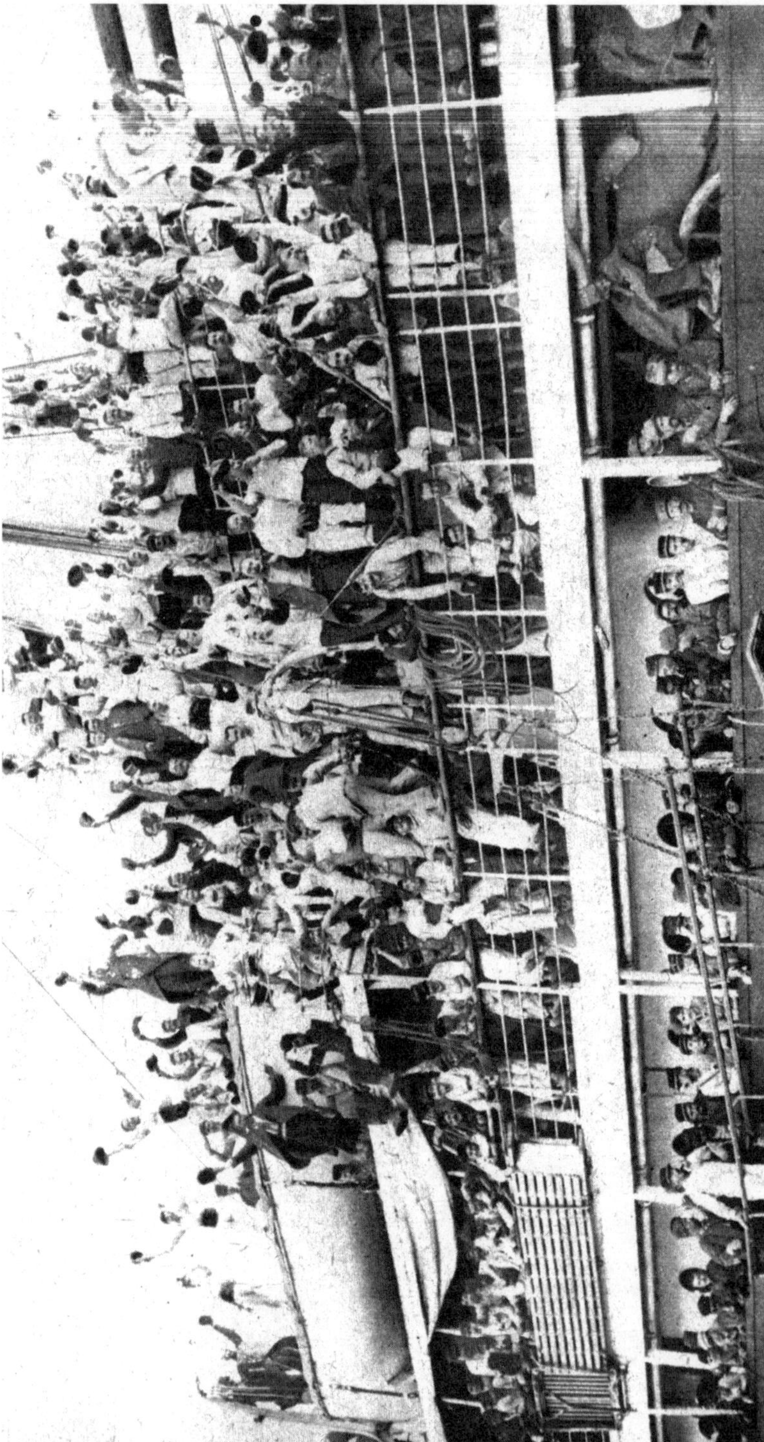

Algerian troops embarking for Europe

From all corners of the world, ships are bringing compatriots with a desire to join their Allies. Algeria sends reinforcements to France. This photograph, taken in Algiers at the time of the departure, shows the soldiers' enthusiasm.

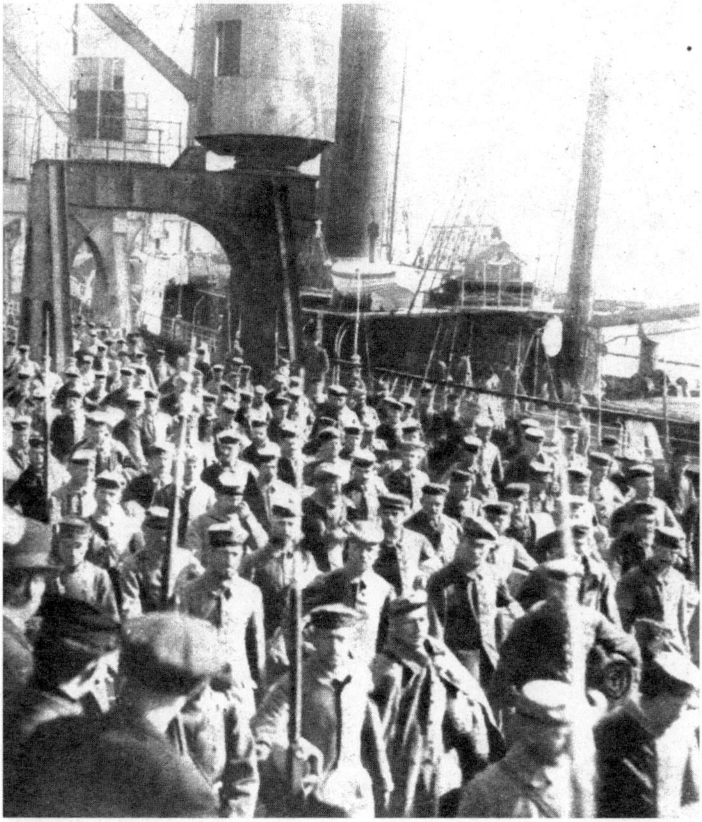

German prisoners leaving for Morocco

Captured German prisoners are sent to Algeria and Morocco. The first convoy was recently embarked for Casablanca.

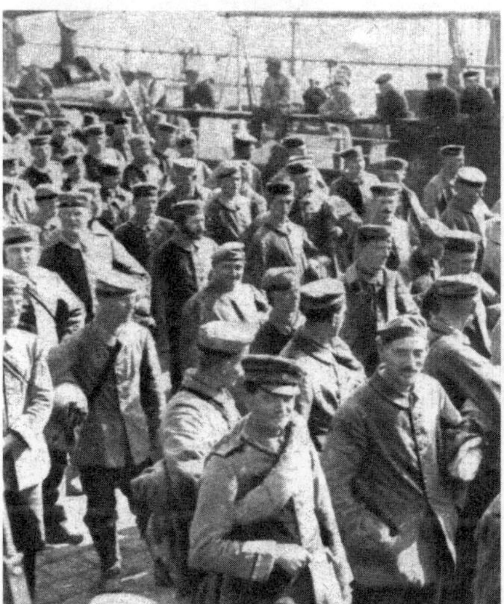

A modification of the 'Voyage to Paris '

The German officers assured their men that the war would be a "walk in France". This walk, for many, suddenly changed, and they are now going to Morocco. They didn't think their dream would end this way!

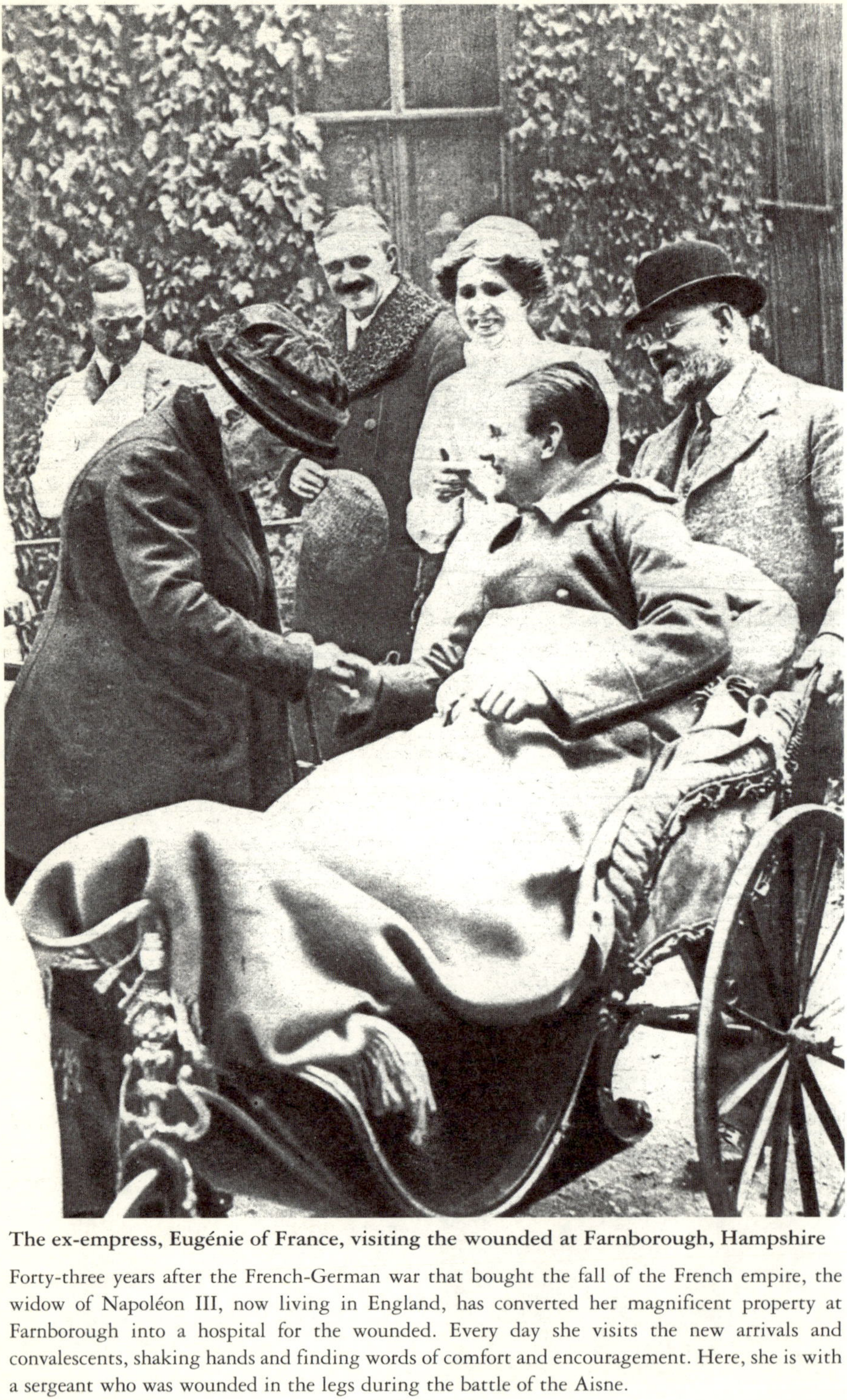

The ex-empress, Eugénie of France, visiting the wounded at Farnborough, Hampshire

Forty-three years after the French-German war that bought the fall of the French empire, the widow of Napoléon III, now living in England, has converted her magnificent property at Farnborough into a hospital for the wounded. Every day she visits the new arrivals and convalescents, shaking hands and finding words of comfort and encouragement. Here, she is with a sergeant who was wounded in the legs during the battle of the Aisne.

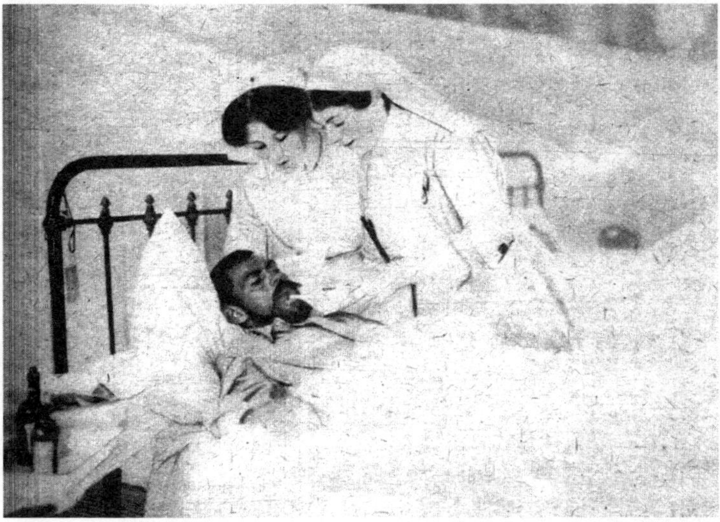

Ladies of the Red Cross with a Turkish soldier

African soldiers, accustomed to a rough life, are especially appreciable of the maternal care offered by nurses.

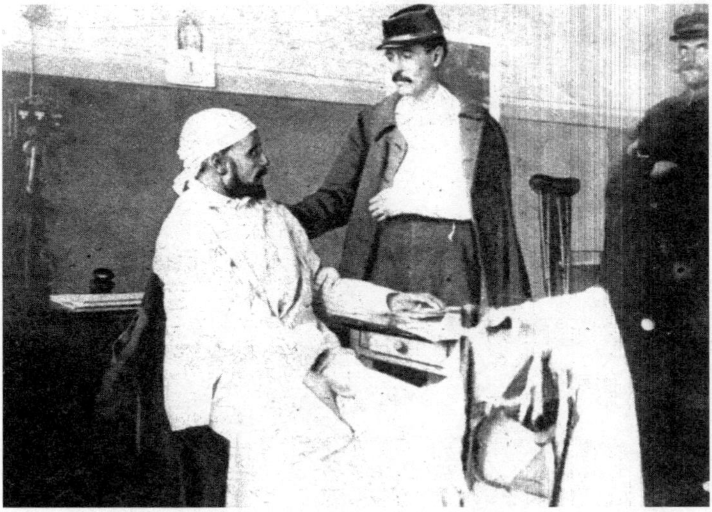

Two injured soldiers compare thoughts

From separate battlefields, two soldiers compare their views on the war.

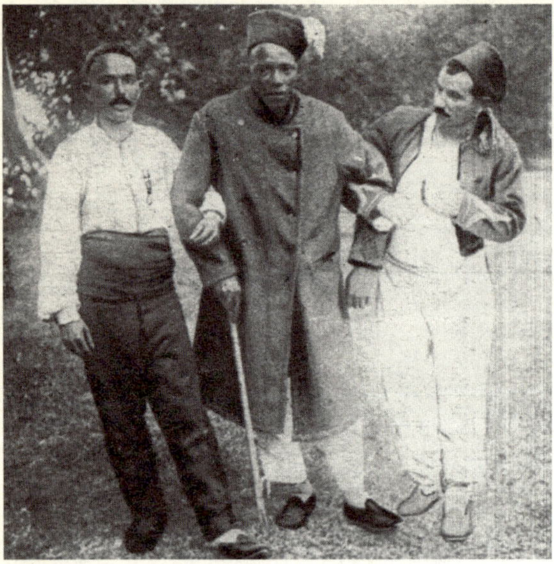

Three friends taking some fresh air

'That's good' he says, smiling, as brave Ouolof from Senegal enjoys convalescence, but can only speak about leaving!

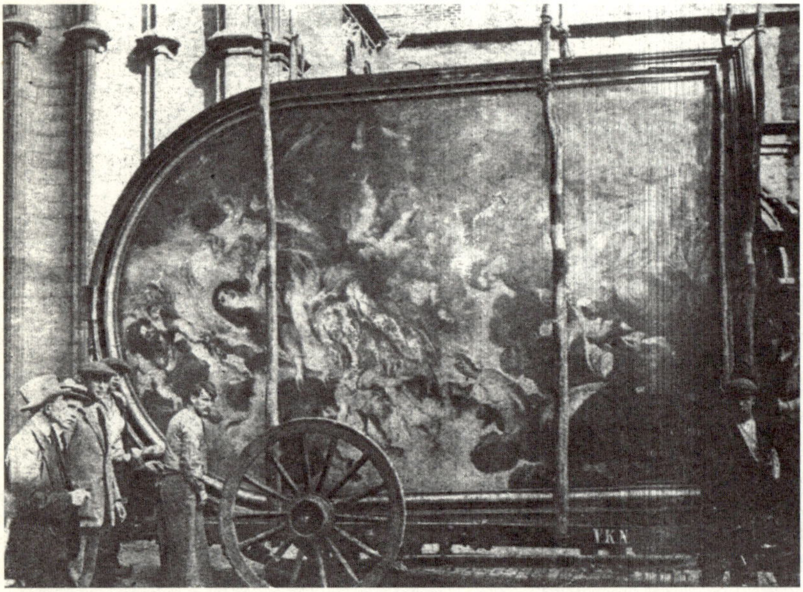

The transportation of a Rubens painting from Antwerp

In Antwerp, the Belgians are moving pictures for safety. This photograph shows the transportation of "Assumption of the Virgin ' by Rubens.

- NEWS REPORTS -

Tuesday October 20, 1914

Land battles have begun near the coast of the North Sea. The German heavy artillery has guns in the vicinity of Dixmude in Belgium, but the Belgian army is containing them. The allied forces advanced between Lille and Ostende. The fighting has spread out around Lille and is now on a house-to-house basis.

Dispatches from Petrograde indicate that German troops hold a line on the Vistule but the Russian army has some four million men overall! The Serbians have killed a thousand Austro-Hungarian soldiers close to Sarejevo.

Italy suffers, like all countries, from the lack of cereals, and has decided to cut rations by half.

Wednesday October 21, 1914

Distressing news from Arras. It has undergone the same fate as Louvain and Malines with many districts now in ruins after heavy shelling.

The information from Petrograd confirms the defeat of the Germans on the Vistule, near Warsaw. Czar Nicolas II has addressed Poland in an attempt to quell the disorder that is occuring.

Thursday October 22, 1914

The allied and German forces are fighting on three fronts: Nieuport to Dixmude, Ypres to Menin, and Warneton to Bassee.

The main interest of the day is with the Russian army who have inflicted a major defeat on the Austro-German armies, whose headquarters in Berlin have also taken command of the contingents of Austrians in Galicia. There were between 1,500,000 and 1,600,000 Russians on a huge front stretching from the middle Vistule towards the fortresses of Warsaw and Ivangorod. Guillaume II (Kaiser Wilhelm II) has, as ever, pressed his generals to advance and enter Warsaw, but his plans may have to change. A consequence of Russian success is that the armies of Grand Duke Nicholas can progress rapidly towards Silesia in southern Poland. This battle also determines the fate of Cracow.

News of this big Russian success soon spread amongst German troops in Belgium, according to the Dutch newspapers. It is certain that the Kaiser will move a contingent from Brussels to slow down the Cossack advance so the victory of our allies will have a direct repercussion on our own operations on the western battlefield.

Friday October 23, 1914

England increases precautions against German spies who have swarmed into Britain. We have proceeded with mass arrests and, at the same time, barred

German and Austrian nationals from within five miles of the coast. Belgium publishes a "Grey Book" - a compilation of diplomatic documents relating to the origins of the war, answering the allegations of the German Chancellor, Bethmann-Hollweg, and the Berlin unofficial press, that Belgium violated its own neutrality to benefit a British and French victory.

There is no end to the violent fighting taking place between Lille and the sea. The Germans are shattering the defensive line of British, French and Belgian troops.

Shortages worsen in Berlin, with the price of food becoming more and more expensive. The president of Prussia, in an interview, acknowledged that the days are hard and bad for Germany.

Saturday October 24, 1914

The German army doesn't seem to tire of its attacks between the North Sea and Lille. We have given up some ground in this area, but three enemy artillery batteries have been destroyed to the north of the Aisne.

Important Austrian contingents have once again attacked the Serbo-Montenegrine troops to the north of Sarajevo in Bosnia. In Cattaro, the Franco-Montenegrine batteries continue their destruction of the Austrian strongholds.

Sunday October 25, 1914

The British admiralty announced that 70 British, French and Japanese cruisers are at sea in search of seven or eight German cruisers. They recognise that the E-3 submarine must be presumed lost.

The Russians have now have pushed back the Germans some 160 kilometres (100 miles) to the west of Warsaw and some 50 kilometres (30 miles) from Ivangorod. Through his intermediary, the ambassador to Rome Mr. Kroupenski, the Czar offered to return the Italian speaking Austrian soldiers captured by his army. Mr. Salanadra (Italy) thanked the ambassador and said that he would give consideration to the proposal.

Monday October 26, 1914

England, previously a big customer for sugar manufactured by Germany, Austria and Hungary, has just barred imports of sugar from these countries. England will not suffer though, with a contingency in the Antilles - a group of Caribbean Islands. This is another move that will undermine German trade.

Germany is preparing to move troops towards Austria to defend the Trentin region against Italy. The government of Petrograd has passed new laws so that Germans and Austrians cannot become owners of buildings in the western part of the region.

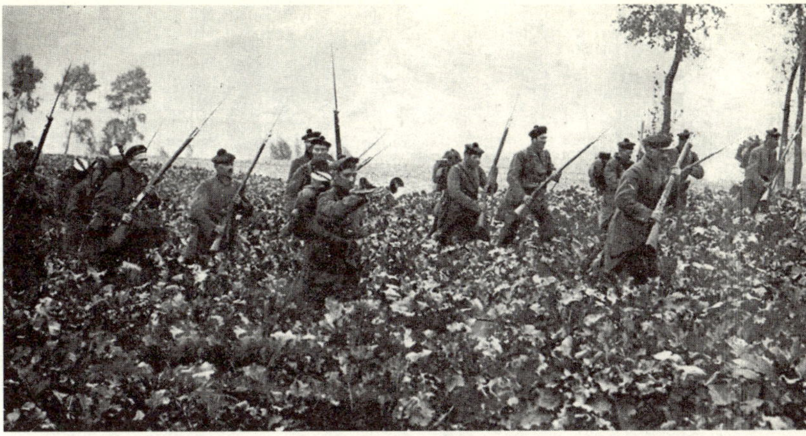

French marines commencing a bayonet attack

The blue collars of sailors are mingling with the uniforms of soldiers of all nationalities. These brave troops have just encountered their first meeting with the enemy in the north of France.

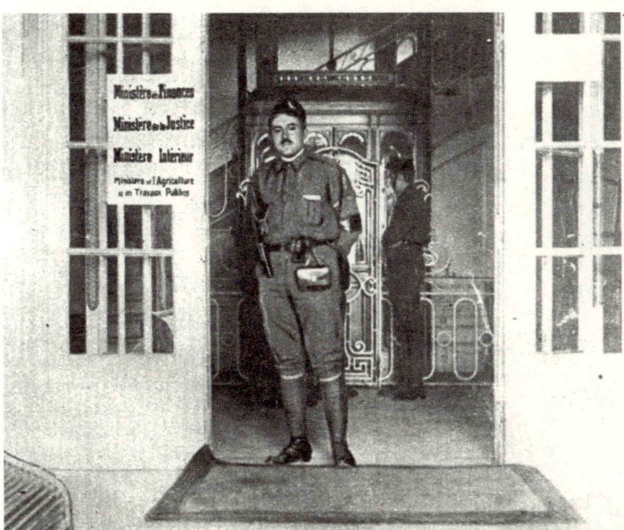

The entrance to the temporary Belgian ministry offices at Le Havre

There is something curiously moving in the simplicity with which our Belgian friends adapt to a new home.

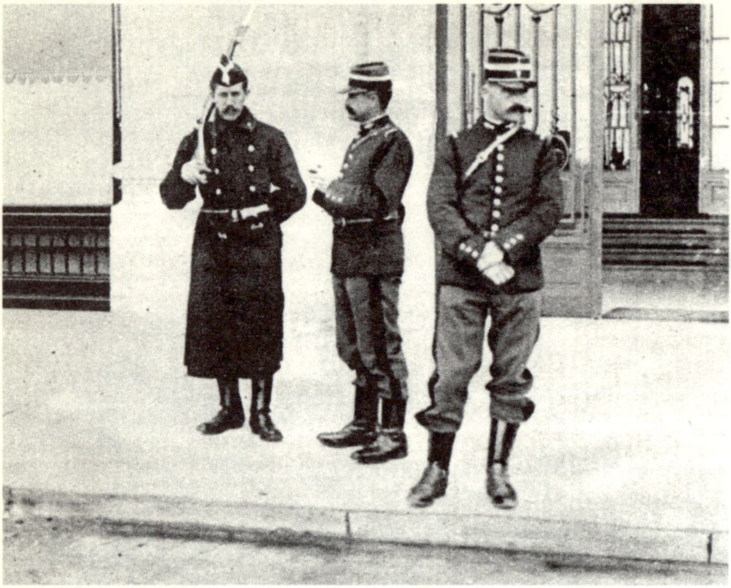

French policeman and Belgian soldiers

A straightforward friendship exists between the two nations.

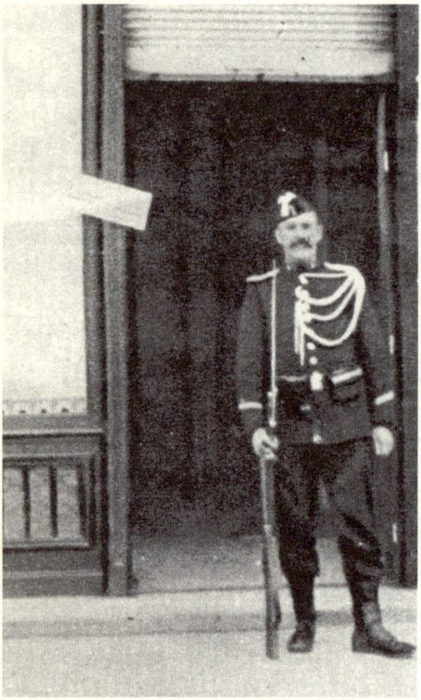

The Belgian Foreign Ministry, now based in a shop

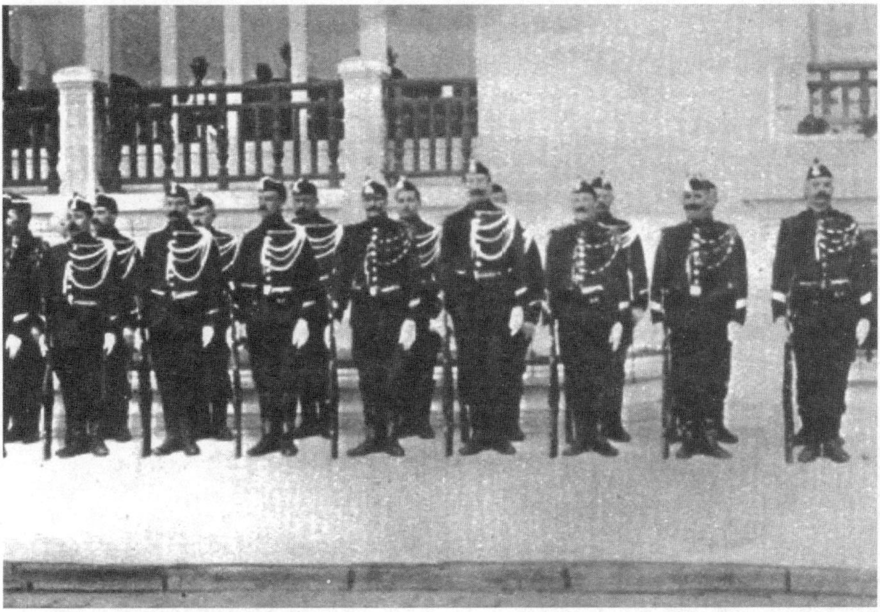

Changing of the guard at Le Havre

Despite its temporary location, the Belgian Government retain the formality of guarding their offices.

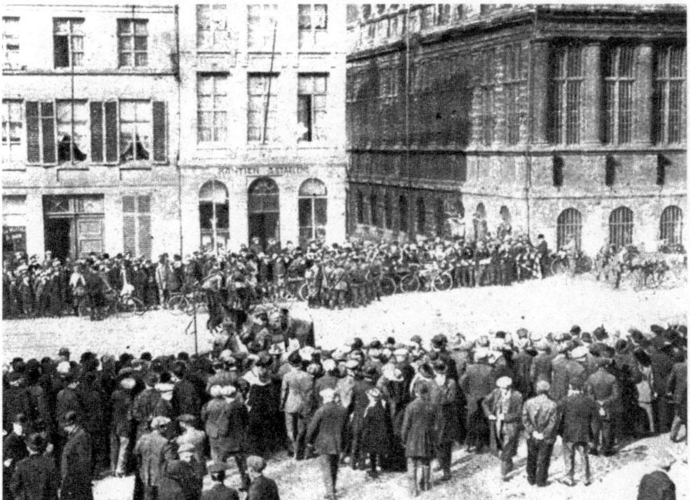

The city of Ghent on the day of occupation

This photograph has been taken at the moment the first soldiers of the Kaiser made an appearance in the streets of Ghent.

The Principle German Generals

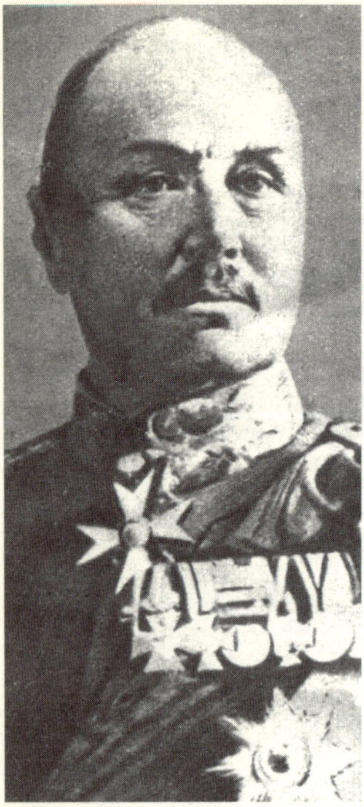

General Von Kluck

Von Kluck has ordered the march on Paris, then the retreat on the Marne, the battle of the Aisne and operations between the Oise and the Somme.

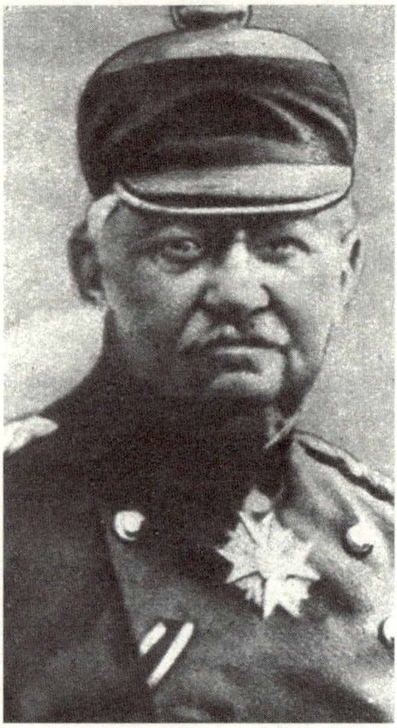

General Von Bulow

Von Bulow, colonel general, commanded the 3rd German division before the war. He played a very important role in the battle of the Marne.

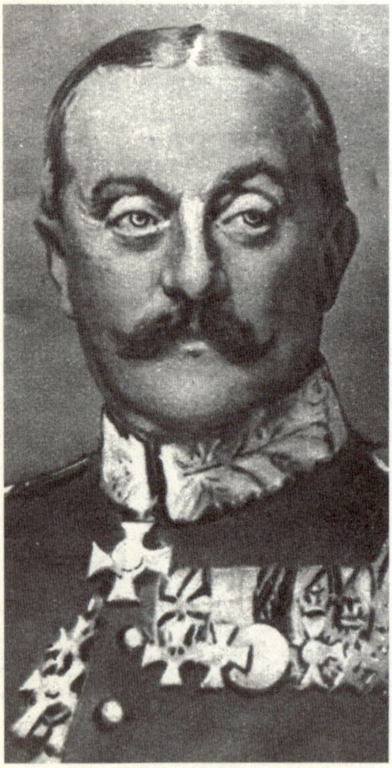

General Von Voigts-Rhetz

Von Voigts-Rhetz was, before the war, the regimental adjutant. He replaced General Von Stein in the middle of October.

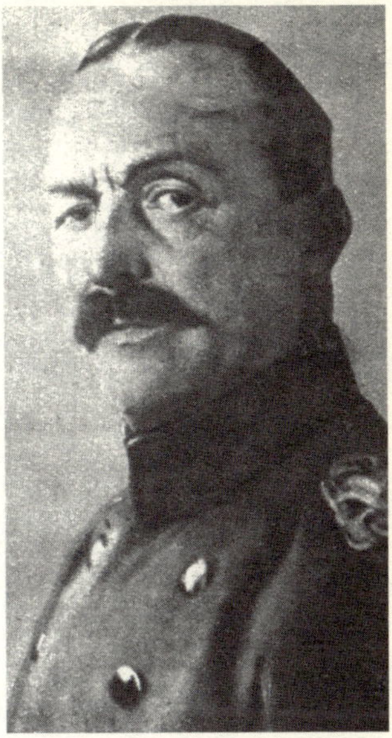

General Von Stein

Von Stein was thought to be out of touch with reality - hence his replacement.

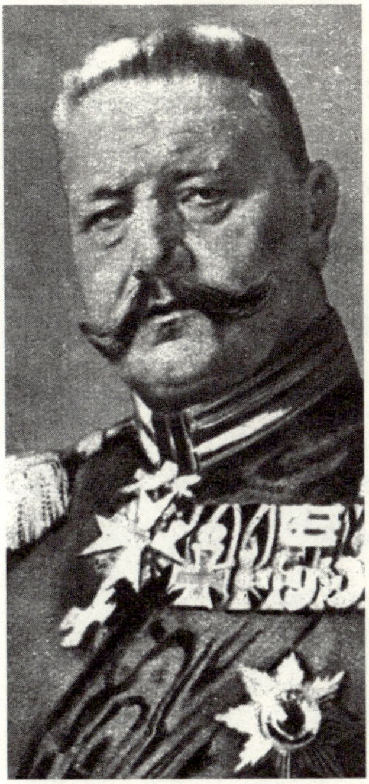

General Von Hindenberg

Von Hindenburg has been called the liberator of Prussia. He was in command when the Russians were defeated at the battle of Tanneberg, but since then, he has had a number of defeats.

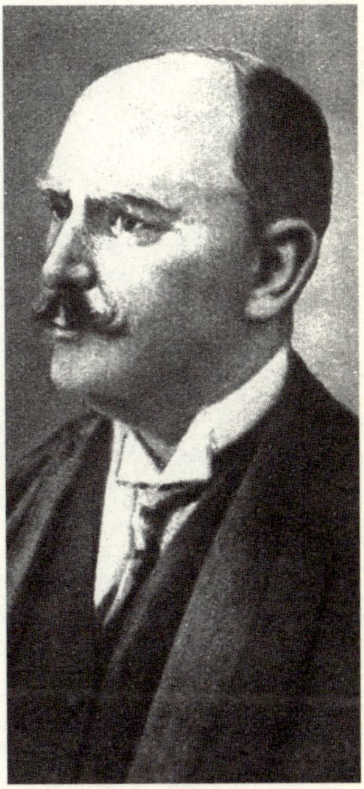

General Von Beseler

Von Beseler directed the attack on Antwerp and succeeded in taking the city. He claimed it was won by good planning. Taking the big Belgian port on the Escaut has cost the Germans dearly, and they lost many lives there.

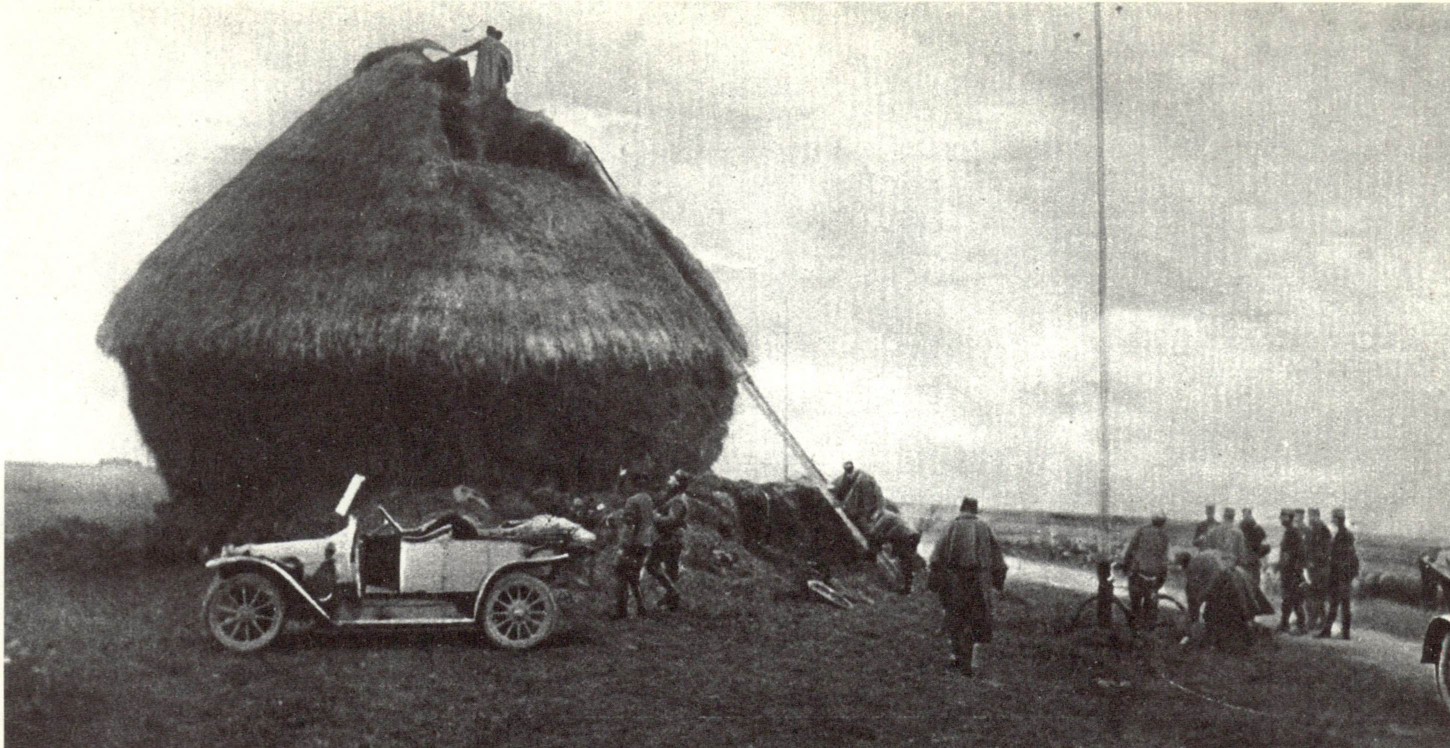

A General climbs down from an observation post in a haystack

This photograph has been taken within sight of hostile lines, during the battle of the Aisne. A general descends from the haystack using a ladder borrowed from a neighbouring farm. It was converted to a observatory, allowing him to monitor the movements of the troops under his command. The car is used to tour the lines quickly, and is waiting for him to go back, with his officers, to headquarters.

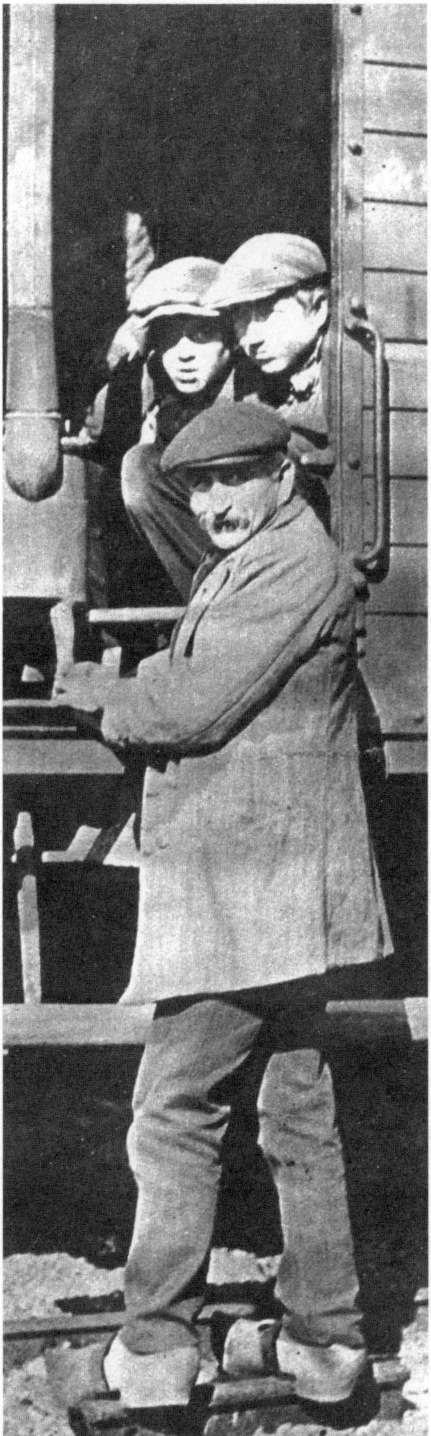

Refugees in a wagon

When Antwerp fell, hundreds of Belgian railway wagons were taken to Holland where they are used as temporary dwellings.

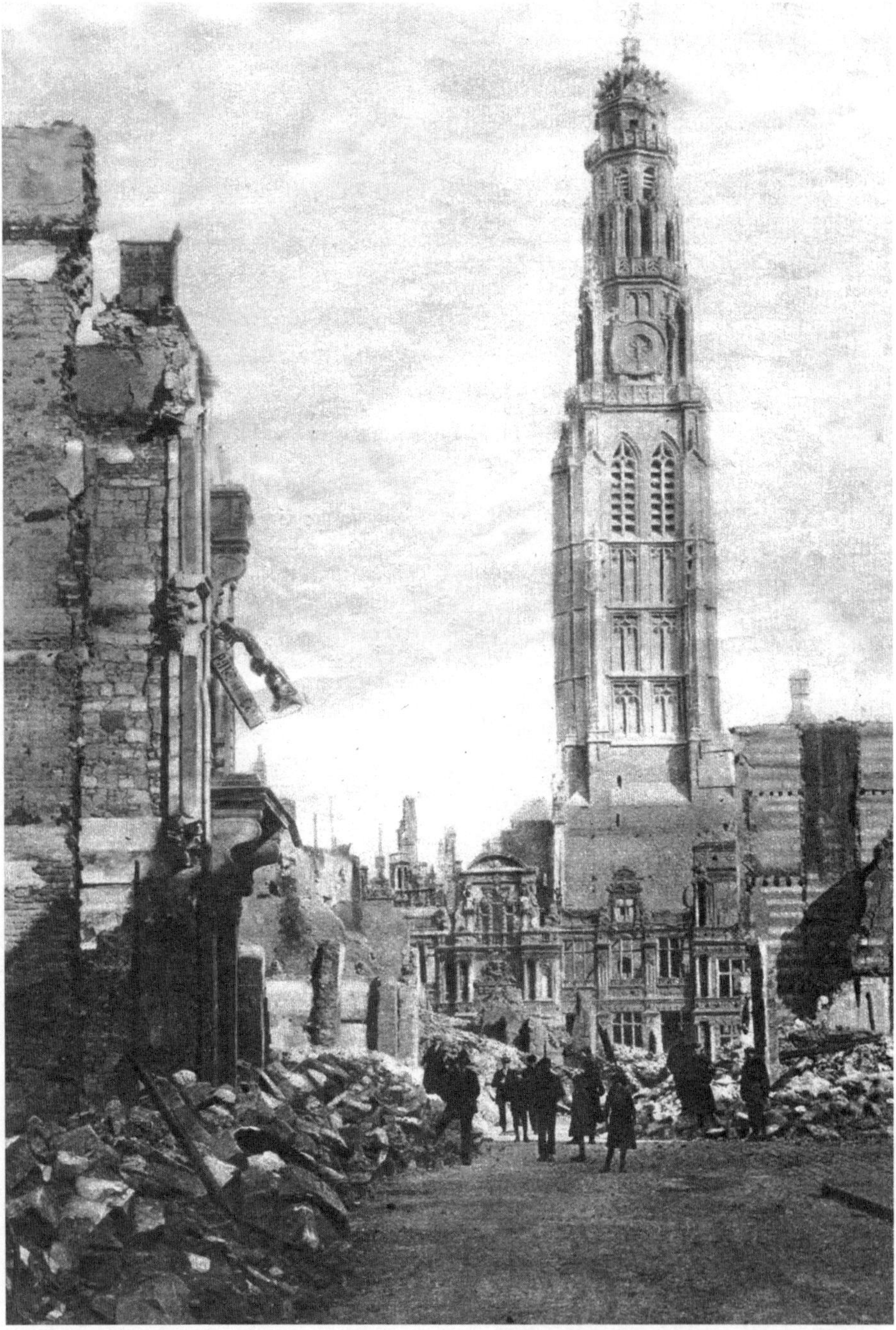

A last photograph of the belfry at Arras

The Germans have used the belfry of the city hall at Arras as a target. During the first attack the shells only skimmed it, but destroyed the old Flemish-Spanish style houses that were the pride of the city. In the middle of the ruins, the belfry still stands proudly.

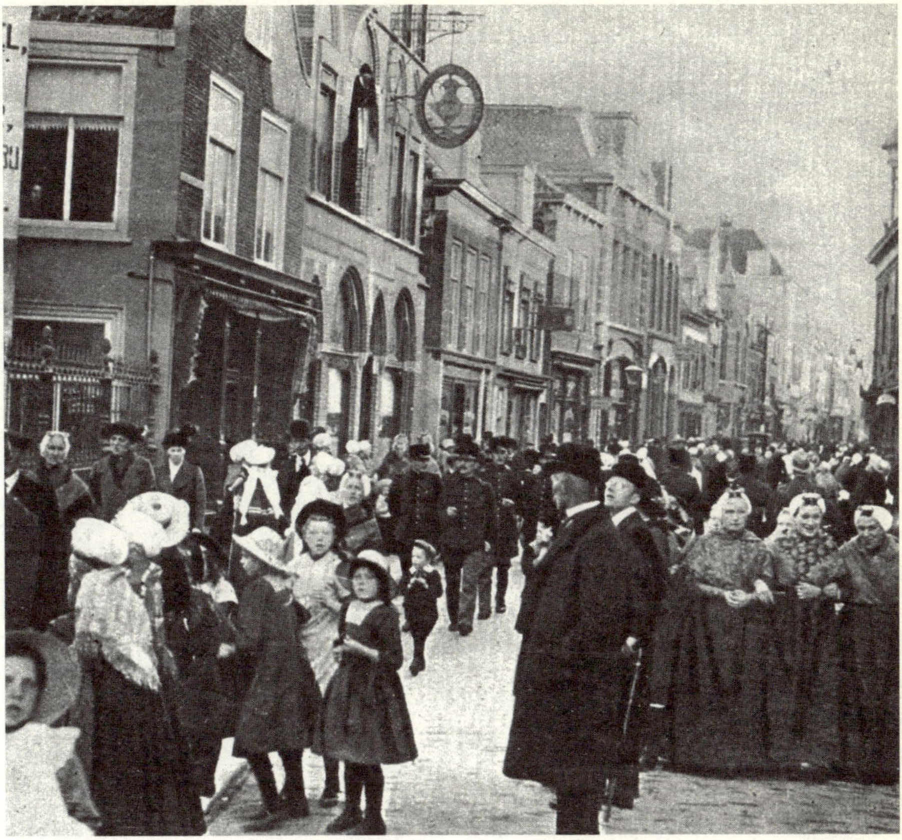

A normal Sunday on the streets of The Hague in November 1914
Although Holland is neutral, she is only a few kilometres from the battlefields. Those sheltering here have found a warm welcome. In the streets of The Hague you often see Belgian and French soldiers, mainly male nurses who help the prisoners that the Germans send back from France.

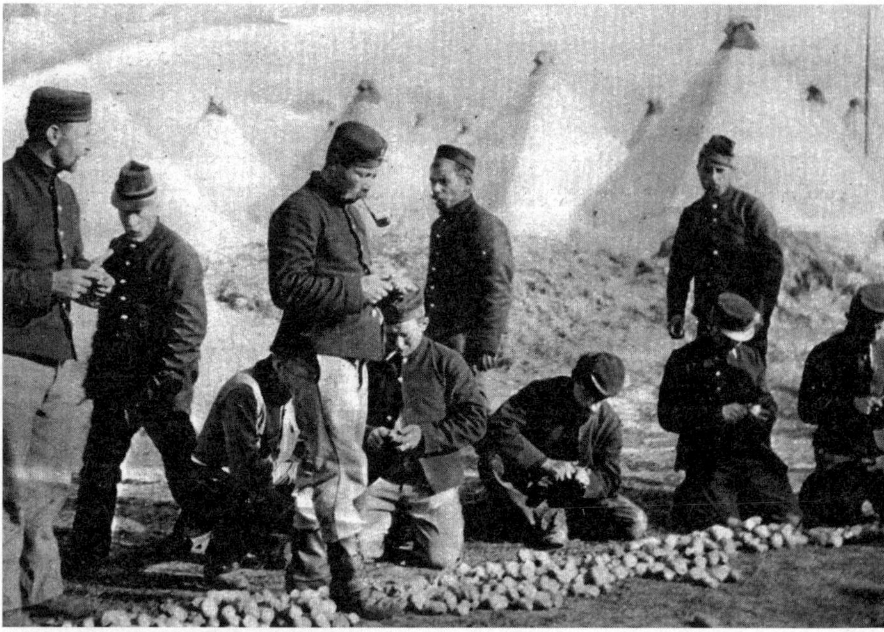

Belgian soldiers preparing their meal in Holland

When soldiers of the fighting nations move to neutral countries, they are disarmed. This was also what happened to the army of Bourbaki (a French General and mathematician commanding the army on the Rhine) that crossed into Switzerland in 1871. Belgians currently in Holland still enjoy many privileges. Here, they are at their camp preparing their lunch. .

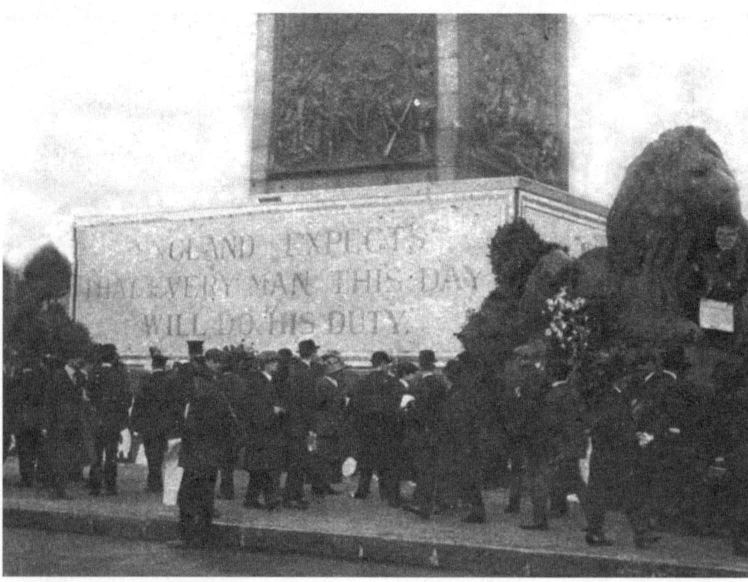

The anniversary of the battle of Trafalgar

This year Nelson's monument was covered in patriotic emblems.

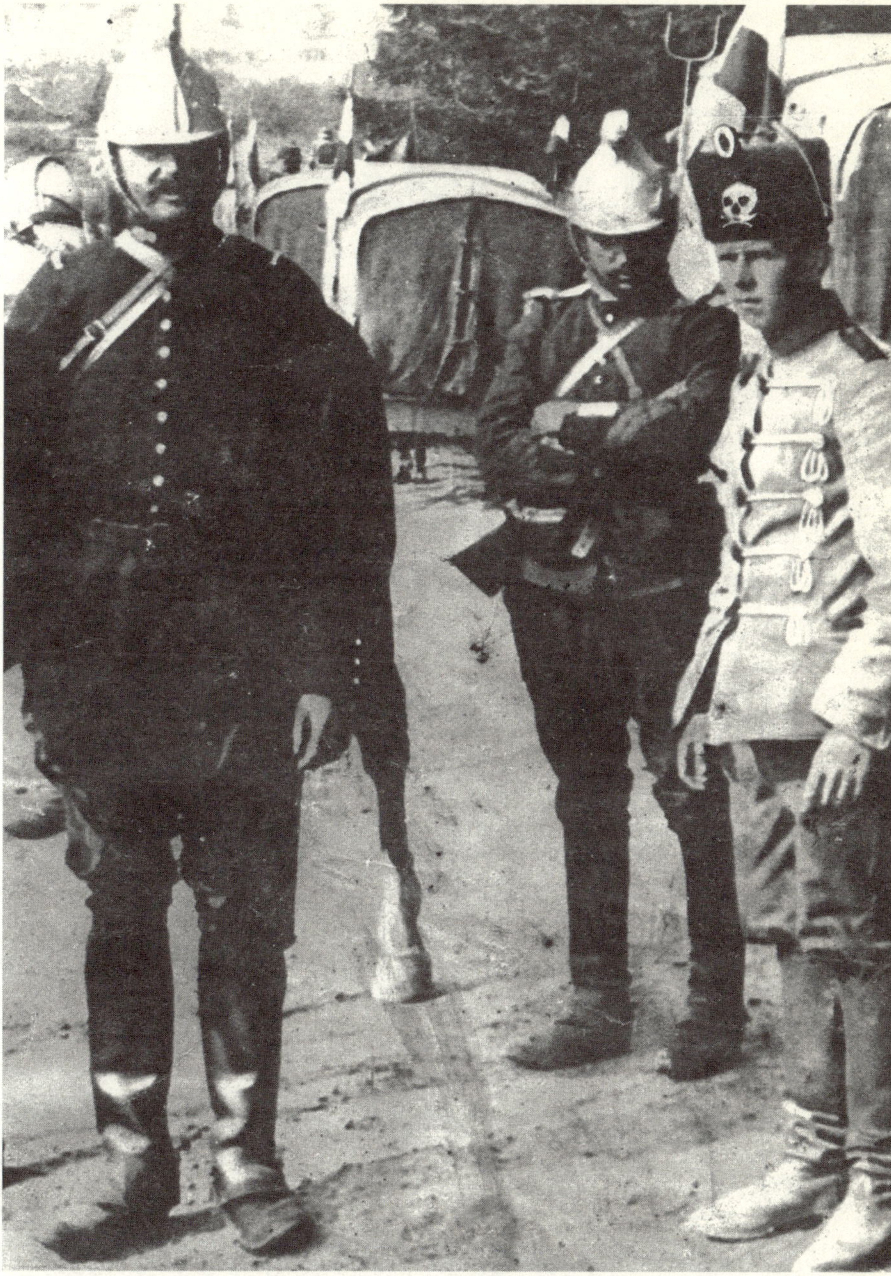

Hussar captured by French Dragoons near Armentieres

Before the war the German Kronprinz was Colonel of the famous 'Hussars of Death'.

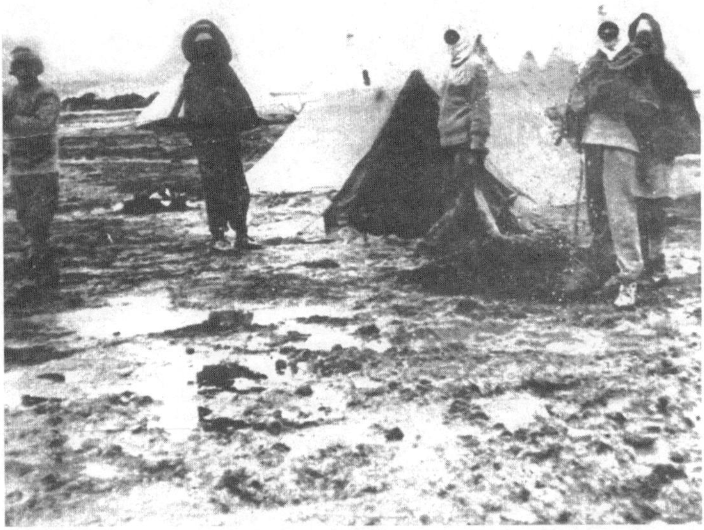

A Gurkha camp

Some seasons are ominous to the Hindus. They are ill equipped to meet the rigors of our climate. In their country, the Gurkas are used to heat in summer and cold weather in winter.

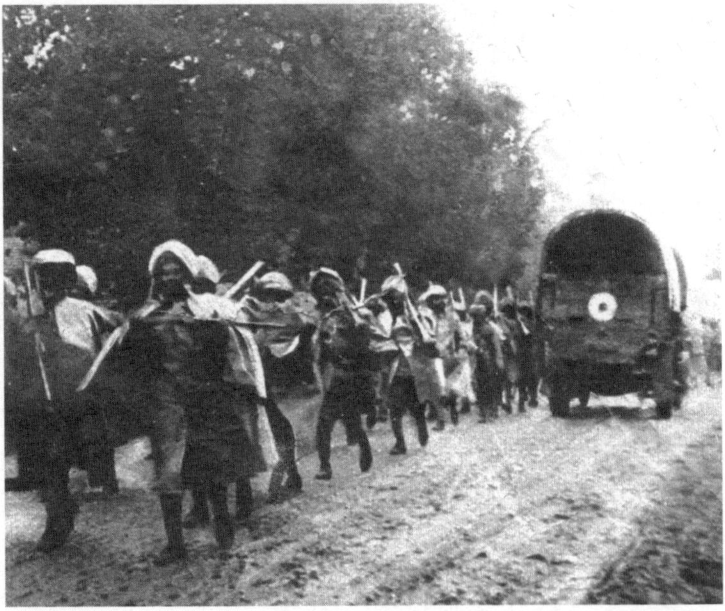

The Sikhs walking in the rain

Clothed warmly, well heeled, fed according to their tastes and their habits, these soldiers come from India. They are committed to their beliefs, their talismen and their fakirs.

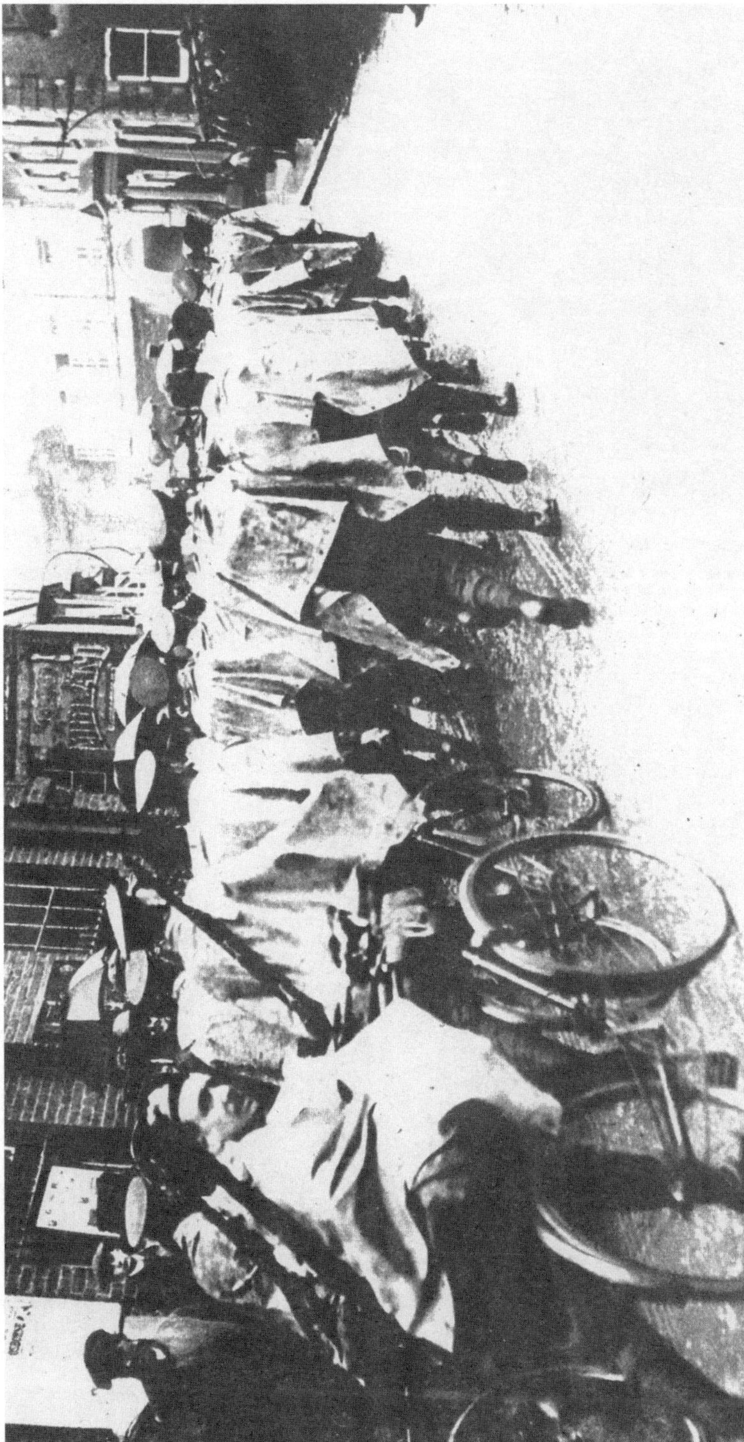

British troops, provided with raincoats, ready to embark for France

Not that the English soldiers ever complain about rain, they are accustomed to it! Covered against the rain and mud, their main thoughts are of getting back home again.

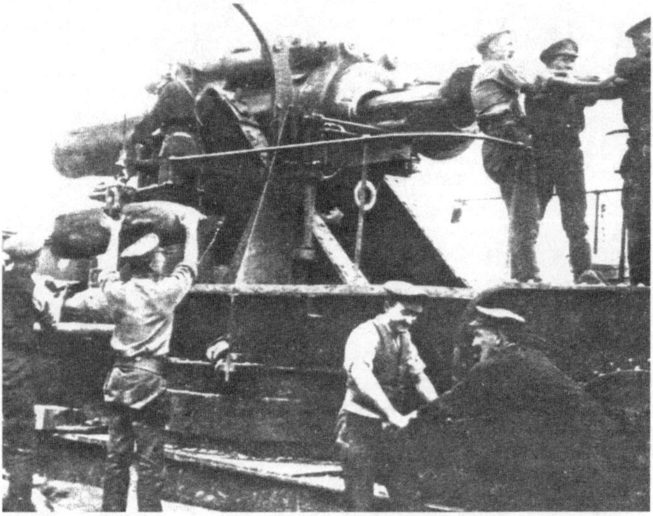

British heavy artillery in action

At Bassee in the Somme, the intensity of the shooting by British artillery is continuous. This railway mounted gun fires every few minutes, with railwaymen assisting their army colleagues.

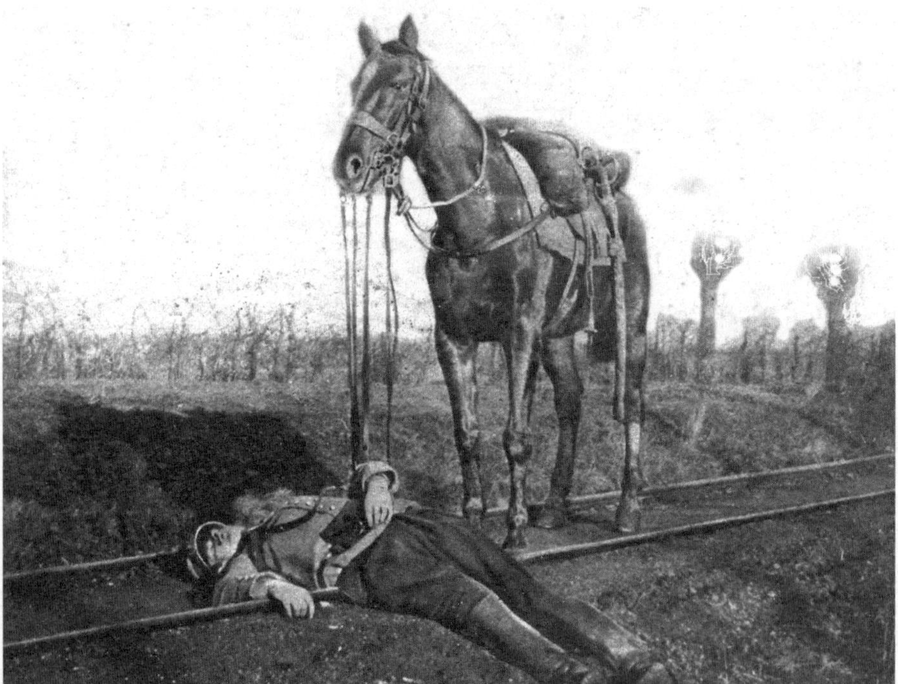

A Hussar killed by the railway track while on reconnaissance

Some photographs, as this one, are complete in themselves. The rider has been shot while he was walking with his horse - the animal remained immobile, quivering with concern.

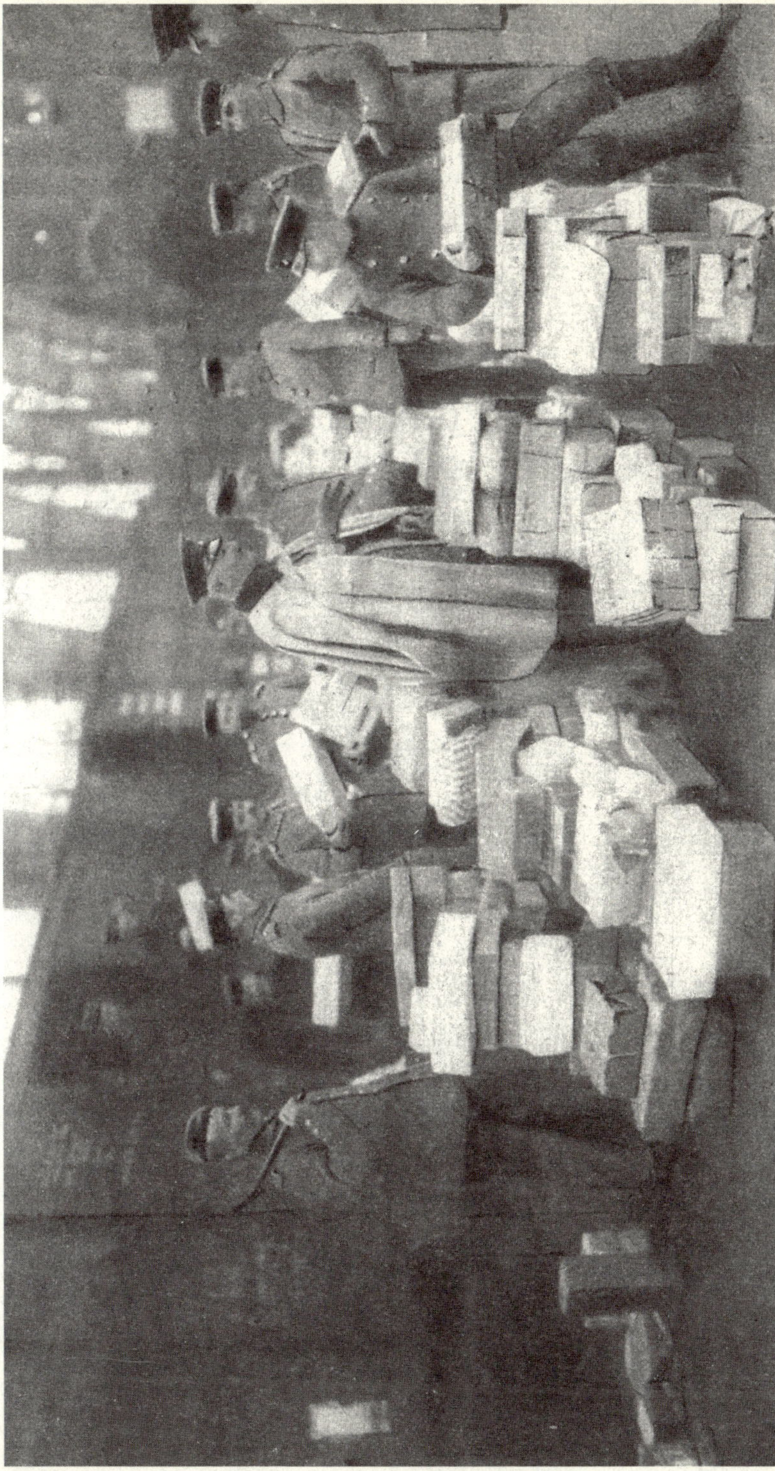

German customs-officers in Antwerp inspecting packets for Christmas addressed to soldiers

The garrison of Antwerp is mainly composed of Bavarians, who currently cost the Germans 80,000 francs per day. The Germans have reinforced the outskirts of the city with a deep trench and networks of barbed wire. Some 150 men desert on average per week to cross over to Holland.

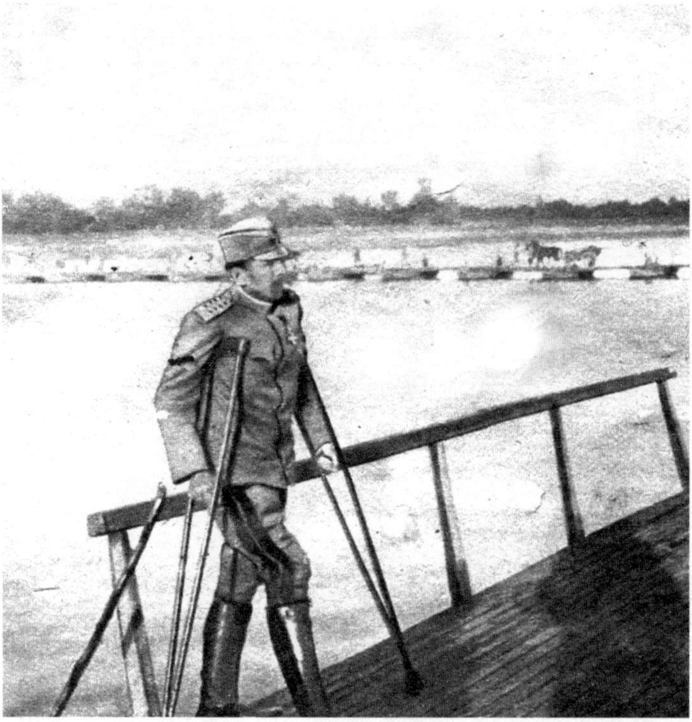

General Bayovitch crossing the River Save

While commanding the First Serbian Army, General Bayovitch was severely wounded near Chabatz. Here we see him crossing the River Save, while his army moves into Austrian territory.

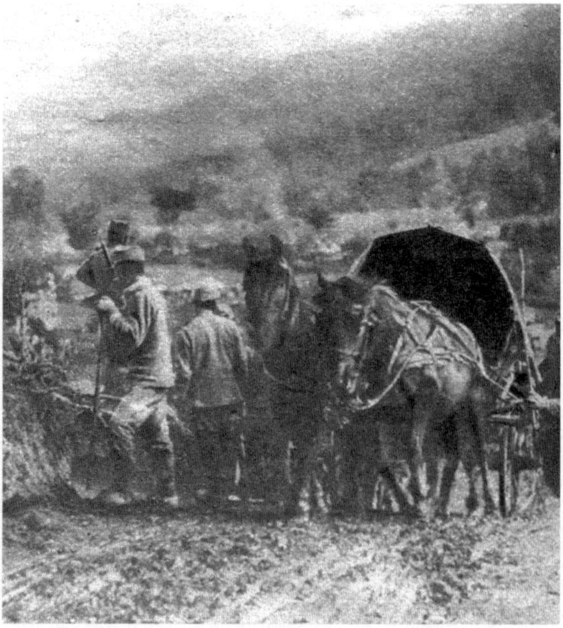

A Serbian munitions convoy in the mountains

With roads often soaked by rains, the Serbian convoys negotiate the mountains. One can only imagine the energy and courage demanded for their valiant fight.

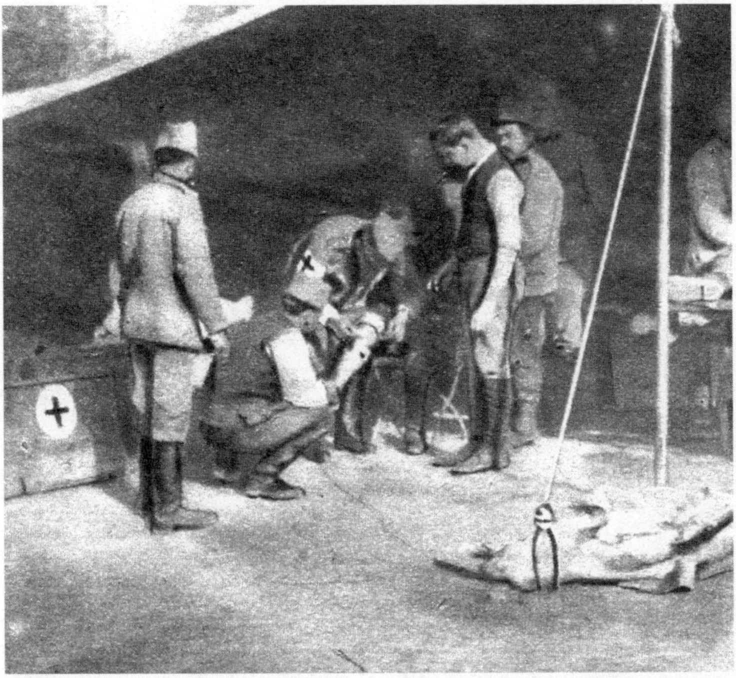

A Serbian field hospital

To take on the Austrians and succeed, the victorious Serbian army made sacrifices and the wounded were numerous. Injuries were mainly caused by the enemy's bullets.

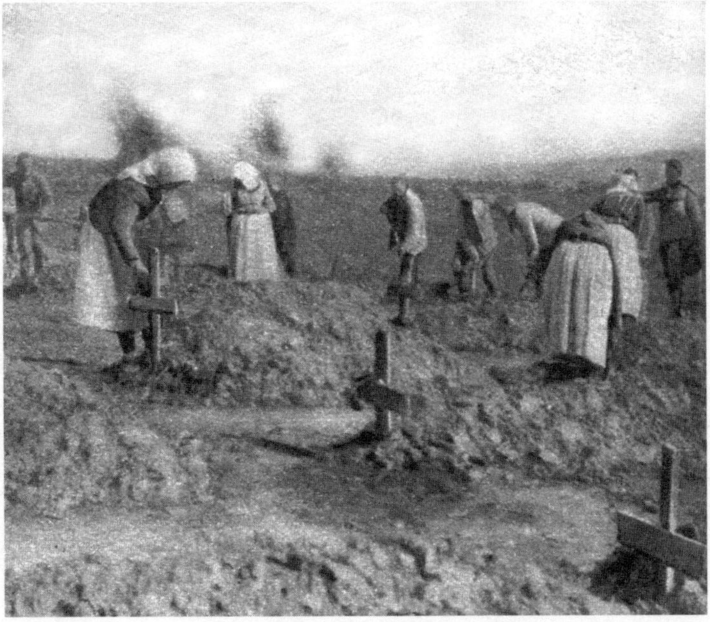

Serbian women decorate graves

Girls dressed in their best costumes, devoutly decorate graves with flowers and wreaths.

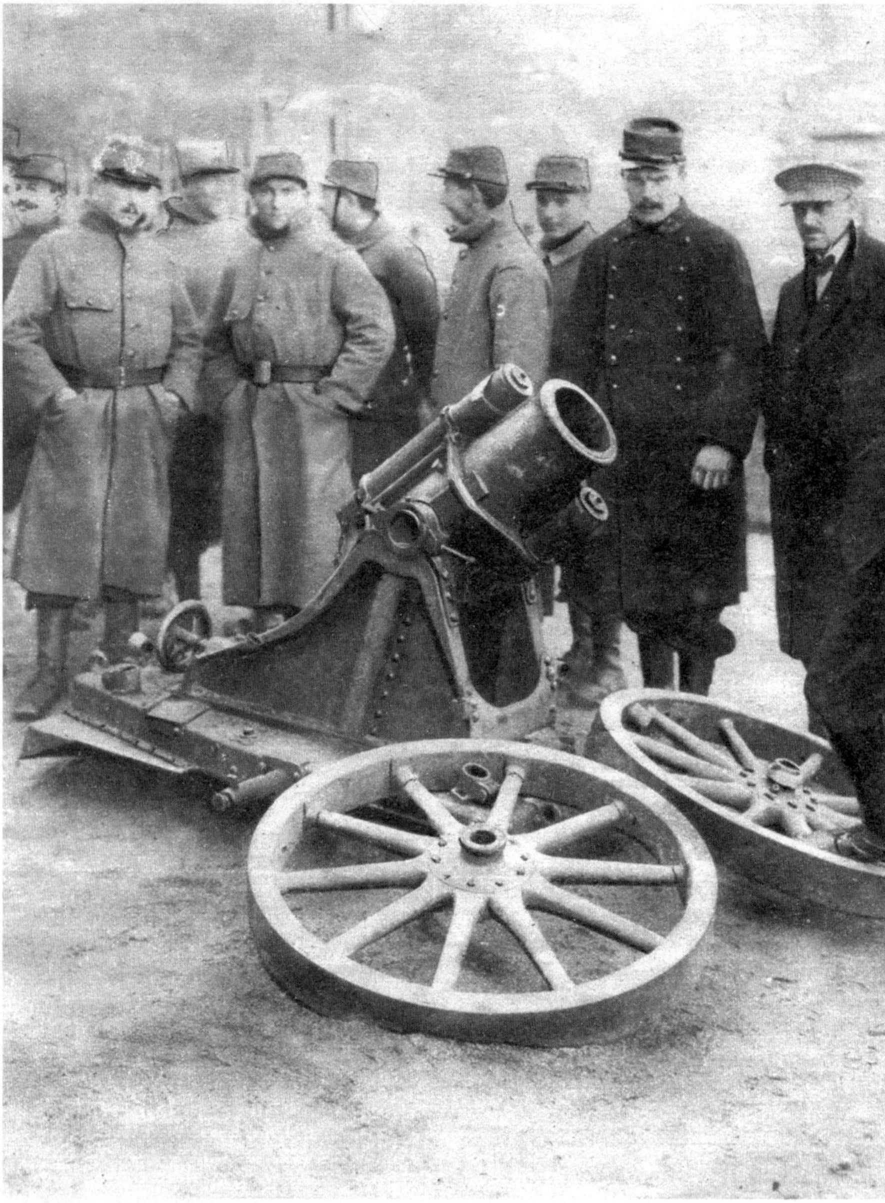

A captured mortar from the trenches near Dixmude

We often wonder what the 'Minenwerfer ' uses in German trenches. It is a contraption destined to fire haphazardly from afar, but we know little about it. It is a mortar of 18cm that includes two pneumatic rams, one above, the other underneath. In the vertical position it tilts to 90' ; the horizontal aim is made on the platform by means of a crank. Removable wheels permit it to be harnessed to a limber or to be pulled by hand.

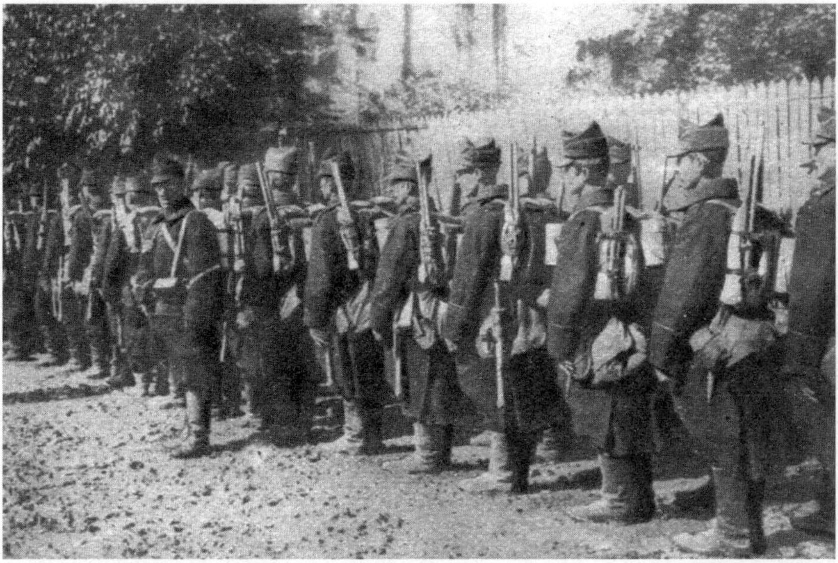

Romanian Infantry Soldiers

Romania can raise 5,000,000 men of which forty regiments are infantry [Dorobantzi].

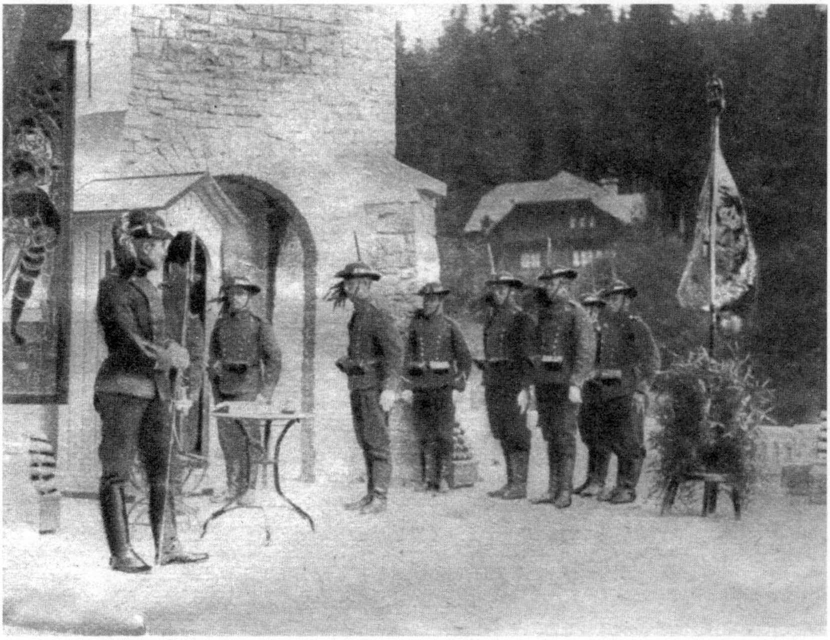

Romanian mountain troops

The Romanian army has nine battalions of 'hunters', mountain infantry specialists with Mannlicher rifles, type 1893, 6.5 mm calibre.

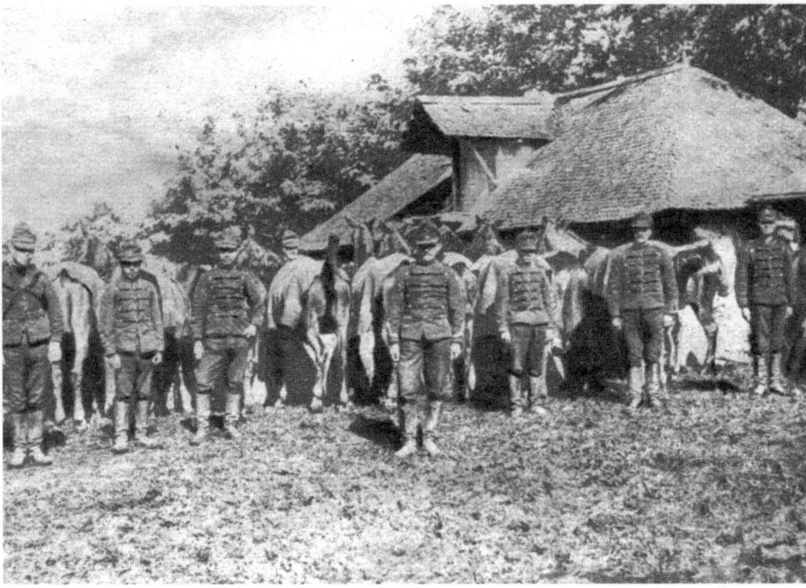

Romanian cavalry [Calarasi] on manœuvres

Hussars form eleven regiments, each with four squadrons. Cavalry service is for three years.

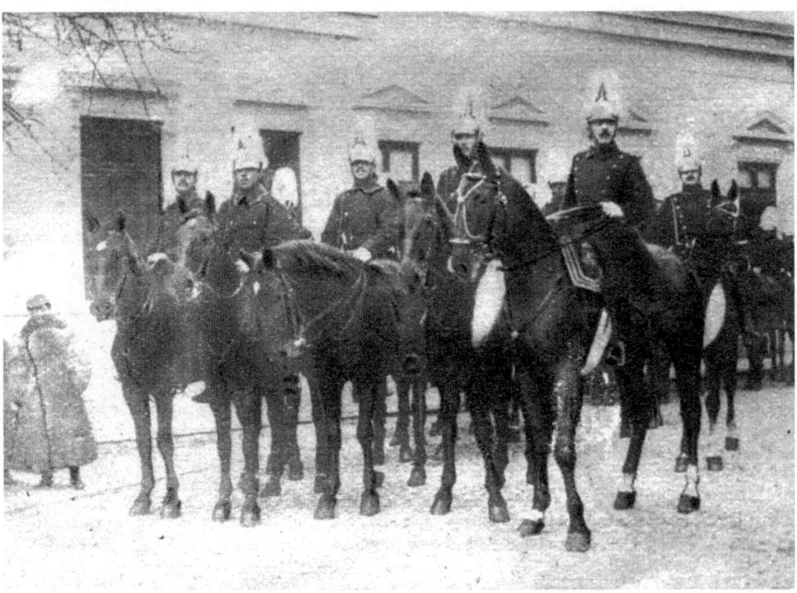

Riders of the royal escort at Jassy

The nine regiments of cavalry include one for royal escort duty, of which part is at Bucharest and the remainder at Jassy.

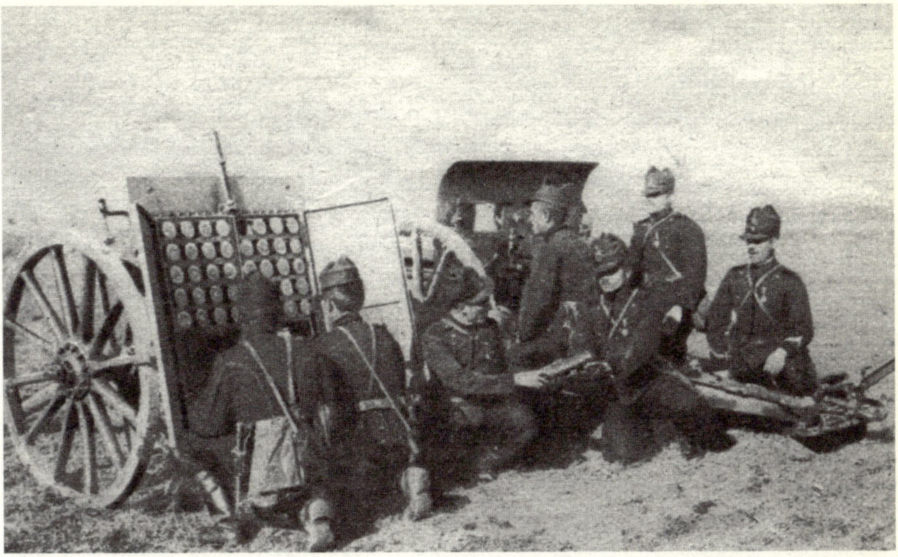

A 75mm Romanian gun in action

Each of the twenty regiments of artillery have five batteries. Cannons are the 7.5 cm model 1908.

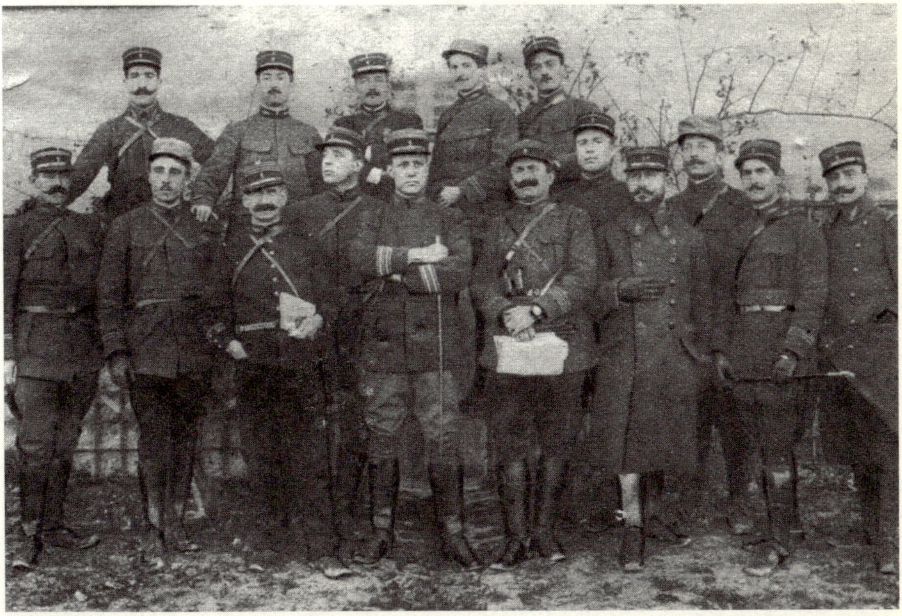

A group of officers from the Italian foreign regiment

Two thousand Italians from overseas have returned home to form a regiment fighting for the allies. They received a baptism of fire in Argonne. This noble cause lost forty who fell in the field with honour during the first engagement.

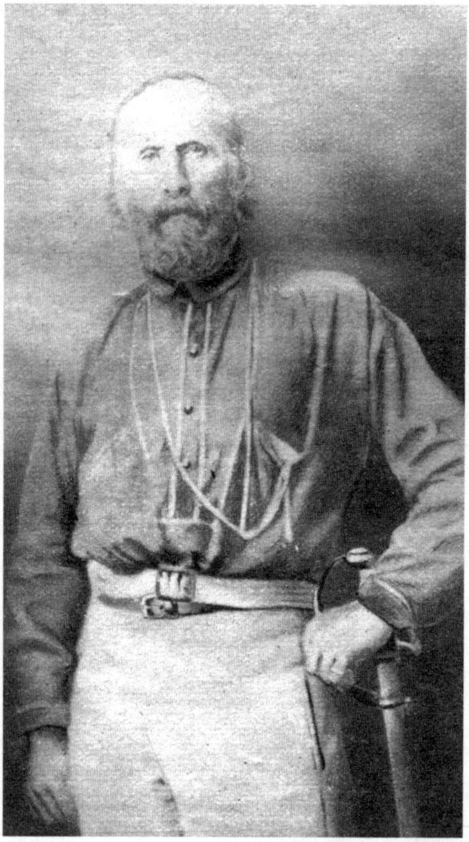

Guiseppe Garibaldi

The memory of the hero, who died in 1882, lives on. His followers fight on, proudly worthy of him.

Garibaldi's six sons of whom two have already been killed by the enemy

The emotion caused by the heroic death of Bruno Garibaldi was remembered when his brother Constantin also fell under fire from German bullets in Argonne. In the centre, lieutenant-colonel Peppino Garibaldi surrounded by his brothers. The first left is Bruno, the last right the adjutant-chief Constantin.

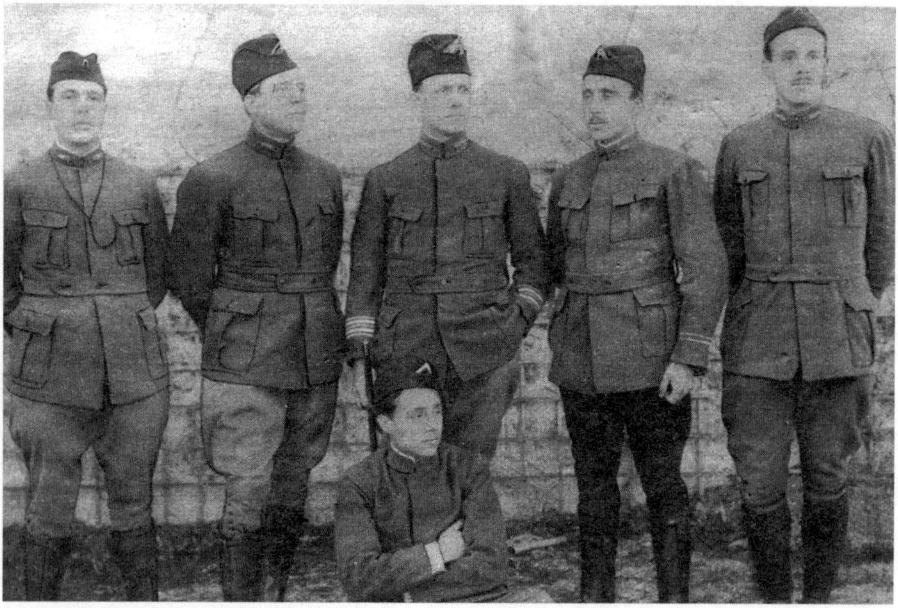

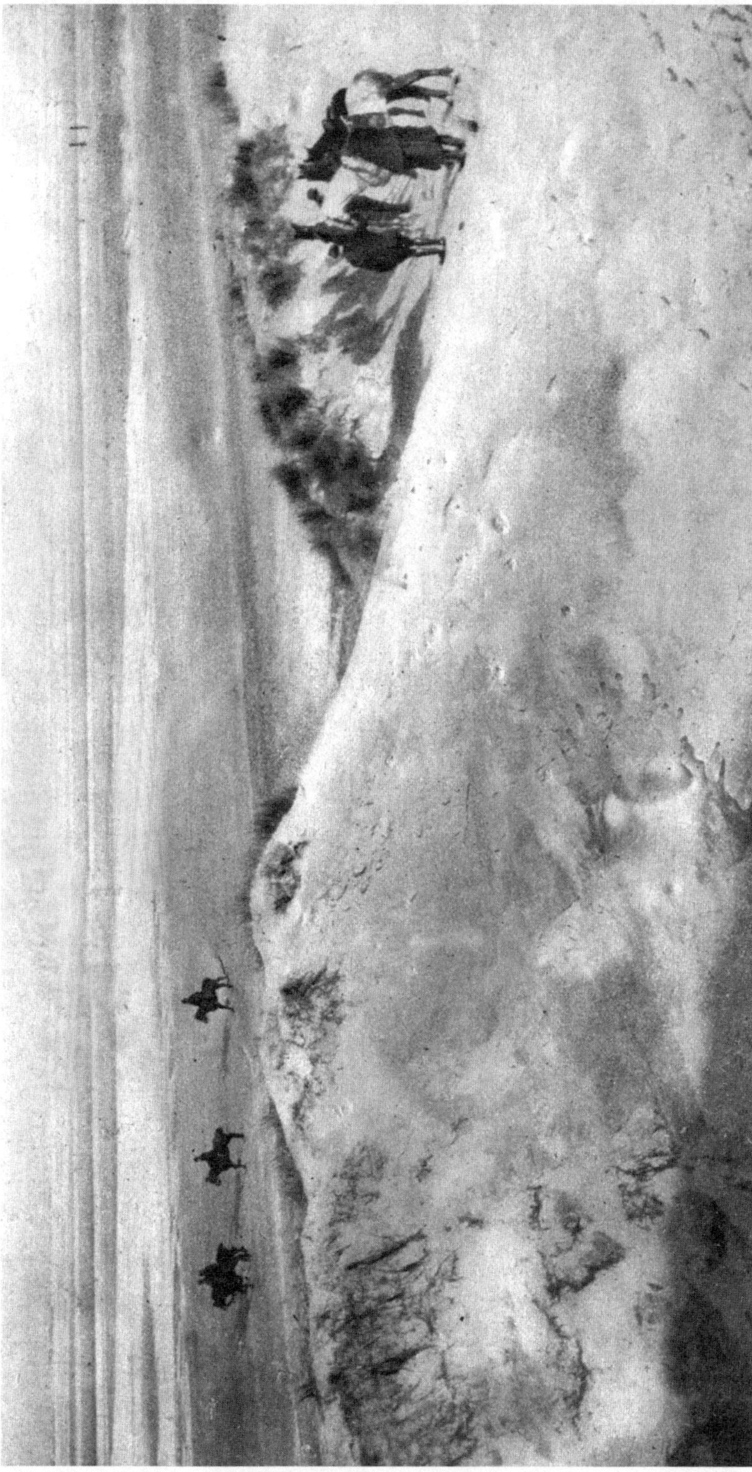

Belgian riders in patrol on the coast to the west of Nieuport

Allied troops have, during these last weeks, made appreciable progress, but communication is often difficult. We publish here some photographs that give an idea of this region and the land which leaves our troops open to ambush. The nature of soil permits entrenchment and the men don't suffer from damp or water, which quickly drains away.

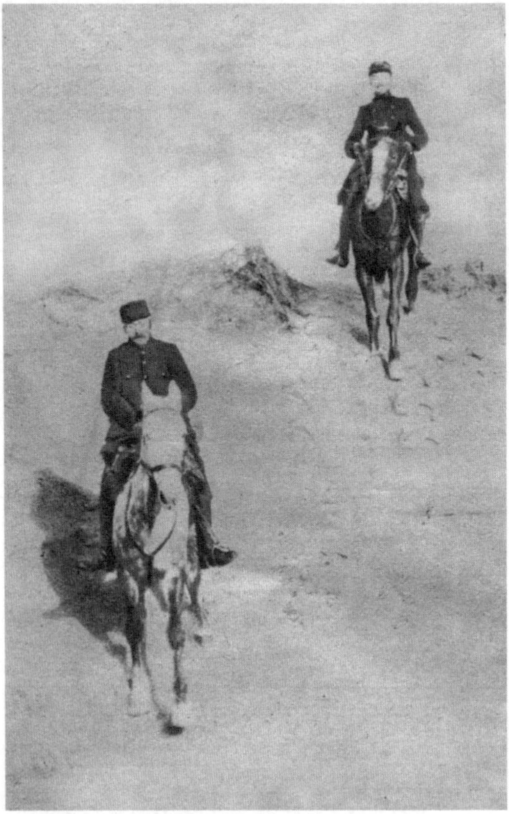

Belgian officers on reconnaissance

Several times recently, the Belgian army have made some very daring cavalry raids to the west of Nieuport, towards Ostende.

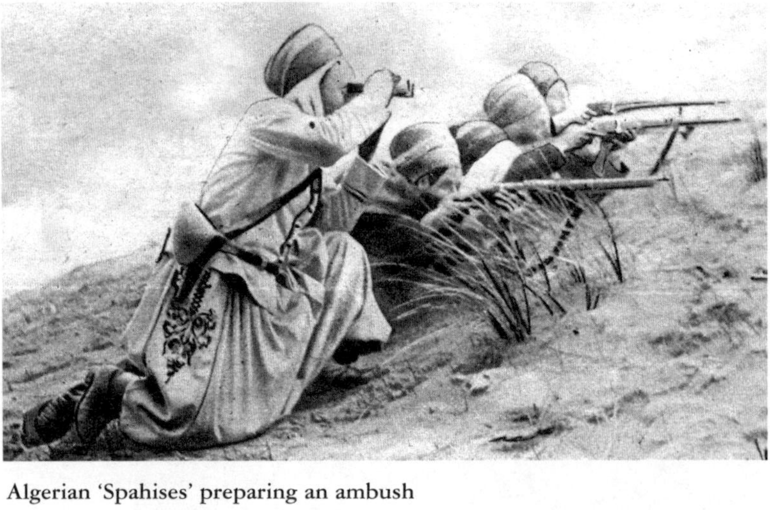

Algerian 'Spahises' preparing an ambush

In the sand, these 'Spahises' are quite at home. They have proven their ability in this kind of warfare. On the left is lieutenant Ferhat Aissa who leads a contingent of Algerian volunteers.

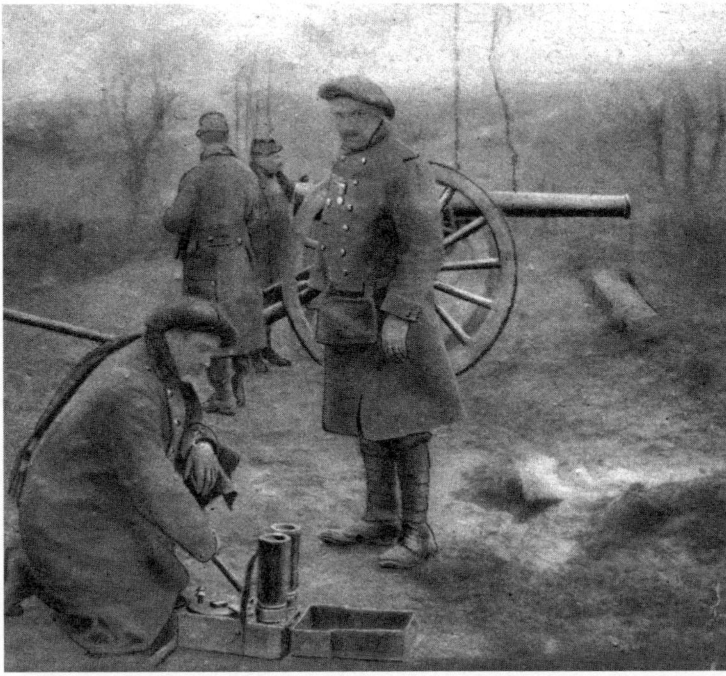

French alpine troops practice with 90m cannons.

In the Vosges these troops, more used to ski shoes in the Alps, are learning to use cannons instead of bayonets.

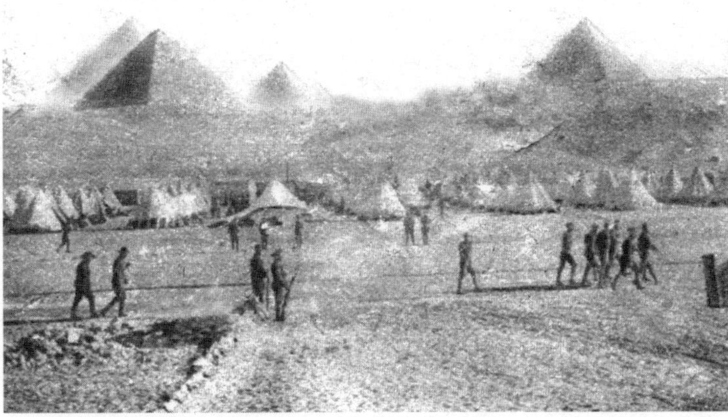

An Australian camp by pyramids

The Australian contingent establish a camp at the foot of Pyramids, that over the centuries have seen so many warriors and battles.

- NEWS REPORTS -

Thursday 11 February, 1915

Allies have secured the village of La Boisselle, having crossed three mine fields and now occupy new ground in spite of a counter attack that was defeated by a bayonet charge. In Argonne, shellfire and bombing in the region of Bagatelle and Bolonte. A violent attack, but fruitless for the Germans.

In Lorraine, a German offensive was contained near Manonvillers. The Germans are increasing their offensive against the Russians in Oriental Prussia. Russian successes in Galicia and the Carpathians. M. Déclasse, French Minister of Foreign Affairs, came to London for discussions with Sir Edward Grey, British Foreign Secretary, but has now returned to Paris.

In Prussia, the socialists have protested against the indefinite length of the war.

Friday February 12, 1915

Mr. Asquith, British Prime Minister, declared to the House of Commons that sterner measures should be applied against German trade as the enemy were systematically breaching all of the laws of war. The United States sent a note to England to make some observations on the use, by the British merchant navy, of their (US) neutral position. They sent another note to Germany saying that the attack on an American ship by a German submarine would require some detailed explanation!

The Germans have bombard Nieuport with little success, while French artillery returned fire. The enemy, in the north, is using planes to operate over allied lines but without any effect. They attacked French positions in Champagne but this was decimated by artillery fire and infantry, leaving many bodies scattered across the land.

The Bulgarian ambassador in Rome, Mr. Risof, stated that their cabinet in Sofia, was making a loan to Berlin from Vienna, but suggests that it would not compromise their political liberty.

Saturday February 13, 1915

A German submarine pursued the British steamer, Laertes, in Dutch waters. The American government published the text of the note that it sent to Germany on the topic of the destruction of their neutral ships. This note sounded a distinctly threatening tone, while the memorandum sent to England about neutrality is viewed as friendly. The Dutch government in The Hague wants an investigation into this.

Heavy fire around Reims. In Argonne, a light break, with the Germans limiting themselves to throwing hand grenades. In Woevre, shellfire in several localities. Italy has a squadron of several new ships. The Russians move back in Oriental Prussia, adopting a new tactic. It seems that von Hindenberg has modified his programme to crush Poland, and is now concentrating on its left front. In the Carpathians, the battle continues without interruption.

Sunday February 14, 1915

The United States have just asked for an explanation, from Germany, on the difficulties that their ambassador in The Hague has in communicating with Luxemburg. Italy and the Scandinavian states have protested, with America, against the decision of the admiralty in Berlin to threaten their neutrality.

The Germans have shelled Nieuport once again, also Ypres and the area surrounding the city but they have not advanced. German planes flew over Verdun. In Alsace, the enemy has shelled the new allied positions. The Russians are also gaining ground in the Carpathians. A Greek naval attachment has been held in Constantinople, the Greek ambassador wants to know why. If an explanation is not forthcoming, he has threatened to leave the capital.

Monday February 15, 1915

The cabinet in Berlin has just sent a new letter to Holland about the blockade in the North Sea. This text differs somewhat from the one that had been sent to the United States. The German chancellery, at the same time, has forbidden Danish and Norwegian boats to enter the high seas - establishing a blockade of Denmark and Norway towards the North Sea and hindering the vital trade of these two countries.

The Giornale d'Italia (newspaper) that speaks for Rome and is edited by Mr. Sonnino, Italian Foreign Minister, has published a call for unity and intervention in the European crisis. He suggests that Italy is not able to do more, without compromising its future and its national rights to neutrality. On the eve of the return of Italian parliament, this article is sensational - it appears to be the answer from the Salandra cabinet to criticism of Mr. Giolitti, the Italian Prime Minister.

Germany has sequestrated the monument of Turenne in Salzbach, a French monument that was erected on German soil in 1675. It stands on the right bank of the Rhine near Strasbourg. The Albanians, probably at the suggestion of Austria, have made an incursion into Prizrend on the Serbian border. The German shelling continues at Ypres with return fire by our artillery. In Champagne, Reims which had been quiet for some days, was shelled again.

Tuesday February 16, 1915

Count Bernstorff, German ambassador in Washington, has resorted to blackmail, announcing to the American government that the German admiralty would renounce its threat against the neutral countries if England agrees to allow cargos and supplies into Hamburg.

Italy has confirmed its solidarity with Romania. The Greek ambassador has left Constantinople, not having received a satisfactory answer regarding his naval squadron.

Wednesday February 17, 1915

A German submarine has sunk the coal steamer Dulwich, of 2,115 tons, off the coast of Etretat, Normandy. The majority of the crew were saved. A favourable day for allied armies. Artillery fighting in Belgium; the British bomb Ostend and the French attack the German airfield at Ghistelles, Belgium. The British army takes trenches at Ypres. French dissipate enemy troops at Bailly, between the Oise and Aisne, more progress in Loivre, Reims; three kilometres of trenches taken in Champagne with several hundred prisoners; in the Argonne, a successful fight concluded.

Switzerland has demand an apology from the German cabinet for a German plane flying over Swiss territory. An unofficial newspaper in Vienna, the Nouvelle Presse libre (New Free Press), has warned Italy to remain friends with them.

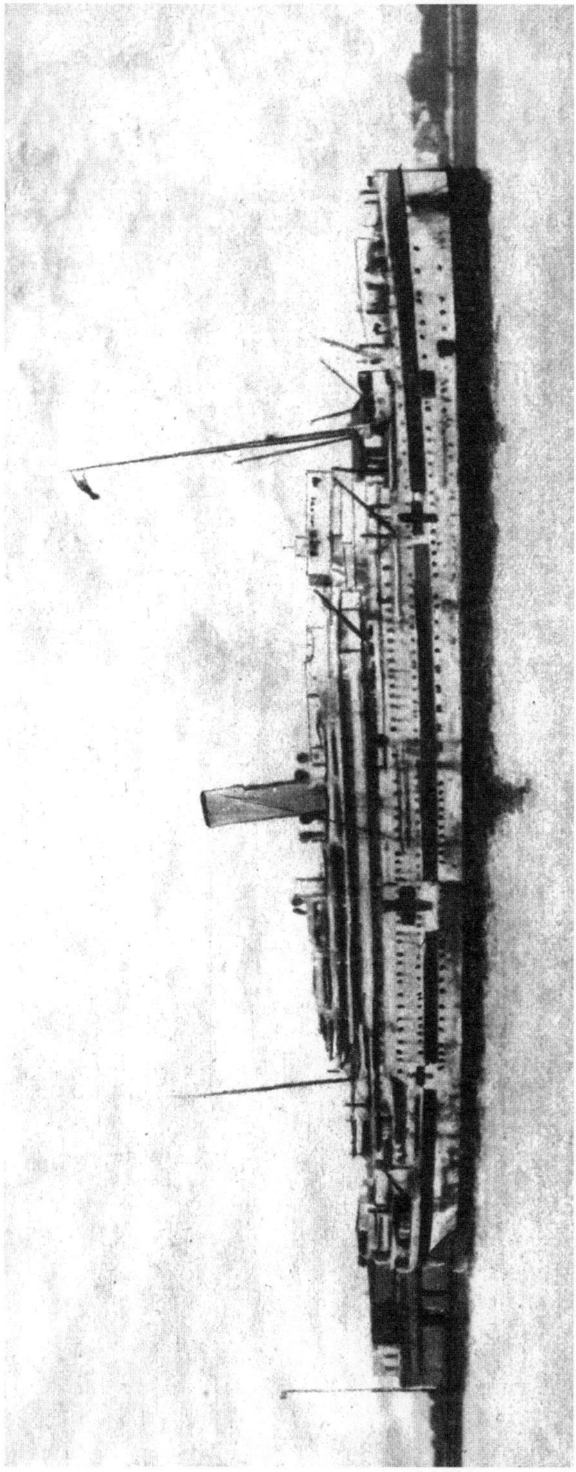

The British hospital ship "Asturais"

The 12,000 tonne English steamer, converted to hospital ship 'Asturais', was torpedoed by a submarine at the entrance to Le Havre.

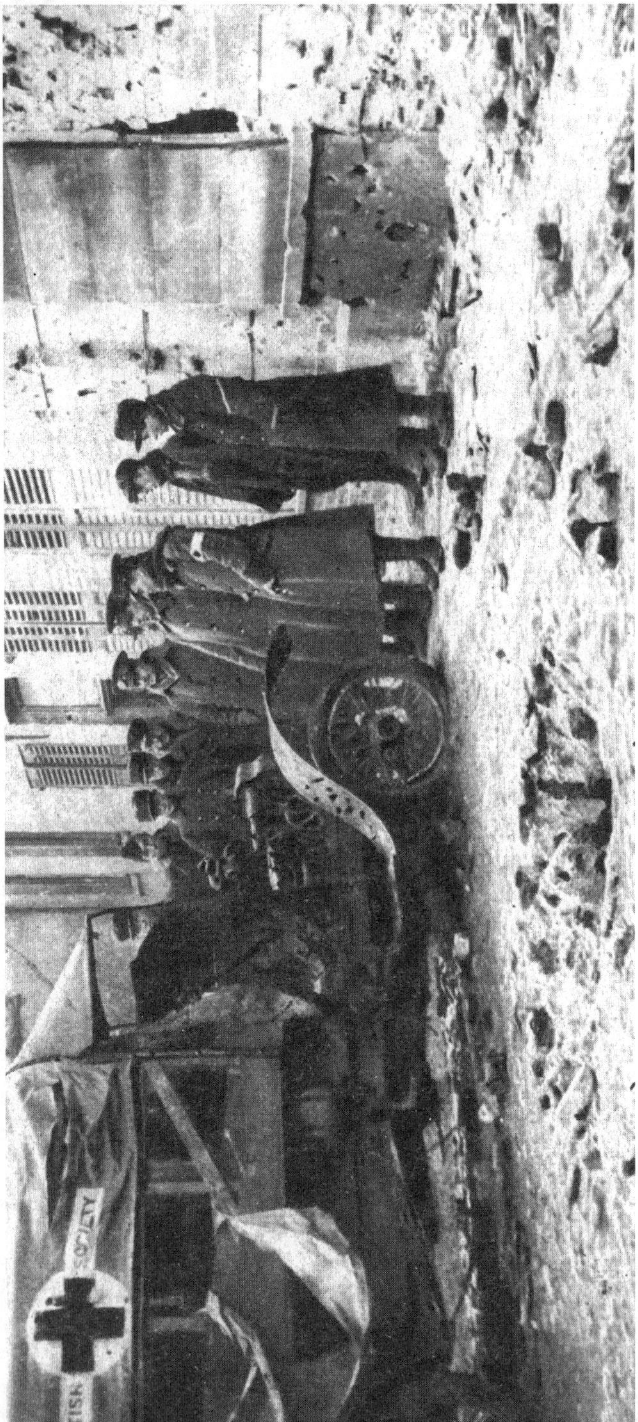

A British Red Cross car that came under fire at Furnes

Germans have shelled Furnes and this car, killing the driver and the wounded that were carried in it.

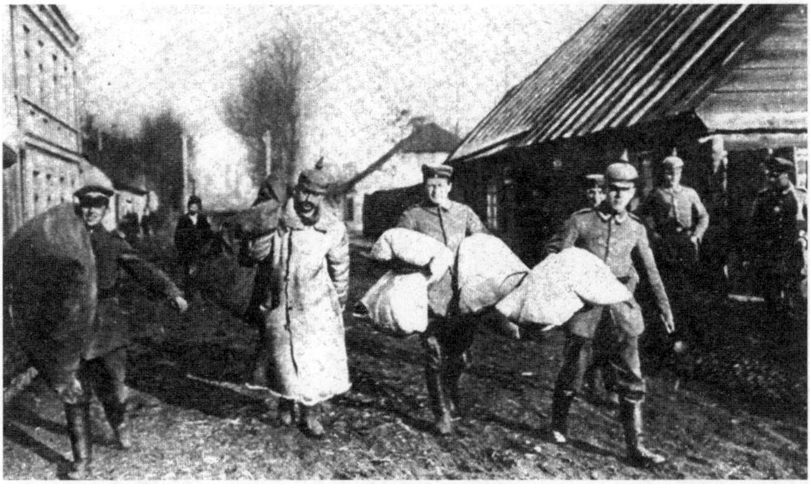

German pillagers carrying away bedding in Alsace

Having ransacked houses, soldiers remove covers, pillows and bedding without asking for permission.

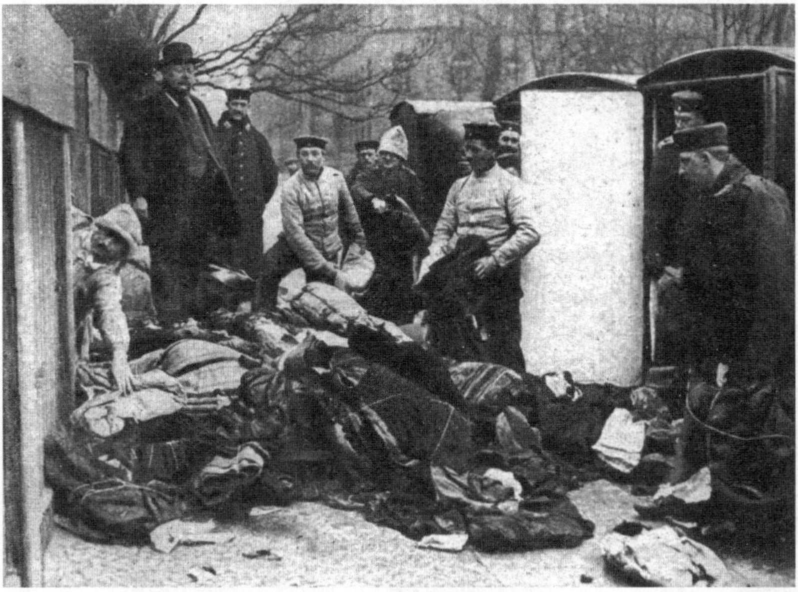

The loot from France and Belgium arrives in Berlin

With no wool available in Germany, collections in the regions are sent to Berlin. The material is disinfected in steam before being reused.

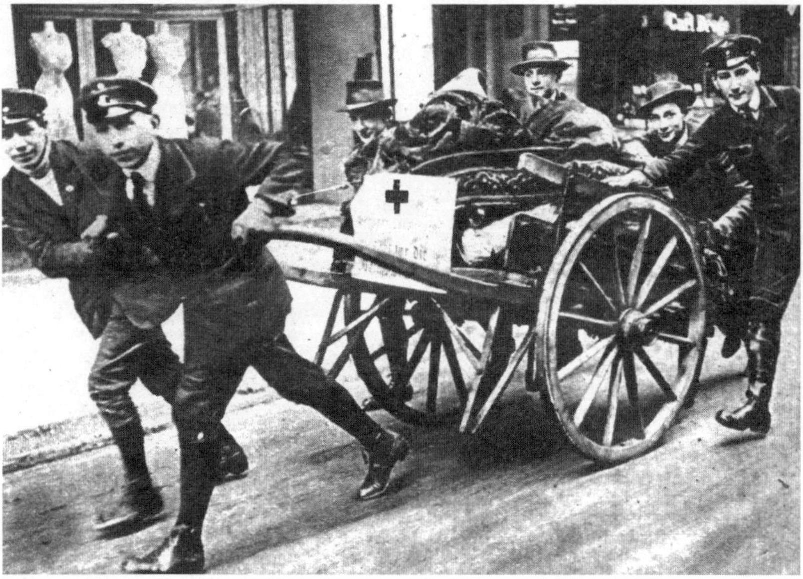

How Germany teaches its children integrity

These young boys transport the material, unaware of the honesty of their parents.

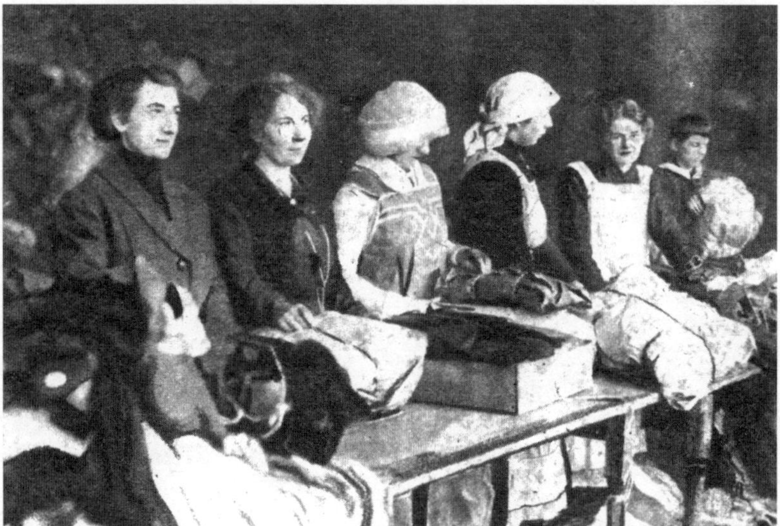

A shop of "transformed goods" in Berlin

Disinfected and sorted, clothes are brought to shops, transformed for the use of soldiers.

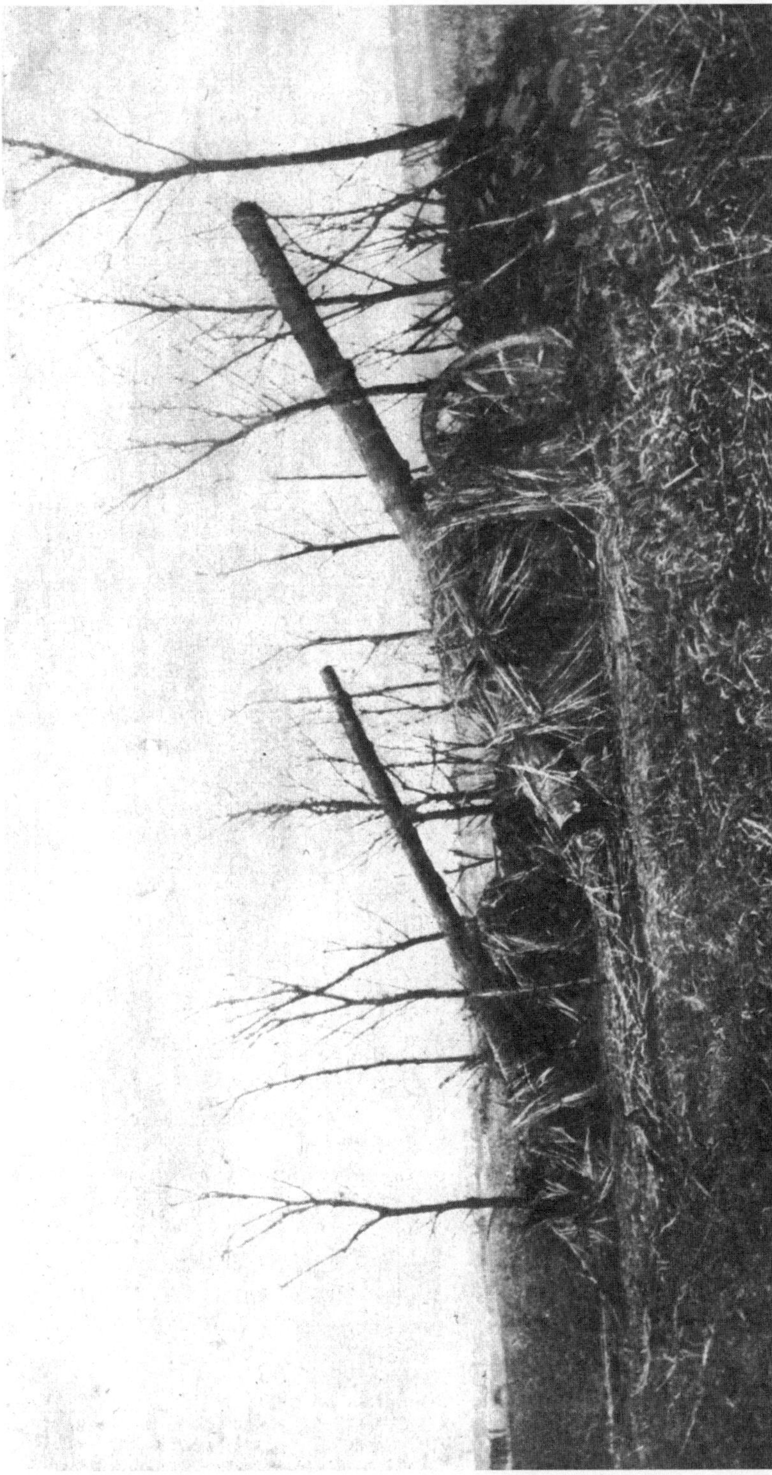

Funny tricks used by the Allies - Two false 155mm cannons [Les Marmites]

A classic trick played on the enemy is to construct dummy cannons, concealed enough to attract the German aviators attention. These decoys, their position quickly marked, draw enemy fire from our troops.

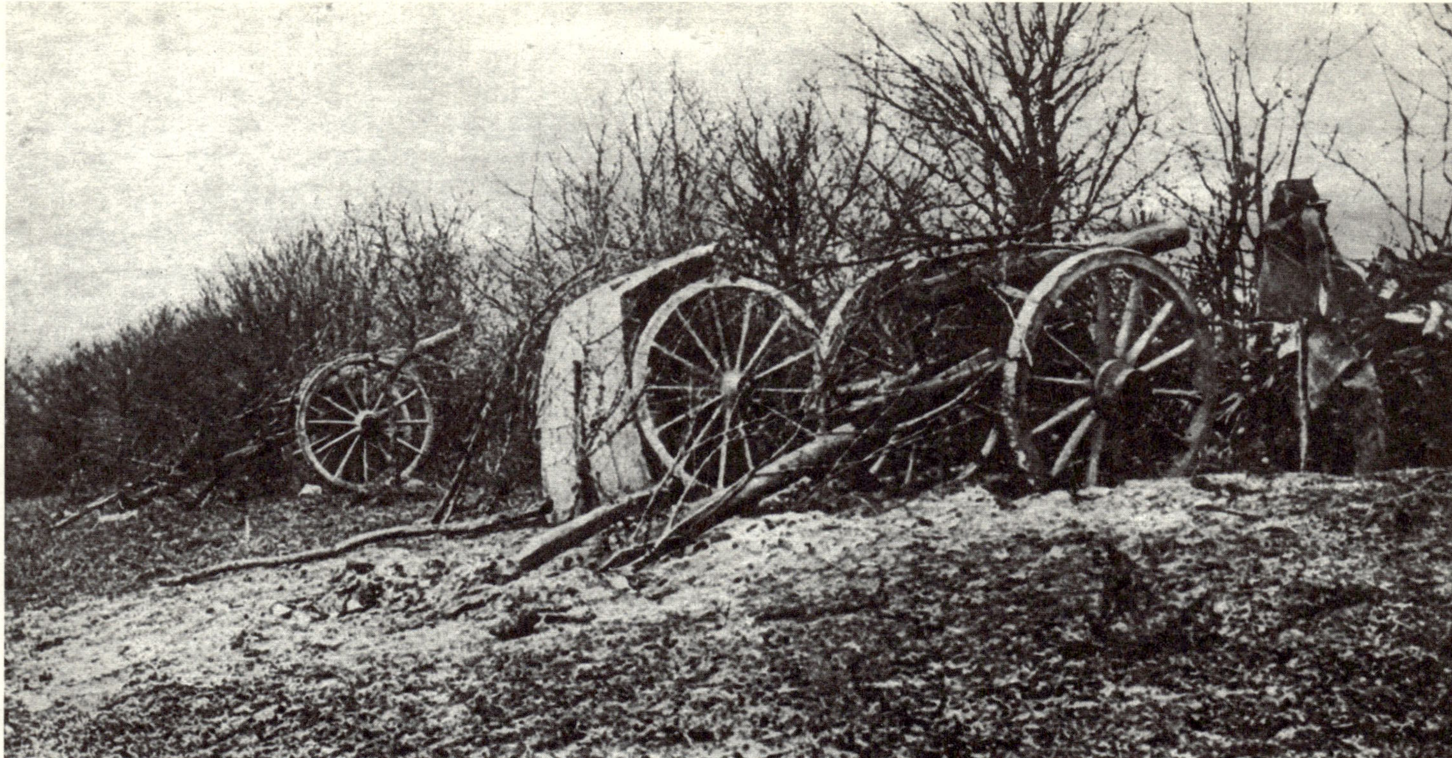

A joke 75mm battery, its destruction cost the enemy dearly

Ingenuity and a legendary joke. From afar, the appearance of a real battery but without so much as being able to fire at the enemy. Although this battery was near the front line, the Germans shelled it continuously, using hundreds of pounds on shells to destroy it.

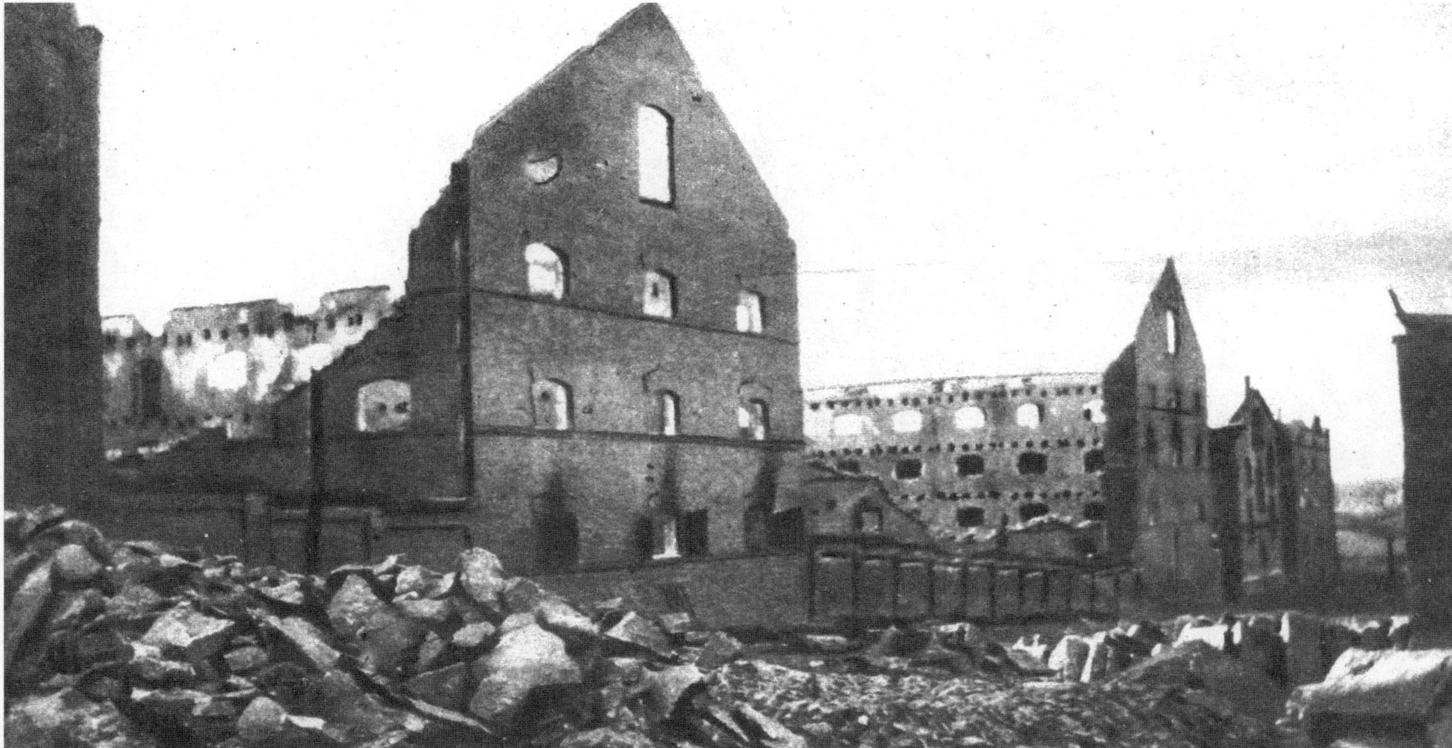

The Belgrade tobacco factory destroyed by incendiary shells

Batteries of Austrian artillery, on the opposite bank of the Danube outside Belgrade have shelled the capital that was evacuated at the beginning of the war. They succeeded in causing a number of fires that were quite intense in some districts. The 'white city' defended itself valiantly. During this long bombardment, Prince George, son of the King Peter 1st of Serbia, was wounded but he has since recovered.

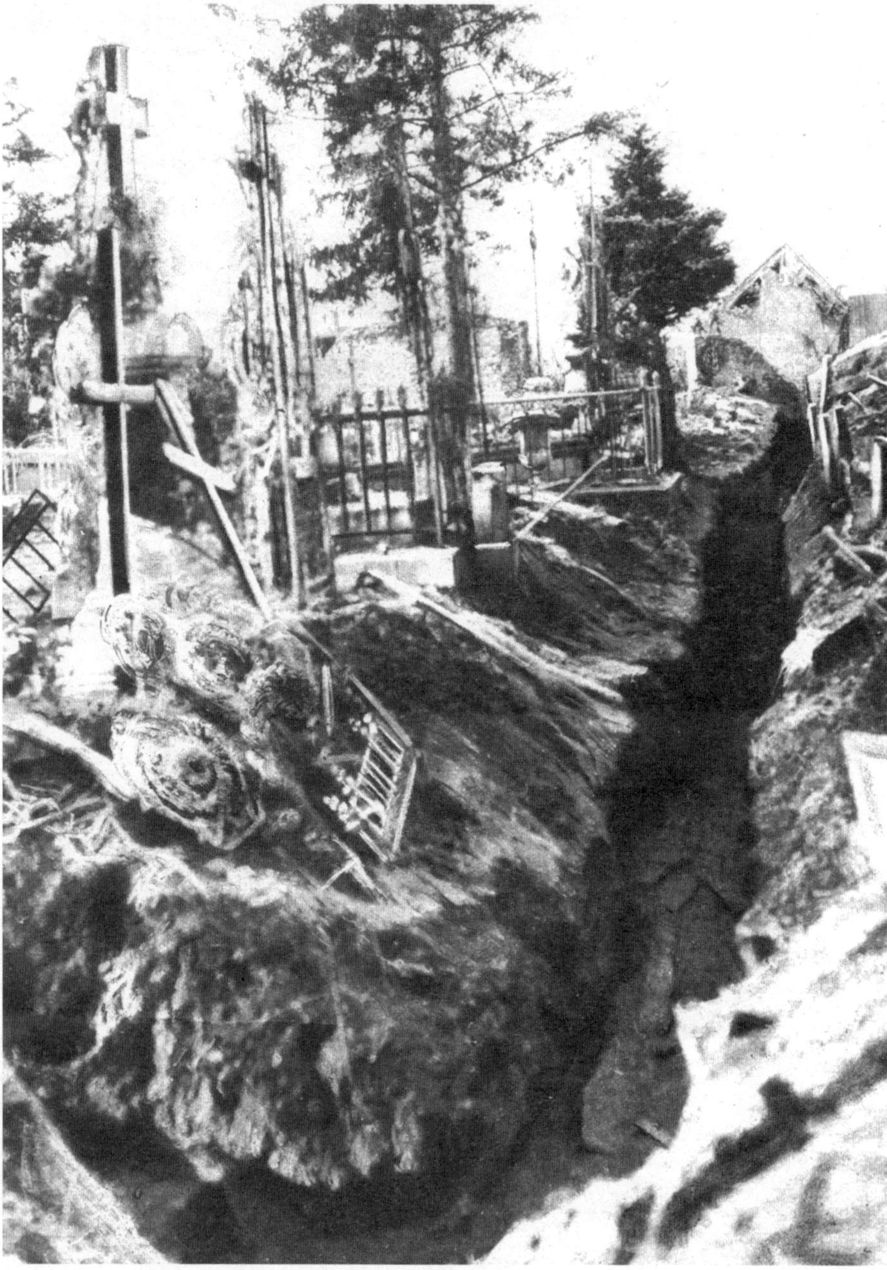

A German trench cuts through a cemetery

Without respect for death, they have cut a trench across graves. The Germans are not content with abuse, they desecrate as well. In this small village cemetery they have ravaged crosses and funeral stones.

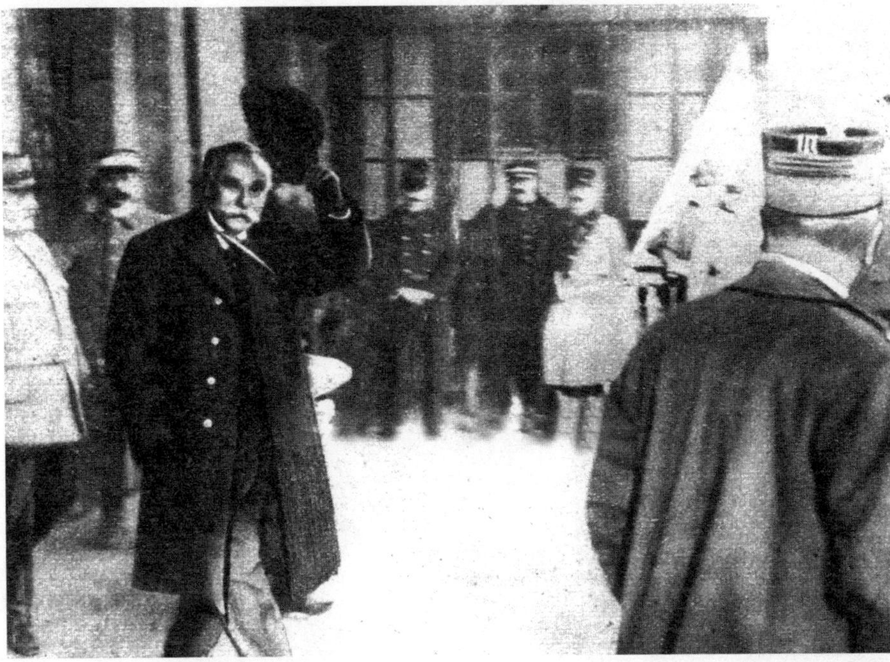

On his way to Athens, General Pau passes through Marseille

General Pau, on his way to Russia via Greece, was cheered heartily as he embarked at Marseille. In civilian clothes, he is seen leaving the station.

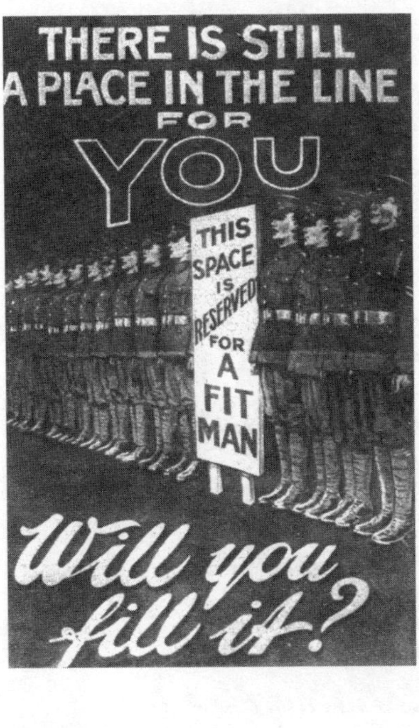

A British recruitment poster

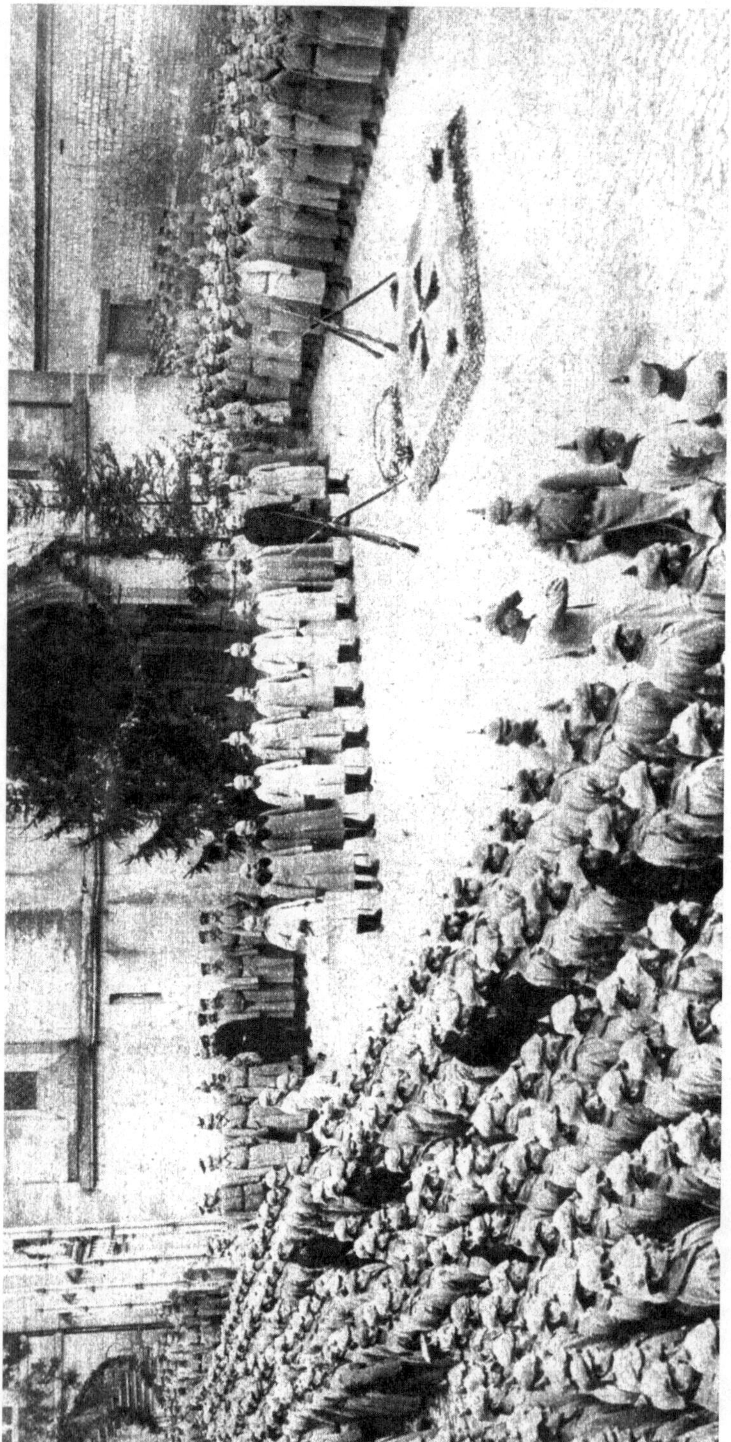

The Kaiser's birthday celebrated in France

This photo, taken in front of the church at Neufchâtel, near Laon, shows the ceremony that took place on occasion of the Kaiser's birthday. It presents an interesting sight because it will never happen again.

-NEWS REPORTS -

Thursday April 15, 1915

A British torpedo boat and cruiser are now off the Dardanelles shelling the coast. A French pilot dropped some bombs on the stronghold of Smyrne. In Champagne, allied firing has stopped and a detachment of infantry advanced forward. In Eparges, allied artillery has halted a counter attack, capturing soldiers, their rifles and munitions. A Zeppelin dropped some bombs on Bailleul killing three civilians. Two German planes landed behind allied lines, near Lunéville; the avaitors have been taken prisoner. A third plane was damaged by our fire to the north of Verdun.

Italy vigorously pursues its military preparations. A women's revolt took place in Prague and some Czech regiments are also rebelling in Hungary.

Friday April 16, 1915

German submarines have torpedoed a British cruiser and a Dutch steamer. German cruisers seized four Dutch trawlers at Cuxhaven. A Zeppelin dropped a number of bombs on the British coastline at Northumberland, the damage to property was small, no-one was killed. The official total for British losses to April 11 is 139,147 men killed, wounded, taken prisoner or missing.

Saturday April 17, 1915

Zeppelins have flown over the British coast in Essex and Suffolk, but their bombs didn't produce any significant results, their only victim was a hen!

French troops have stopped three German counter attacks. Their pilots dropped ten bombs on the workshops and railway at Leopoldshohe, another ten nearby plus forty on the electricity plant at Maiz-les-Metz.

An incident occurred on the Austro-Italian border where fifteen Austrian soldiers and customs officers have crossed onto Italian soil. The government of Rome has changed some members to those who favour the German empire. A French cruiser destroyed a bridge and railroad track on the coast of Syria. The situation has become very critical in Constantinople, the lack of supplies making itself felt now. During a council of war, Sultan Mehmed V, ruler of Turkey, let slip the possibility of his abdication.

Sunday April 18, 1915

In northern France, three successive German counter attacks have been defeated and our positions strengthened.

Monday April 19, 1915

New British success in Mesopotamia. A British submarine, caught in a minefield off the Dardanelles, is stranded near the beach at Kephis. The crew may have been captured by the Turks, under instruction from Constantinople. The battle of the Carpathians seems to be in a lull.

A Greek ship, the Ellispontos, was torpedo in the North Sea. In Champagne, the enemy has retreated slightly following a land mine explosion; we have gained a few score yards of trenches.

Tuesday April 20, 1915

The British troops in Belgium have taken 200 metres of trenches and strengthened their position. In Alsace, an allied advance is confirmed, taking two cannons and two machine guns.

French pilot Garros has landed in Flanders and has been taken prisoner. The battle of the Carpathians is momentarily suspended. Up to now, the Russians have captured 70,000 Austro-Germans, 30 cannons and 200 machine guns. Some Bavarian reinforcements are approaching Cracow.

The shellfire has restarted in the Dardanelles. Austria and Germany have recalled their steam ships that were in Italian waters. New riots took place in Austria, especially in Trentin, bought on by hunger.

The Gazette of Frankfurt questions the expense of the war, to April 1st, costing the country some 42 billion deutschmarks.

Wednesday April 21, 1915

In London, Mr. Lloyd George declares to the House of Commons that conscription may be superfluous because of the good results of volunteer recruitment.

The Germans fired fifty incendiary shells on Reims. Artillery struggles in Argonne and Champagne. The demonstrations, discouragement and general war-weariness increase in Austria and Hungary.

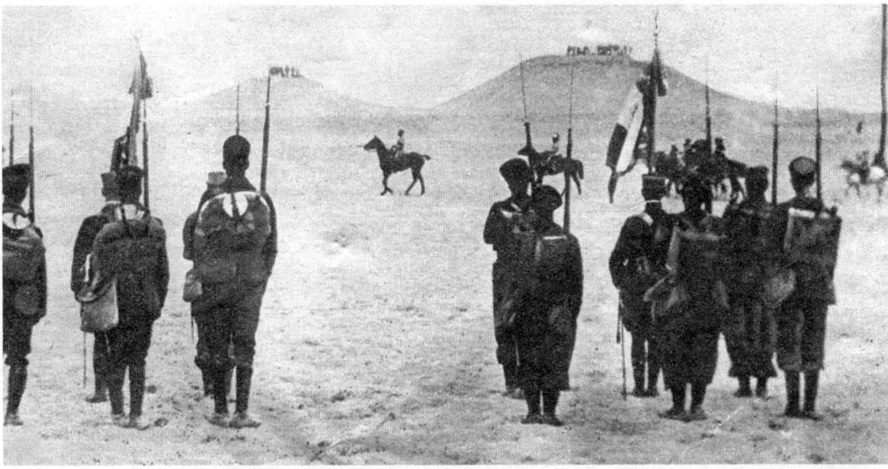

Oriental troops receiving their battle flags

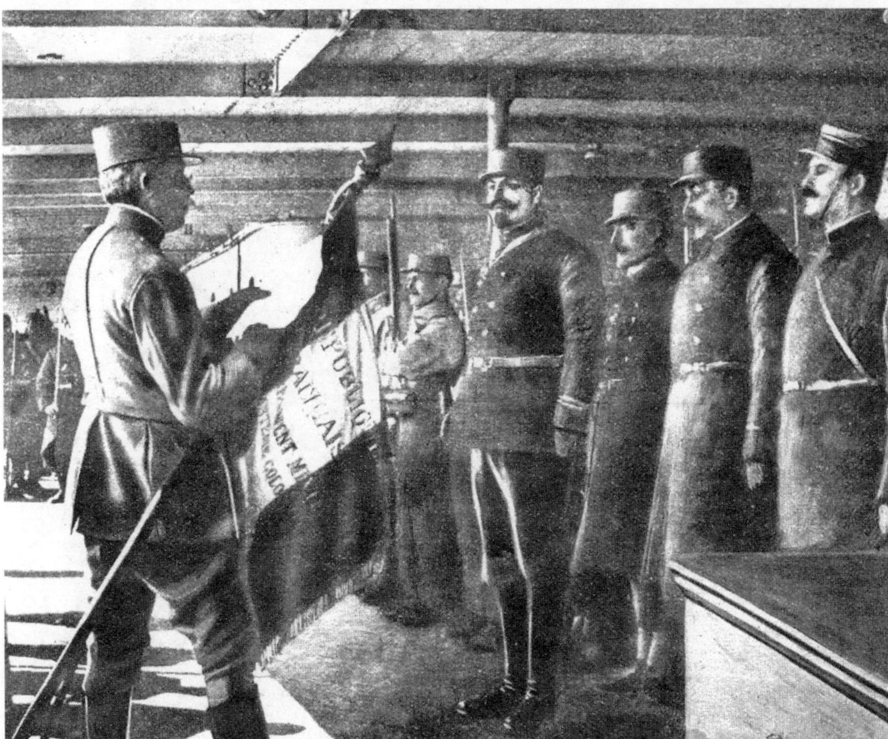

The Oriental troops are based largely in Alexandria, where the population gave an enthusiastic welcome. General Sir John Hamilton (British) and General Amade (French) are seen reviewing the troops after presenting the flags to two colonial regiments. The second picture shows General Amade reading a speech to the troops with orders regarding the enemy, and presenting the flag that he holds in his hand.

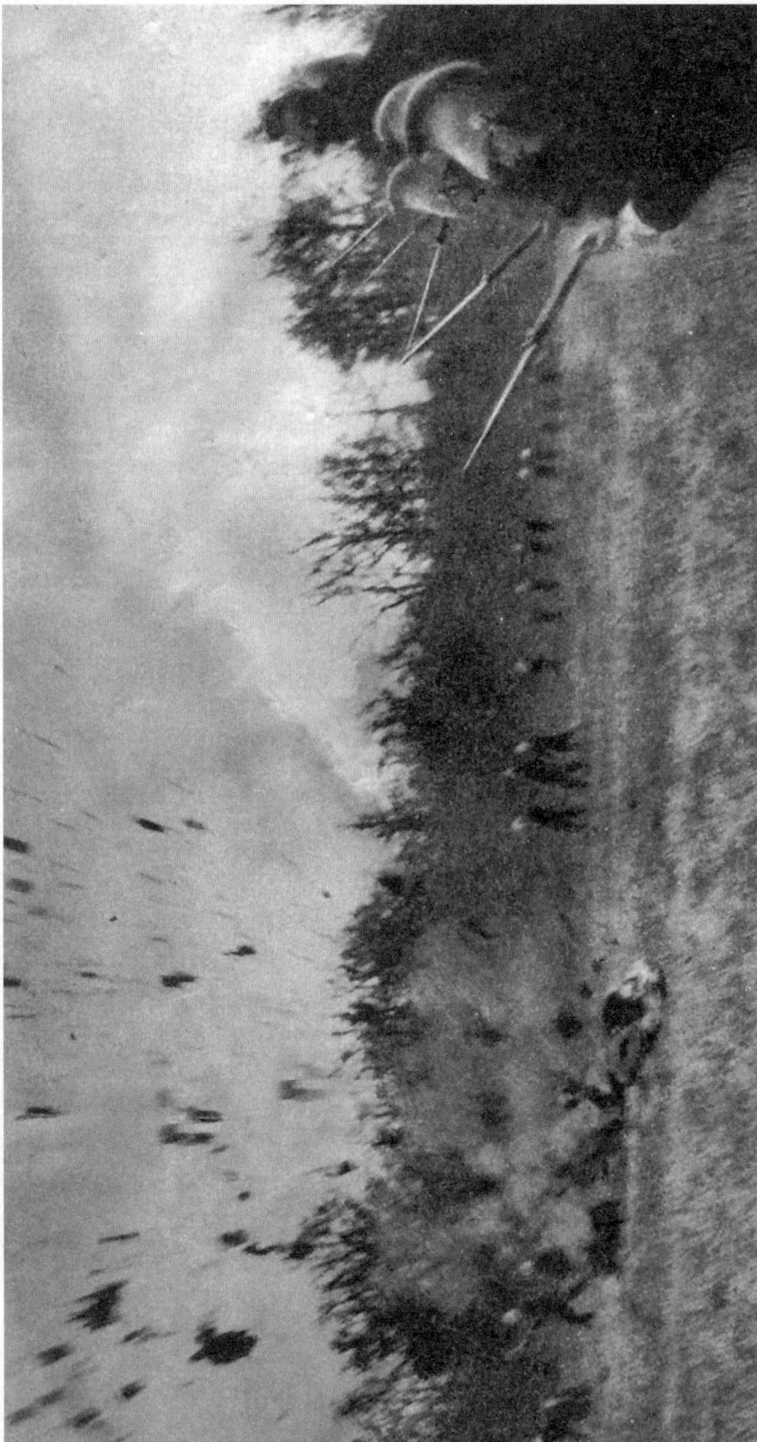

A photograph taken in battle conditions

A shell explodes in the Pas-de-Calais, between two lines of dragoons on foot, with bayonets fixed. Shells scream overhead with the noise of a motorcar, so everyone knows that they are coming. One can only imagine the composure needed by this photographer who, during the battle took this picture as the shells burst around him.

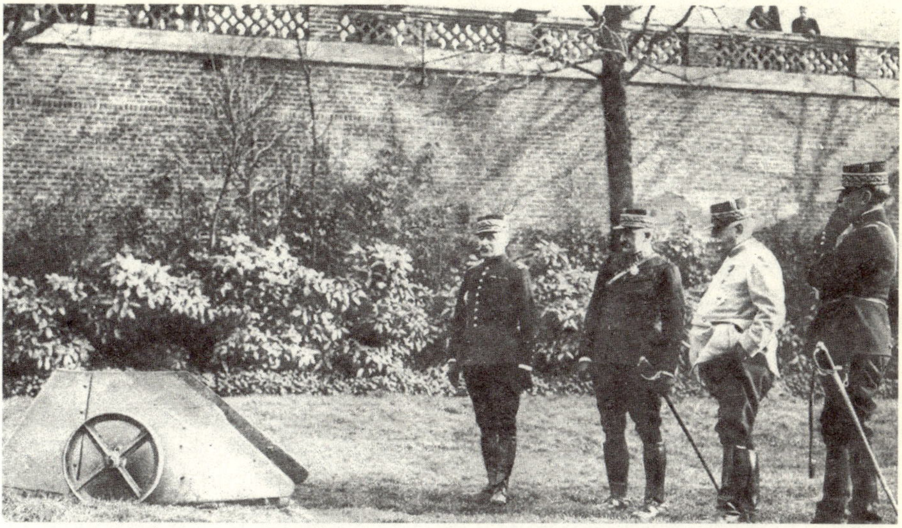

French generals examine a new gun

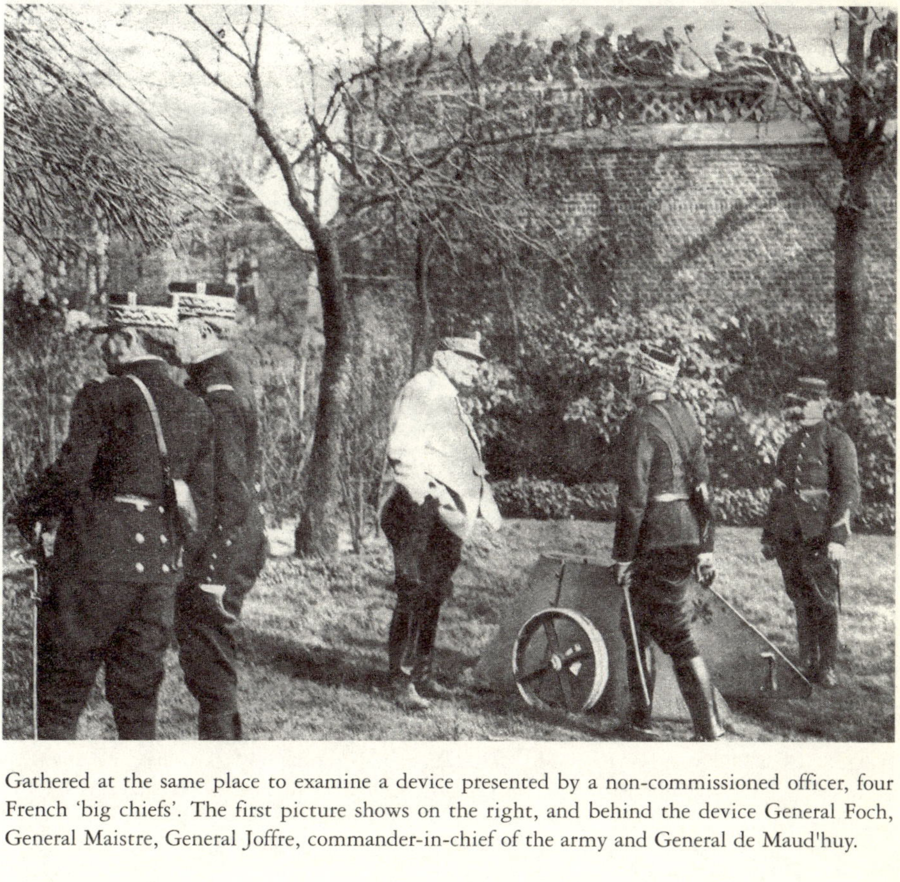

Gathered at the same place to examine a device presented by a non-commissioned officer, four French 'big chiefs'. The first picture shows on the right, and behind the device General Foch, General Maistre, General Joffre, commander-in-chief of the army and General de Maud'huy.

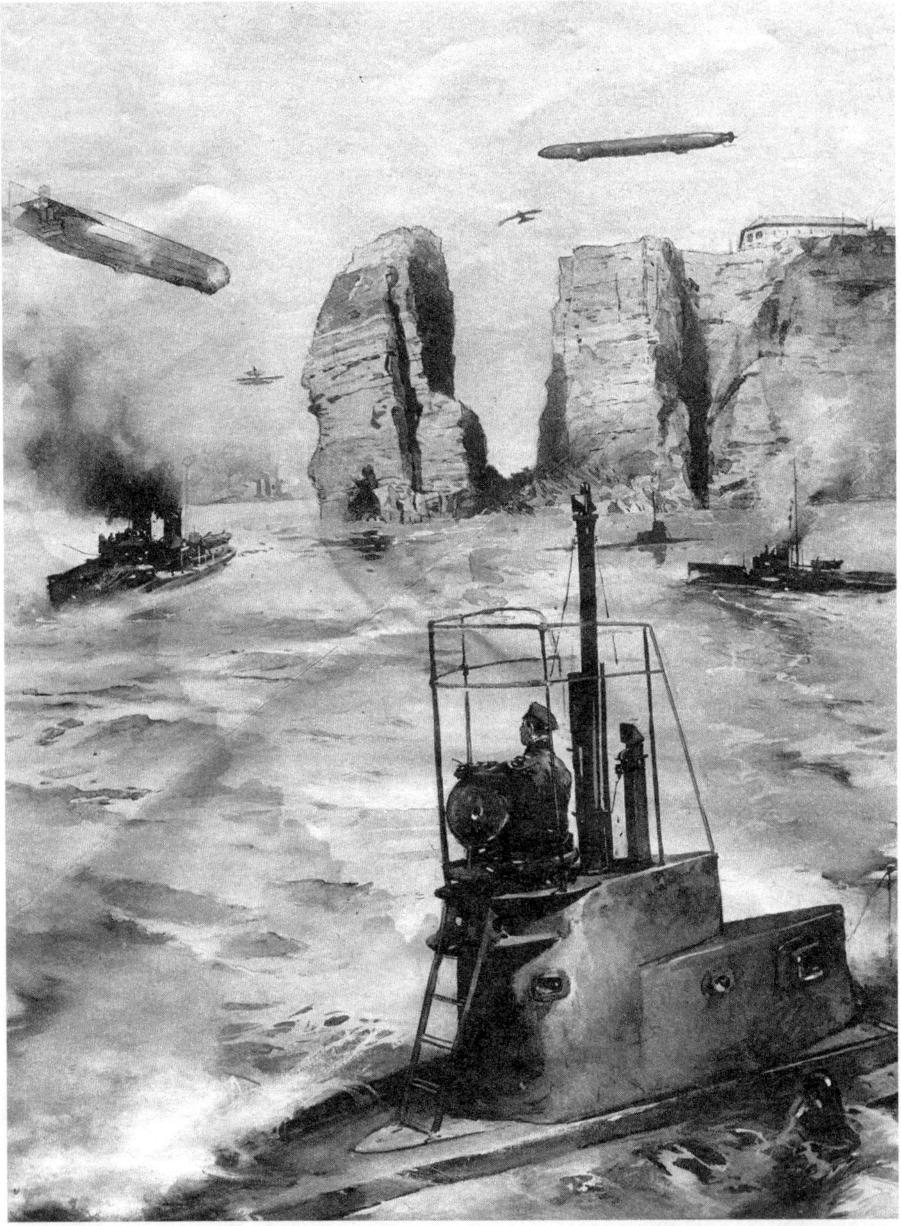

The lair of sea and air bandits - the island of Heligoland

A base for German airships and submarines, Heligoland is a rocky outcrop in the North Sea, situated at the mouths of the Elbe and the Weser. This island, that belonged to the United Kingdom in 1890, is today, ironically, the main base of the fleet of Zeppelins that operates against England. The submarines are also based there, close to Emden, Wilhelmshaven and Cuxhaven. [artists impression]

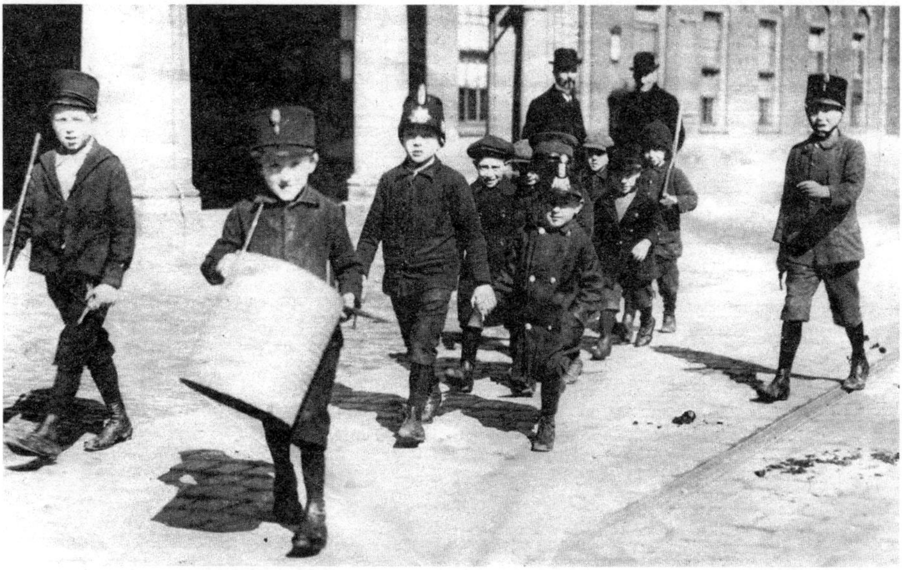

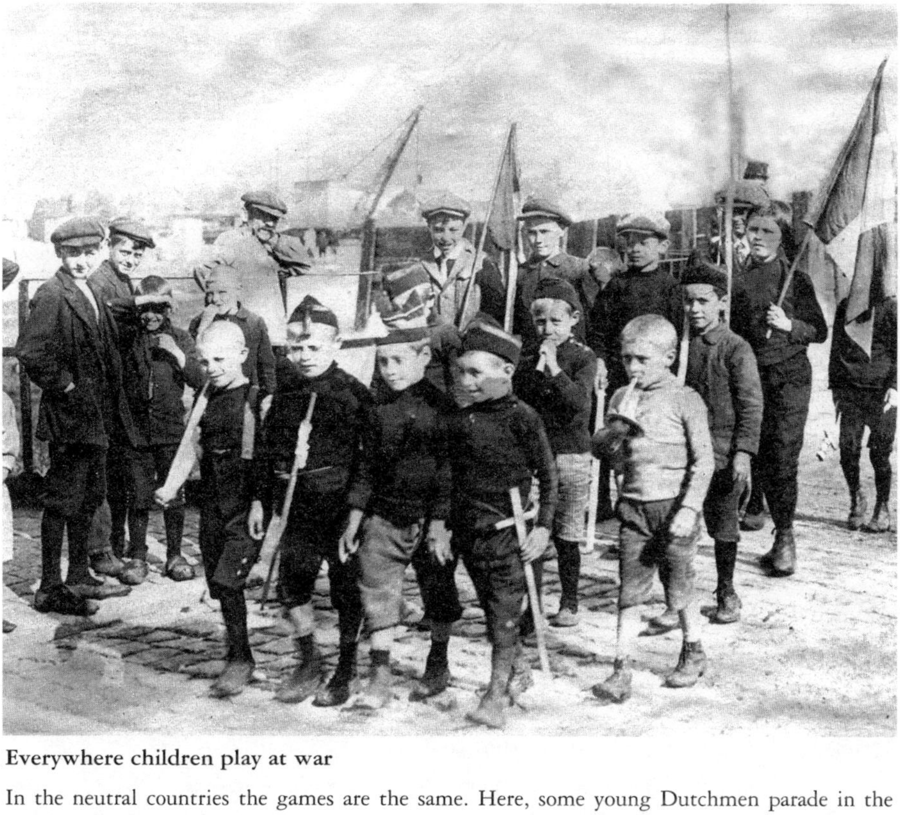

Everywhere children play at war

In the neutral countries the games are the same. Here, some young Dutchmen parade in the streets of The Hague, to the sound of a drum and wearing cardboard hats.

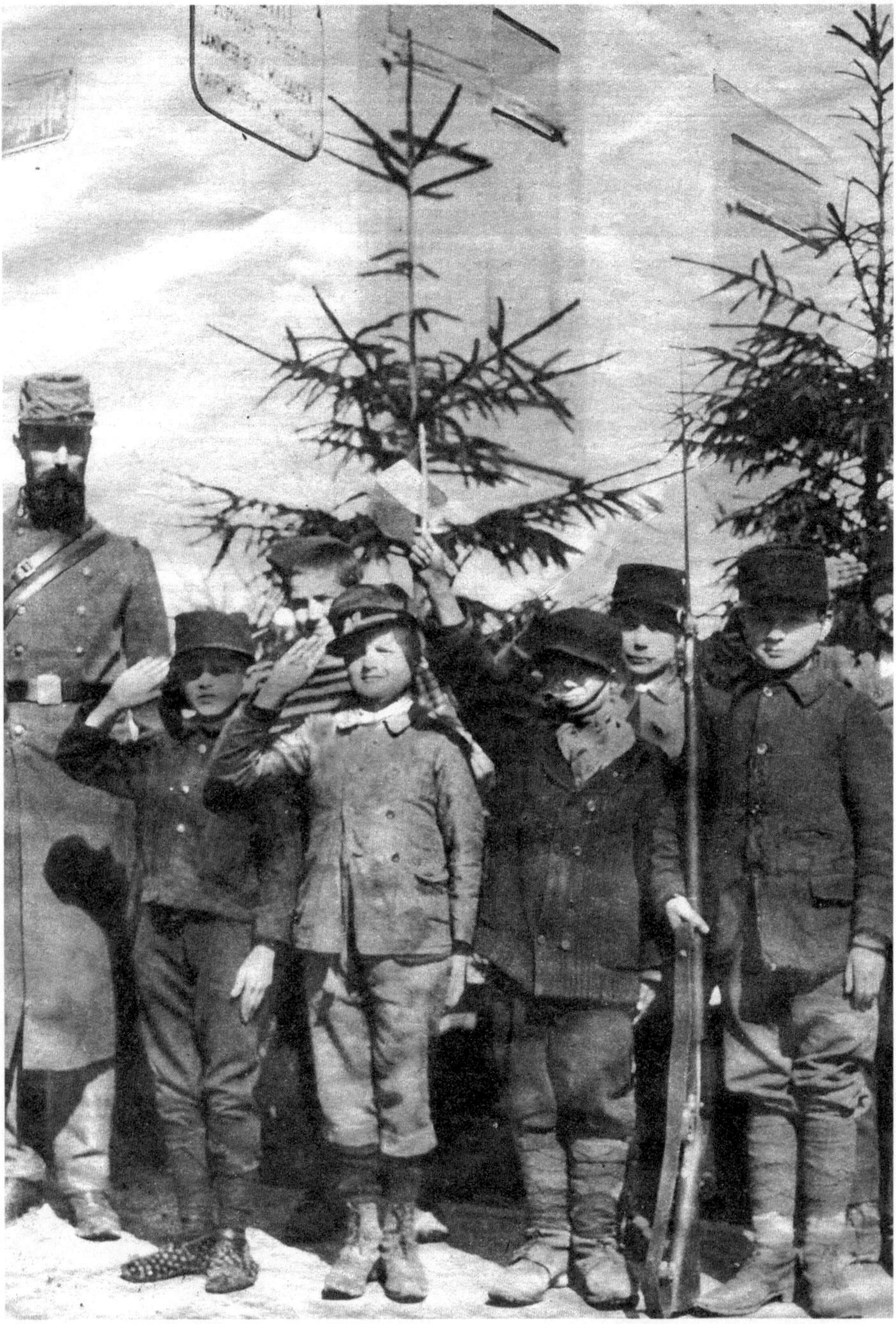

Young children in Alsace playing at being soldiers

In the retaken countryside of Alsace we can see the joy on the children's faces. With uniforms made from old clothes, they happily wave their flags.

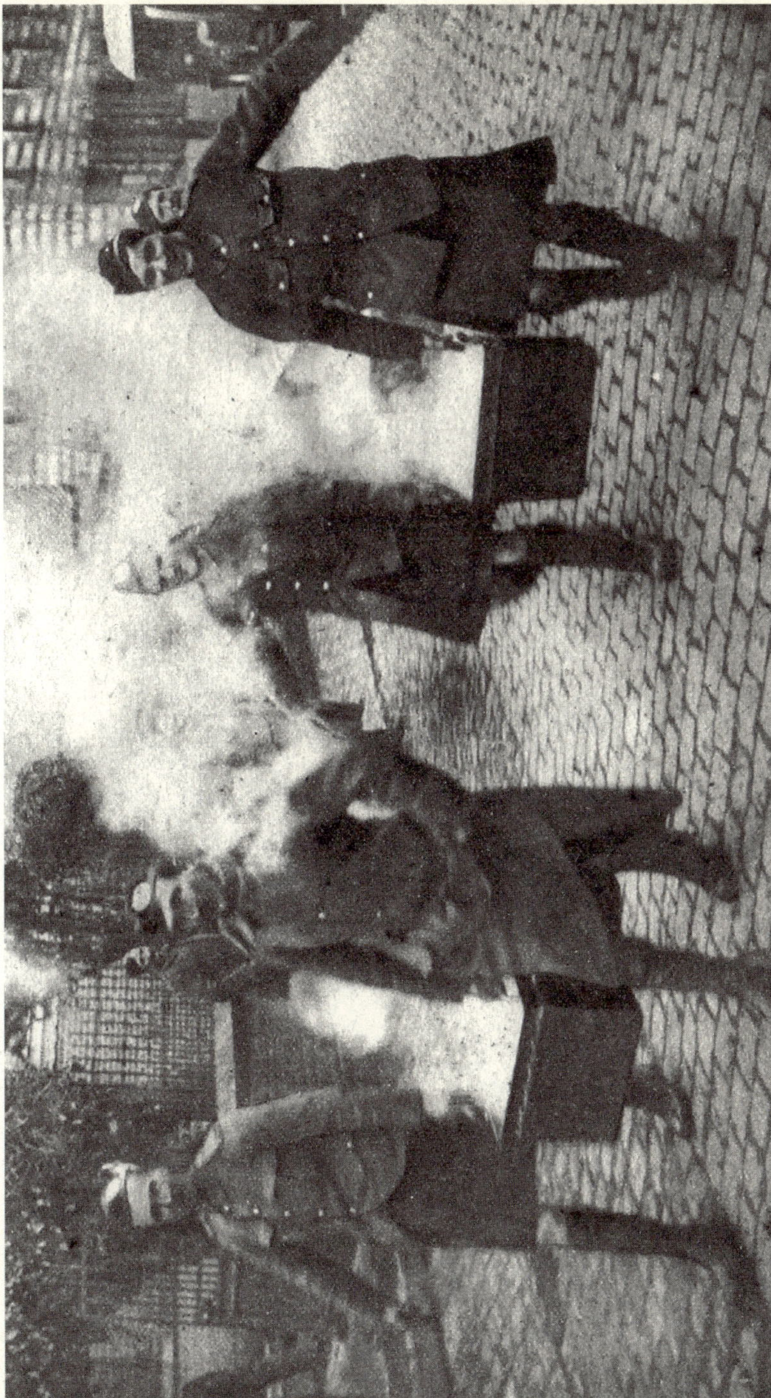

Scottish troops carrying soup to the camp

Ever popular in their colourful uniforms, the valiant highlanders are seen taking steaming soup to their colleagues. They still sing and laugh on occasions and their camps are especially cheerful.

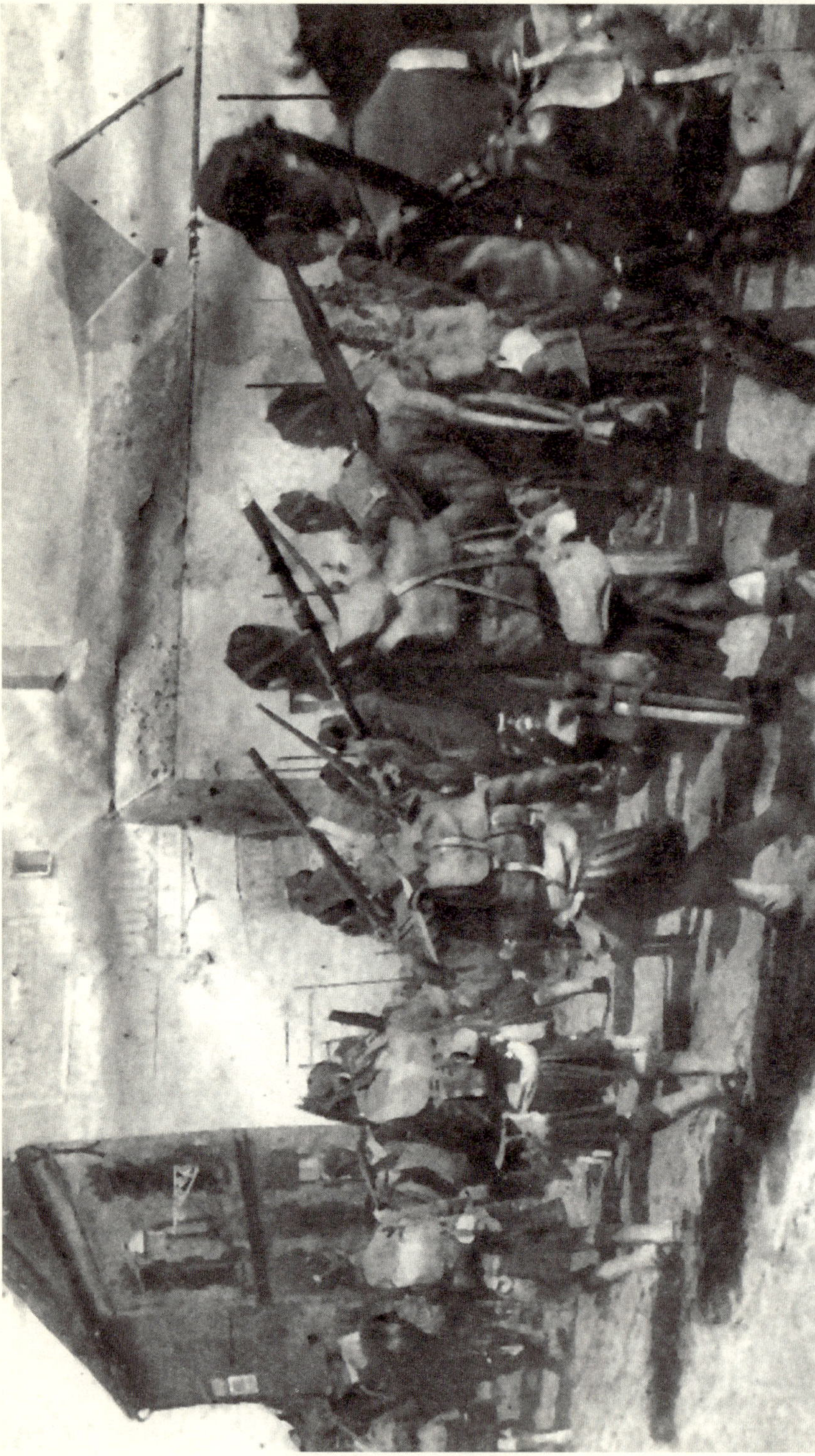

Following a hearty meal the brave highlanders march off to the front.

- NEWS REPORTS -

Thursday May 27, 1915

In Sheerness harbour, the British auxiliary cruiser Princess Irene was blown up and 400 lives lost. In the Arras-Lens sector, the enemy has made concerted efforts to retake the positions that they had lost. They broke through allied defences at many points.

Violent fights took place on the Oriental front in the Baltic provinces, around the Vistule and San. The Italian army penetrated into Austria along its western border. King Victor-Emmanuel III of Italy, joined the troops on the front line having delegated control of the kingdom to the Duke of Gene.

Friday May 28, 1915

The British cruiser Triumph was torpedoed off the Dardanelles. Two Zeppelins have flown over Southend (Essex), dropping bombs. There were two deaths. Close to Arras, allies have defeated two attacks and inflicted heavy losses on the enemy. Close to Ablain, several trenches were taken, then the cemetery and surrounding ground that had previously been a German strong-hold. Troops took 400 prisoners, including several officers. An artillery battle began further south. A squadron of French planes has bombard Ludwigshafen, on the Rhine, the large Badische-Anilin factory which was converted to manufacture explosives.

Saturday May 29, 1915

The Russians have advanced in the region of Chavli (Courlande), where they took 1,000 Germans; 6,000 Austro-German were captured in Galicia, and to the north of the Sieniawa a further 1,000 prisoners. In Armenia, allies have entered Van. After engaging the Italian navy the Austro-Hungarian fleet has several damaged ships. The Italian army has occupied Grado, in the Frioul. The 12th Austro-German army is held at Botzen, in the Trentin.

Sunday May 30, 1915

Germany has replied to the American letter about the Lusitania. A submarine has attacked the British steamer Ethiopia. In the region to the north of Arras the enemy continues with shelling. The French shot down a German pilot who was firing on their lines.

Italian artillery fire has damaged several Austrian positions near Torsala. They have taken the city of Ala, on the border of Tyrol, near Verona and continue their advance. They have also captured an Austrian seaplane. Mr. Bethmann-Hollweg, German Chancellor, has made a strong speech to the Reichstag directed against Italy.

Monday May 31, 1915

The German letter arrived in the United States. The President, Mr. Wilson won't be content with an evasive answer and he will ask for the cessation of the German naval piracy against the American ships. It is now established, according to the experts, that the Nebraska was torpedoed.

The Italian army operating in the Trentin surrendered ground at Brescia but also took an Austrian stronghold in the north at Asiago. Arch Duke Eugene is now the commander in chief of the Austrian troops. Allies have advanced two kilometres near Gallipoli.

Tuesday June 1st, 1915

The American government has considered the letter from Berlin about the destruction of the Lusitania. The content is evasive and delaying, provoking irritation across the Atlantic. In France, some progress in the region between Souchez and Carency, with 50 prisoners taken, after seizing the mill at Malon. Trenches were dug towards the sugar refinery at Souchez.

The Russians have advance significantly on Doubissa, also to the northeast of Przemysl. They have taken more than 15,000 Austro-Germans during the last fifteen days' march. German airships have appeared over the coast of Finland. After a long lull, fighting has resumed between Austrians and Serbians.

Wednesday June 2, 1915

Zeppelins appeared over the suburbs of London. The British public is irritated by these, and demanding attacks against the German towns. There is confirmation of the presence of German submarines in the Oriental Mediterranean. General Maxwell, commanding the Anglo-Egyptian army, took some precautions at the entrance to the Suez canal.

In spite of repeated offensives by the enemy, near Arras, allies have kept the trenches that were earlier conquered. We have taken the sugar refinery at Souchez, moved back, then taken it a second time. The enemy suffered heavy losses. We have also progressed to the southeast of Neuville, in the fortified area called the "Labyrinthe" and taken about 150 prisoners.

The Montengrines have had more success in Hercegovina. Count Bernstorff, German ambassador has asked for an audience with the president of the United States. He wants to influence the attitude of Mr. Wilson towards the Germans. The American opinion requires strong government politics, and no procrastination.

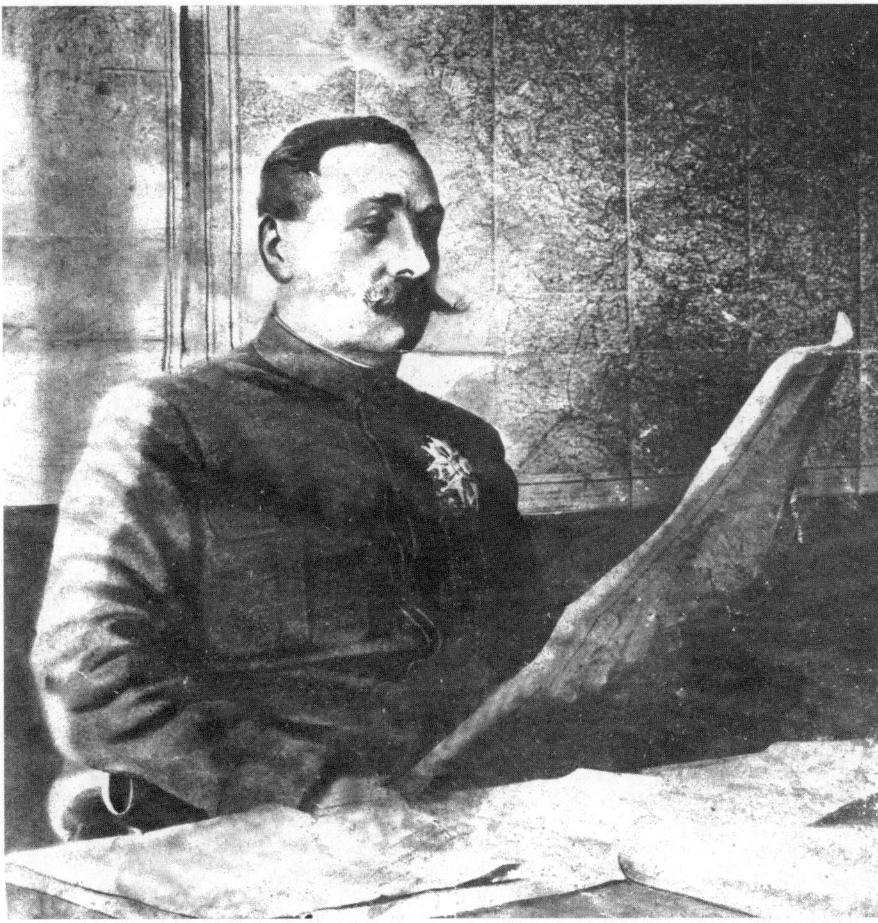

General Dubail, Commander-in-Chief of the troops on the French eastern front

Before commanding the armies in the east, General Dubail, led the 1st army. Here we see him reviewing plans for the next stage of the battle. Last month his plans halted the enemy between the rivers Meurthe and Mortagne.

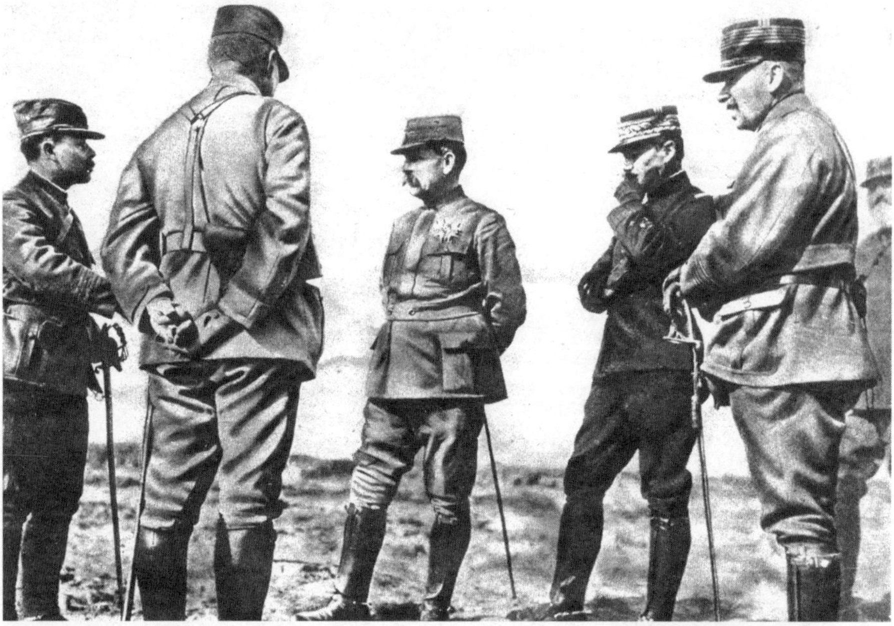

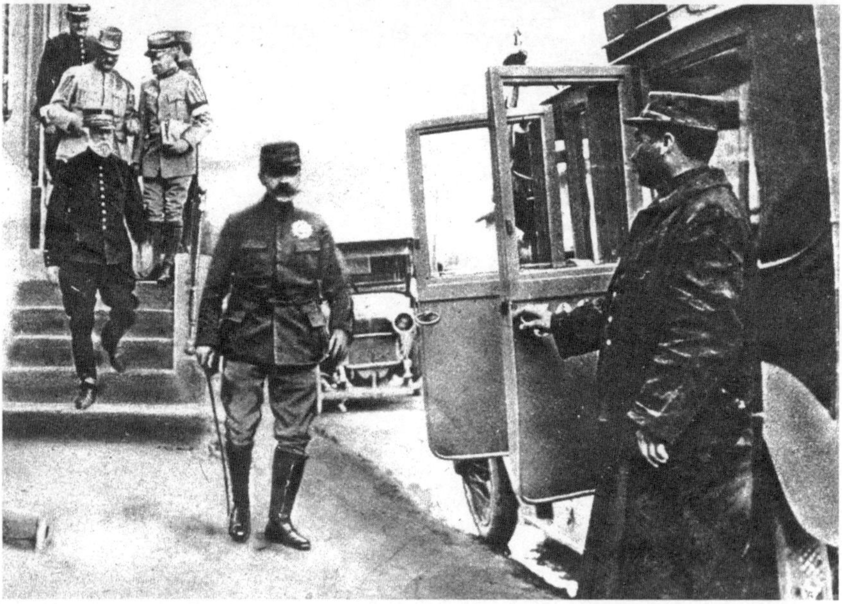

General Dubail at a command station for discussions on tactics

From Alsace, he has always tirelessly opposed the German attacks. Here we see him leaving a command post in Argonne; followed by General Sarrail. In the top photo General Dubail (on the right) is in conference at an observation station commanded by General Humbert. Behind him, General Heimann.

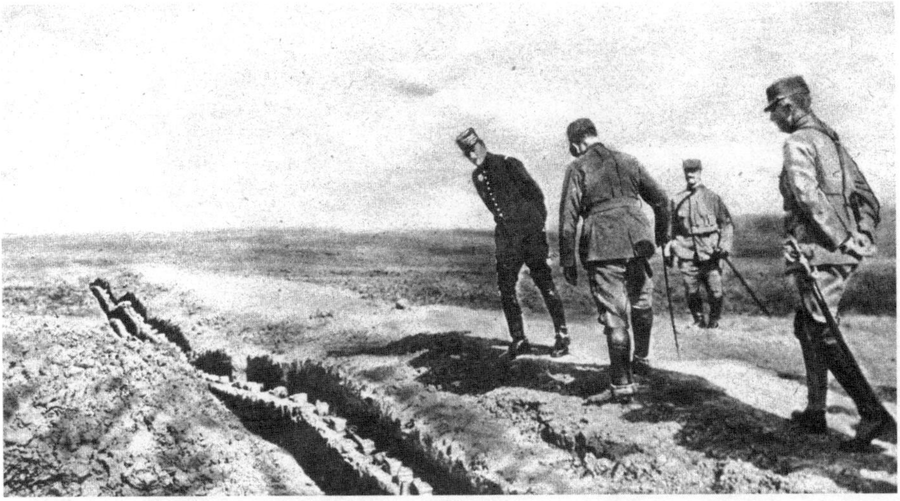

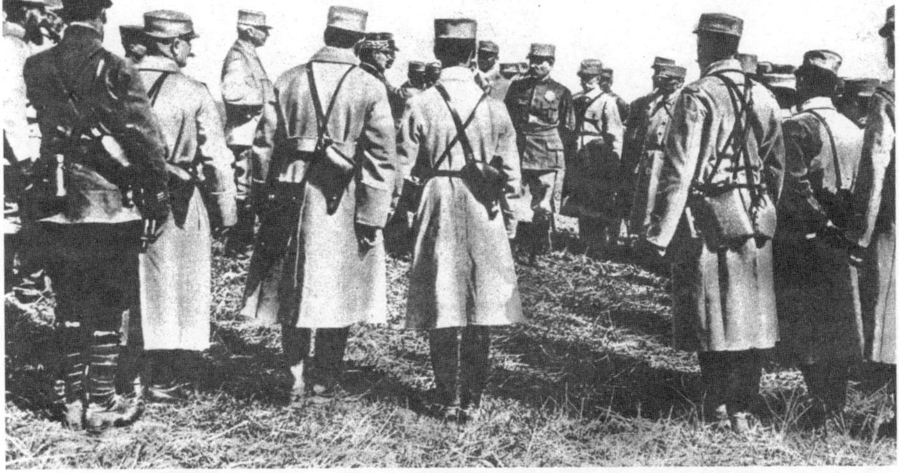

The inspection of defence lines and final recommendations to officers

After an attack, Generals Dubail, Humbert and Heimann inspect a gulley running towards the forward trenches. A store of ammunition ready for the soldiers can be seen on the edge of this. In the second photograph we see officers at a briefing for the following days attack.

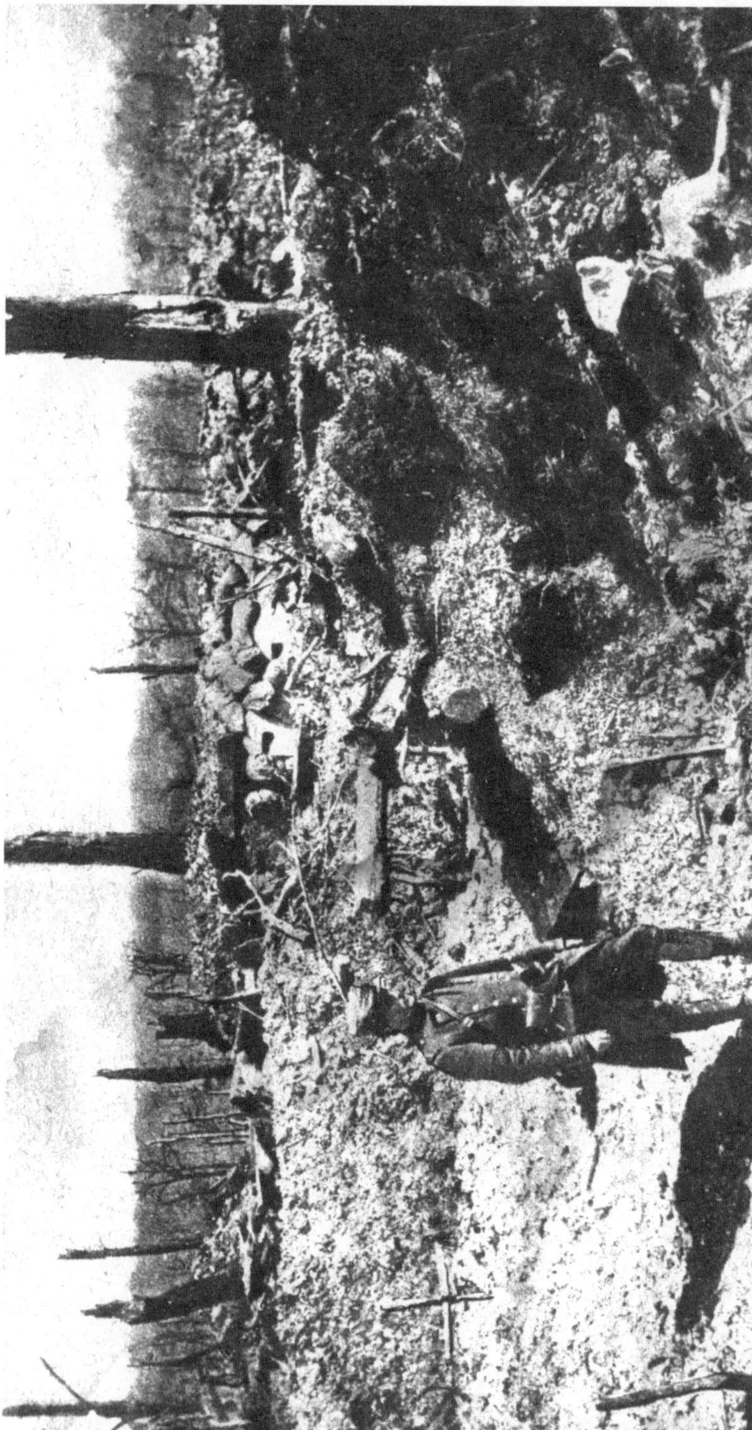

A view of "Priest Wood" [bois Le Pretre], which the enemy call "Wood of Death".

The edge of Priest Wood at crest 372, an important westerly point. After an unceasing and extremely hard fight, troops recovered the crest in a bayonet attack on May 12.

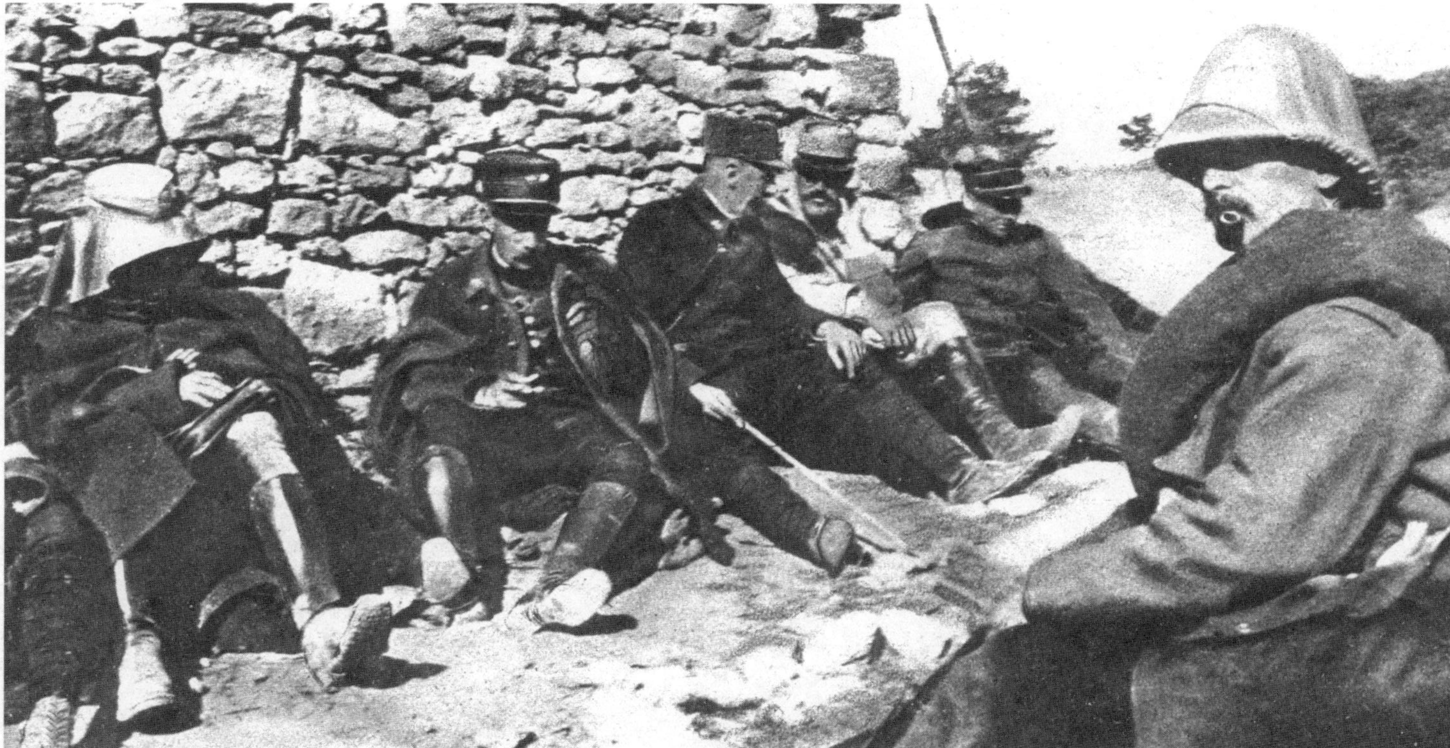

The battle of Krithia

The village of Krithia, situated five kilometres from Seddul-Bahr, on the island of Gallipoli, was the background to a battle where troops took several lines of trenches with a bayonet attack, an act of indescribable bravery. This photo, taken during one of the engagements, shows a general and his team sheltering behind a wall of a building.

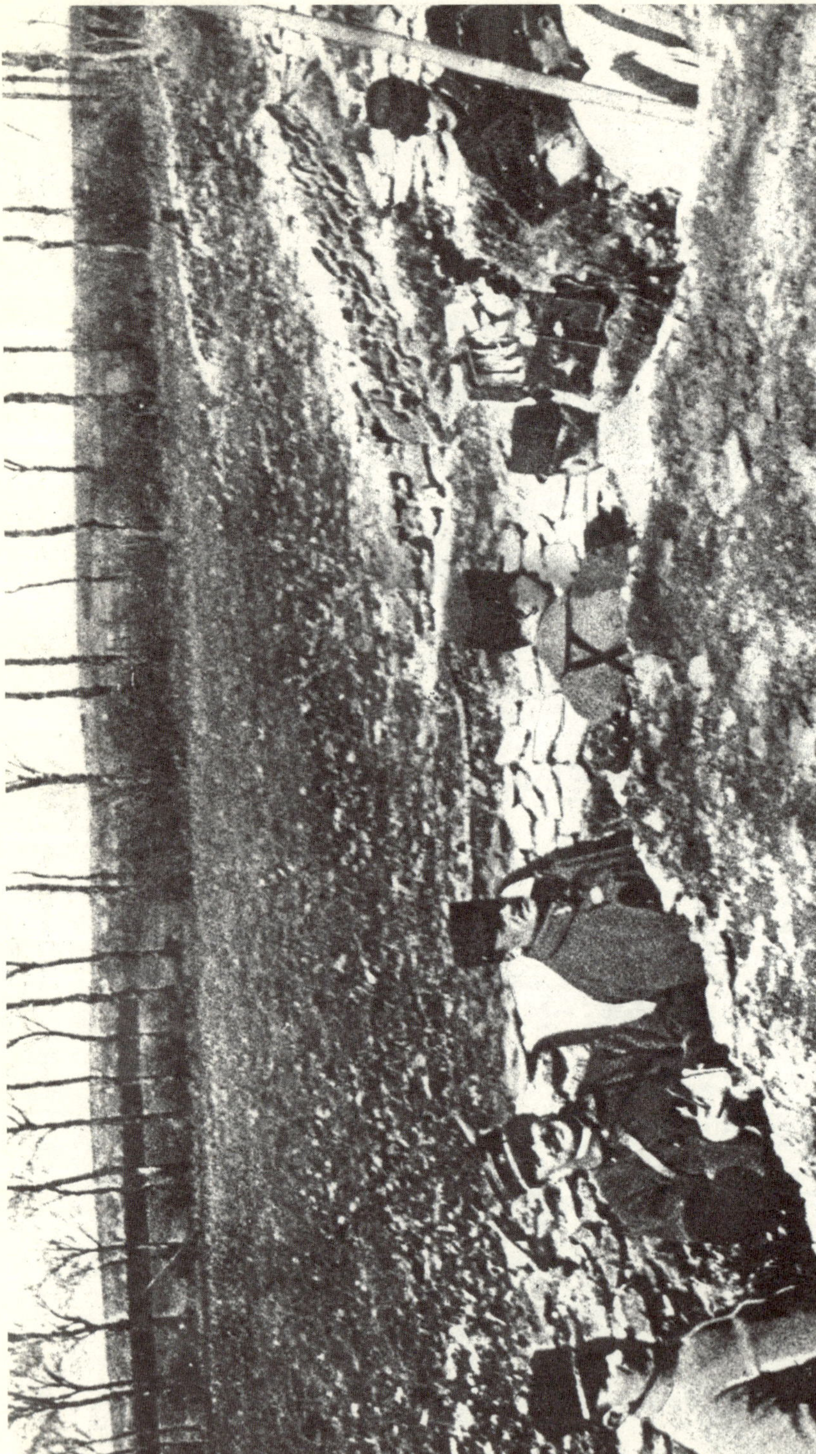

Another view at Krithia showing a forward observation post in a trench near the front line.

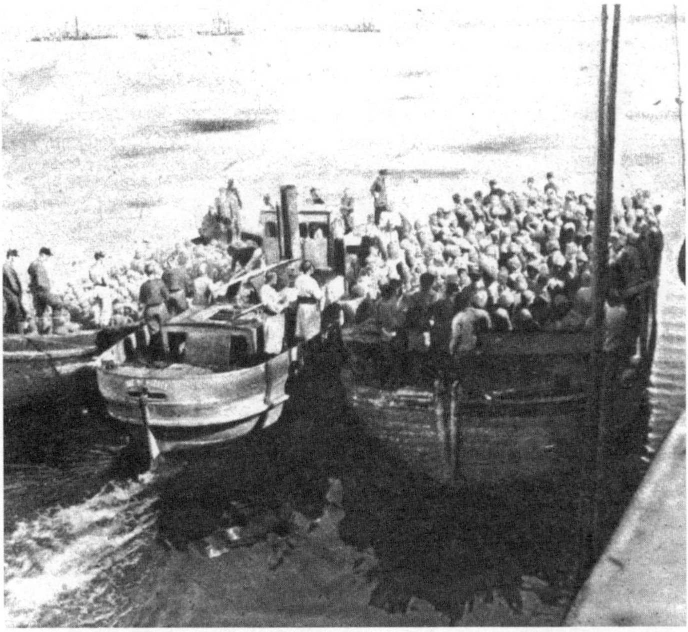

Current operations at Gallipoli

Five hundred Turkish prisoners, captured in engagements at Krithia, are embarking onto barges to be taken to Moudros, Greece.

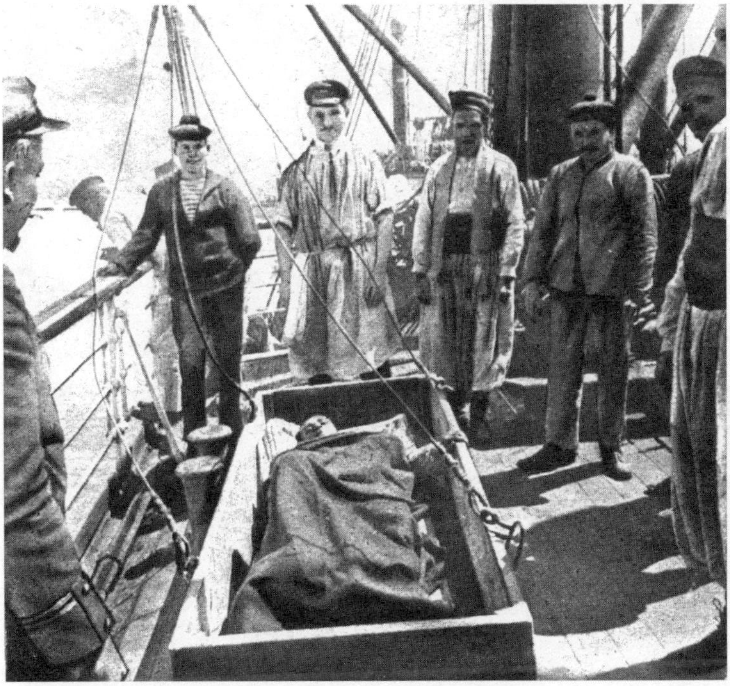

A severely wounded French sailor being lifted from a rowing boat, after the battle of Krithia.

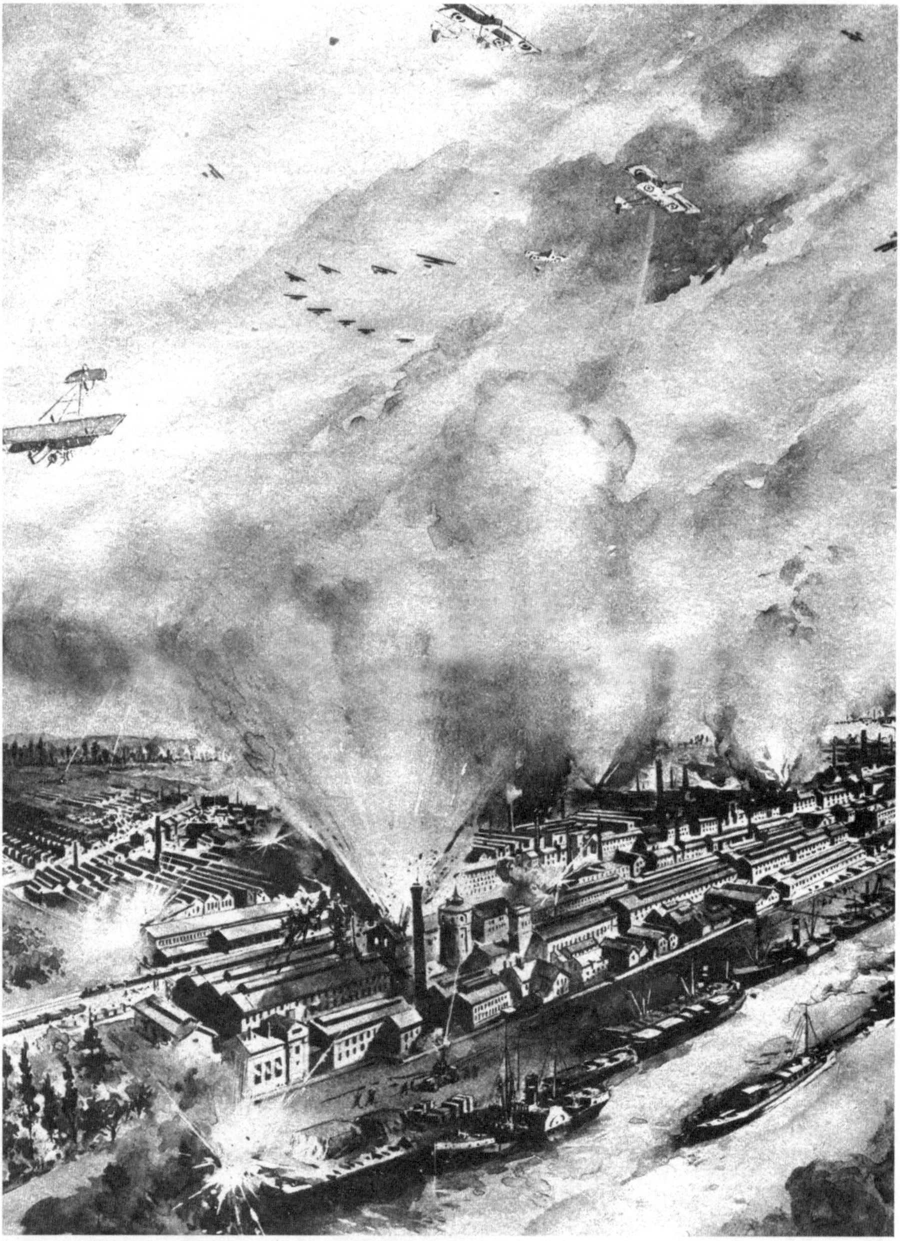

The bombing of Ludwigshafen by aviators [artists impression]

Eighteen French planes have dropped 49 shells on the Badische Anilin factory, a German armaments manufacturer. The bombardment of factories in Ludwigshafen, by French aviators, was one of the most successful aerial attacks since the beginning of the war. Leaving in the early hours of the morning, eighteen planes have dropped 47 x 90mm and 2 x 155mm shells on the biggest factories manufacturing explosives in Germany, in Ludwigshafen, on the Rhine, and 16 x 90mm on the Oppau manufacturing plant. All have hit their target, causing a gigantic fire. Only one plane was lost.

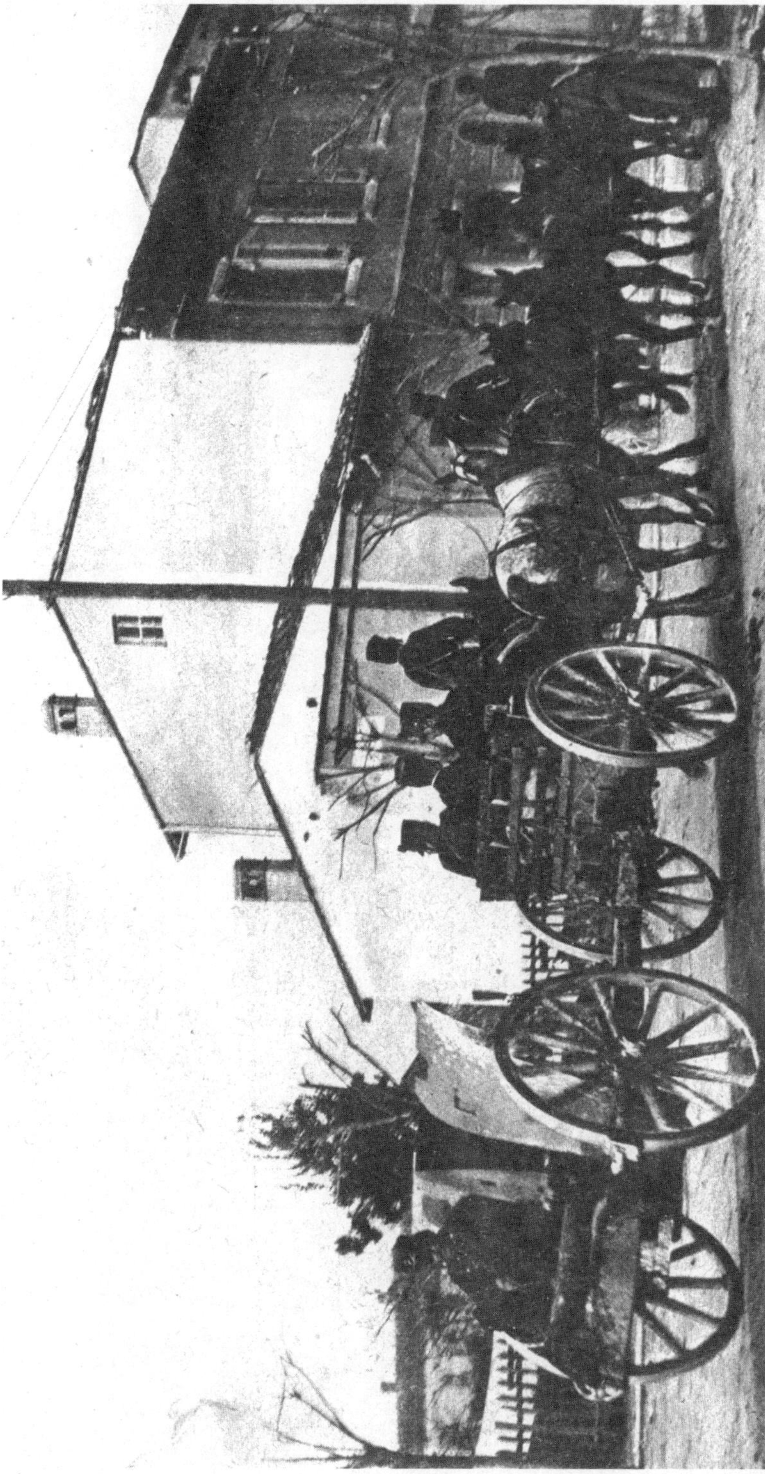

The Italian artillery has been re-equipped with French cannons and is now the most modern in Europe.

Batteries were previously equipped with 6 Krupps (German) guns, but these have been completely replaced with French designed 75mm ones. Italy has prepared, in its factories, a considerable stock of shells.

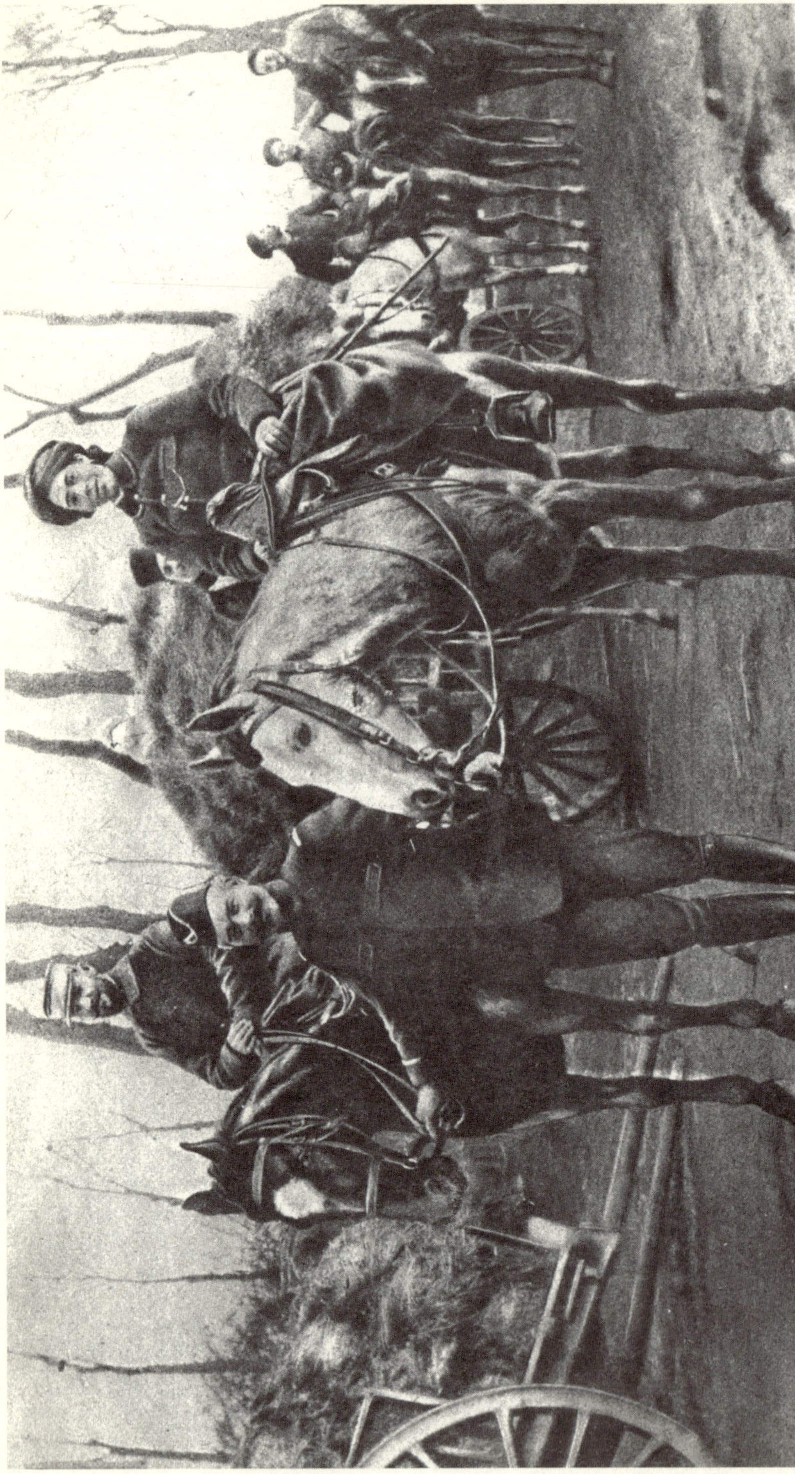

Women fighting as true soldiers - Fathima the Moroccan

Several women have taken an active part in the war since Miss Iovanitch of Belgrade took the first shot in 1912. Fathima, the Moroccan, photographed here, has followed the troops since the beginning of the war, fighting courageously like a man.

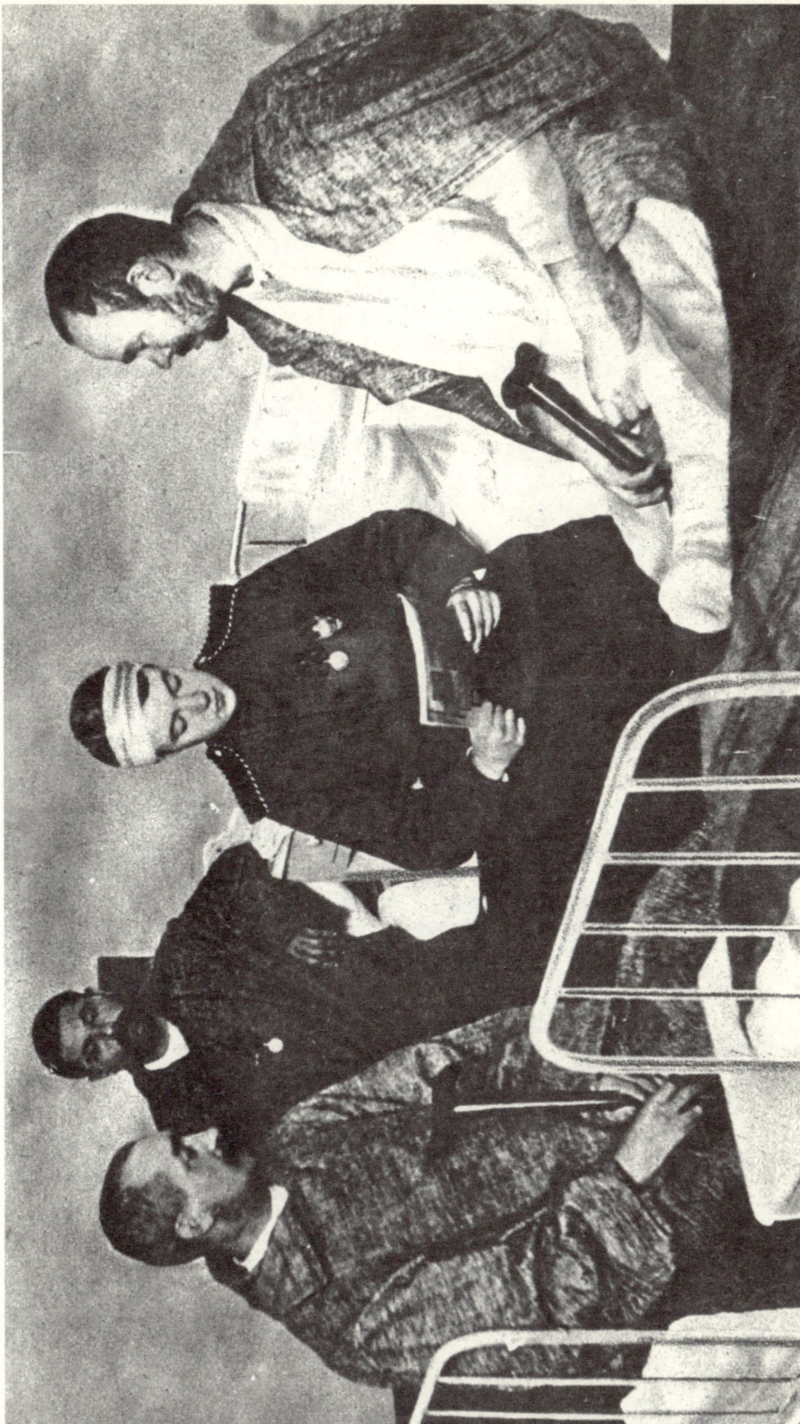

Miss Cokovtseva, the wounded but decorated, Russian heroine

In the Russian army, Miss Cokovtseva has proved her bravery. Wounded twice, she received the George medal. Here she is in a hospital with wounded friends.

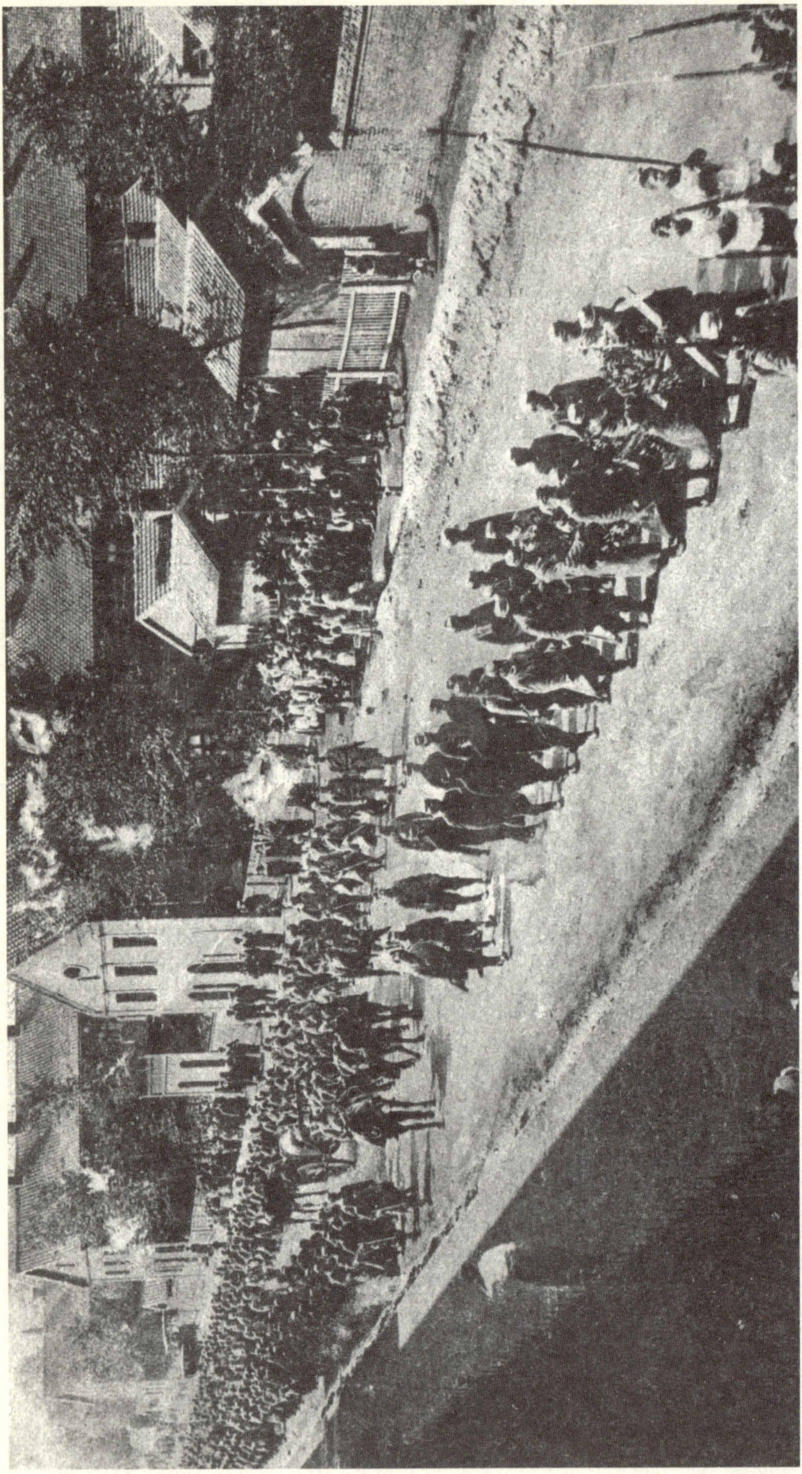

The funeral of a French general, killed at Carency

A funeral ceremony for a French general, killed by a shell burst near Carency, conducted with an imposing yet simple dignity. His regiment parades after the religious ceremony in front of the coffin and surrounded by officers.

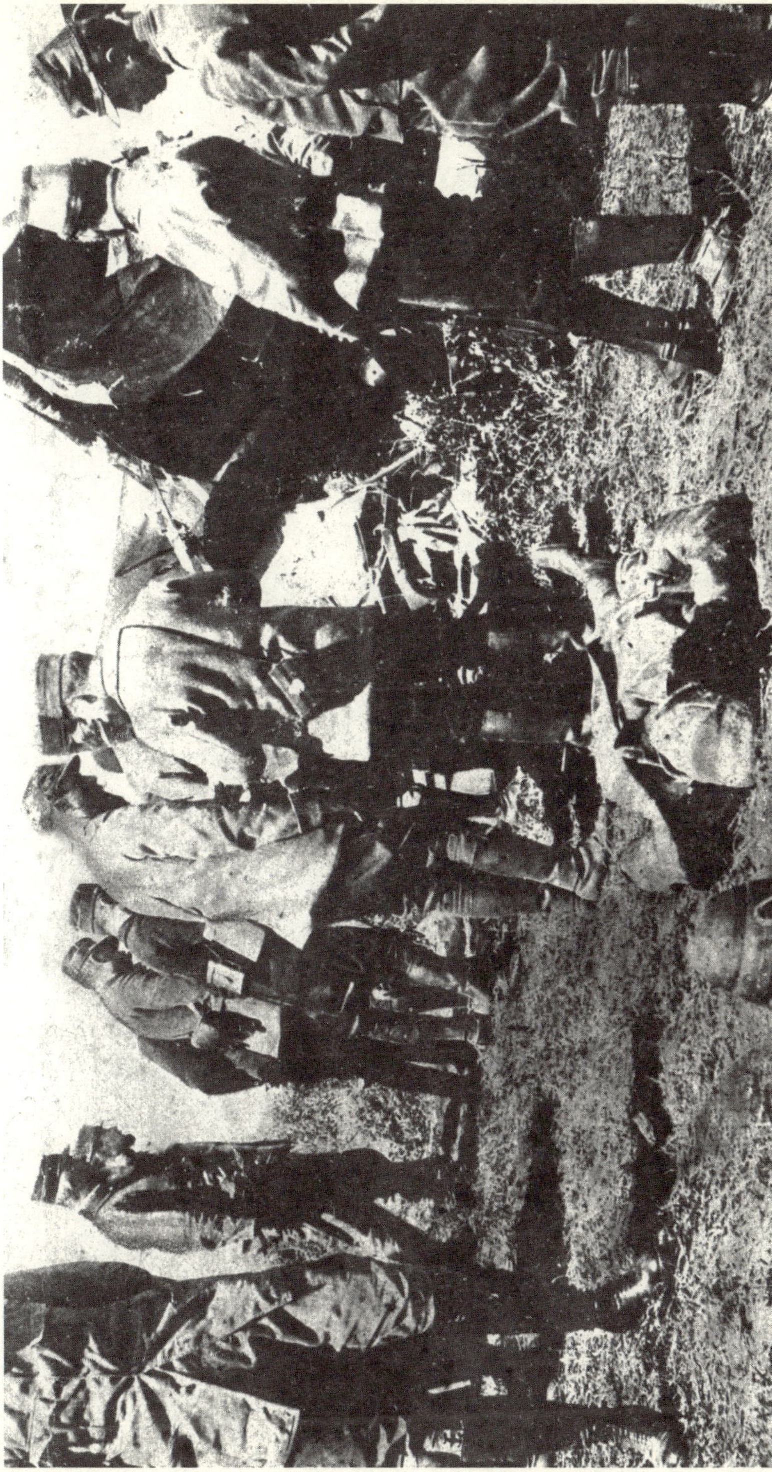

German aeroplane shot down

A photograph of a German aviator shot down near Braine, close to Soissons, by Lieutenant Jaccottet. The plane tried to head on to Paris but the pilot, named Bülow was killed.

- NEWS REPORTS -

Thursday June 10, 1915

Two German planes were shot down in Flanders after crossing British lines. An Italian airship caught fire after having bombed the Hungarian port of Flume. An Austrian plane dropped bombs on Venice. A German plane was captured in Serbia.

Heavy artillery action in the sector to the north of Arras. Allies took the village of Neuville-Saint-Vaast that the enemy had previously retaken - the village is now totally under our control. In the "Labyrinthe", we have advanced towards the south- east.

Friday June 11, 1915

Two British torpedo boats were sunk in the North Sea by a German submarine. A fire destroyed 300 military vehicles in London. Some German ships were sunk or damaged in the Baltic by British and Russian submarines.

The artillery struggle continues in the region around Lorette. The enemy is vainly trying to retake the sugar refinery at Souchez. Further progress in the "Labyrinthe" and a report indicates that, at Neuville-Saint-Vaast, 1,000 German bodies have been found.

Italians have arrived at Falzarego on the border of Carinthia and seized Preitkofel. They have also taken Monfalcone, 35 kilometres from Trieste. In Russia, the fighting continues around Chavli. In Galicia, the Russians have forced back the Austro-Germans towards Dniester, taking 800 prisoners, but the battle continues in Jouravno where the enemy has made advances.

Saturday June 12, 1915

The letter from President Wilson (USA) to the chancellery of Berlin has been published. It presents a solemn representation to Germany, effectively saying that the President is asking for a formal assurance that the attacks on neutral ships will end.

A vast store of enemy equipment was found following the French conquest at Neuville-Saint-Vaast; three 75mm guns, three grenade launchers, fifteen machine guns, 800,000 cartridges, 1,000 rifles, and many shells. Near Hebuterne, the French took 130 prisoners, none wounded. Generally the enemy is limited to shellfire. In Champagne, the trenches are being held.

In the Dardanelles, some progress with heavy losses inflicted on the enemy. On the Oriental front, Russians under attack at Chavli and on the right bank of the Pilitza. In Galicia, they stopped the Austro-Germans near Przemysl; at

Zidaczen, they took 2,000 prisoners. They also took 6,500 prisoners plus 17 cannons and 49 machine guns at Jurawno. The Italians have now occupied Podestagno, north of Cortina; the Austrians have taken Freikopel (Carnie) and moved a strong contingent into the hills over Monfalcone. The city of Gradisca, on the Isonzo river, is now in their possession.

Sunday June 13, 1915

A very violent artillery attack at Lorette where the enemy are trying to retake trenches in the whole sector. The French have replied with heavy shelling. Thick fog slowed progress in the "Labyrinthe". A German counter attack was stopped in the region around Hebuterne, and there was more artillery action near Reims.

The Russians took the superior position on the Oriental front. In Lithuania, they inflicted enormous losses on the Germans who were advancing to the west of Chavli. On the Doubissa, they have captured 500 men and their guns. At Svitza, the enemy came under machine-gun fire with a number of Austro-German losses.

The Italians have strengthened their positions all along the Isonzo and especially in the inshore area of the Frioul. Two Austrian planes have flown over Mola di Bari and Monopoli (Apulie) dropping some bombs. A Swiss spy was executed in the duchy of Bade. Rumours again, that Turkey may be ready to ask for peace.

Monday June 14, 1915

A hostile counter attack has been stopped in Puisieux, France, where rapid shellfire caused a lot of panic. The Germans have also fired 120 shells on Soissons.

The Russians continue to hold the Austro-Germans along the entire Oriental front. The German cruiser Berlin was damaged in the Black Sea by a Russian torpedo boat. The Italians took new ground in the middle and lower Isonzo. They now occupy significant positions along the Austrian border. The general elections took place in Greece, effectively voting for the support of Mr. Venizélos.

Tuesday June 15, 1915

The British government has requested supplementary taxes to support the war. Allies have defeated several further attacks against our trenches in the Aix-Noulette-Souchez region, progressing in the "Labyrinthe" where artillery fire is unceasing. The enemy suffered a serious defeat to the south of Hebuterne. while the French gained ground close to Quennevieres, and decimated the Germans.

General Von Mackensen (Germany) lost 20,000 men in the battle at Jouravno, Galicia. On the Dniester, the Russians have broken through the Austrian lines. The Italian army bombed Malborghetto, an important fortress dominating the railway track from Pontebba to Tarvis.

Wednesday June 16, 1915

Twenty-three French planes bombed Karlsruhe, capital of the Duchy of Bade. They initially dropped flares to indicate positions of the castle, the weapons factory and the railway station.

Two shells landed without exploding near Compiègne, fired by a new, long range German cannon.

The Italians have recorded excellent results from the artillery bombardment of Malborghetto. The Russians have regained the advantage in Poland while on the whole front in Galicia the battle has increased in intensity. In Greece - the elections have assured an important majority to M. Venizélos, Prime Minister, and the King's health remains precarious. The Crown Prince of Bavaria is also seriously ill.

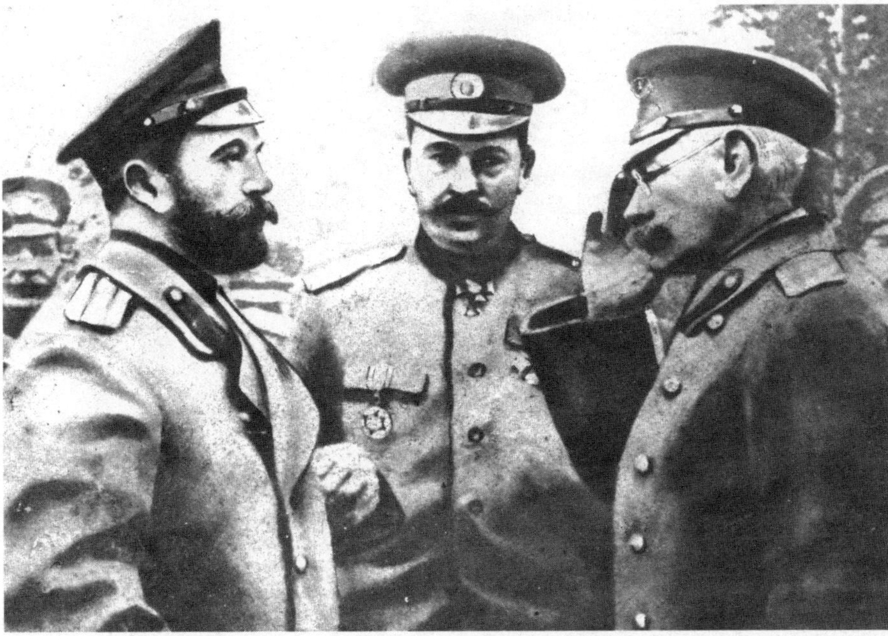

The Czar in conversation with Generals Janouchkevitch and Rouzsky

The Emperor Nicolas II frequently visits the front. During a recent trip in Galicia, he agreed to let himself be photographed with General Janouchkecitch, chief of staff of Grand Duke Nicolas and General Rouzsky.

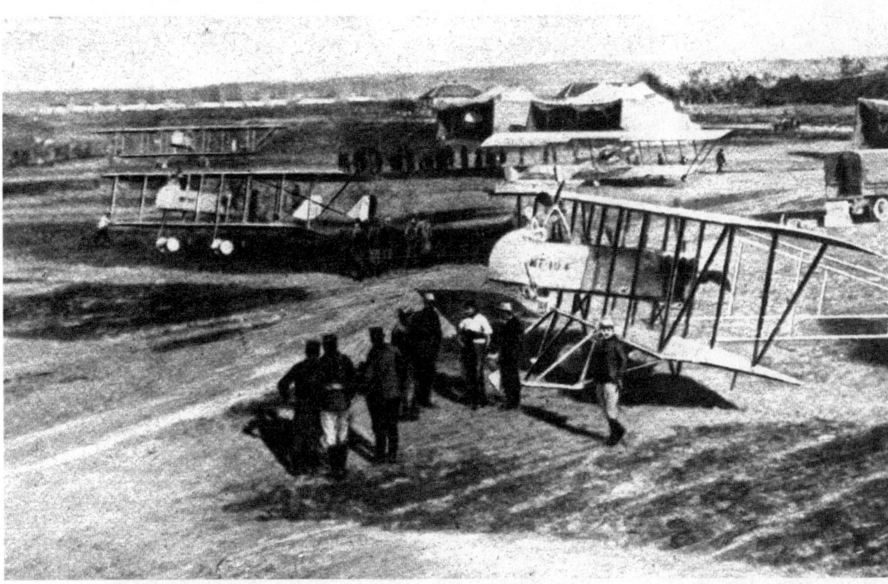

The Serbian airfield in the fields outside Belgrade

French aviators are working closely with the Serbians and have defeated an attack by enemy planes near Kragoujevatx.

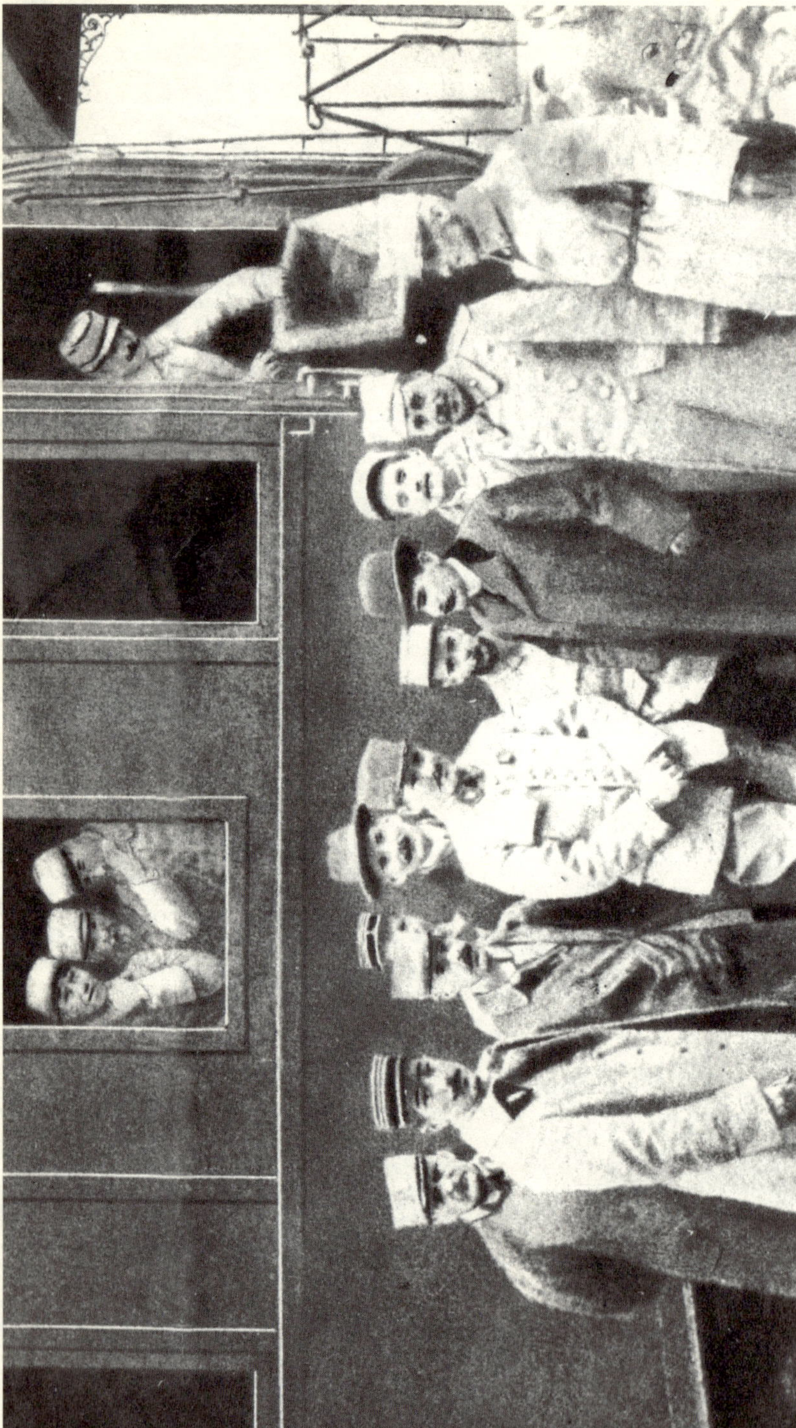

The French pilots

Two very well known pilots are seen arriving at Nisch, meeting Serbian colleagues.

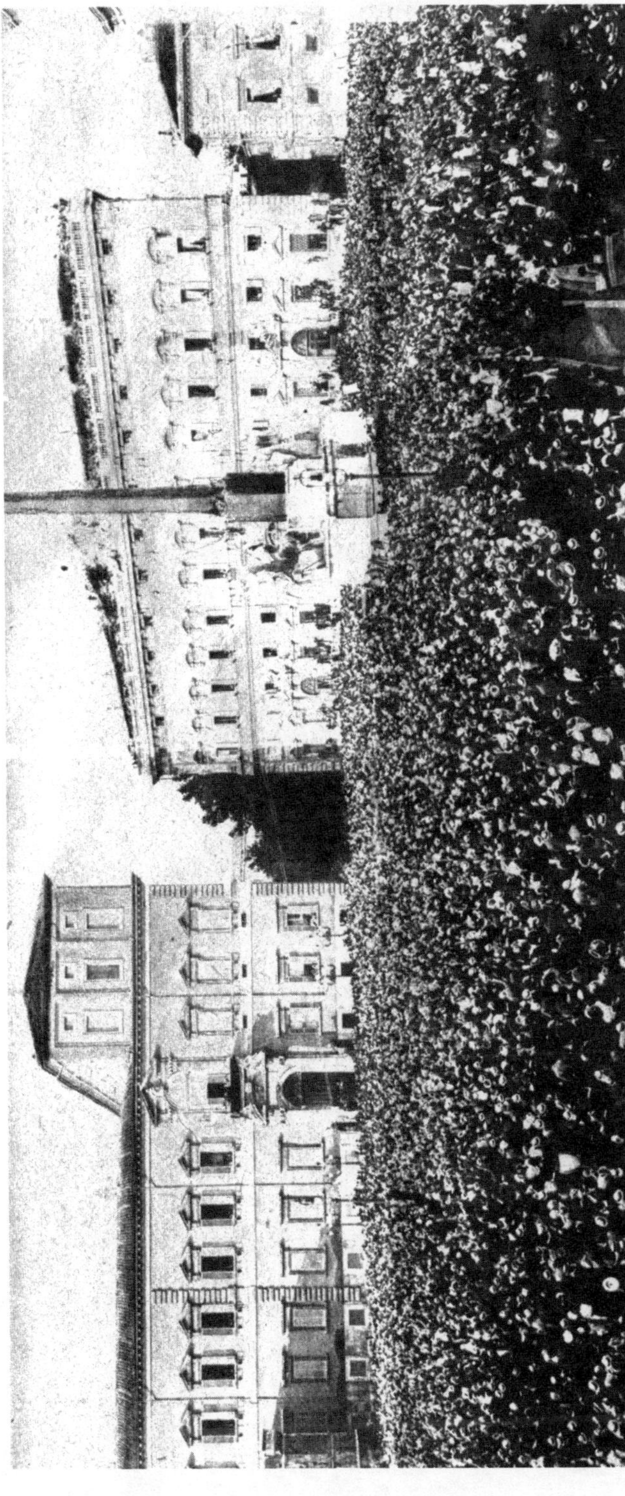

Two hundred thousand people cheer the Italian royal family in front of the Quirinal (royal palace).

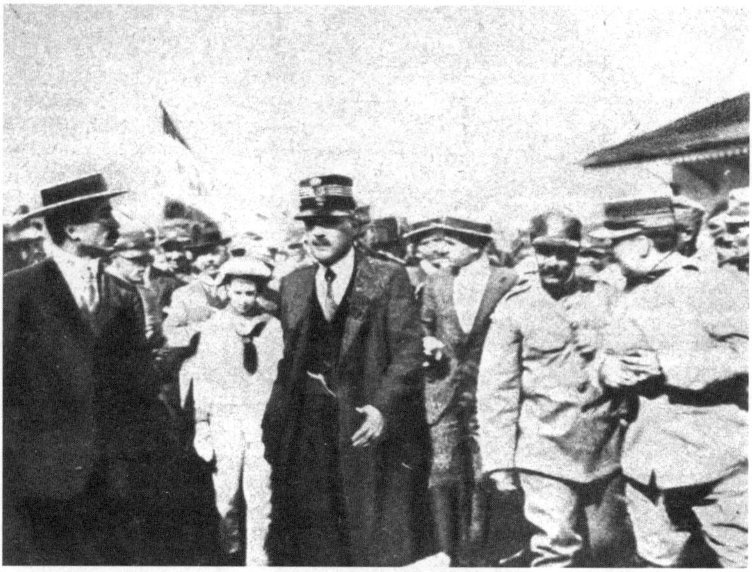

Reactions to the recent Italian success in Rome.

The prince, heir to the Italian throne, meets and encourages the troops in person.

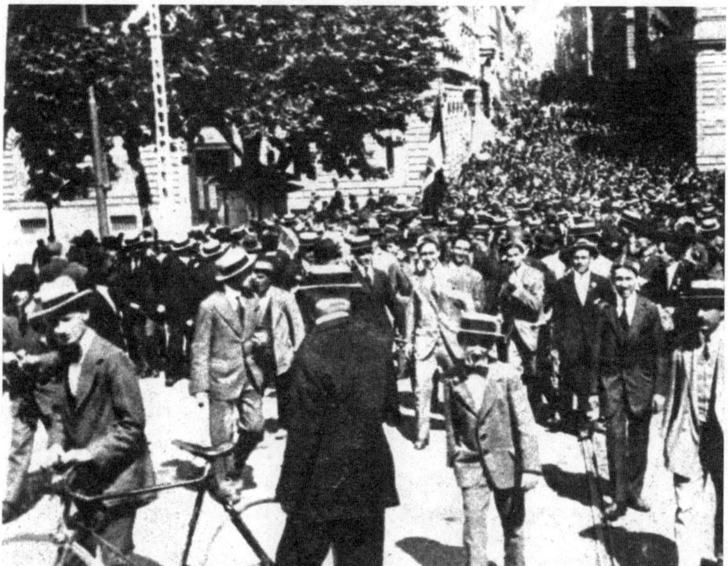

Italian students, preceding their university flag, go to enrol en masse.

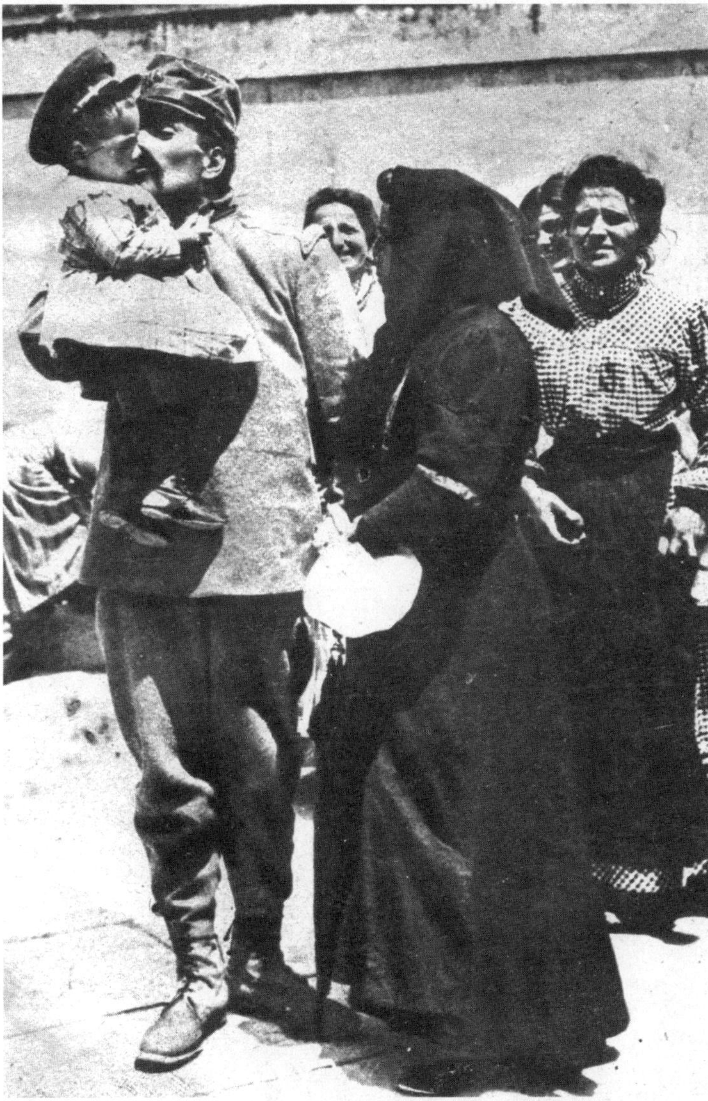

An Italian father kisses his child before being going to fight, a particularly moving scene.

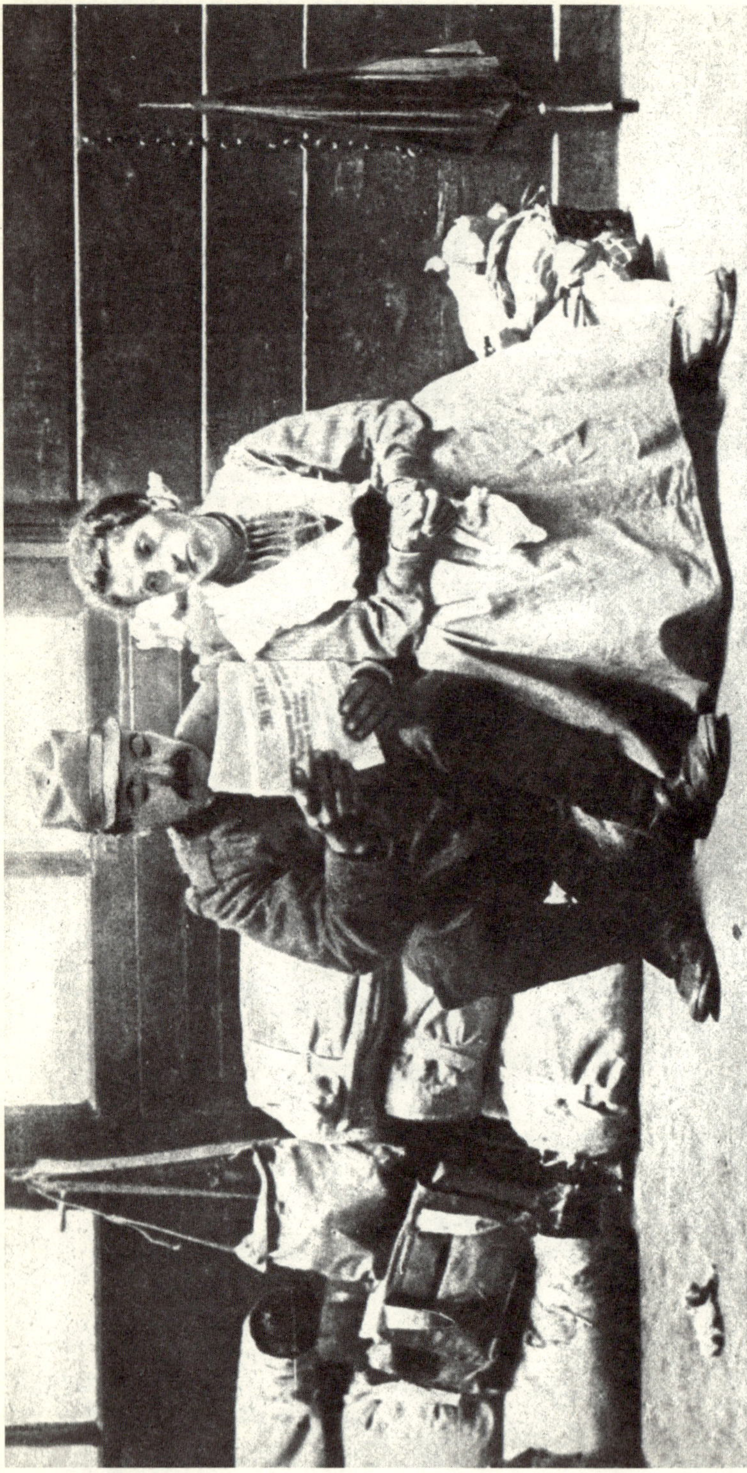

Emotional departures in Italy

Italian pride and sadness of separation at the station during August, repeated across all of the country.

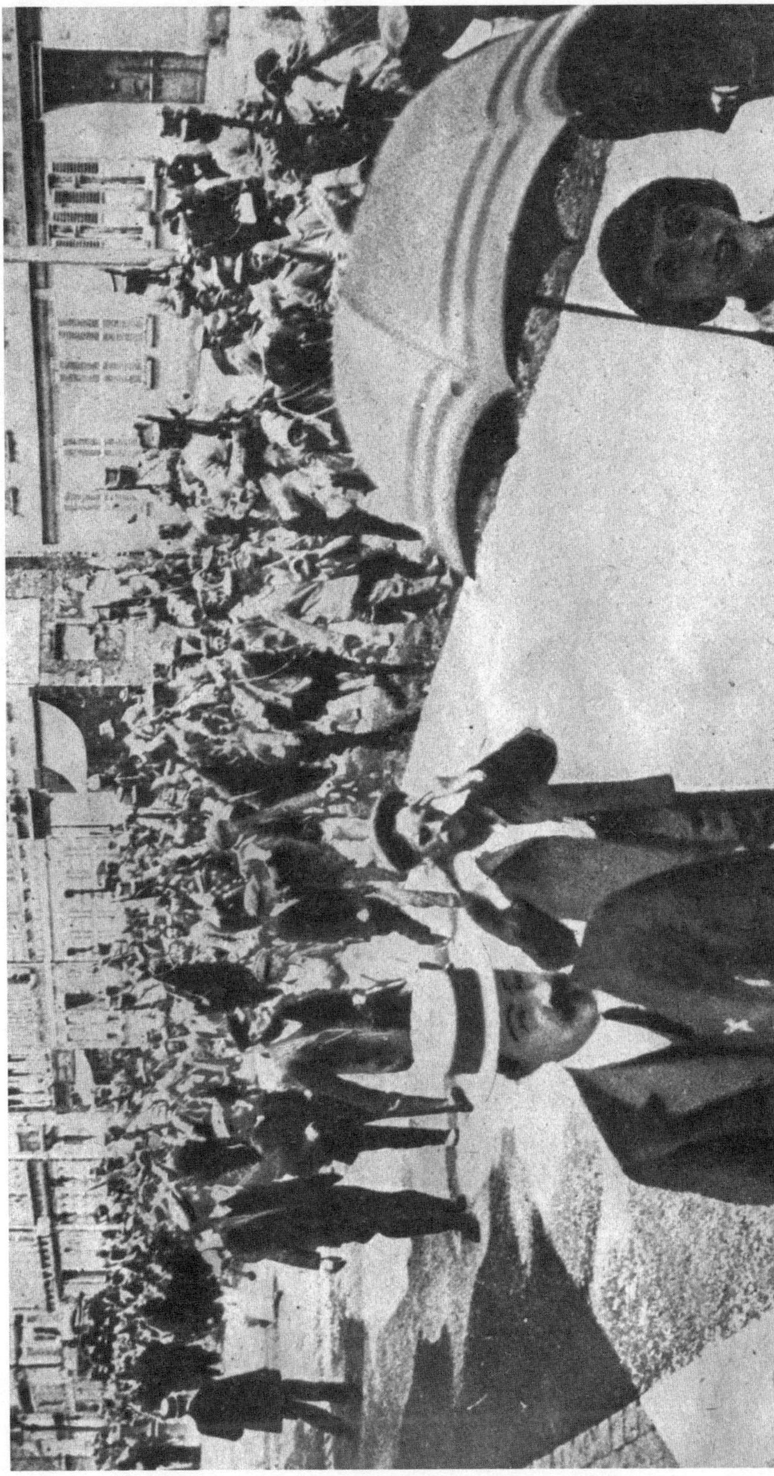

Prisoners captured at Hebuterne

Four hundred prisoners, captured at a farm at Tourvent, are being moved to Amiens.

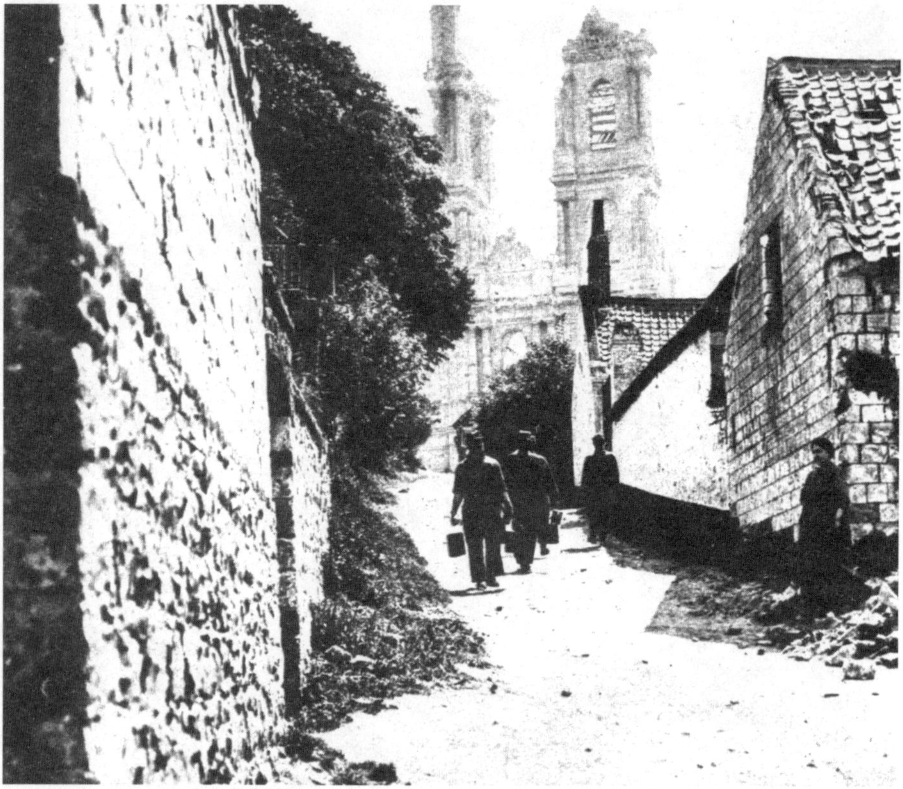

Life under fire in Mont Saint-Eloi

For several weeks there has been heavy fighting in the Arras region. These photographs show Mont Saint-Eloi, a small village of 1,157 inhabitants, who are in constant danger. In the streets of the village life has not stopped, and the children play quietly in the ruins.

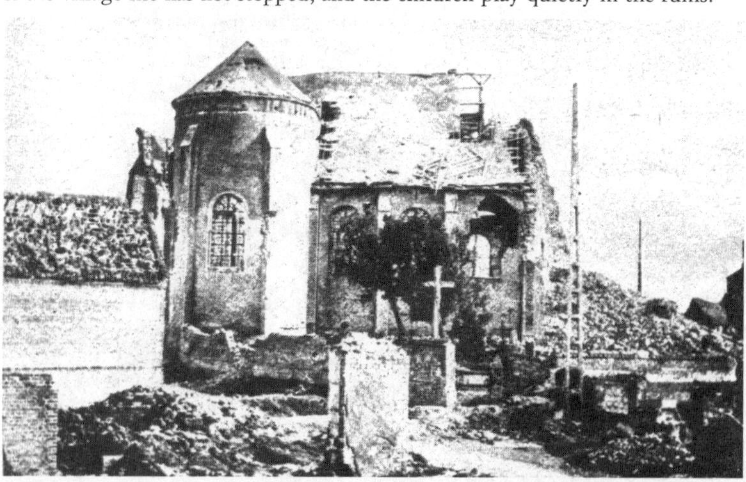

Success at Hebuterne

Hebuterne, where allied troops have retaken several lines of trenches and other key positions. The village of 894 inhabitants was completely demolished. This photograph shows the ruined church.

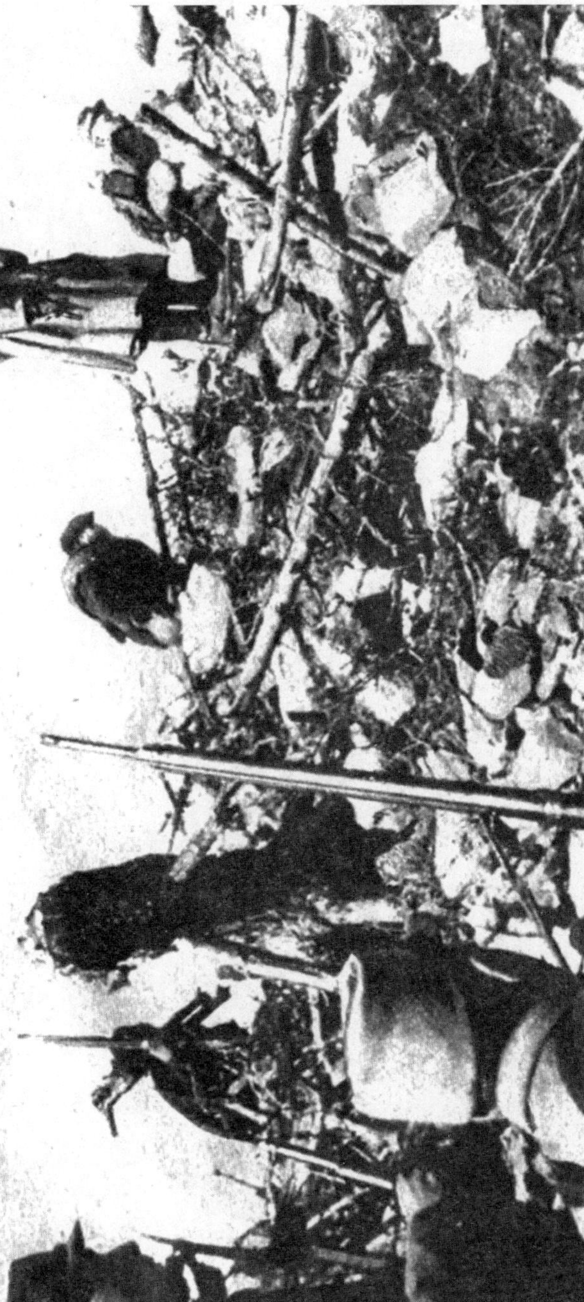

Following the battle, the allied soldiers search for the wounded and hidden enemy.

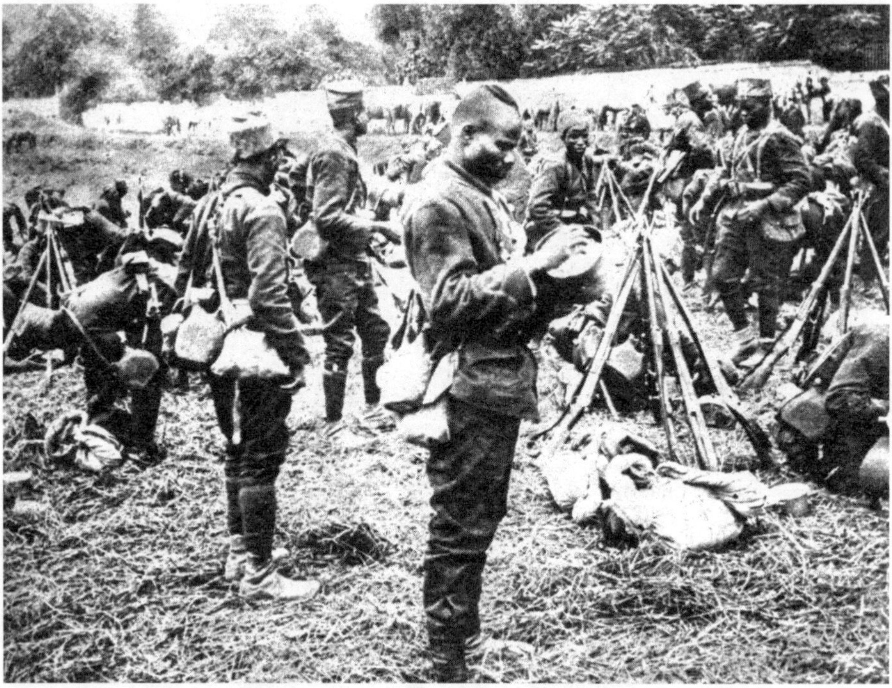

A Senegalese camp in Turkey

Senegalese troops preparing to leave their camp and go into battle. These brave soldiers fight in Turkey under General Gourud, and the Germans have already experienced their skills!

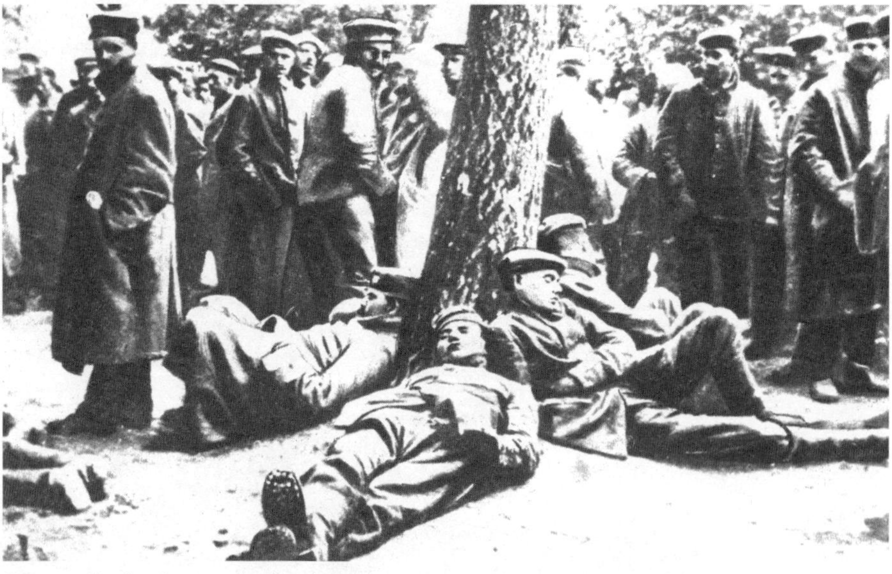

Demoralised prisoners in Artois

Exhausted, starving, falling asleep, the German soldiers don't have confidence anymore. Many German soldiers taken prisoner during the fights near Arras were pleased to surrender.

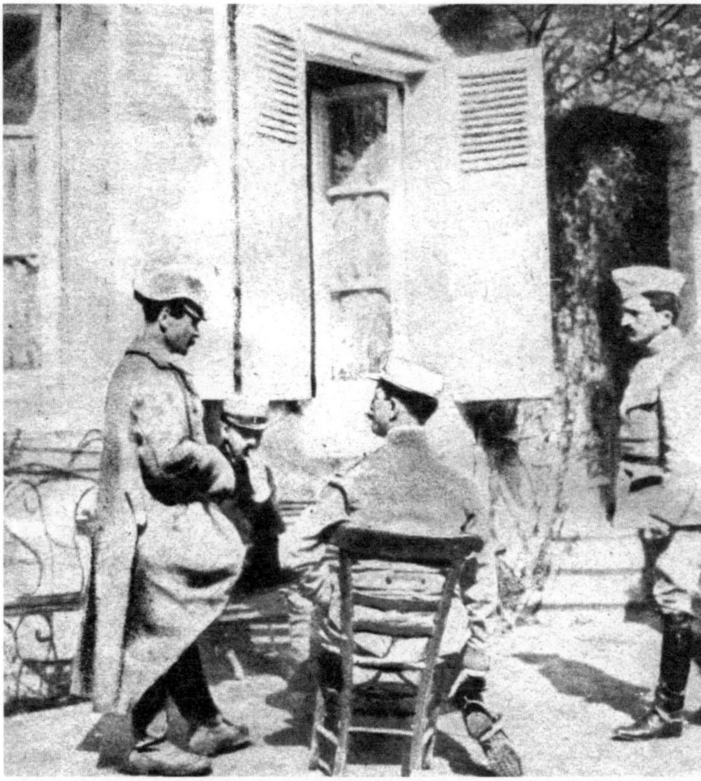

Cross-examination in a prisoner of war camp in Artois.

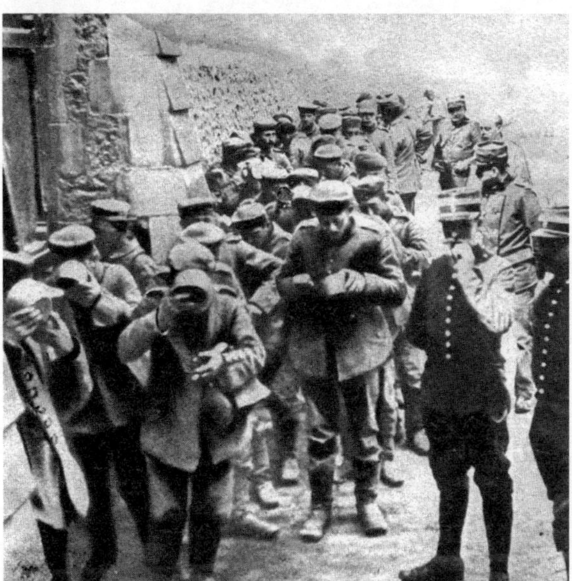

The first step on the road to exile

These starving Germans, recently taken prisoner, are pleased to receive a meal.

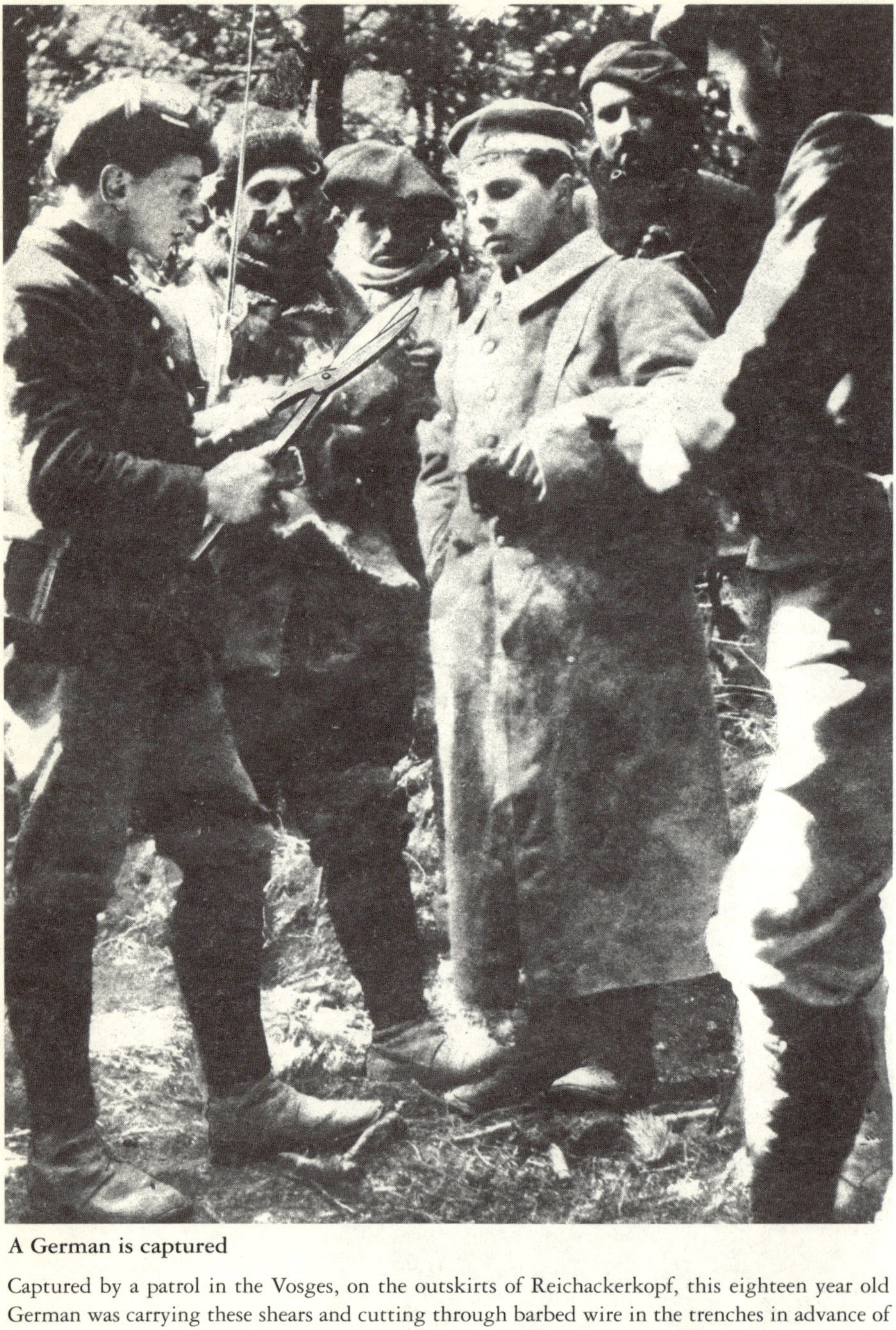

A German is captured

Captured by a patrol in the Vosges, on the outskirts of Reichackerkopf, this eighteen year old German was carrying these shears and cutting through barbed wire in the trenches in advance of an attack. Here he being is questioned before being sent away for interrogation.

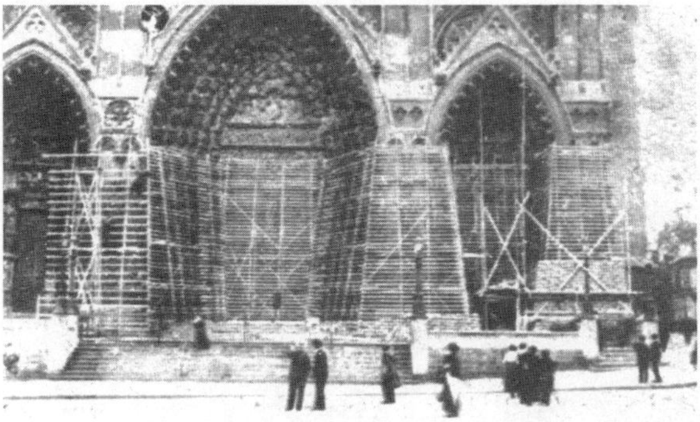

Protection around Amien cathedral

Because of possible bomb and shell damage, the cathedral of Amiens is protected by sand bags and shuttering.

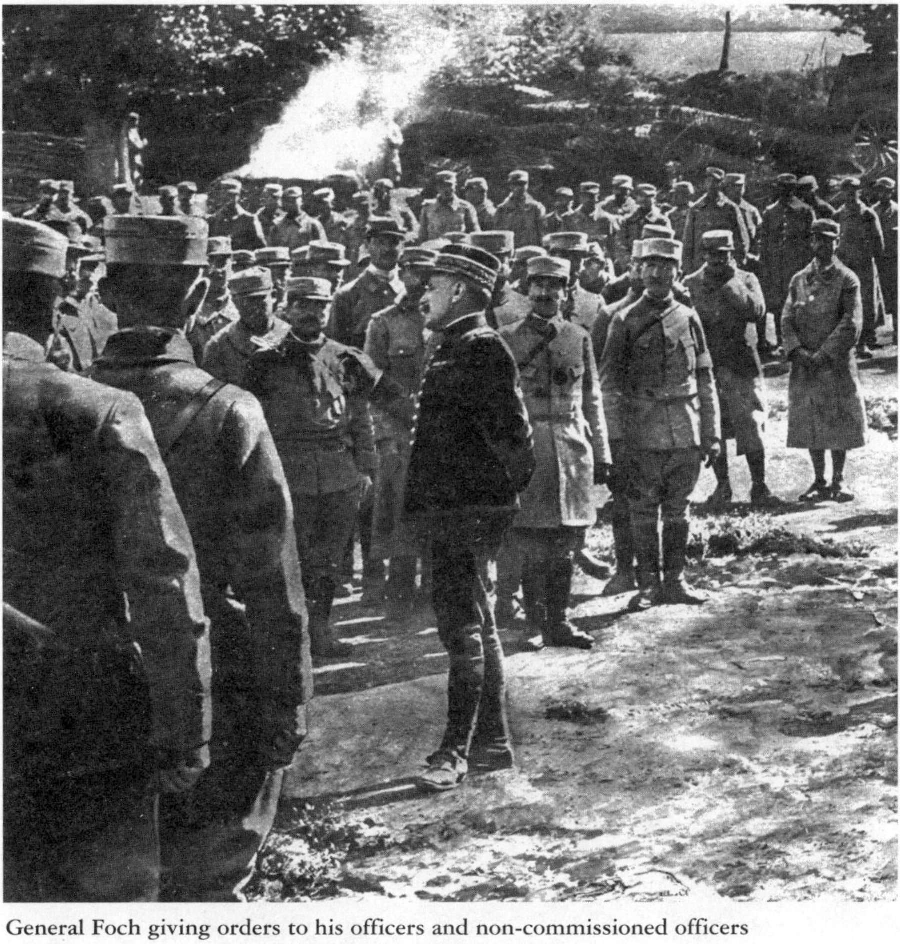

General Foch giving orders to his officers and non-commissioned officers

Having reviewed the regiments in Artois, General Foch gathers with his officers to explain, in strong words, how he has absolute confidence in the future.

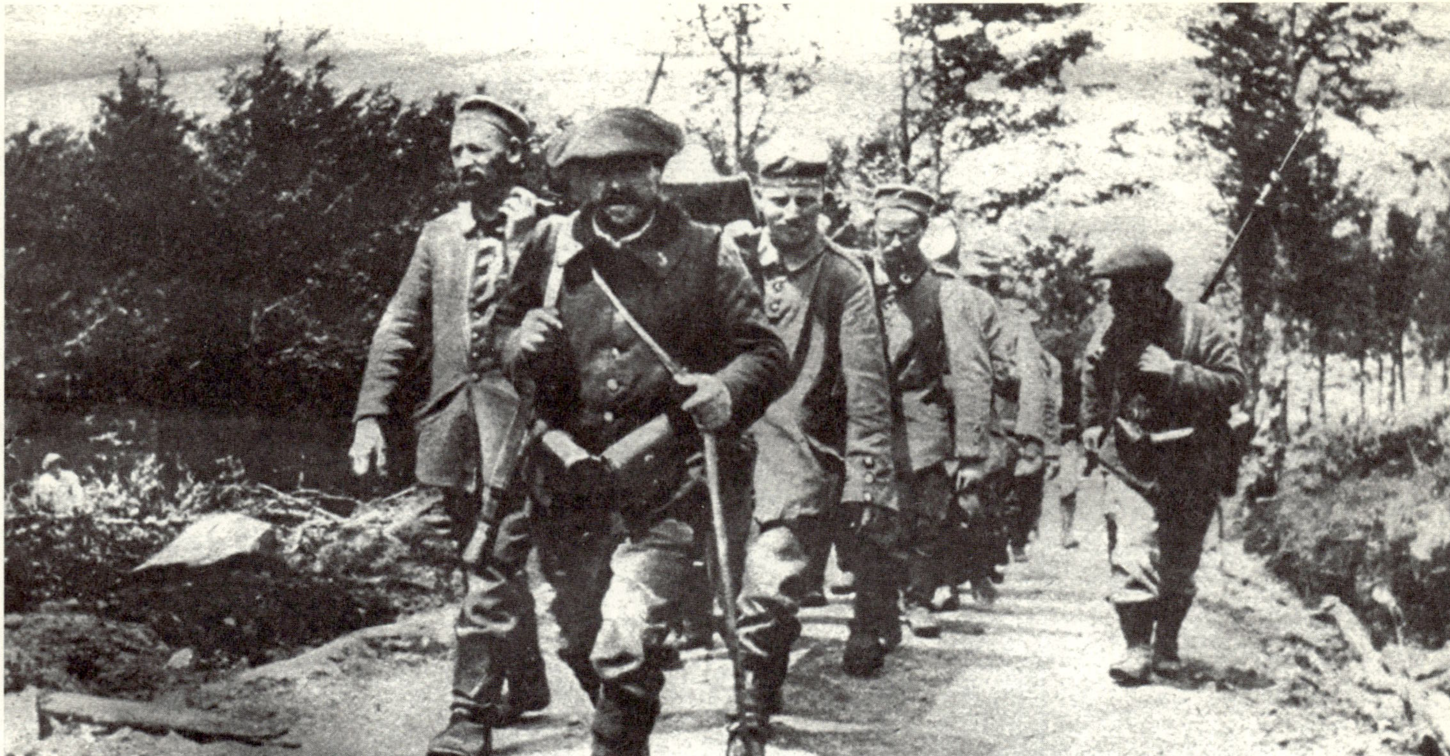

Prisoner captured after an attack in Alsace

Allied soldiers have recently captured 276 prisoners of which five were officers and an important stock of material including hand grenades.

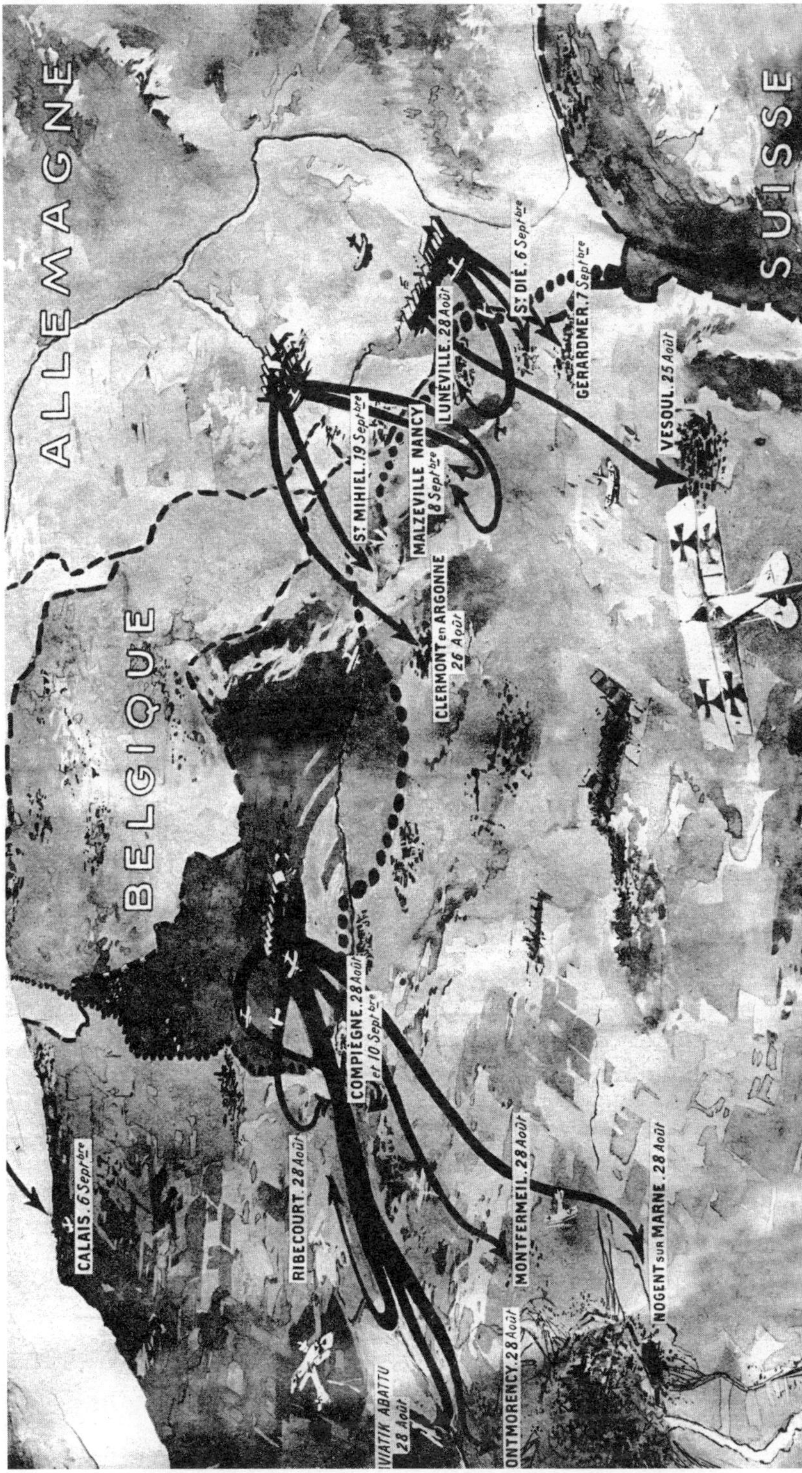

Raids by enemy aircraft from 20 August to 20 September

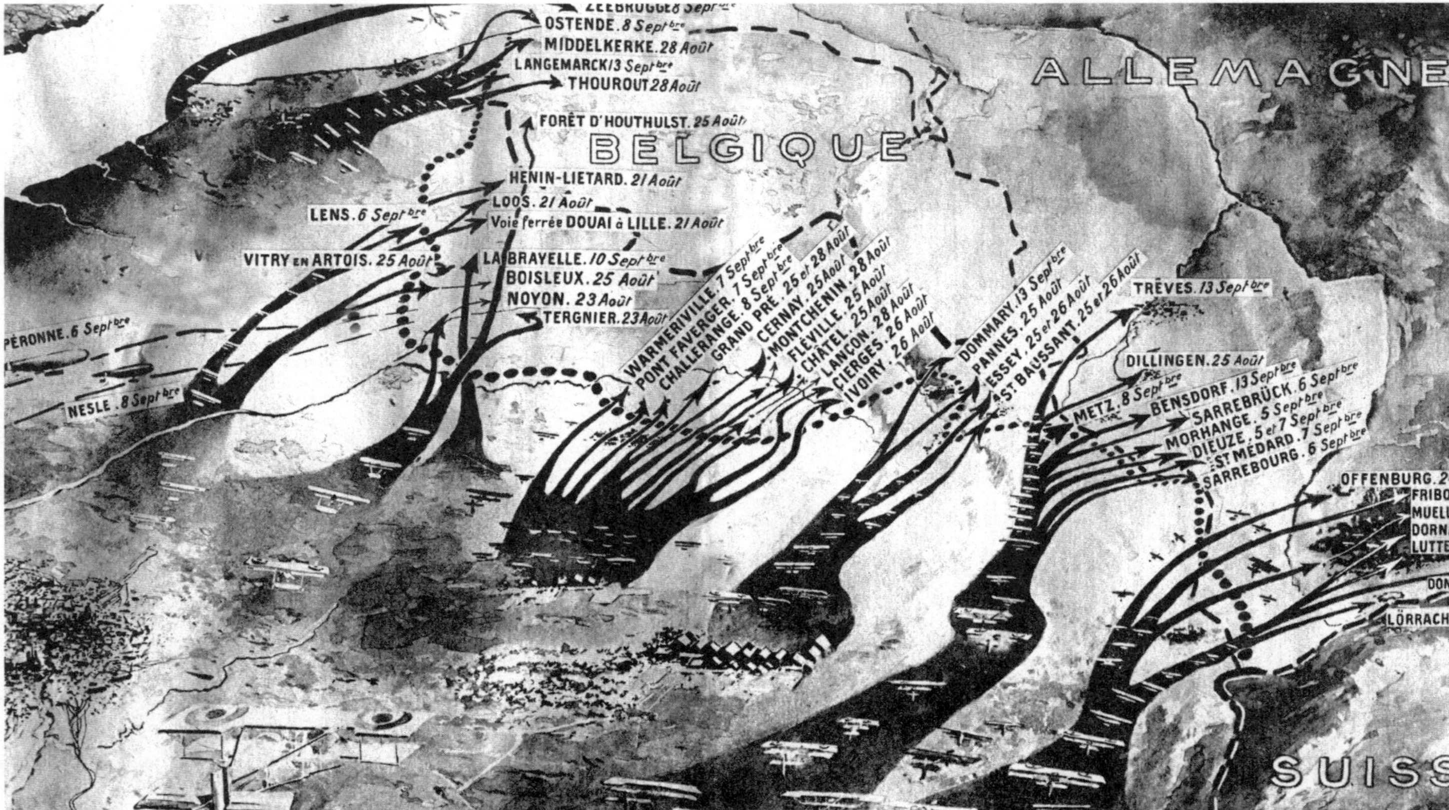

Raids by Allied plans from 20 August to 20 September

The fronts are shown by dotted lines, and the country frontiers by broken lines. Arrows indicate the points of attack.

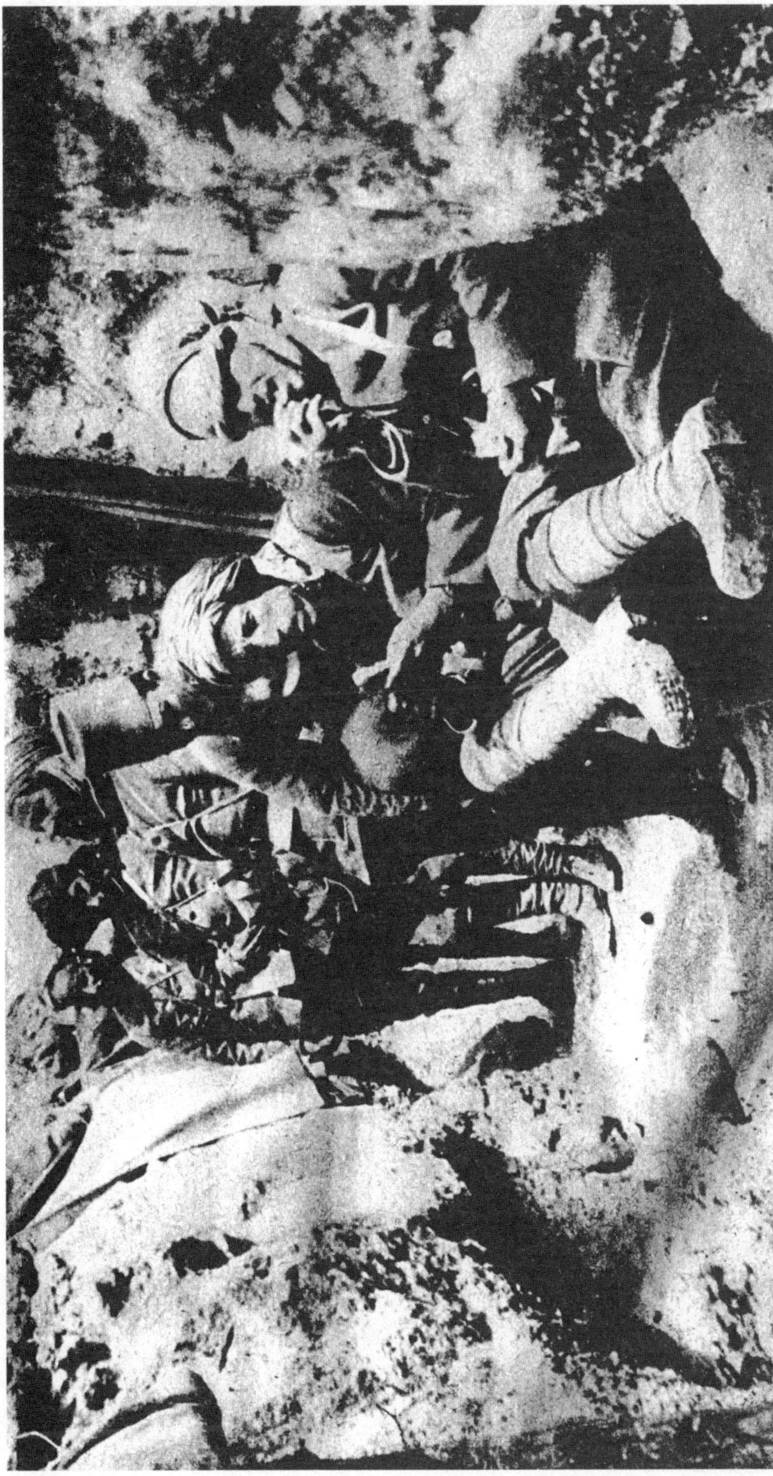

Moroccans in their trenches

These African riders have left their fast horses behind and now take their places in the trenches alongside infantrymen. Although this is not their ideal way of fighting, they are quickly adapting to it.

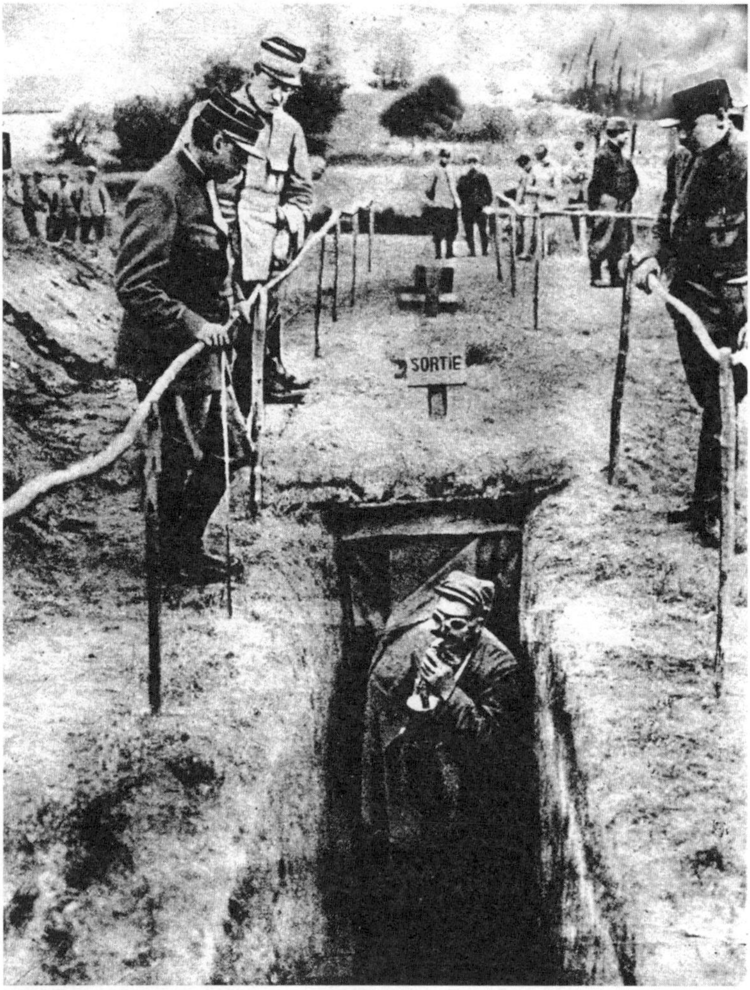

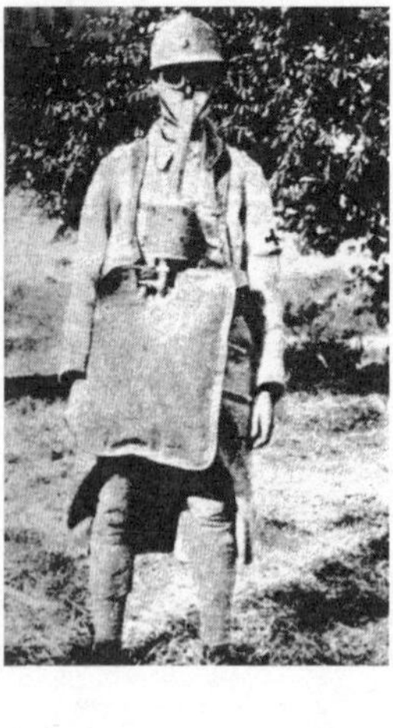

Lessons in the use of gas masks

With more gas masks available, soldiers don't dread the asphyxiating gases quite so much. Both French and British troops receive practical training in their use.

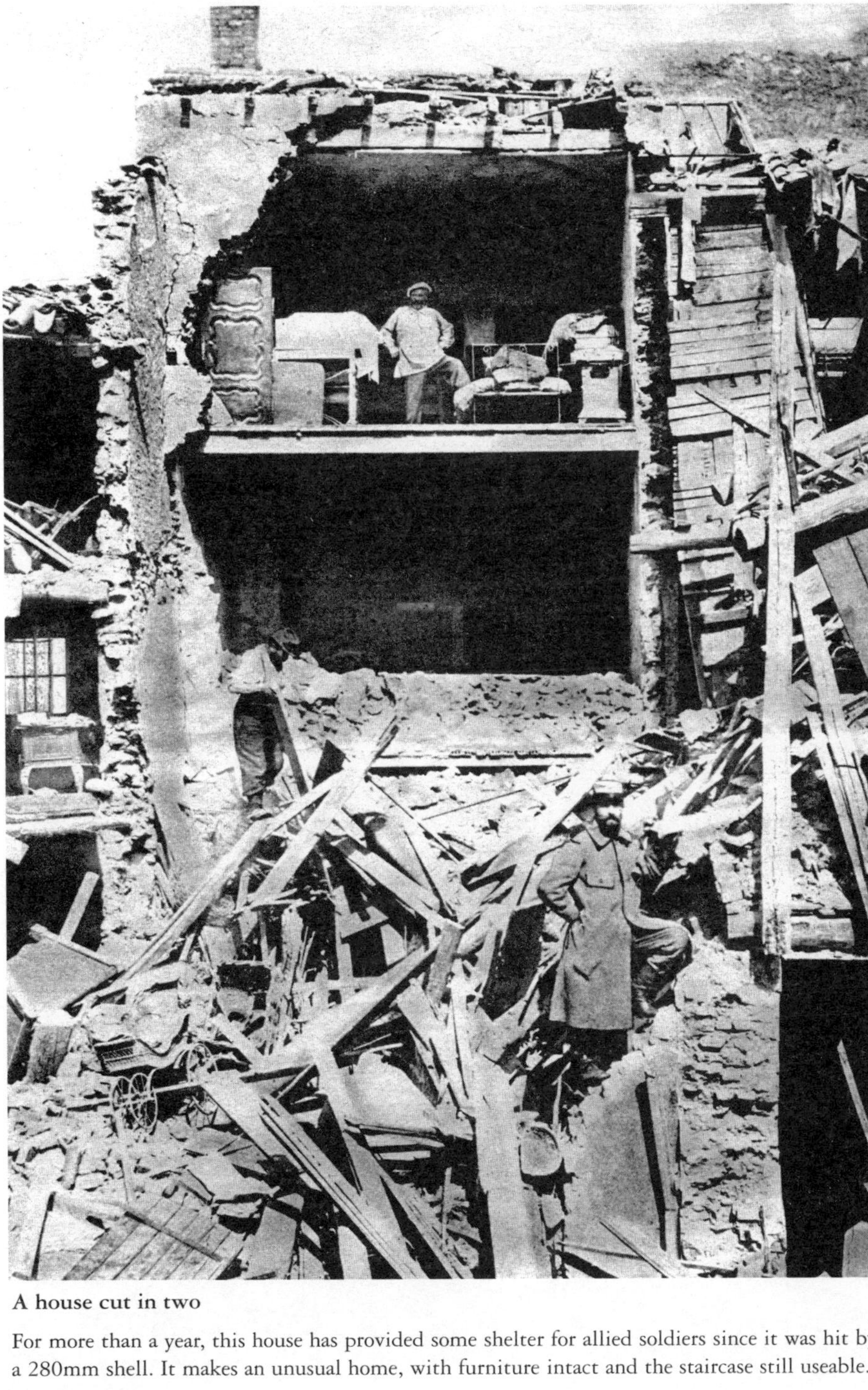

A house cut in two

For more than a year, this house has provided some shelter for allied soldiers since it was hit by a 280mm shell. It makes an unusual home, with furniture intact and the staircase still useable.

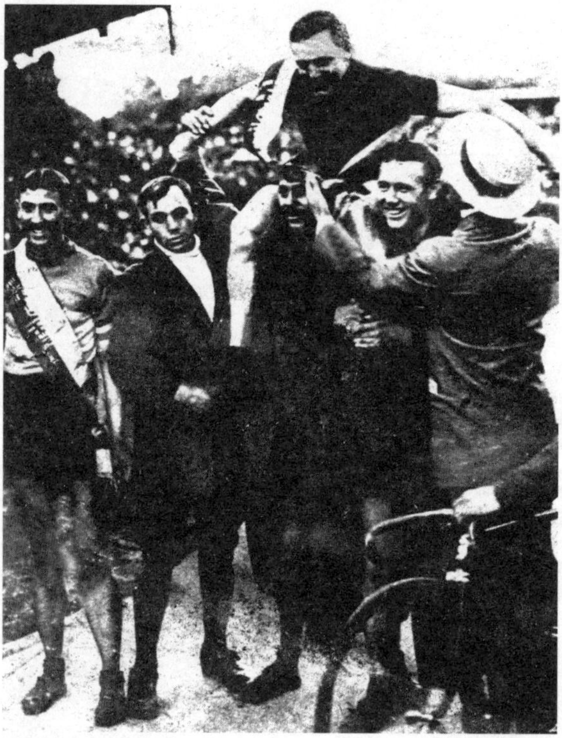

Rutt, the grand prix cyclist of 1913 in the German army

German bicyclist Rutt, who won the Paris grand prix in 1913, and was in America when the war started, has reached his homeland via Sweden. He is now a motorcyclist and messenger on the eastern front.

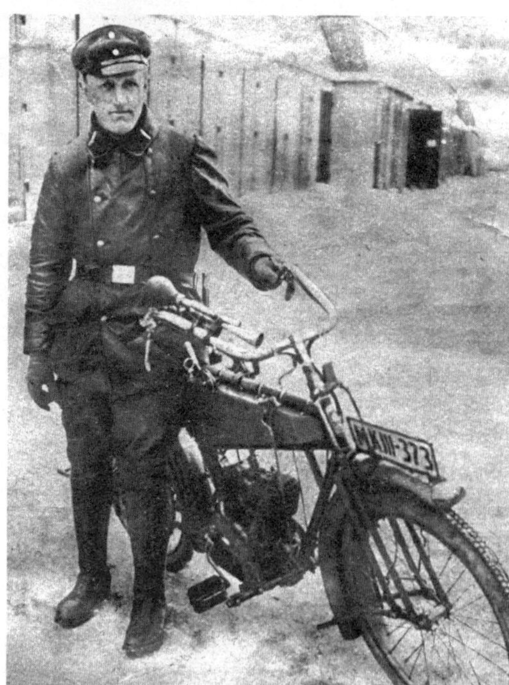

- NEWS REPORTS -

Thursday March 16, 1916

Shooting has stopped in the trenches in Belgium. To the west of Meuse, the shelling has slowed down between Bethincourt and Cumieres. The French have also re-taken parts of trenches lost earlier. Shelling continues around Woëvre.

Friday, March 17, 1916

In Woëvre, intense shelling by the Germans. General Roques replaces General Gallien in the French ministry of the War. The Italians, despite violent Austrian attacks, have maintained their position at the Carso front in the Adriatic. Admiral Tirpitz, minister of the German navy, has resigned. His successor is Von Capelle.

Saturday, March 18, 1916

To the north of the Aisne, the French have defeated a hostile attack. In Argonne, they attacked the enemy's communication centre behind the front lines. Violent action overnight, to the East of the Meuse, with the Germans mounting five strong but unsuccessful attacks. Artillery destroyed an important enemy munitions dump near Champneuville. Reciprocal shelling in Woëvre, and German prisoners taken in the woods at Mortmare. The German Treasury secretary made an optimistic speech to the Reichstag.

Sunday, March 19, 1916

In Belgium, artillery has disrupted the enemy trenches in the region of Boesinghe. The Germans have moved east, after bringing forward additional artillery during the day near Haudremont. They were held back by allied batteries which were very active in Woëvre. A German attack occurred in Lorraine against French positions of the region of Thiaville. An immediate counter offensive has driven the enemy back to their trenches.

The Russian artillery has attacked near Dviftsk. Our allies have occupied Malsamohun, some 90 kilometres to the west of Erzeroum, on the Euphrates. They have taken more than 800 Turkish prisoners.

Monday, March 20, 1916

Artillery has destroyed enemy trenches near Neuville and Godat, north of Reims. The Germans have completely failed to gain any ground in this region. Five French planes have bombed the stations at Metz-Sablons, the depots at Castle-Saline and the airfield at Dieuze. Twenty-three other planes operated from Habsheim airfield, attacking the goods yard at Mulhouse. Four were lost during the aerial fight that followed, three having landed behind enemy lines. The French torpedo boat, Renaudin, was hit by a submarine in the Adriatic.

Tuesday, March 21, 1916

To the west of the Meuse, the Germans are using large calibre shells in an attempt to widen their front. A new enemy division is using flame throwing equipment on positions between Avocourt and Malancourt. Planes have dropped twenty-five bombs on the station at Dun-sur-Meuse, totally destroying it. General Cadorna, Italian Chief of Staff, has arrived in Paris.

The German Chancellor's financial proposals were defeated by his budget committee and he was strongly attacked by both the liberal conservatives and national press.

Wednesday March 22, 1916.

Sixty five allied planes have been in a raid on Zeebrugge. In Belgium, the enemy broke through allied lines to the north of the bridge at Boesinghe, but were immediately driven back by a counterattack. On the left of Meuse, the Germans renewed their attempts on the Avocourt-Malancourt front and a detachment of their soldiers used flame throwers while, at the same time, their batteries shelled allied lines.

The Russians have progressed on the Dniester and taken Ispahan, in Persia. The heir Prince of Serbia and Mr. Pachitch, president of Serbia, have arrived in Paris.

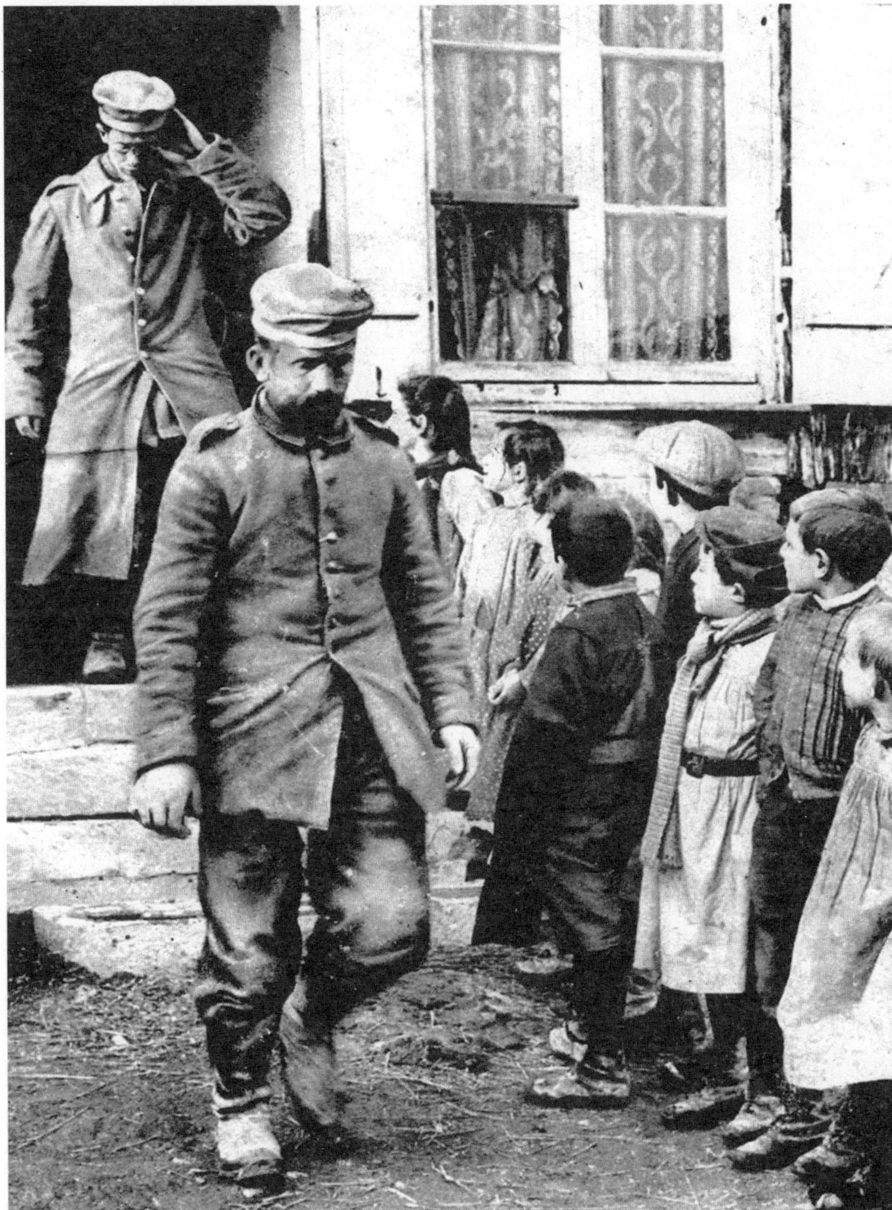

They will keep an indelible memory of German aggression

Enemy prisoners at Verdun, returning from cross-examination, passing curious children. These small people will never forget.

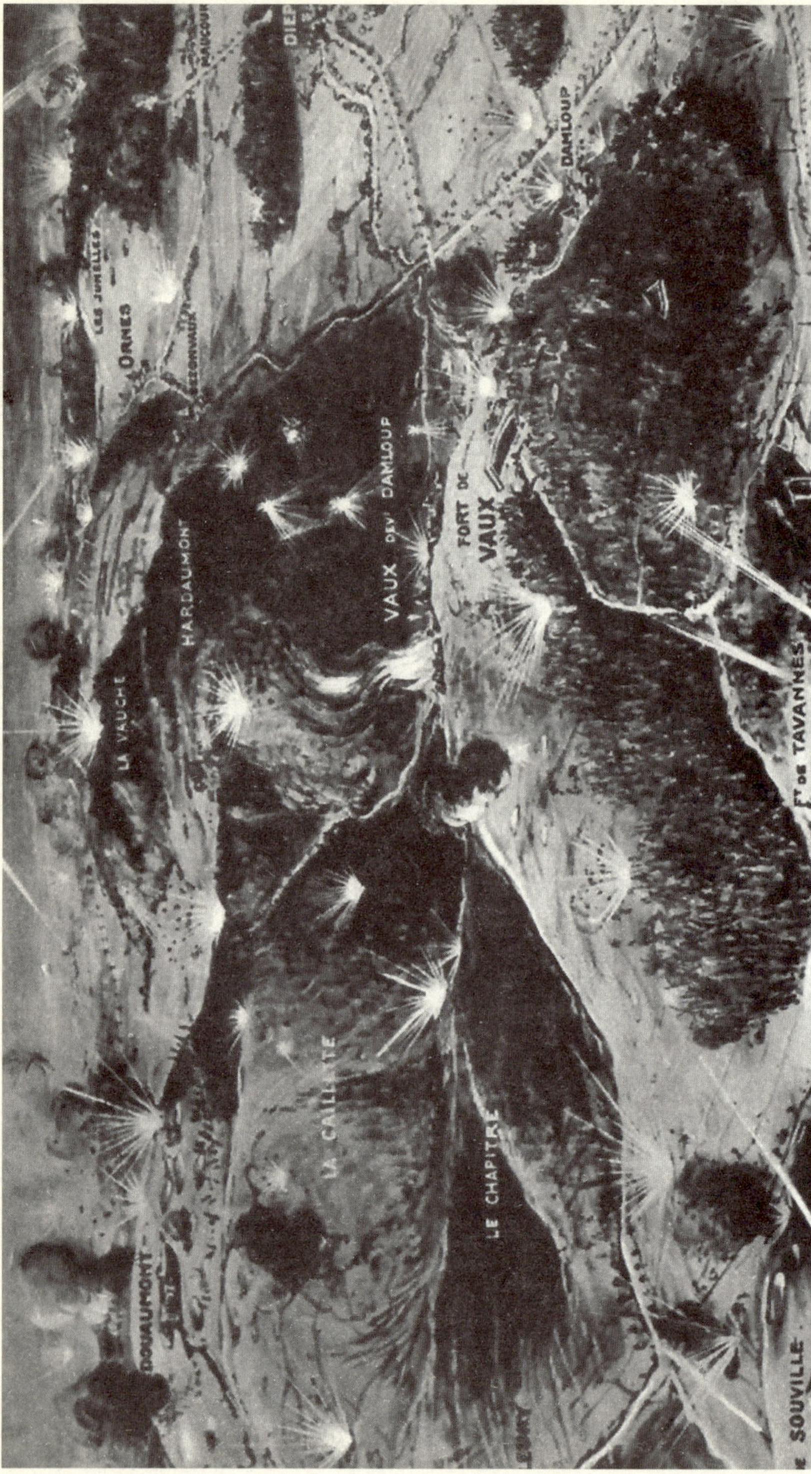

The north east front

A drawing to show the areas of nightly shelling on the battlefield

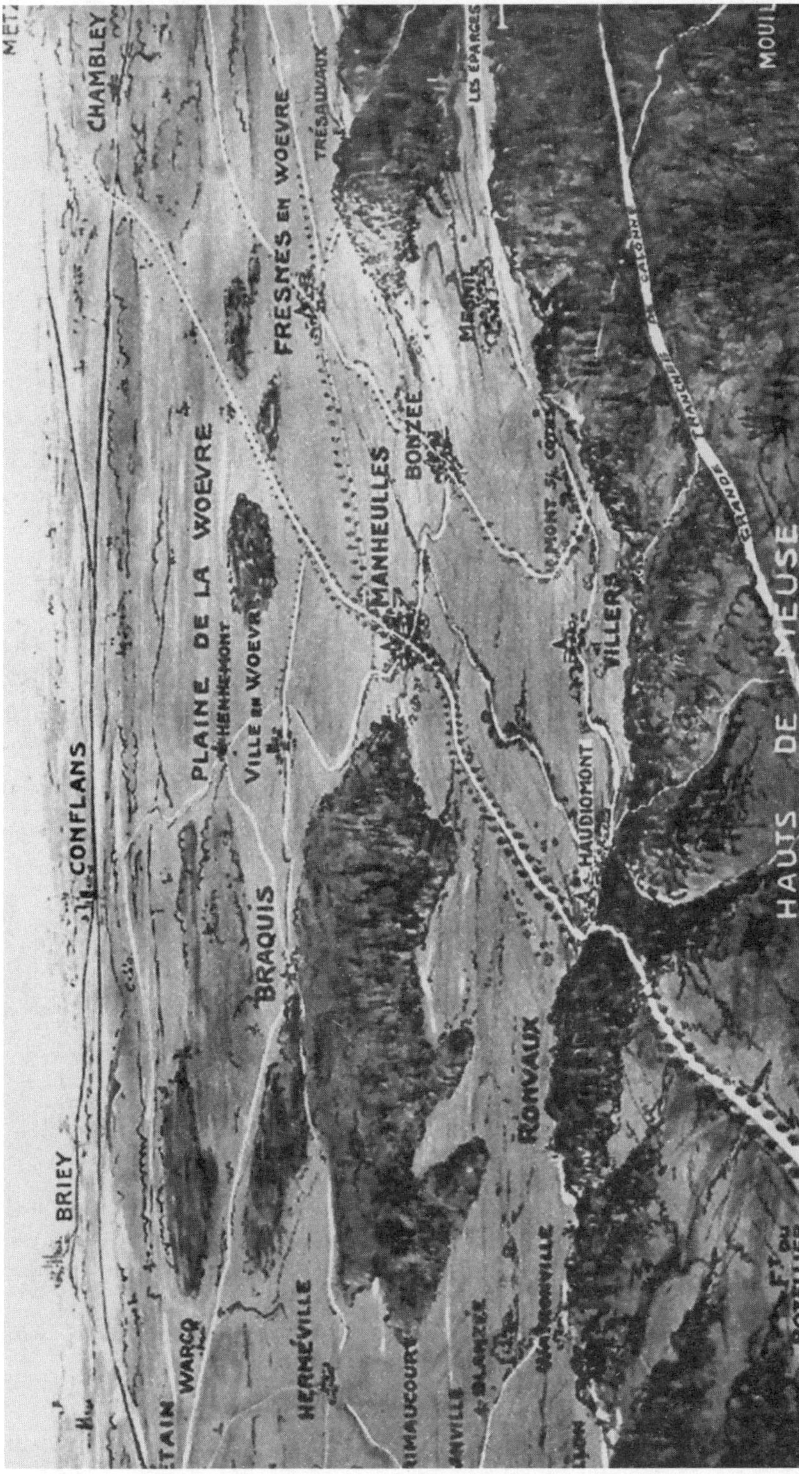

Area to the east of Verdun

A drawing of locations in the plain of Woëvre, at the foot of the Hauts-de-Meuse, viewed from Rozellier.

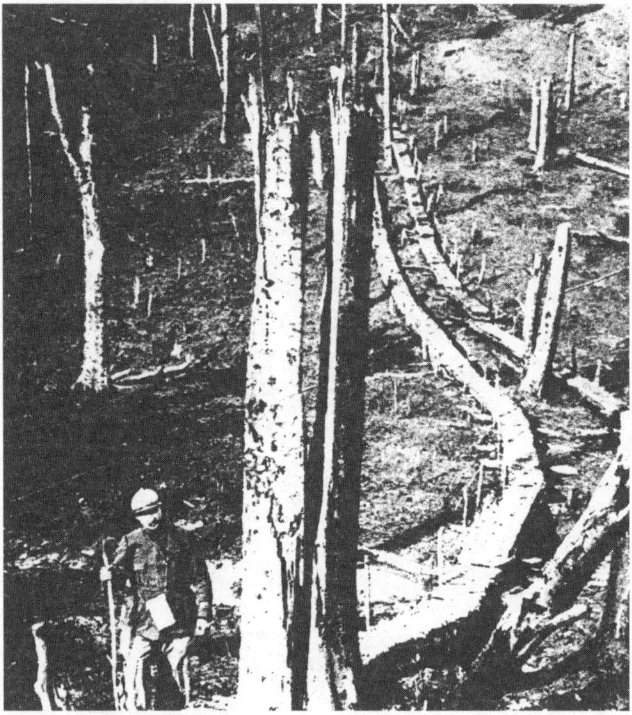

The strong allied position on the Hauts-de-Meuse

Progress in the small, muddy valleys has been difficult but allied attacks in the Woëvre have now stopped the enemy's furious assaults. The offensive developed on the right bank of the Meuse.

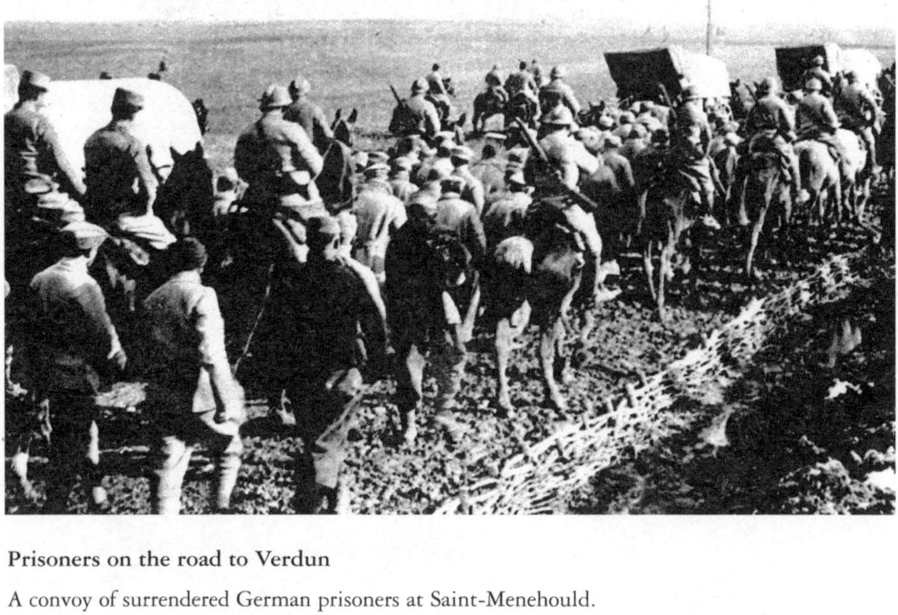

Prisoners on the road to Verdun

A convoy of surrendered German prisoners at Saint-Menehould.

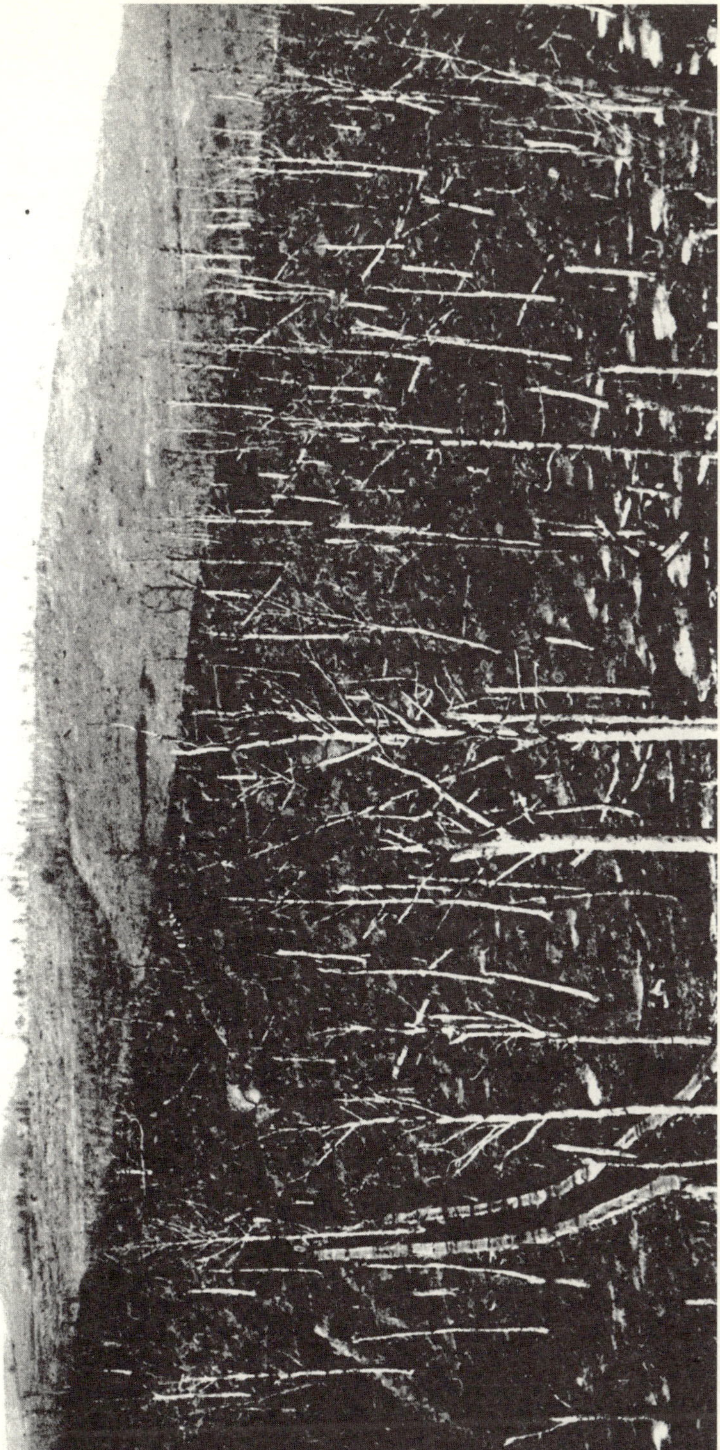

The operations on Verdun were made very difficult by the state of the swampy land. This view, shelled for months, offers an aspect not usually seen.

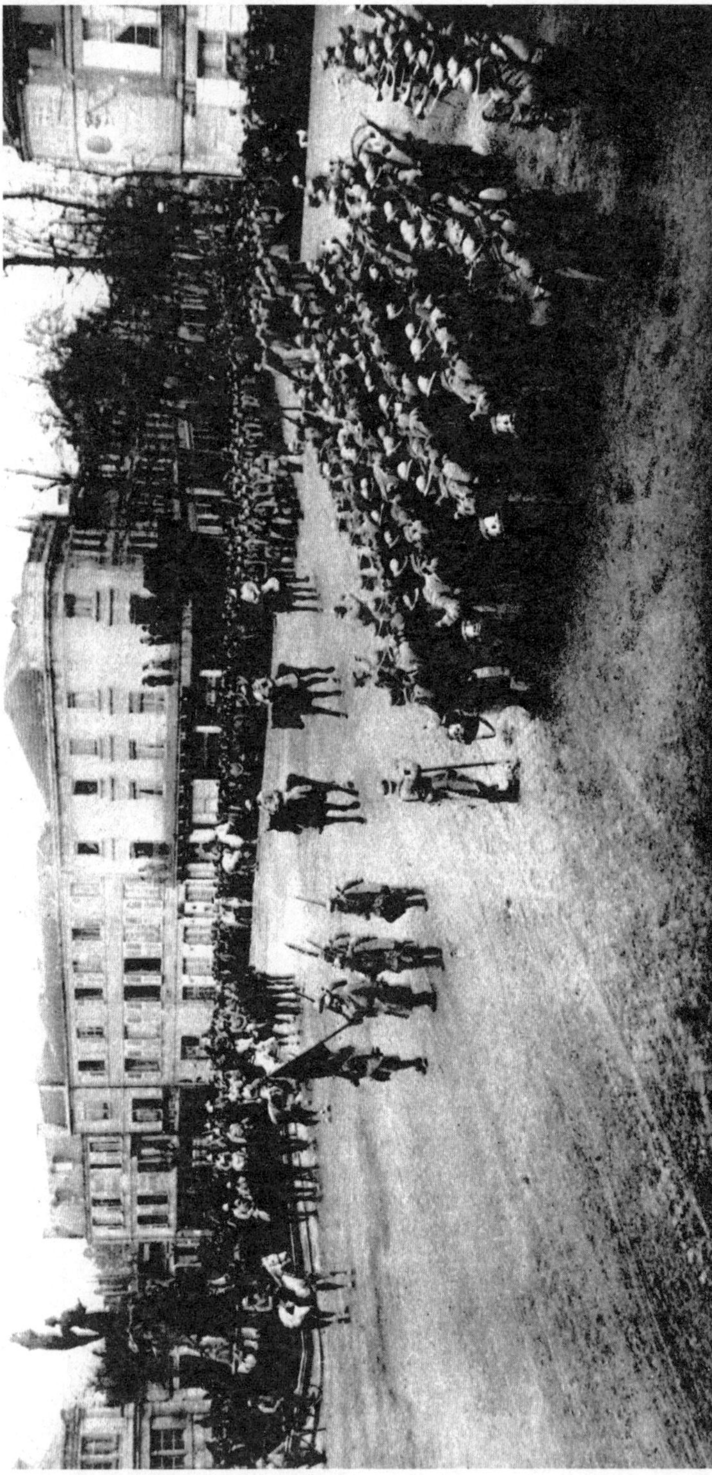

A review of troops near Verdun

A lot of those who, in the last days of February, were involved in the German offensive, are receiving medals - a reward for their heroism.

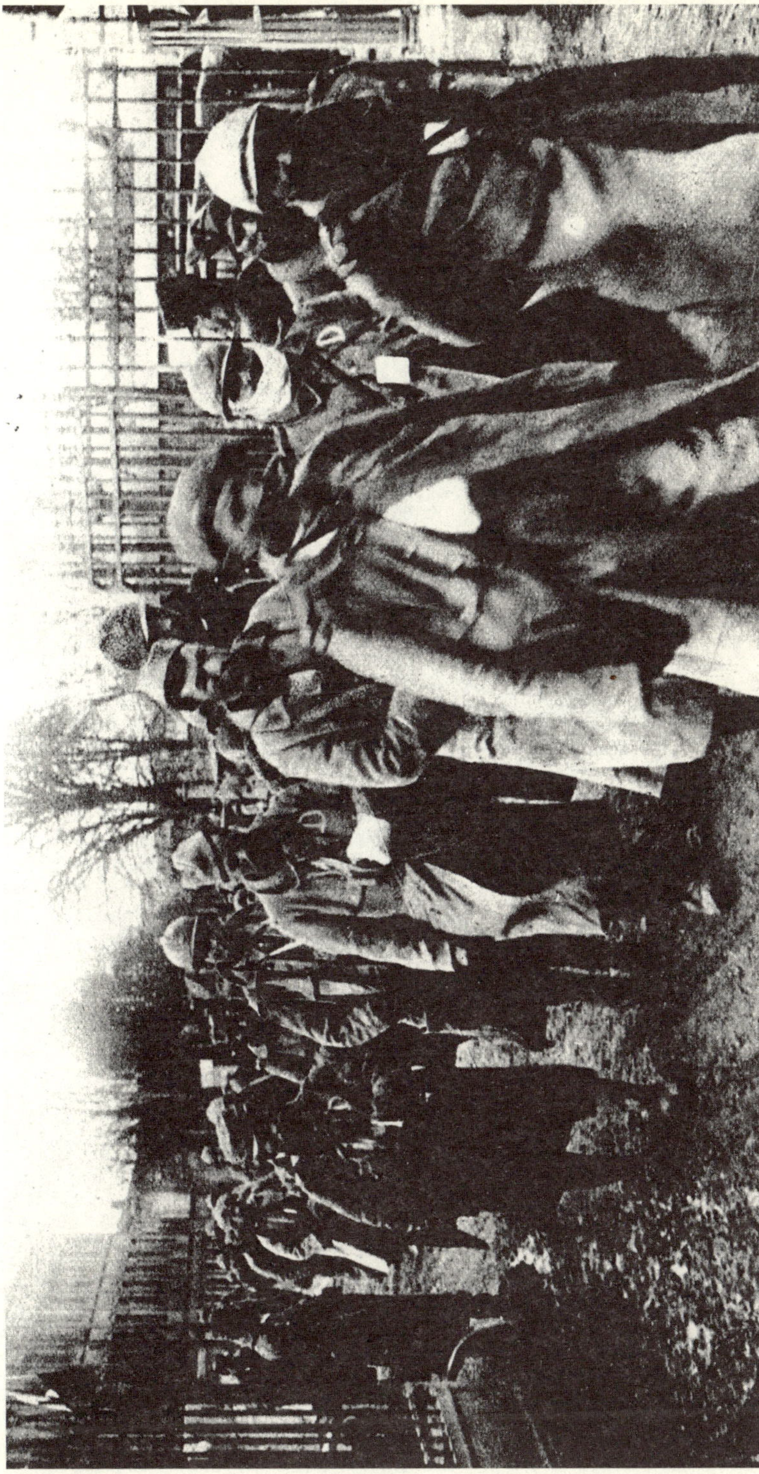

Wounded return to Verdun

Compared to those slaughtered at Verdun by the Germans, these soldiers are only slightly wounded. Here are some of the French heroes coming to embark for home at the station of Bar-Le-Duc.

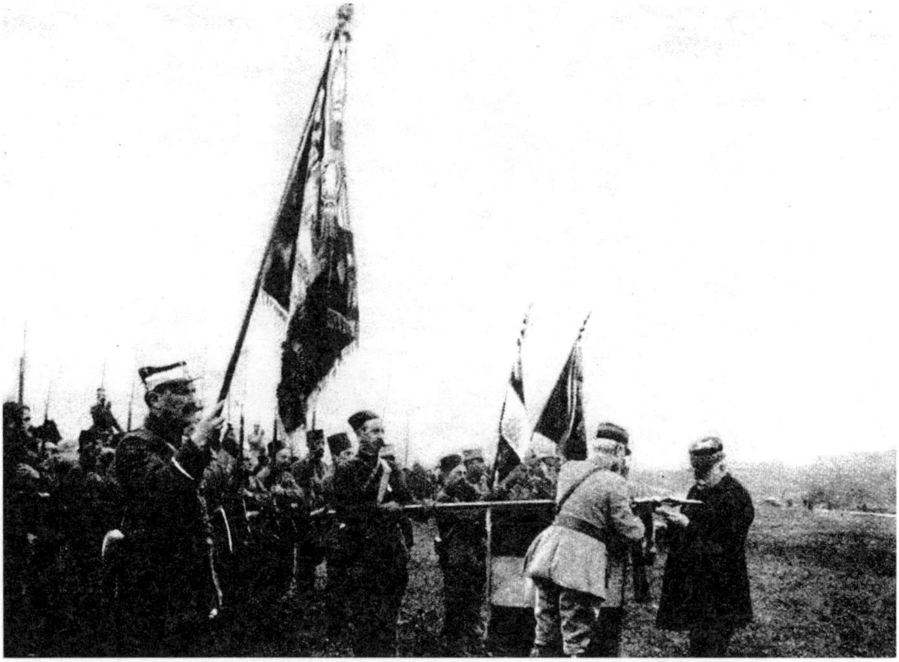

Decorating the regimental flag

These are Algerian mercenaries. The flag of their regiment has already been decorated with the Legion of Honour, and General Joffre now adds the cross of war.

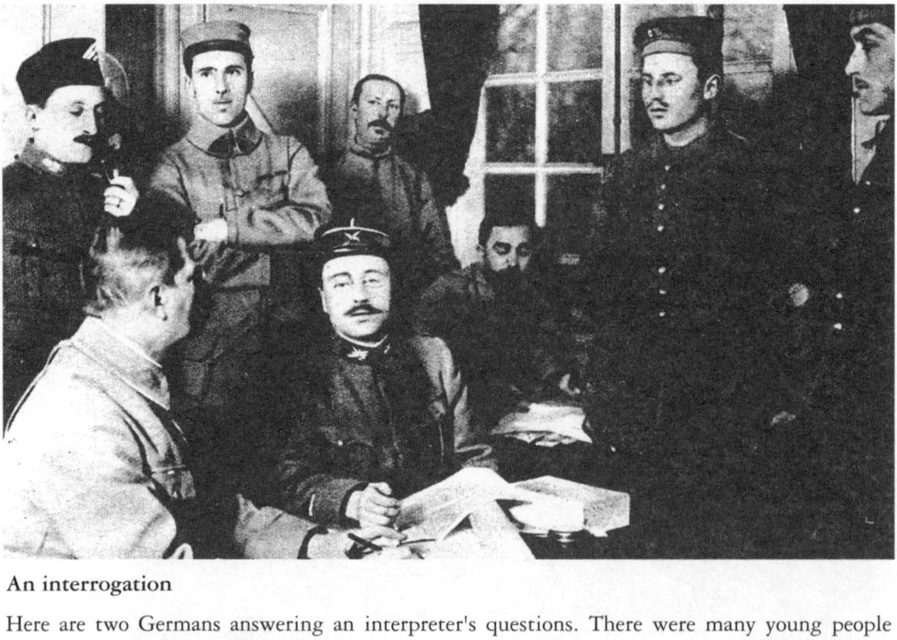

An interrogation

Here are two Germans answering an interpreter's questions. There were many young people amongst the Germans captured at Verdun and in the assault on the city, some regiments included up to a third who were aged only 16.

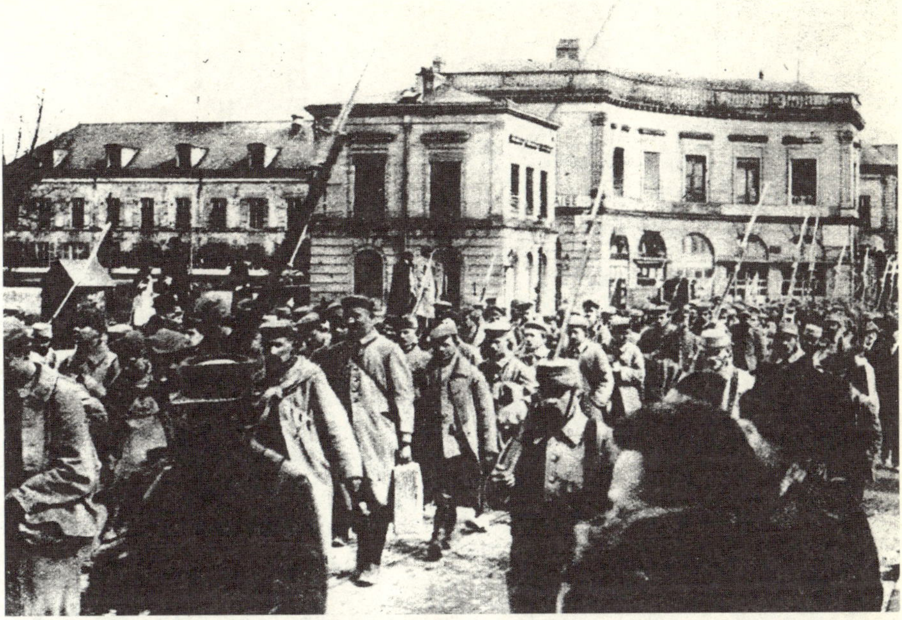

950 prisoners, recently captured, are marched through the streets of Chalons

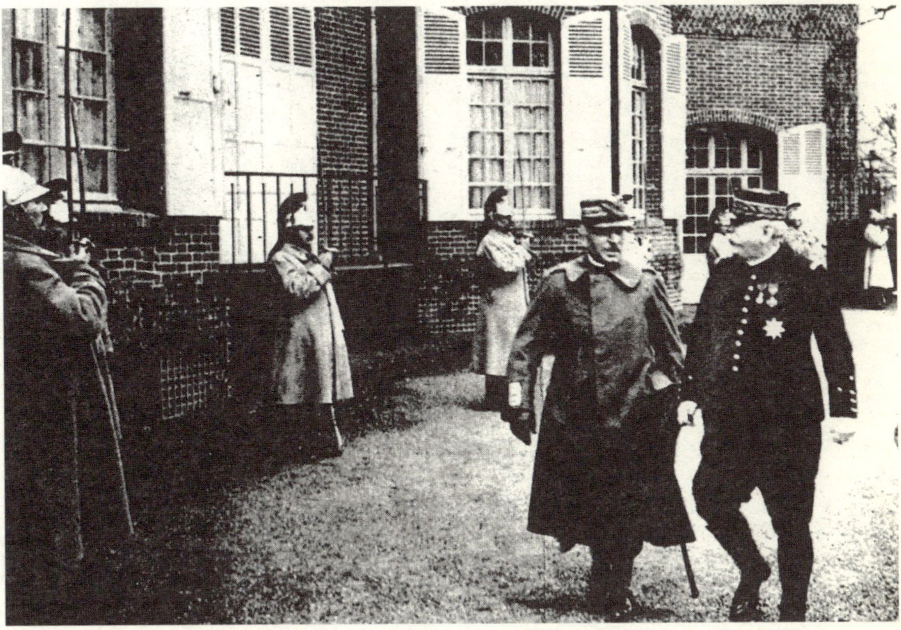

A demonstration of collaboration

A conference in Paris with delegations representing all of the Allies. Here, Generals Cadornas and Joffres from the French delegation.

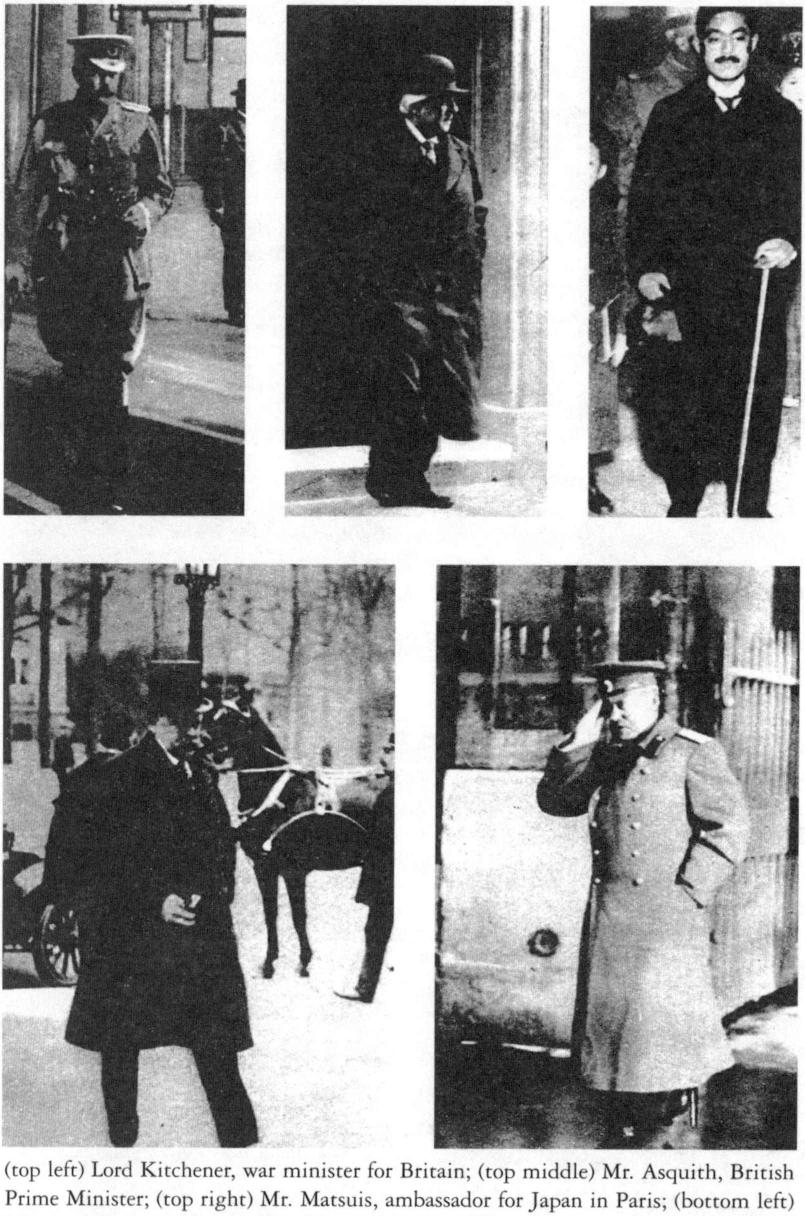

(top left) Lord Kitchener, war minister for Britain; (top middle) Mr. Asquith, British Prime Minister; (top right) Mr. Matsuis, ambassador for Japan in Paris; (bottom left) Mr. Isvolskies, ambassador for Russia in Paris; (bottom right) General Gilinsky, permanent delegate for Russia at allied headquarters.

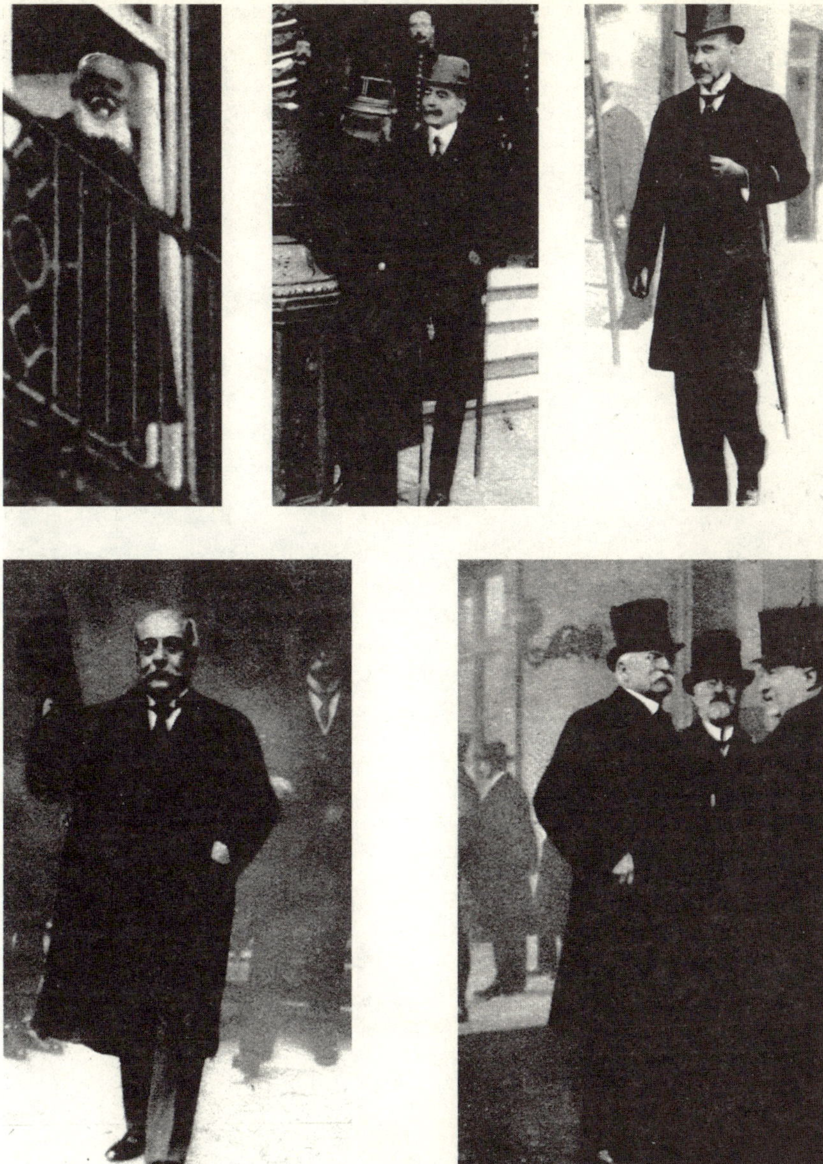

(top left) Mr. Pachitch, president of the government of Serbia; (top middle) Mr. de Broqueville, president of the government of Belgium; (top right) Baron Beyens, foreign minister for Belgium; (bottom left) Mr. Salandras, president of the Italian government; (bottom right) Mr. Sonninos, foreign minister for Italy.

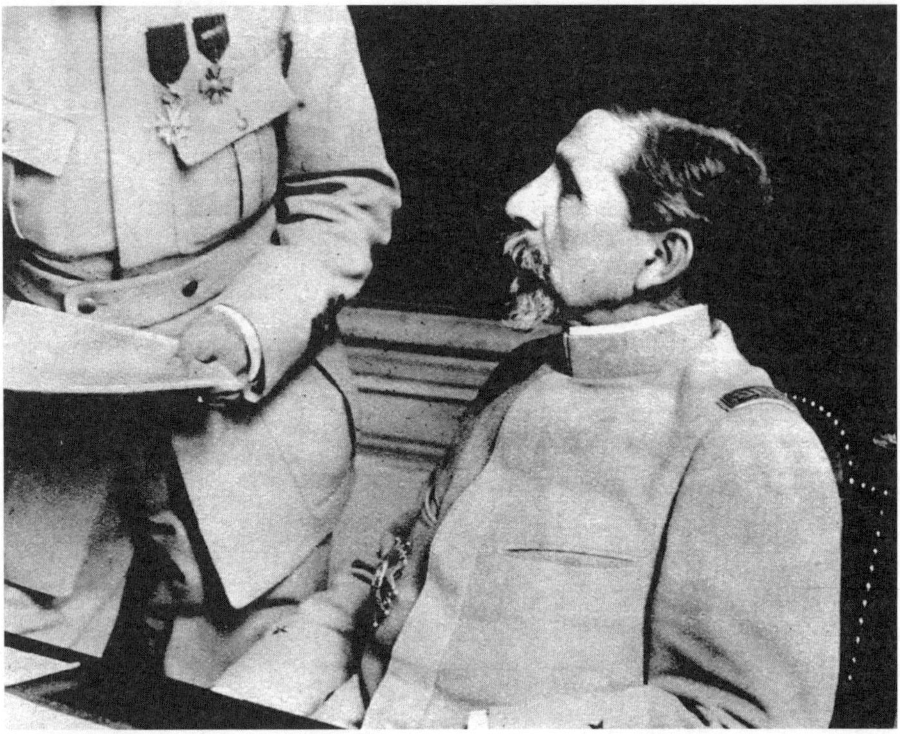

General Roques, the new French war minister

Prior to his appointment, the general directed the army in the Woëvre district. He succeeds General Gallieni in the ministry of the War. Aged sixty, he has directed campaigns in Algeria and Madagascar. From 1910 to 1912, he was inspector of aeronautics.

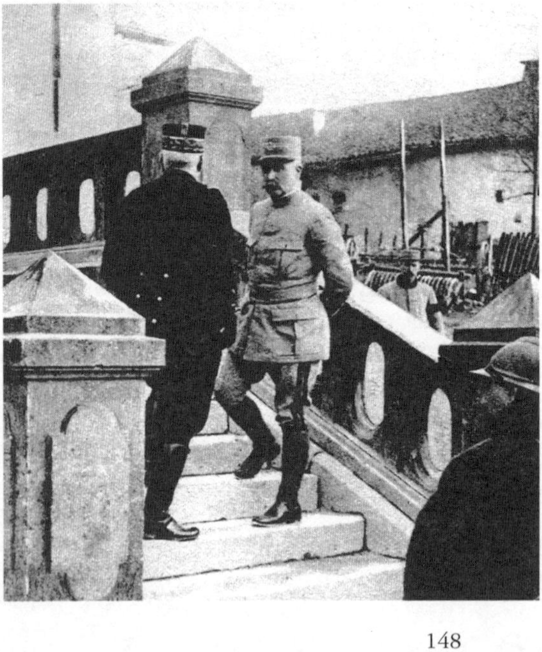

General Joffre

This photograph, taken during the general's recent journey, shows him with General Pétain (facing).

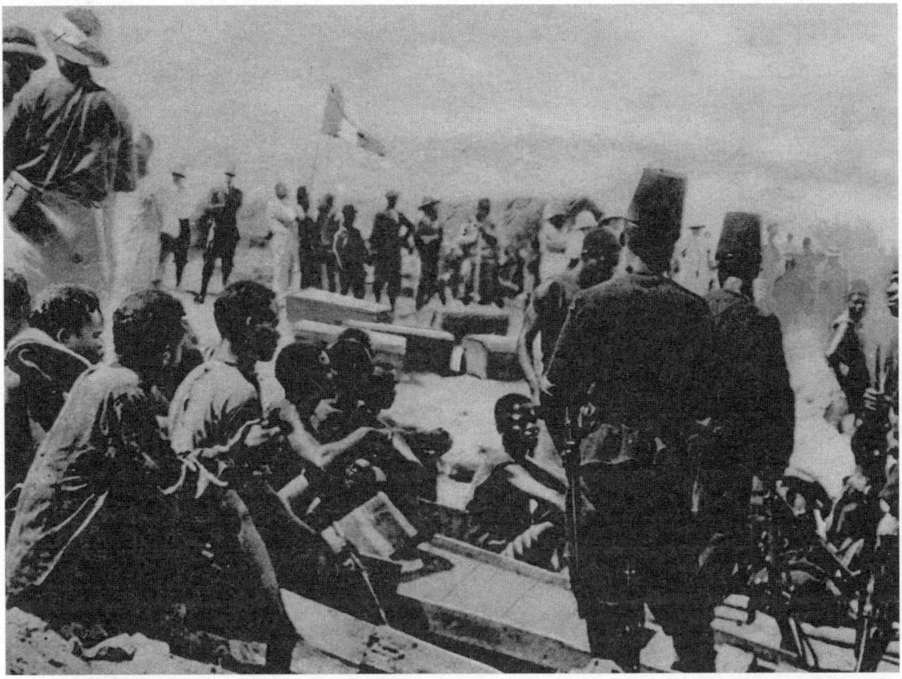

British success in Tanganyika

Having declared war on Portugal, Germany has closed access to its last colony. Attacked to the north and the southwest by the English, the west by the Belgians, and soon to the south by the Portuguese, Tanganyika will then be surrounded. Here we see troops guarding prisoners.

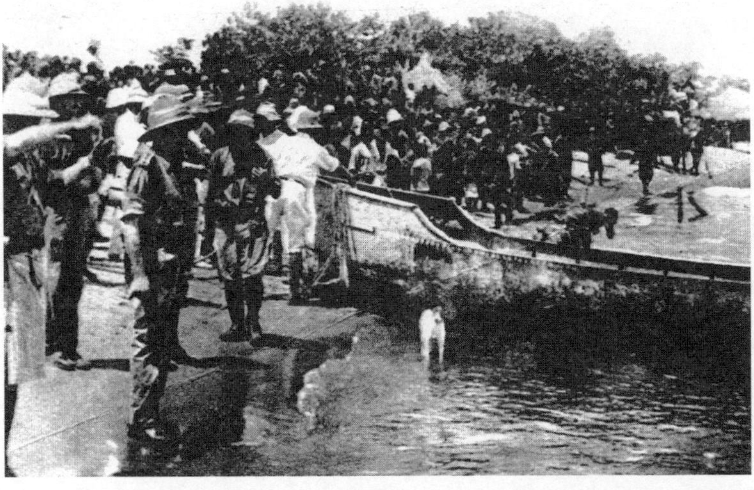

The British have already demonstrated their success, and on December 26th, they captured an arms ship, the "Kingani" on lake Tanganyika. Here a crowd waits for the it to arrive on the beach.

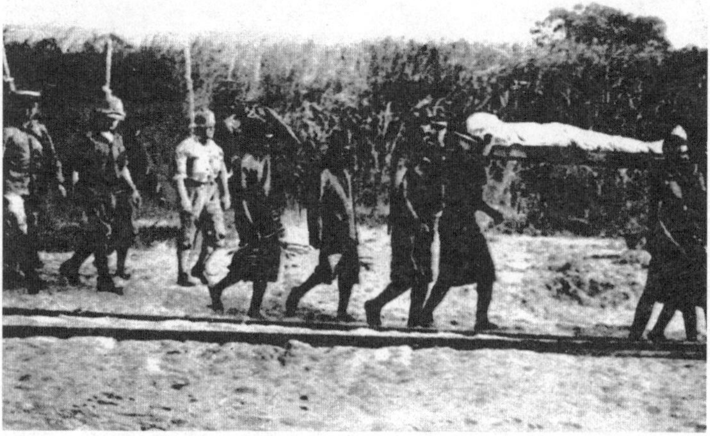

A victim of the fighting, a German officer receives a funeral ceremony.

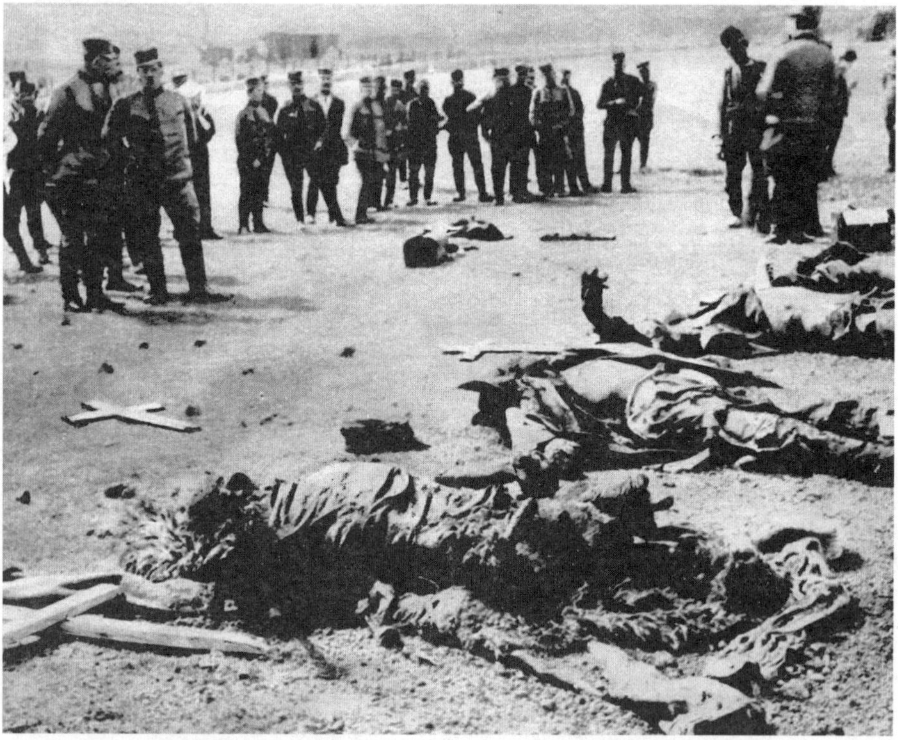

The atrocities of Bulgarian soldiers in Serbia

Photos taken last October (1915) in Stiplie, on the Bregalnitza, are formal testimonies of the Austrian and Bulgarian atrocities.

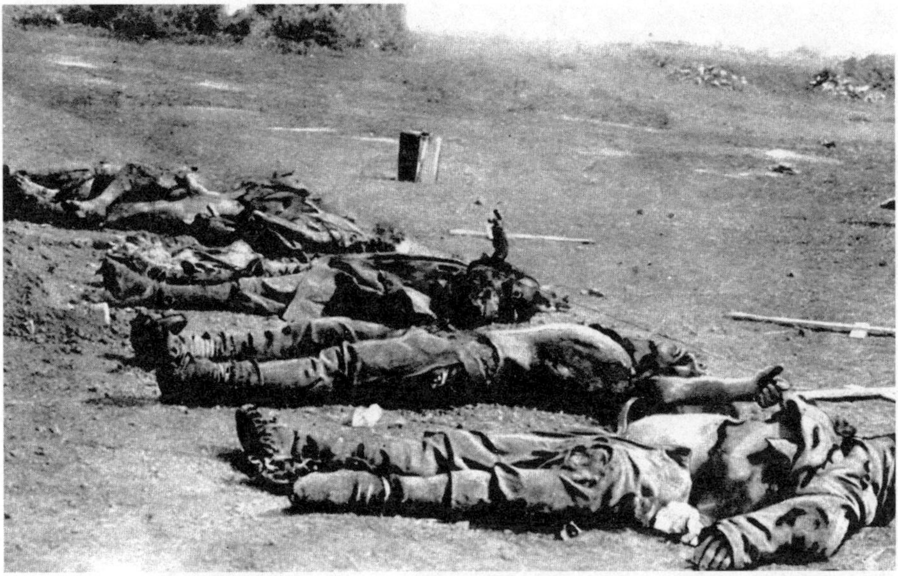

Bodies of soldiers tortured by the Bulgarians at Stiplie in October 1915

Many Serbs were slaughtered following an incursion by Bulgarian soldiers, resulting in several bodies being partially burnt on a fire. A colonel, a commander and his Serbian soldiers are going to bury their comrades.

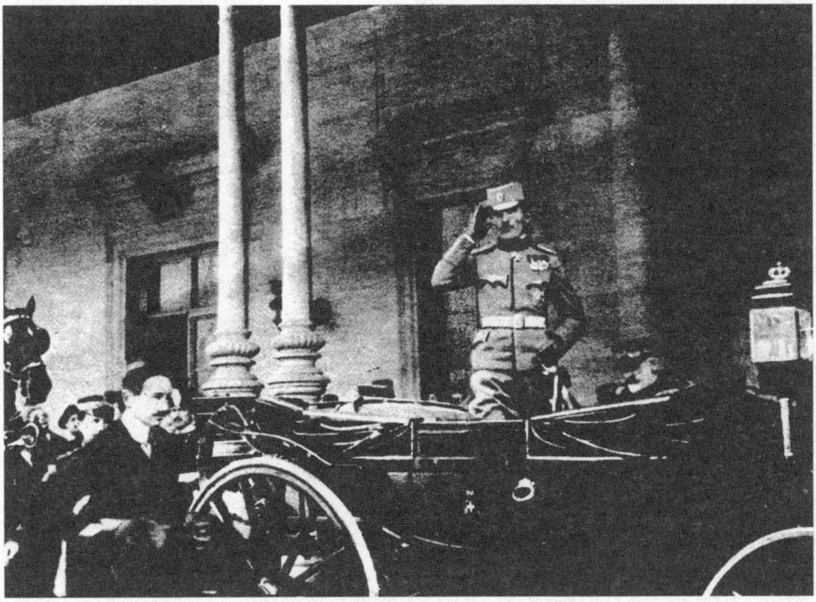

Prince Alexandre of Serbia in Rome

The prince boards a coach and salutes the crowd.

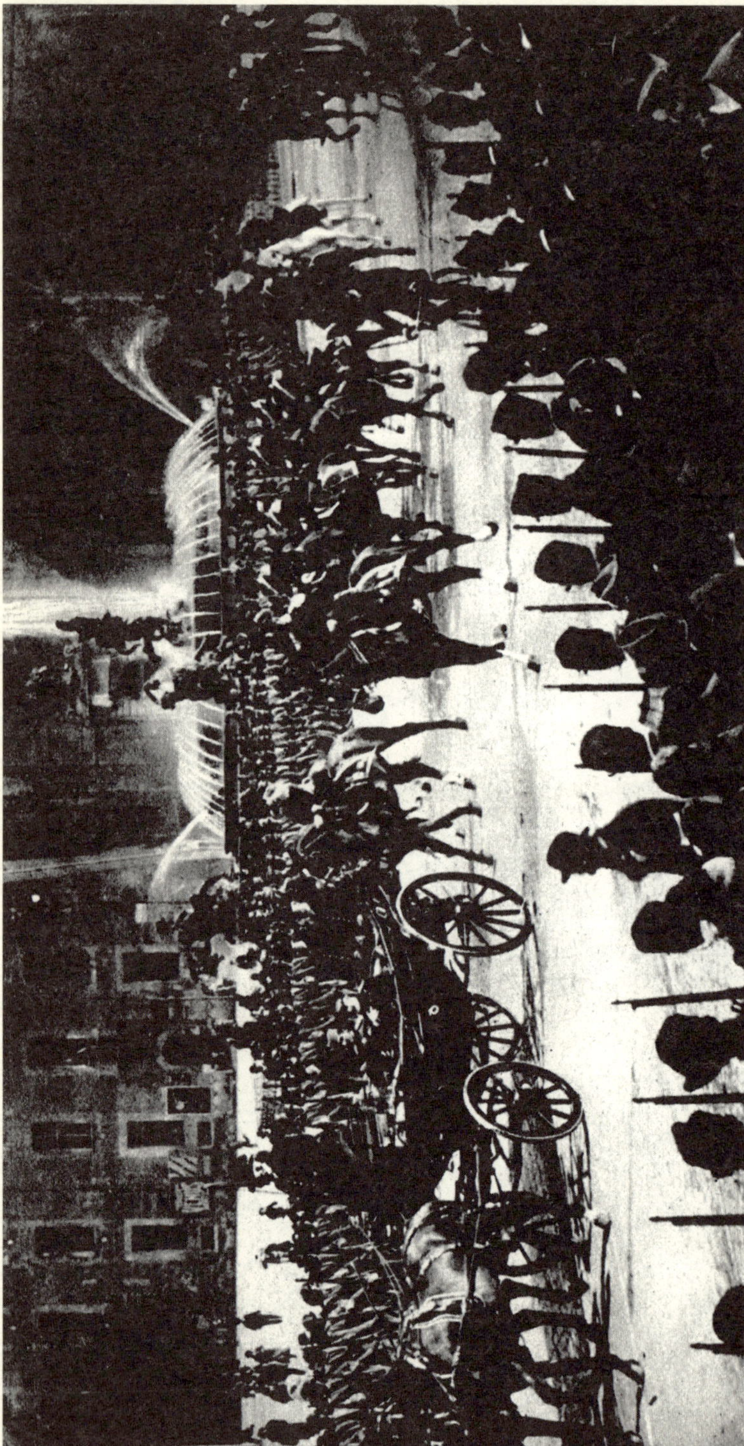

Prince Alexandre and the Duke of Gene drive to the Quirinal

Received at the station in Rome by the Duke of Gene, cousin of the king, all of the Italian ministers, Mr. Pachitch (president) and numerous personalities, the Prince Regent of Serbia is taken by carriage to the Quirinal, cheered by a large and enthusiastic crowd. The troops of the garrison of Rome were guard of honour.

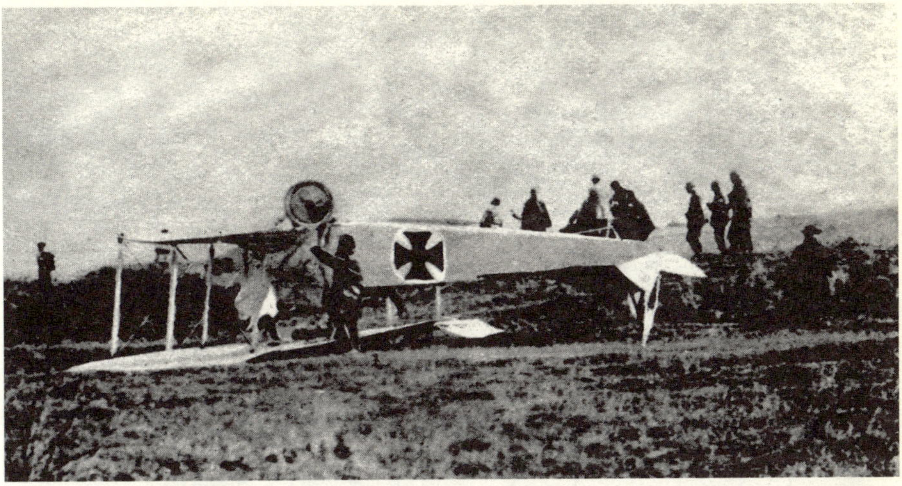

Air defences in Salonika

On February 17th (1916), an enemy aeroplane flew over allied lines at Salonika. Pursued by an allied plane, piloted by French officer Fétu and lieutenant Minteguyaga, he was obliged to land following 50 machine gun bullets hitting the plane and 11 hitting the pilot, although he crashed on landing.

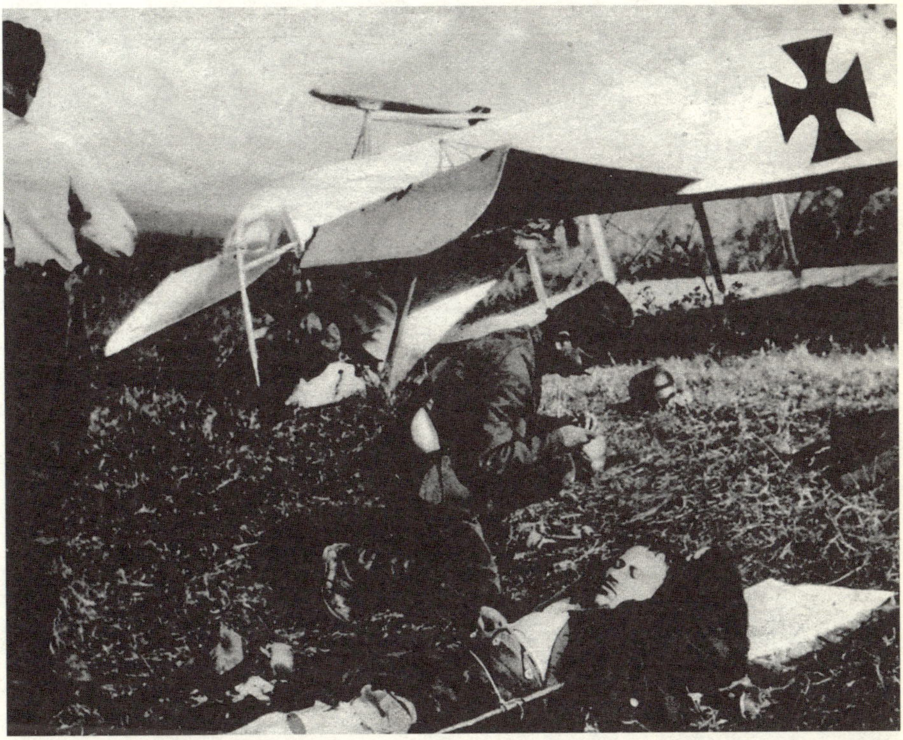

An enemy observer, severely wounded in the thigh, receives medical attention. He was subsequently taken prisoner.

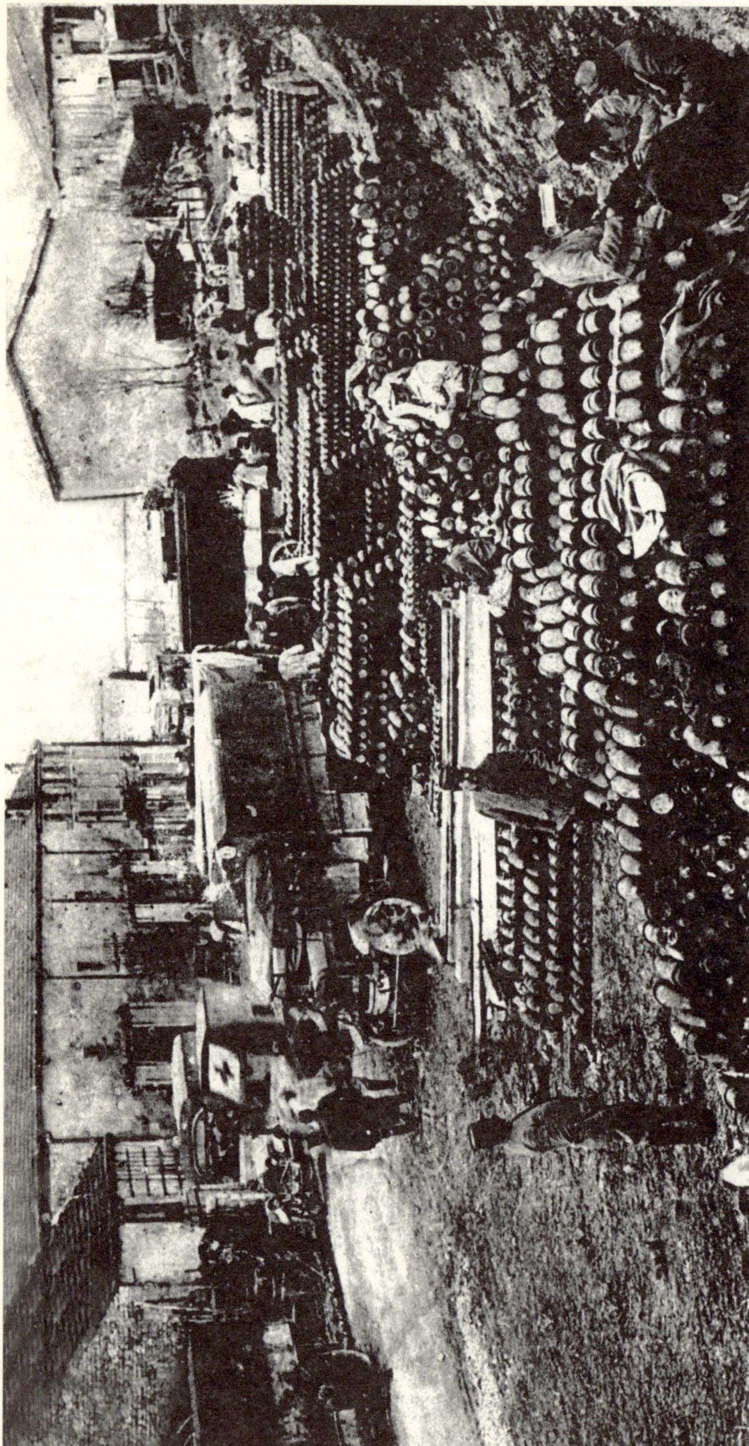

Allied ammunitions dump

The Germans amassed 3,000 artillery guns at Verdun, for their unprecedented bombardment. The allies, who have significant stores of ammunition, replied with an equal deluge of fire.

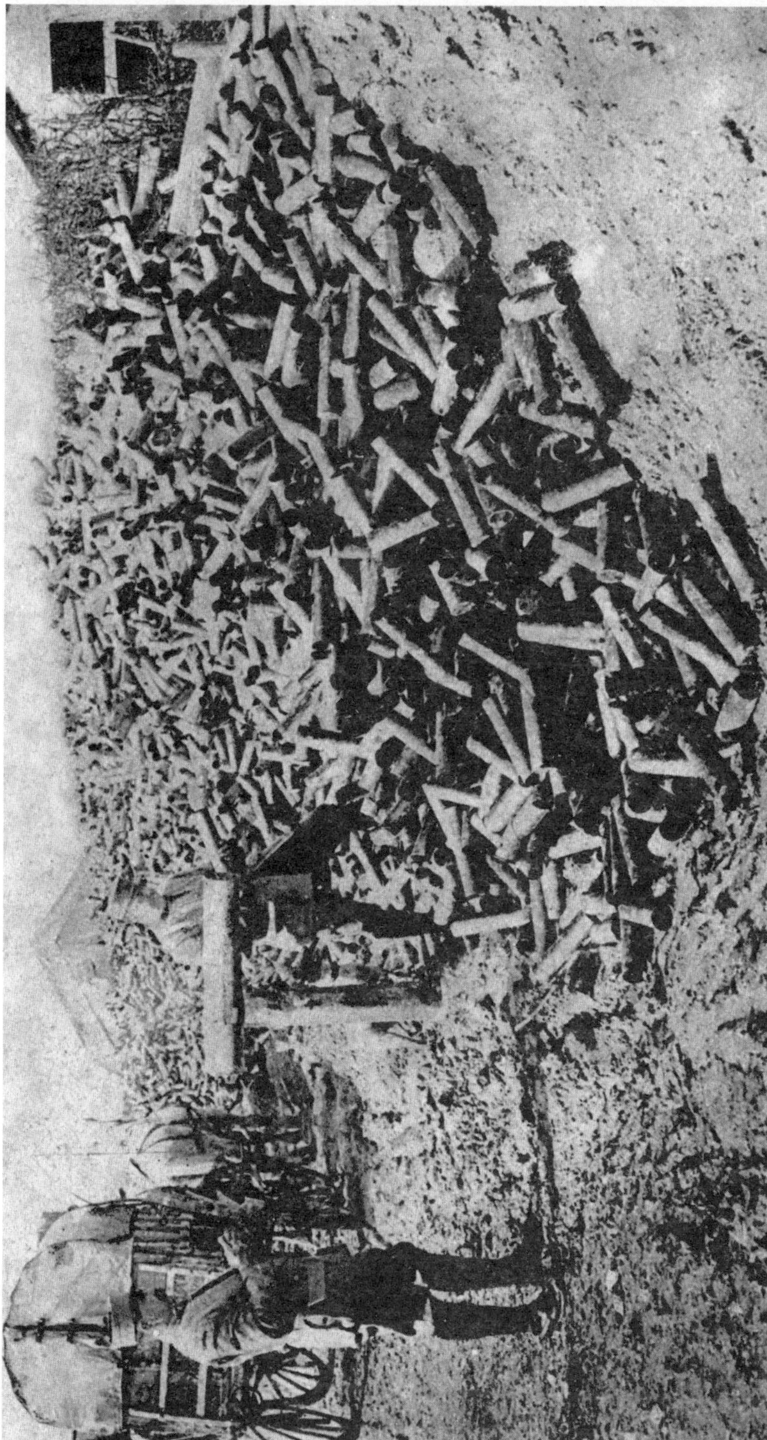

Shell cases from 2 hours firing

In this war, the consumption of shells is beyond imagination as we see from these empty cases, which represent 2 hours shelling in one sector.

- NEWS REPORTS -

Wednesday 3 May, 1916

The British Prime Minister, Mr. Asquith, in the House of Commons, proposed a bill to enable servicemen to get married.

French gains in Champagne where they have severely damaged a German battery near Moronvilliers and another to the north of Massiges. To the East, they gained 500 metres of trenches and took a further 100 prisoners south of Douaumont. The Germans were driven back by the Belgians following an attack to the east of the Yser.

Thursday May 4, 1916

The House of Commons has voted on the first reading of the bill to enable conscripted men to get married before leaving for war.

Three leaders of the Irish revolution were executed, following a court martial in Dublin. Mr. Birrell, Secretary of State for Ireland, has resigned.

Signals received suggest more serious disorder in Berlin.

A gas attack was followed by the enemy attempting a small incursion into French trenches. The French attacked the German positions to the northeast of the Dead Mans Hill and captured 100 prisoners and four machine guns.

Friday May 5, 1916

In Belgium, artillery fire caused a munitions explosion in the enemy camp at Grande-Dune.

In Argonne, the French have shelled the enemy in the woods near Cheppy, while in the air their planes have shot down a German aircraft. Fighting continues at Dead Mans Hill while, to the East of Meuse and in Woëvre there is intermittent artillery action.

A Zeppelin has sunk a Norwegian vessel in the North Sea. Allied troops now occupy Florina in Greece.

Germany has announced that civilians are to be evacuated from Metz. In Berlin, Mr. Liebknecht has stopped the demonstrations that began on May 1st. While the country is under mobilisation he can justify this, but the socialist group in the Reichstag has responded by asking for its independence.

Saturday May 6, 1916

The House of Commons has voted for an obligatory call-up by 328 to 36 votes. A Zeppelin was shot down by a British cruiser in the North Sea off Sleswig. The German Cabinet, in Berlin, has announced that it will only propose to modify the rules of submarine warfare if America persuades England to abandon their blockade. This has been broadcast across the country.

Intense artillery action on the Belgian front, damaging the enemy's defences. Intermittent activity in Woëvre and to the east of the Meuse. West of Meuse, after very heavy fire, the Germans made a strong attack on positions to the north of hill 304. The enemy was defeated along the whole of this front, but managed to get a foothold in some areas.

A Zeppelin, flying over Salonika, was hit by shellfire from the allied fleet. It fell in flames in the mouth of the Vardar river.

Sunday May 7, 1916

America announces that their reply to the German statement will be delayed.

In Champagne, shooting has damaged a German battery. To the west of the Meuse, the enemy shelling reached an enormous intensity in the sector around hill 304. French trenches on the north slope have become untenable. Later, a German attack, to the west and to the northwest of hill 304 was repulsed by a bayonet charge. Intense shellfire to east of the Meuse.

Signals indicate Belgian successes in the Congo.

The German press speaks of further disorder in the Berlin area.

Monday May 8, 1916

Artillery struggle continues on the Belgian front. Reciprocal shellfire in the British sector.

South of the Somme, the Germans, after intense artillery fire, have attacked French trenches. On the left of the Meuse, very heavy and long lasting bombardment of hill 304, followed by a strong German attack between hill 304 and Dead Mans Hill. The enemy, after repeated attempts, has managed to penetrate allied lines on 304 but sustained serious losses.

There was further heavy German fire on trenches between the woods at Haudromont and Douaumont. To the west they gained about 500 metres.

Tuesday May 9, 1916

The American Cabinet in Washington is still deliberating on the German letter.

Intense shelling on the Belgian front around Dixmude. Two German planes were shot down near Verdun, one at d'Ornes, the other south of Azannes.

On the left of the Meuse, the fight continues relentlessly in the region of hill 304. The enemy's furious attempts to attack were again repelled and about fifty German prisoners taken; on the right bank, about thirty prisoners, including two officers. In Woëvre, the artillery action continues. Shellfire also in the woods at Renneres and Jury.

Guillaume II (Kaiser Wilhelm II) has summoned the Prince of Bülow to his headquarters.

Wednesday May 10, 1916

President Wilson has replied to the German letter, noting the Chancellor's promises, but refusing to consider the question of the British blockade with the cabinet of Berlin. The American government has decided to reinforce its strength on the Mexican border.

From France, Messrs. Viviani, Foreign Minister and Albert Thomas, under secretary of War Ministry, have been received by the Czar.

In the Champagne region, allies fired on the German trenches and batteries to the north of Ville-sur-Toube and on their communication routes in the region of Somme-Py. To the left of the Meuse, three German attempts on allied trenches on hill 304; to the right, an allied attack allowed an advance behind enemy lines again. French batteries fired on convoys that were restocking enemy positions on the road from Essey to Bayonville. The artillery battle on the Belgian front continues.

The troops in the Belgian Congo have again progressed in the territory of German Oriental Africa.

The Italians have progressed further in the massif of Tofana (Trentin).

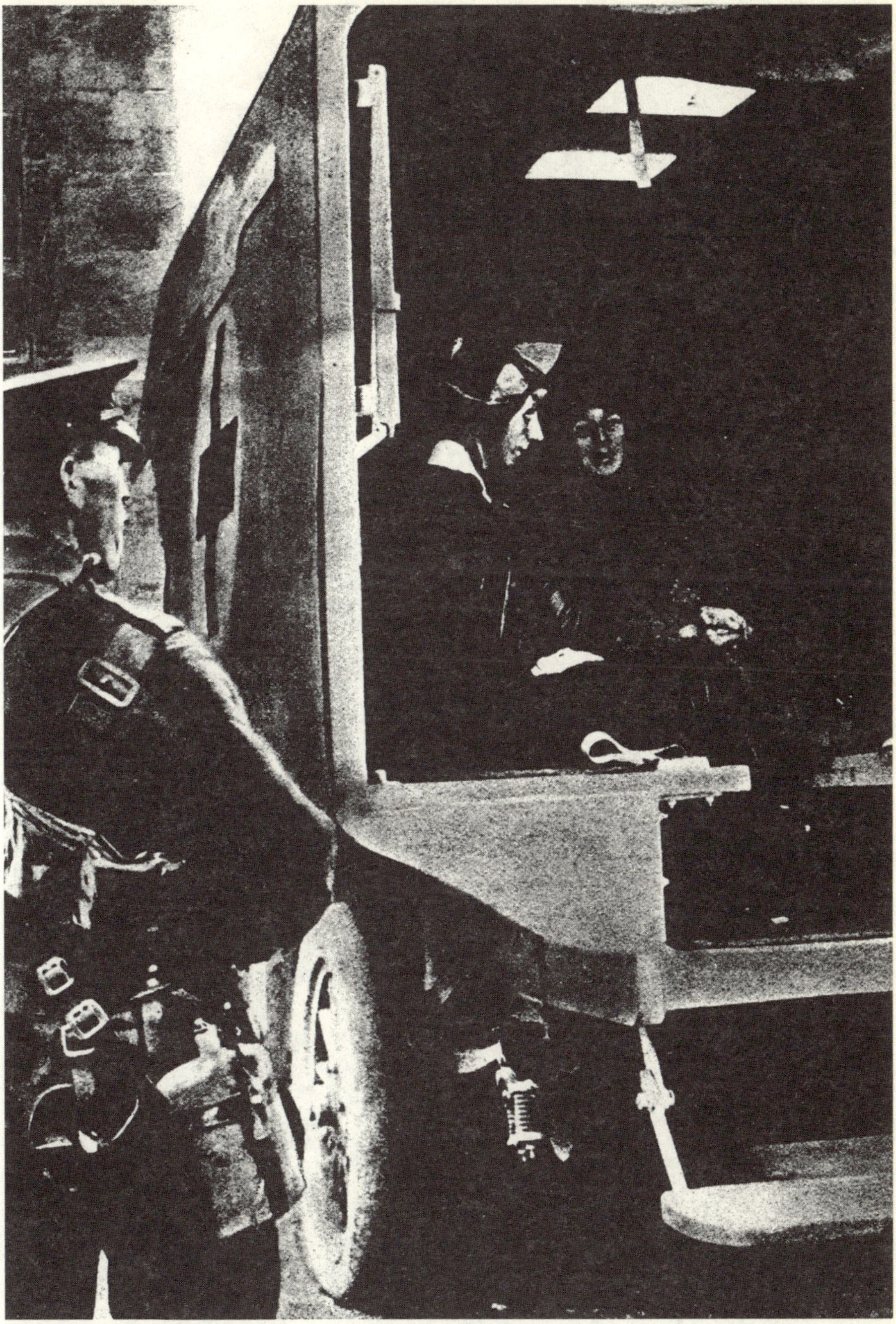

Countess Markievicz returns to jail after conviction

Countess Constance Markievicz, with the nurse supervising her, being taken back to jail following conviction by court-martial. The threat of her capital punishment remains for perpetuity.

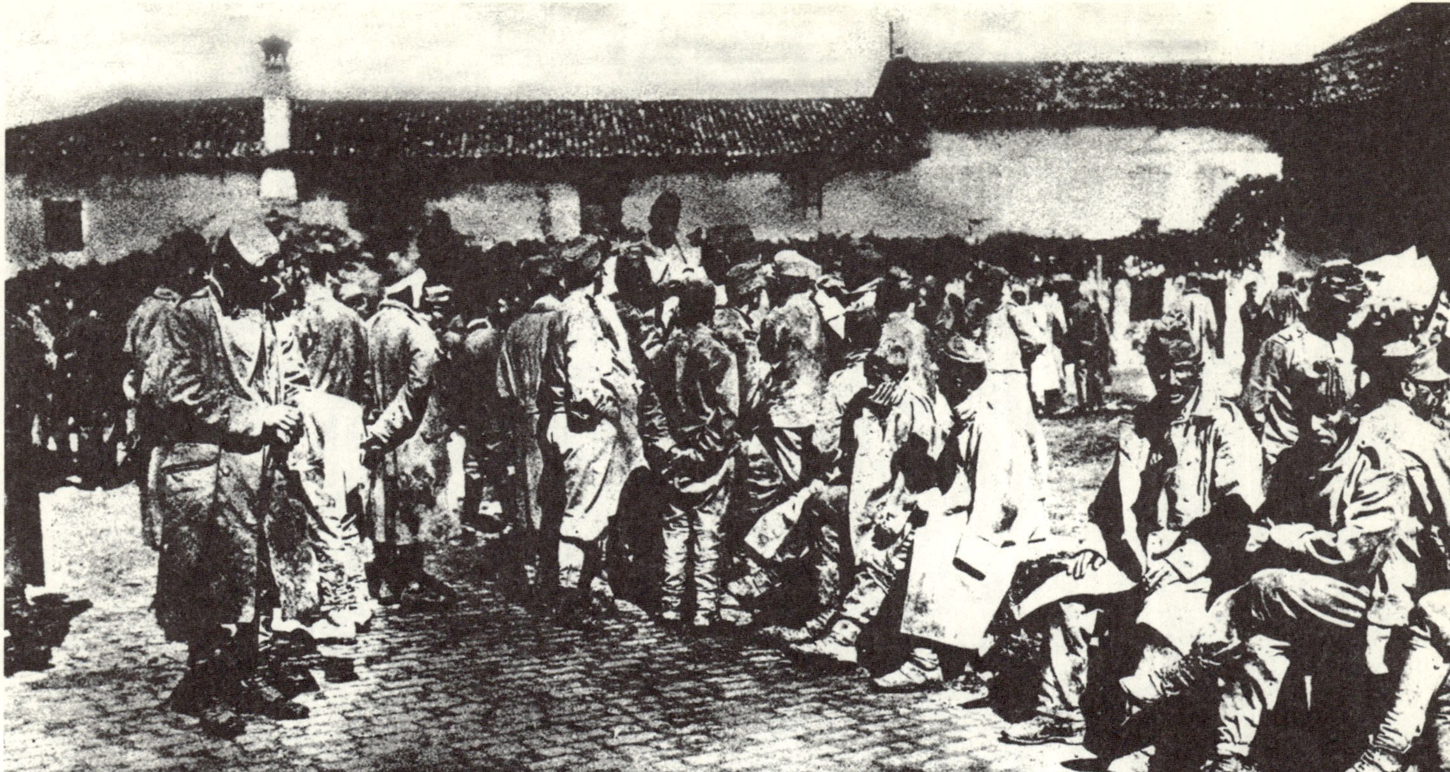

Prisoners gathered together in an Italian village

Different efforts for the Italian armies on their different fronts. They are still capturing numerous prisoners from different nationalities of the Austro-Hungarian empires. Here is a very disparate group waiting to be transferred to the south of Italy.

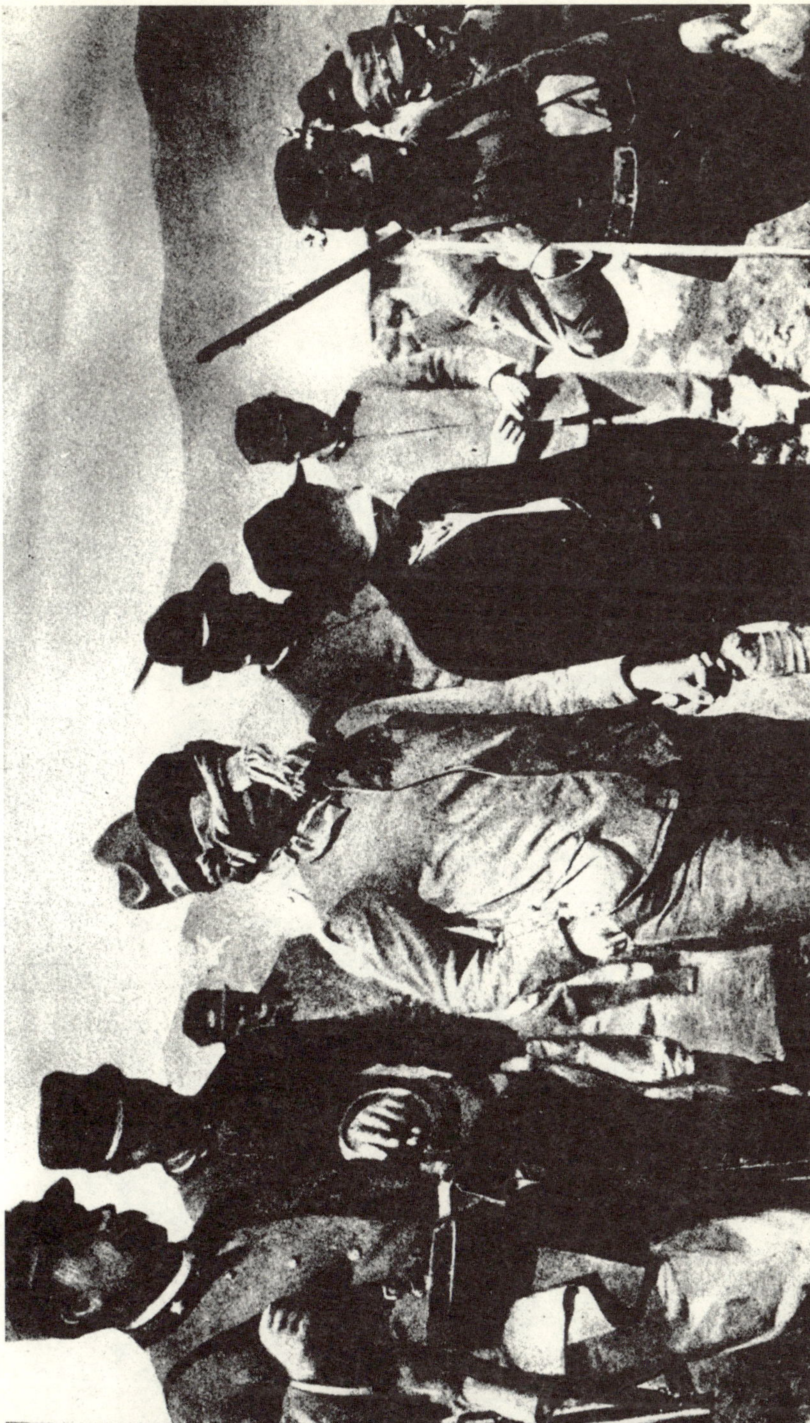

Spies taken to headquarters

Spies, who have just been captured by the Italians, are blindfolded and taken to the nearest headquarters to be interrogated.

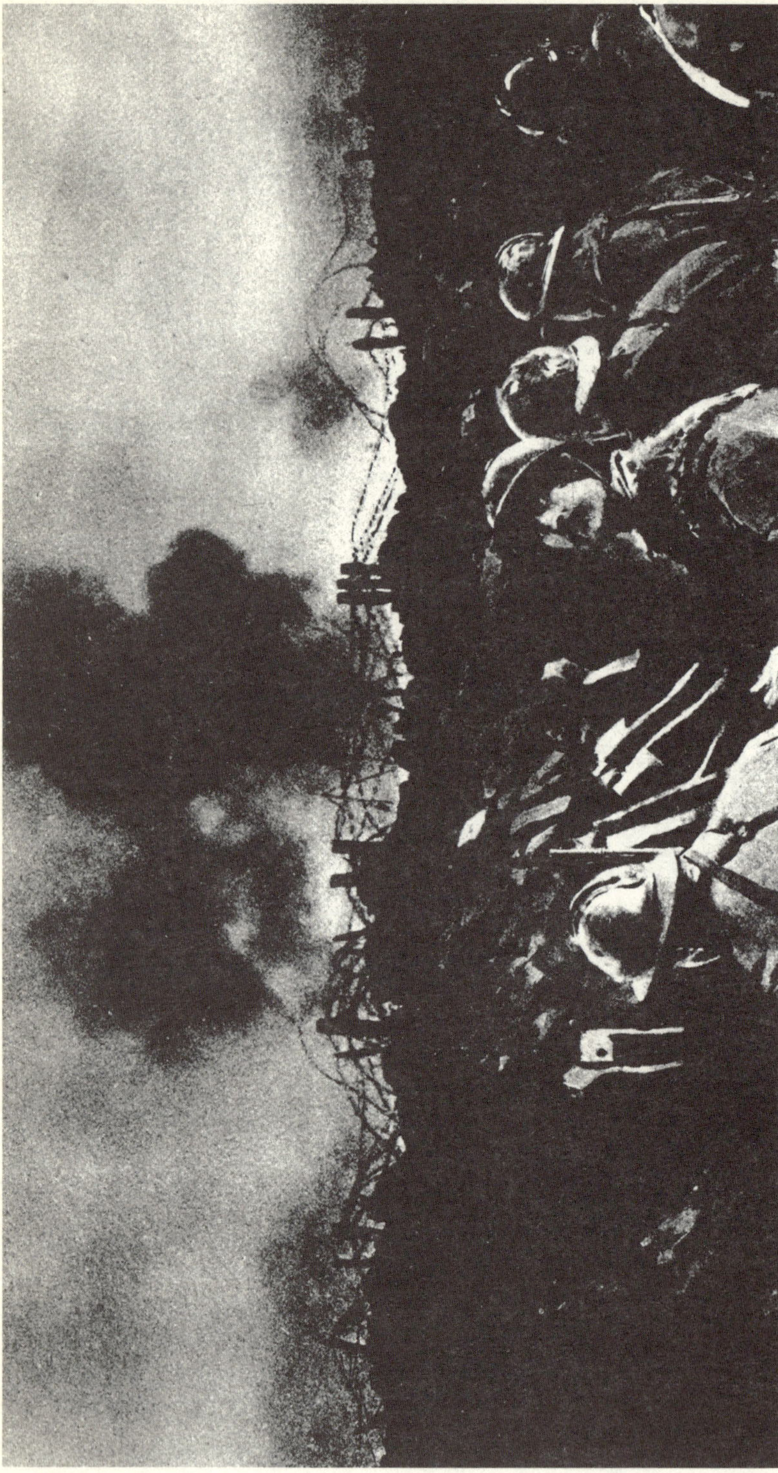

Under shell fire before an attack

The hand grenades are ready, the men wait for the assault, under the cover of gun fire. In the front line no one speaks. The enemy is preparing to attack and the allies are ready for them.

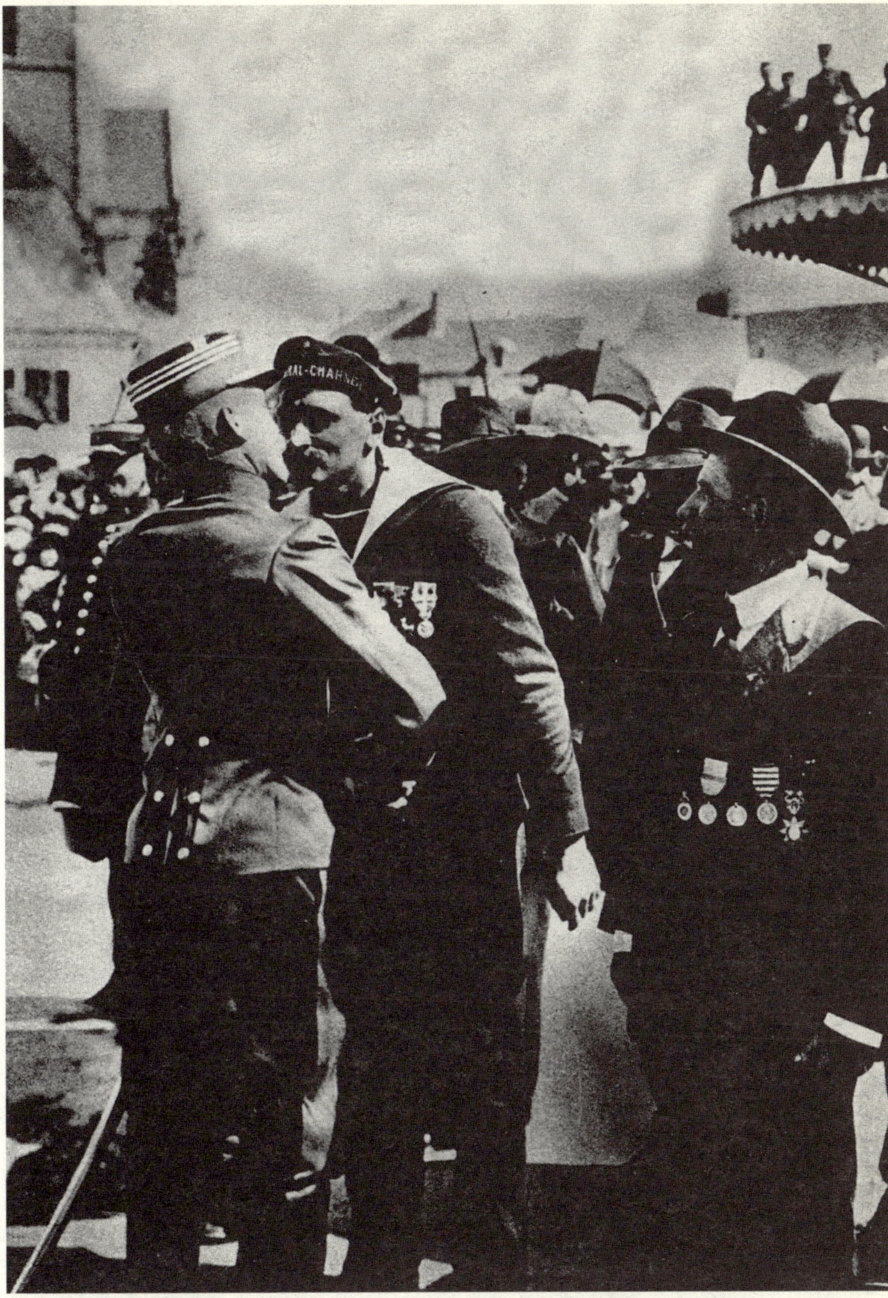

The French leading seaman gunner Cariou receives the military medal

Leading seaman Cariou, sole survivor from the "Admiral-Charner", a French cruiser torpedoed in the Mediterranean on February 8th (1916). One of 14 men who boarded a raft with no food or water for two days and three nights before being found by a trawler. Surrounded by veterans, he has just received the military medal and the cross of war, at Quimperlé.

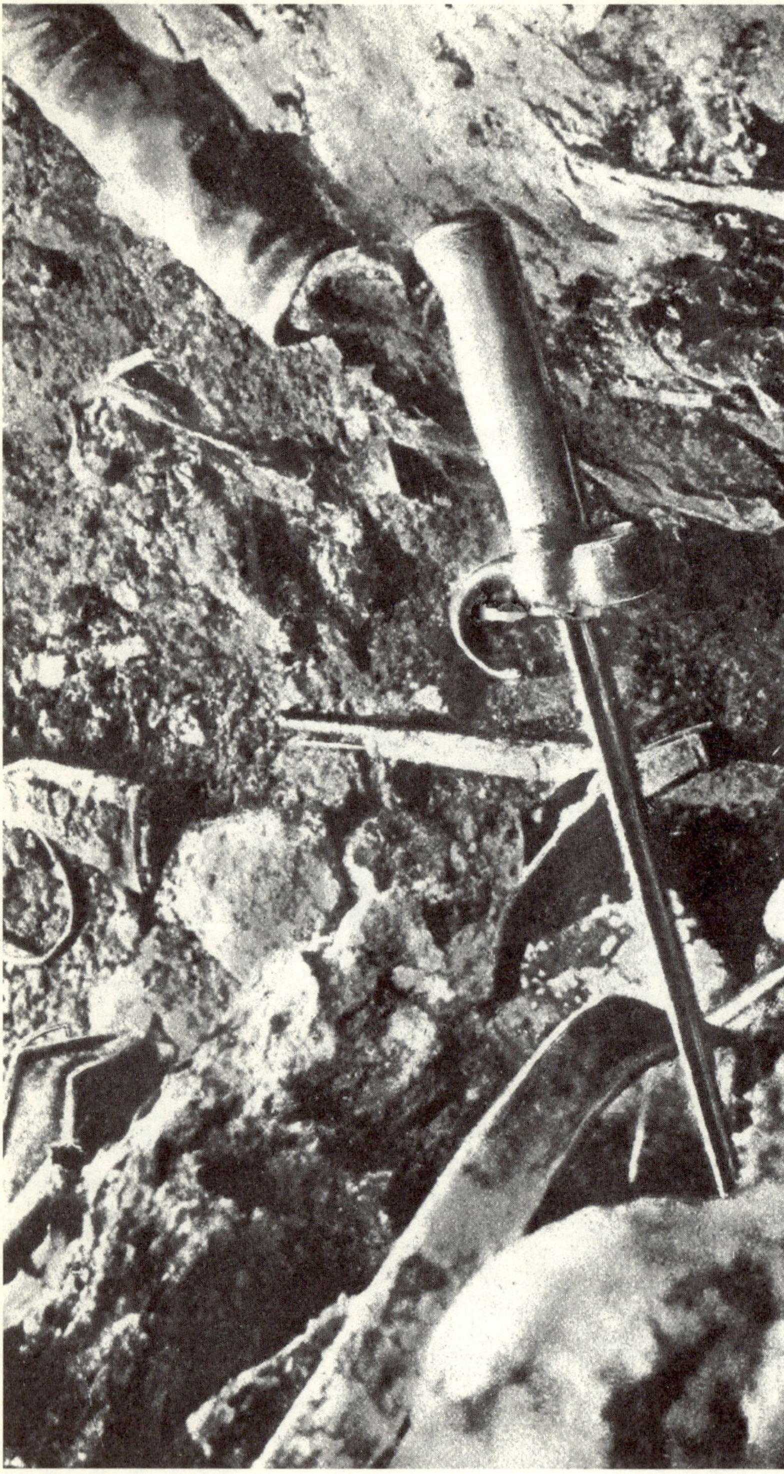

The bayonet - a symbol of war

Symbolically, the bayonet stands to the front of this picture of German defeat, driven boldly by the hand of allied soldiers. Of the bodies, the rifles, the boots, and the supplies of war, the bayonet remains a witness to our successes.

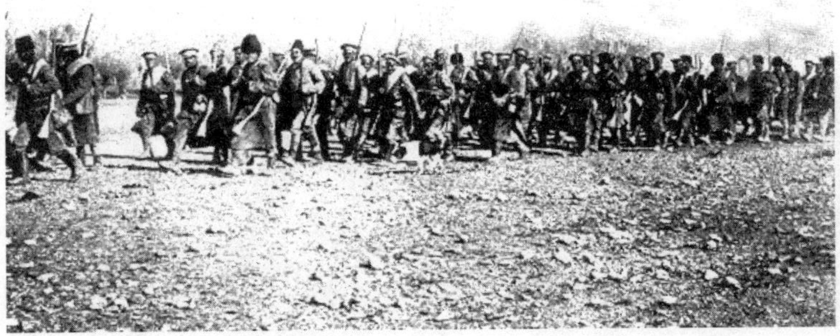

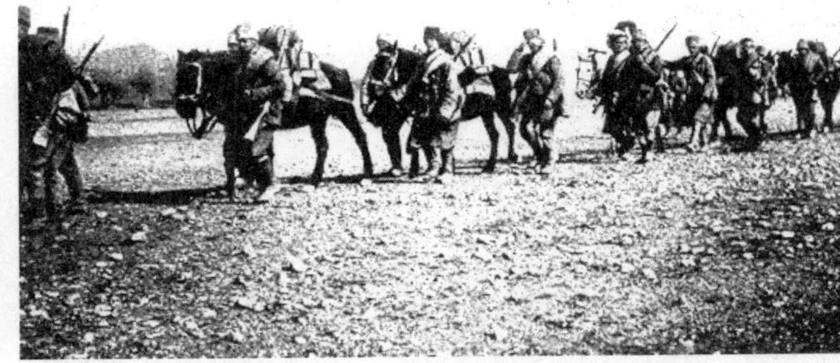

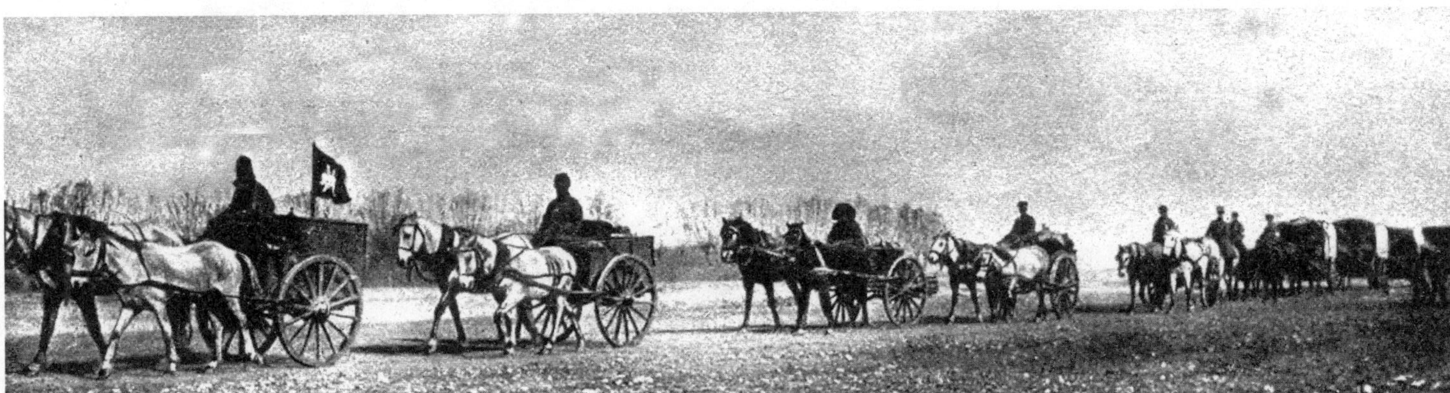

The Russian army advances into Persia

The Russian armies overcame the German plans in Persia. After having taken Kazvin, the Russian troops took Ourmiah, then Saoud-Boulagh, in the province of the Azerberdjan, on the Turkish border. These pictures show the Russian army marching on Ourmiah.

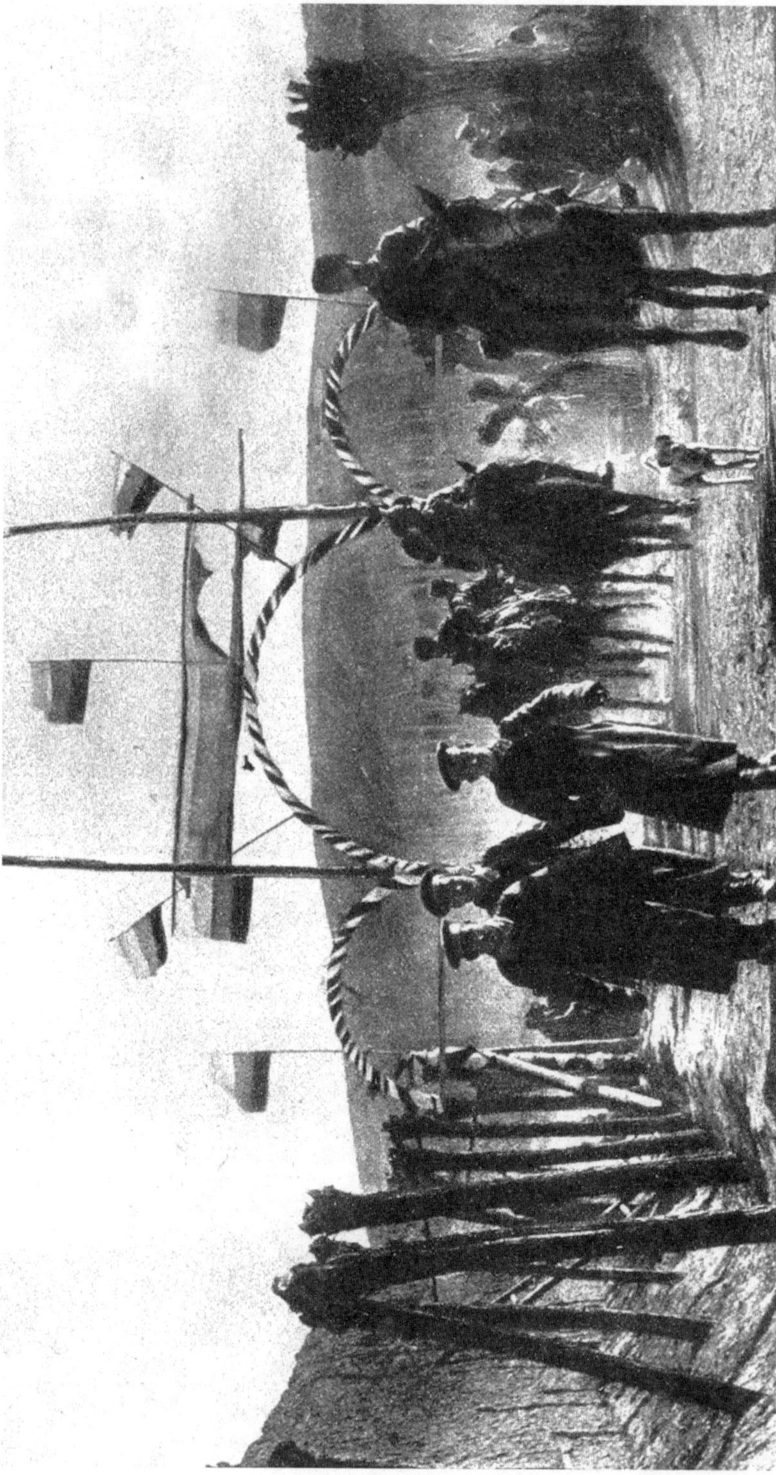

The Russians arrive at Ourmiah

The Russian army arrives under a triumphal arch, erected by the inhabitants,

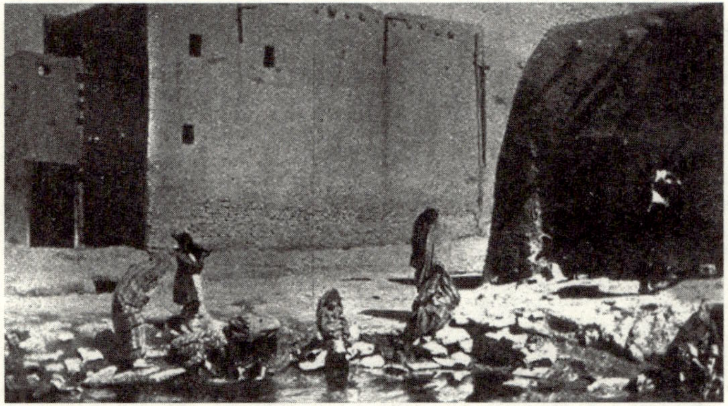

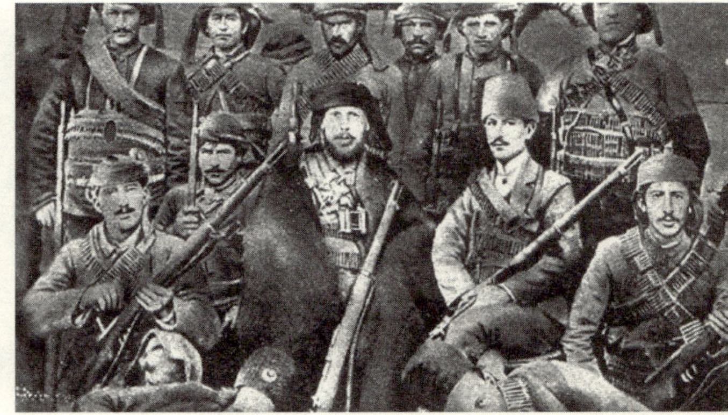

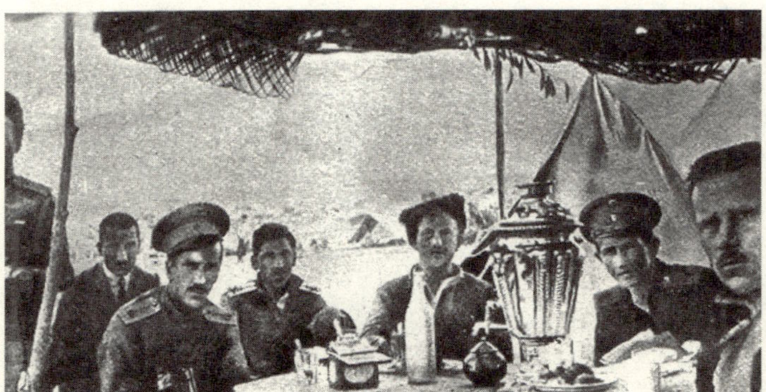

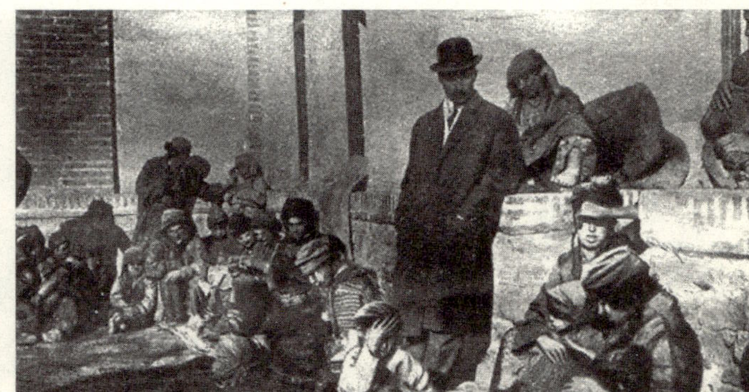

The major stages of a seven month campaign

The Russians have successively fought both Turks and Kurds. (top left) Diliman, where at the end of May 1915, 3,500 Turks fell; (top left) the Turks at Ourmiah, around their chief, Osman-Effendi; (bottom left) a Russian camp to the north of Ourmiah; (bottom right) refugees sheltering at Ourmiah.

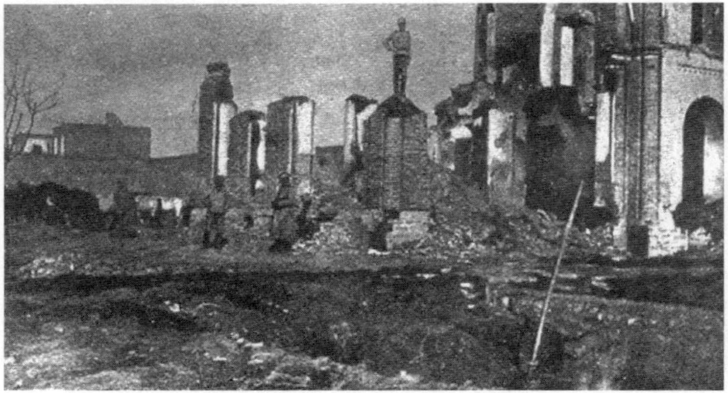

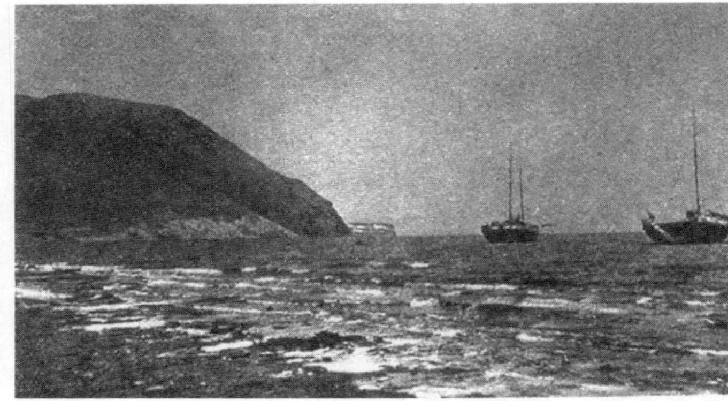

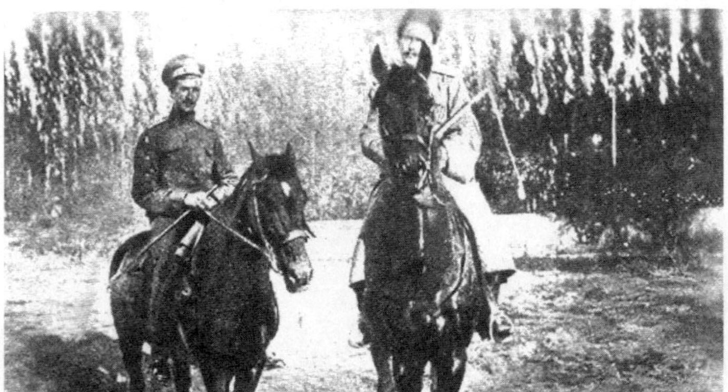

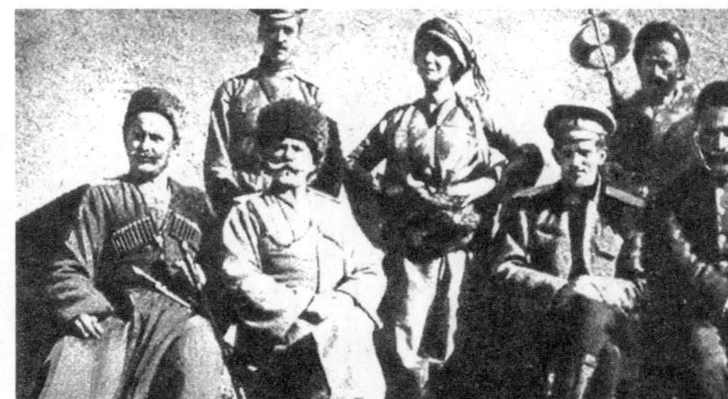

(top left) Russians among the ruins at Ourmiah (June 1915); (top right) the lake to the south of Ourmiah; (bottom left) Russian heroes of the battle of Saoudj-Boulagh (January 2nd, 1916) where 10,000 Kurdish prisoners were taken; (bottom right) group including the female Russian consul in Ourmiah, Mrs. Lora Nikitin, who then followed the army to Saoudj-Boulagh.

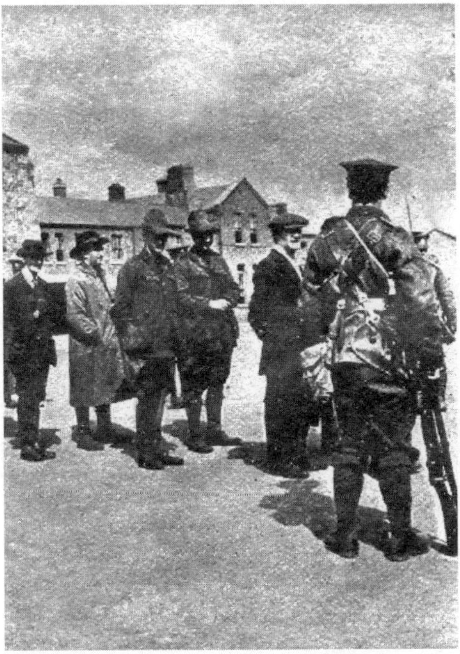

The suppression of the Dublin revolt

The brothers Plunkett, one of whom was married in jail before his execution.

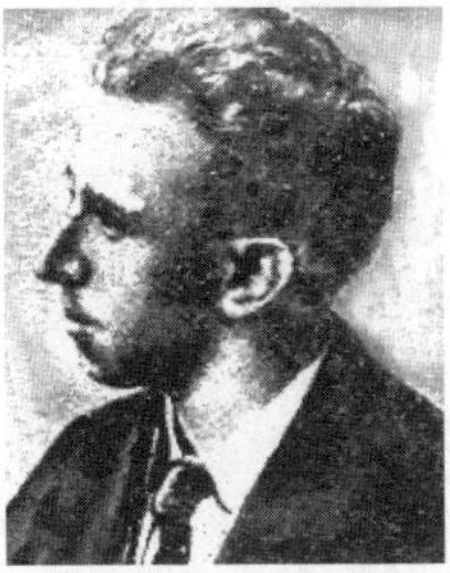

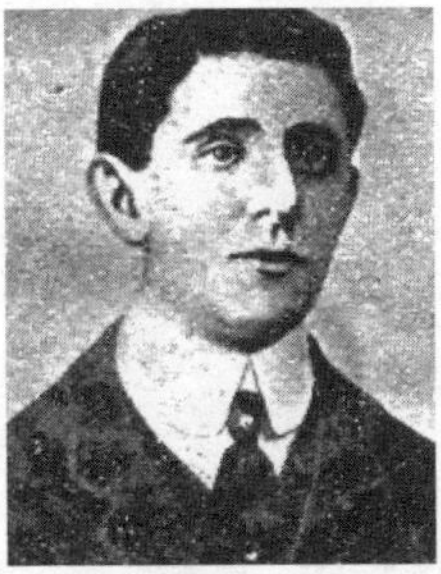

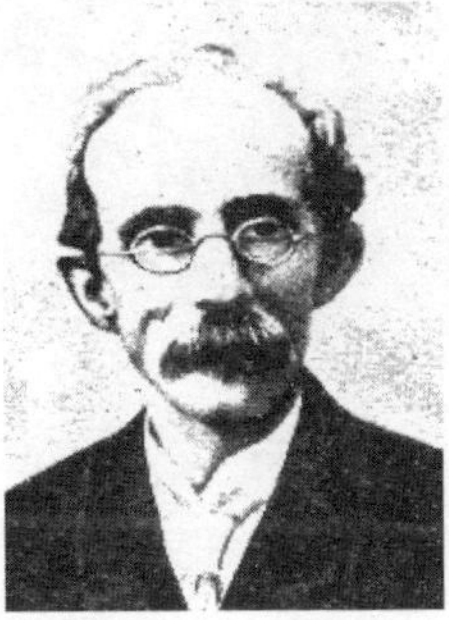

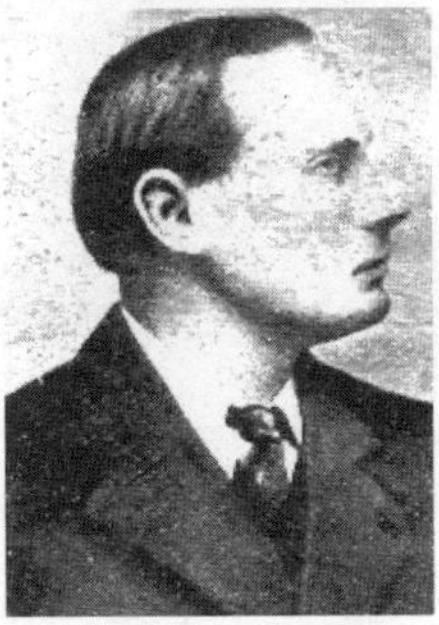

(top left) Thomas MacDonagh, the first rebel executed; (top right) MacDermott, who signed the famous proclamation, executed; (bottom left) Clarke, the "president of the Irish Republic", executed; (bottom right) Pearse, " Commander General of the "Irish Republican Army", executed.

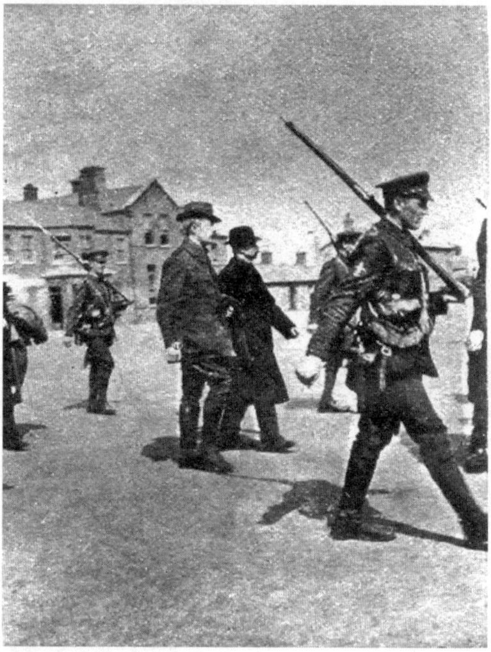

Republican Regimental Adjutant MacBridge, executed.

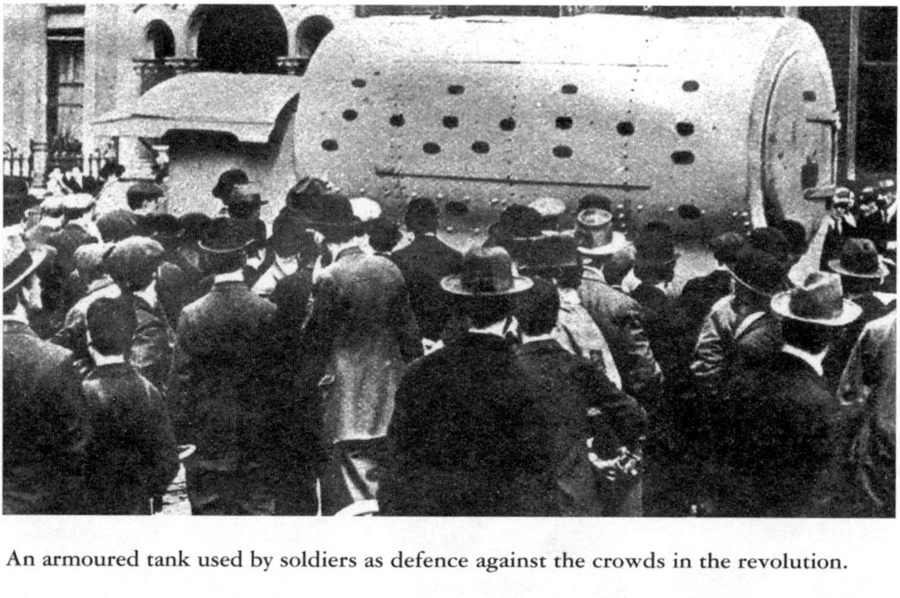

An armoured tank used by soldiers as defence against the crowds in the revolution.

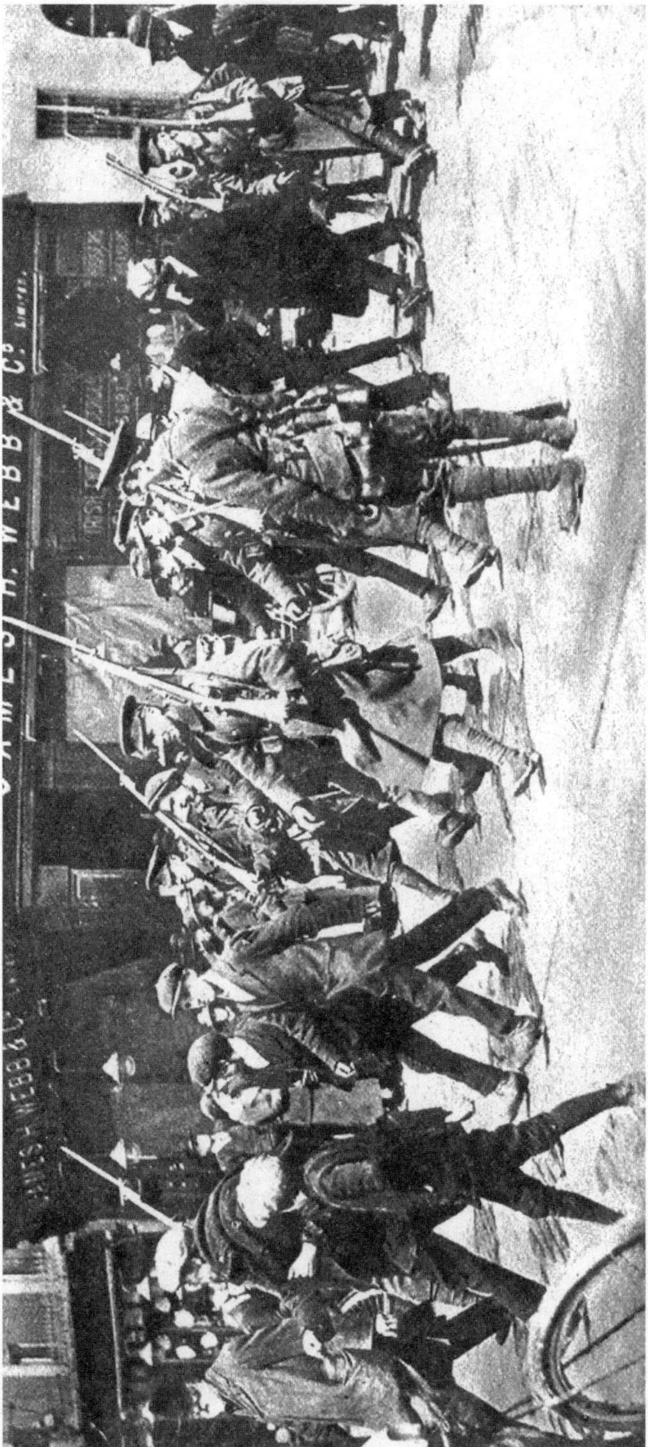

The uprising was condemned and 3,000 Republican prisoners taken. Here, Republican prisoners are marched across Dublin.

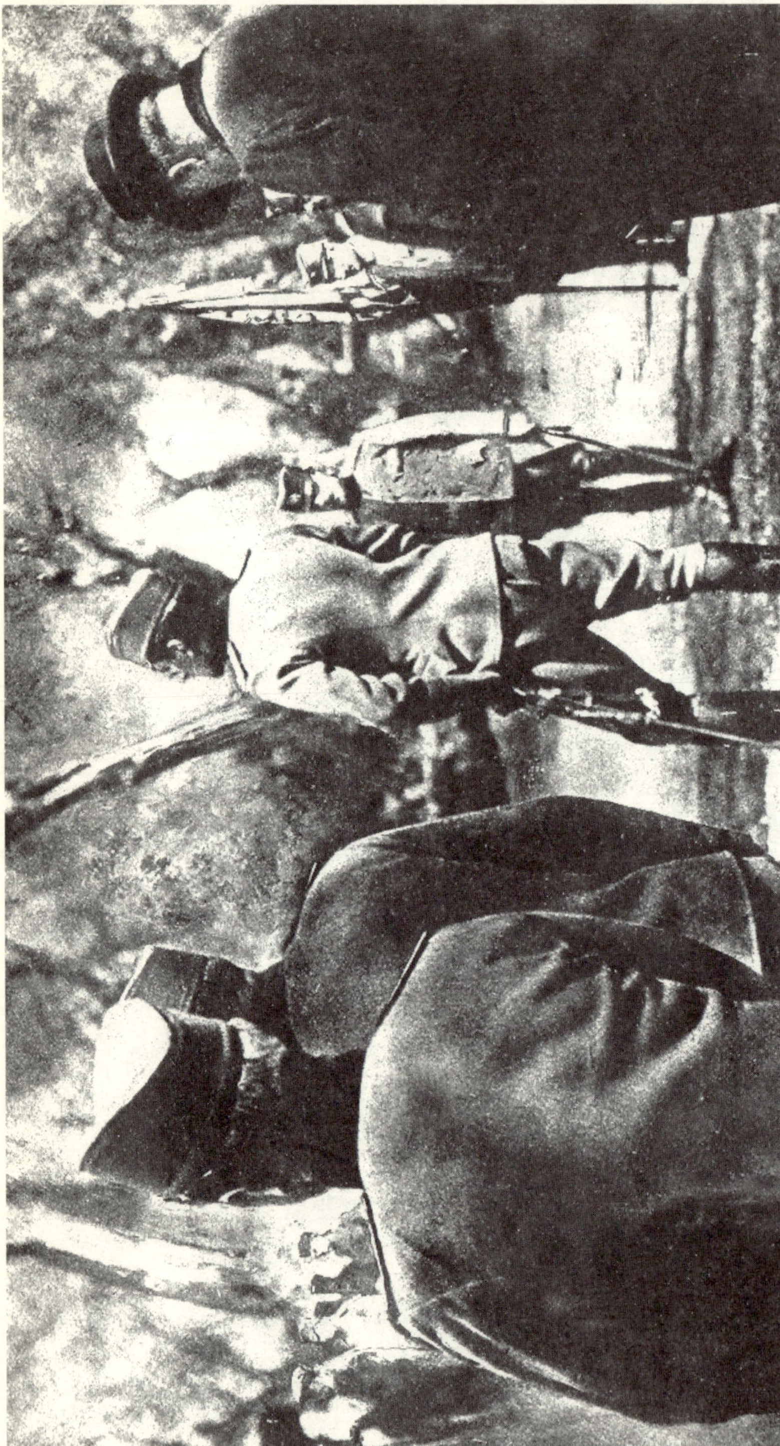

April 17th, Prince Alexandre of Serbia reviews the reorganisation of his army

Before rejoining the allies, Prince Alexander reviewed his troops, recognising that they had recovered all their energy and cheerfulness.

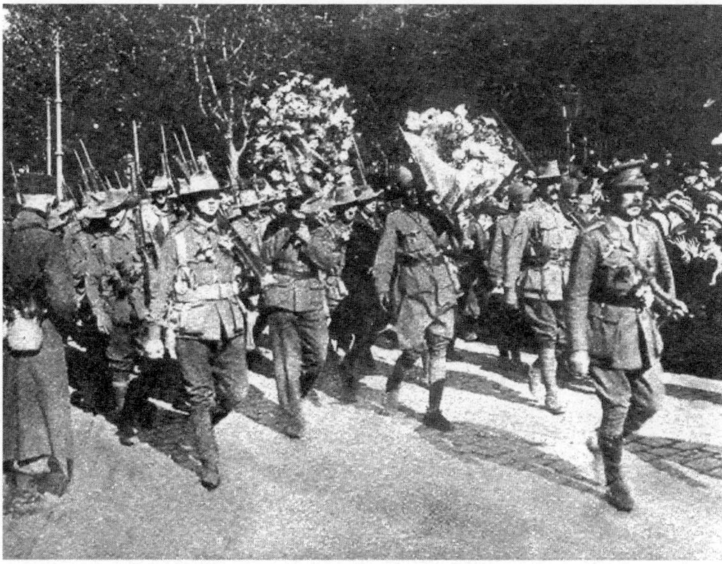

British Colonial Regiments parade in Marseilles

An important contingent of Australians, South Africans and Hindus coming from Egypt, parade in Marseille before returning to the front.

- NEWS REPORTS -

Thursday July 27, 1916

The British forces have occupied the whole village of Pozieres, pursuing the enemy to the west of the town and taking two well defended trenches and some prisoners, including five officers.

The French have taken a hamlet to the south of Estrées, with 117 prisoners, four 105mm cannons and various other equipment. On the right bank of the Meuse, heavy artillery action in the Fleury sector. Hostile enemy fire to the north of the chapel at Sainte-Fine.

The Russians took Erzindjan, thereby completing their conquest of Armenia. The Turks are now clearly uncomfortable. General Zakharof, to the south of the Lipa, has announced that more than 4,000 Austro-German prisoners were taken. Brody and Lemberg are both threatened.

The Italians have defended several attacks in the Posina-Astico region.

Friday July 28, 1916

Activity by the British artillery along the whole front. The Germans resorted to using tear gas shells again.

To the south of the Somme, some French progress to the east of Estrées and to the north of the Aisne, heavy shelling was followed by an enemy attack in the region of the Ville-au-Bois, which failed, driven back under machine gun fire. In Champagne, the enemy shelling concentrated on a 1,200 metre front to the west of Proselles. This ended with heavy losses on both sides and no significant territorial gains.

The Russians have taken a further 6,250 prisoners on the Slonovka, north of Brody. To the west of Erzindjan, the Turkish army is fleeing in disarray. Some Turkish forces, in Galicia, have arrived to help the Austrians.

Saturday July 29, 1916

Allies have taken the whole of Delville woods with 161 prisoners, and achieved progress in Longuevals and in the fields around Pozieres. They have been involved in heavy shelling of enemy trenches to the north of Souchez.

Two enemy planes bought down in the Somme and another forced to land in the Vosges. French aircraft bombed the railway station at Charnies and troop convoys nearby, together with several military establishments between Menneville and Lavannes-Caurel. In the Vosges, the enemy attacked twice to the south of Saint-Marie. The first attack succeeded with them gaining a foothold, despite a French response with bayonets. The second, shortly after, was rapidly driven back under French fire. The enemy's losses were significant.

The Russians have, again, advanced towards Brody, driving back the Austrians. In Champagne, near Auberive, a Russian advance from the north has broken through the German trenches, following a grenade attack, and brought back some prisoners.

Sunday July 30, 1916

Uninterrupted struggle to the north and to the northeast of Pozieres. Allies have progressed in several places under enemy fire. Two or three German regiments seem to have been annihilated during the last fight.

On the Somme, to the west of Vermandovillers, two enemy detachments are approaching French lines. On the left bank of Meuse, a German raid on positions around hill 304 has failed. On the right bank, two German attacks, during the night, on a fort in the ravine to the south. Allied infantry fire inflicted serious losses on the enemy.

The Russians are forcing the Austro-Germans back to the west of Loutsk, towards the Kovel-Vladimir-Volynski railway track. They took Brody, in Galicia, capturing a total of 20,000 men, 400 officers and 55 cannons.

Monday July 31, 1916

The Canadian infantry detachments have broken into enemy trenches in two places to the south of Ypres. The Royal Munster Rifles have executed a similar operation near Loos. In both cases the Germans suffered heavy losses. The enemy has attempted to attack a fort at Hohenzollern. At one point the Germans penetrated our forward trenches but were driven back.

Allies have heavily shelled enemy trenches and their supporting position between l'Ancre and the Somme. During this bombardment a German munitions depot was hit near Courcelettes.

To the north of the Somme, French troops gained between 300 and 800 metres of enemy trenches; have taken the village of Maurepas and hold the wood to the north of Hem. All German counterattacks have been defeated. They have taken more than 200 prisoners.

The Russians have captured up to 32,000 men and 114 cannons over two recent days (28th and 29th July). They are now moving towards Stokhod.

Tuesday August 1, 1916

British pilots dropped 7 tons of missiles on communication posts and enemy gun emplacements. They have blown up a train, set fire to a munitions dump, and destroyed a plane. No infantry action on the British front though.

To the north of the Somme, the Germans have repeated their counterattacks on allied positions at Hem and Monacu, both defeated with enemy losses.

On the left bank of Meuse, a German assault on the slopes of hill 304 has failed under French fire. French pilots have bombed the military factories at Thionville and the railway stations at Conflans and Audun.

The Russians, continuing their move towards Kovel and Stanislau, captured several thousand enemy troops, plus their headquarters.

Wednesday August 2, 1916

The British front was relatively quiet again.

The Germans have attacked French positions on the right bank of Meuse near Thiaumont.

The Russians crossed the Koropecz river, in Galicia, taking another thousand prisoners. The Austro-Germans, while retreating, shelled Brody. The Italians have inflicted heavy losses on the Austrians in the Dolomites.

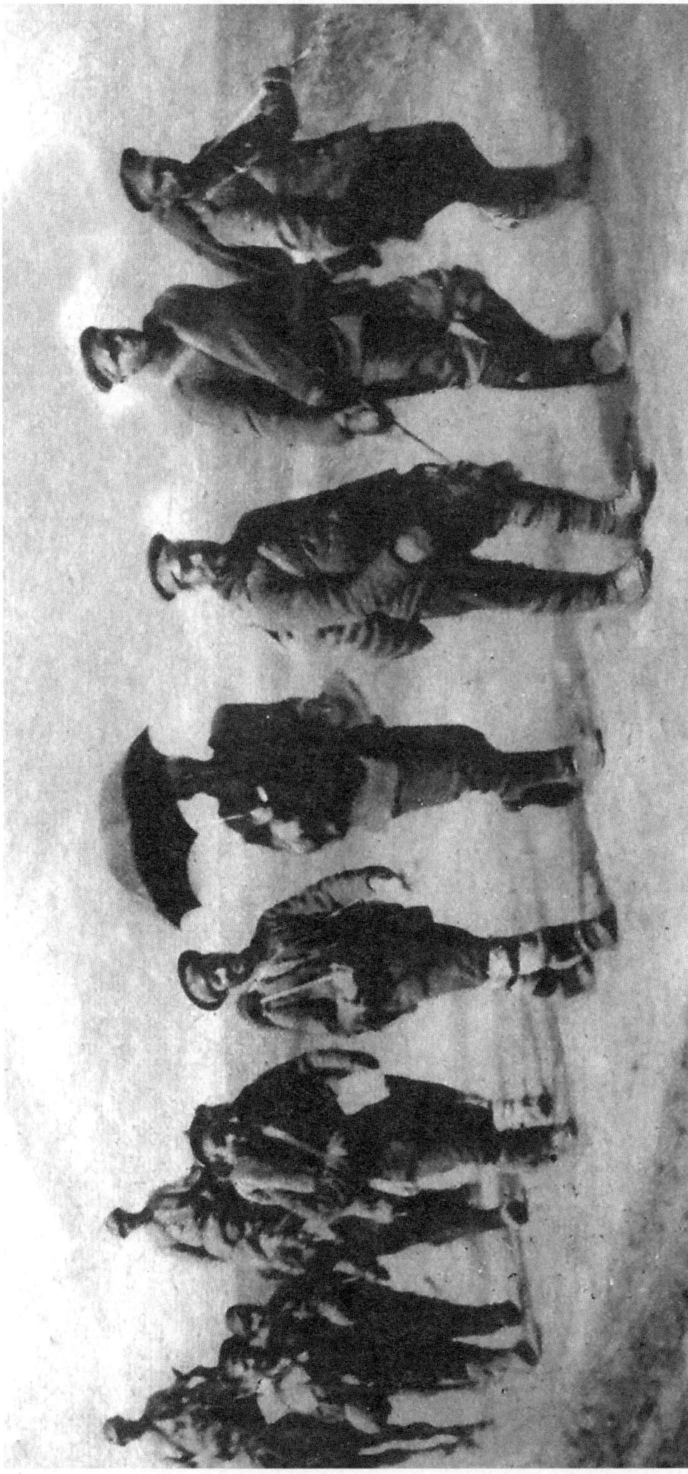

The Serbians action in Macedonia

Following their offensive against the Bulgarians on July 25th, Serbians captured a number of Bulgarian soldiers.

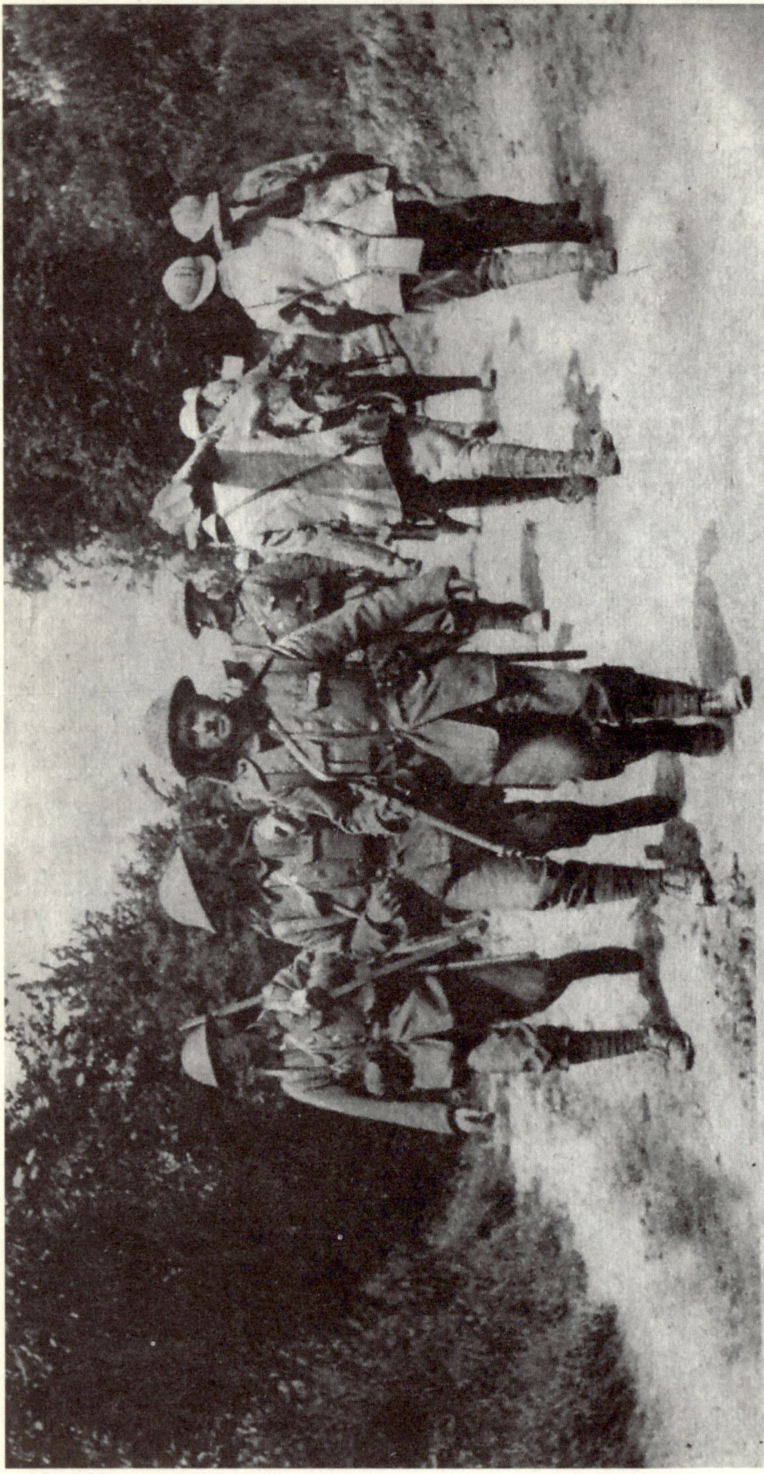

The road to the front near the Somme

July has been marked by a vigorous offensive by the allied armies on the Somme, an offensive that resulted in a major success for the British between Hardecourt and Pozieres, and between the village of Hardecourt and the river for French troops. As here, they often find themselves on the same road.

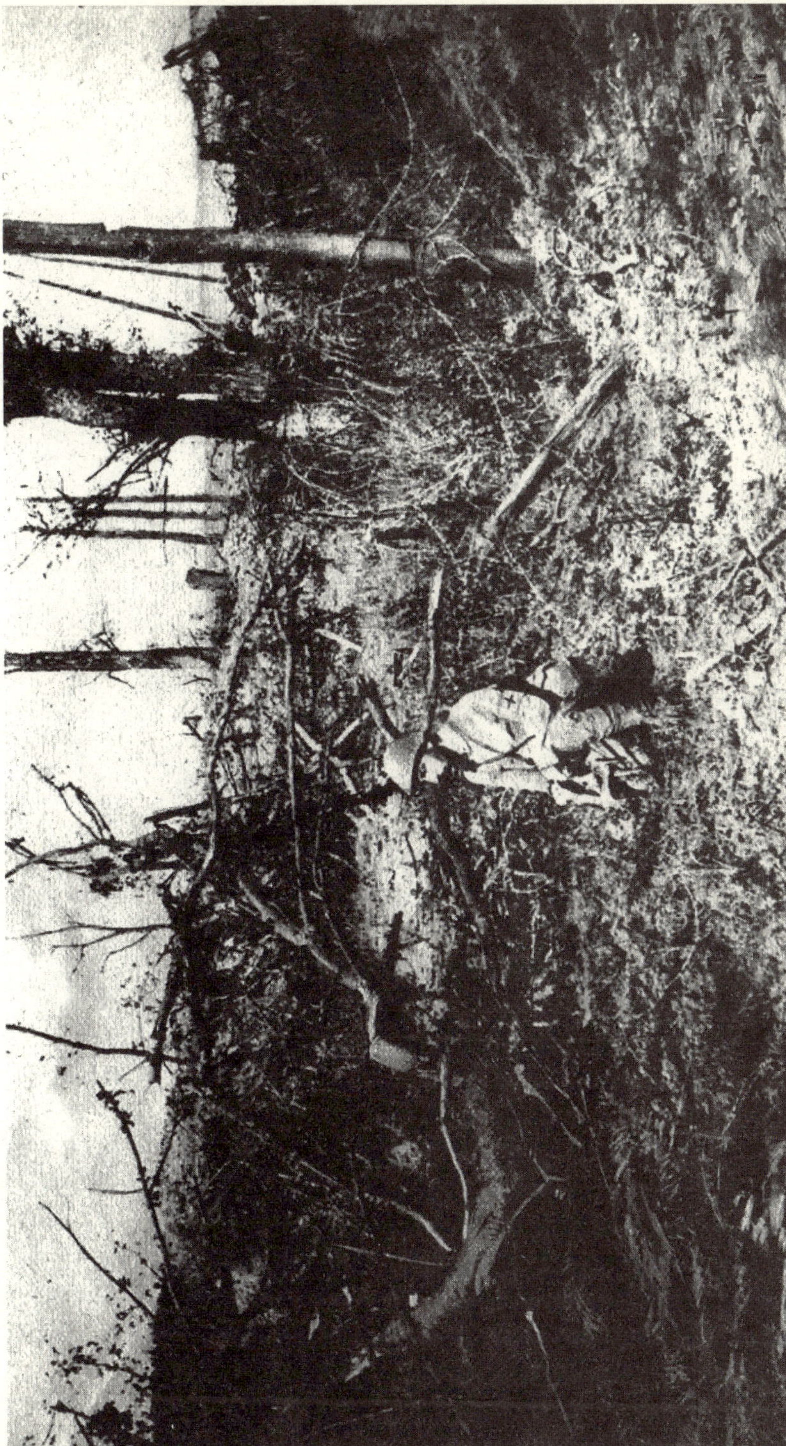

Obstacles on the road to Péronne

A medical orderly shelters on a road leading towards Péronne which has been disrupted near the allied front lines.

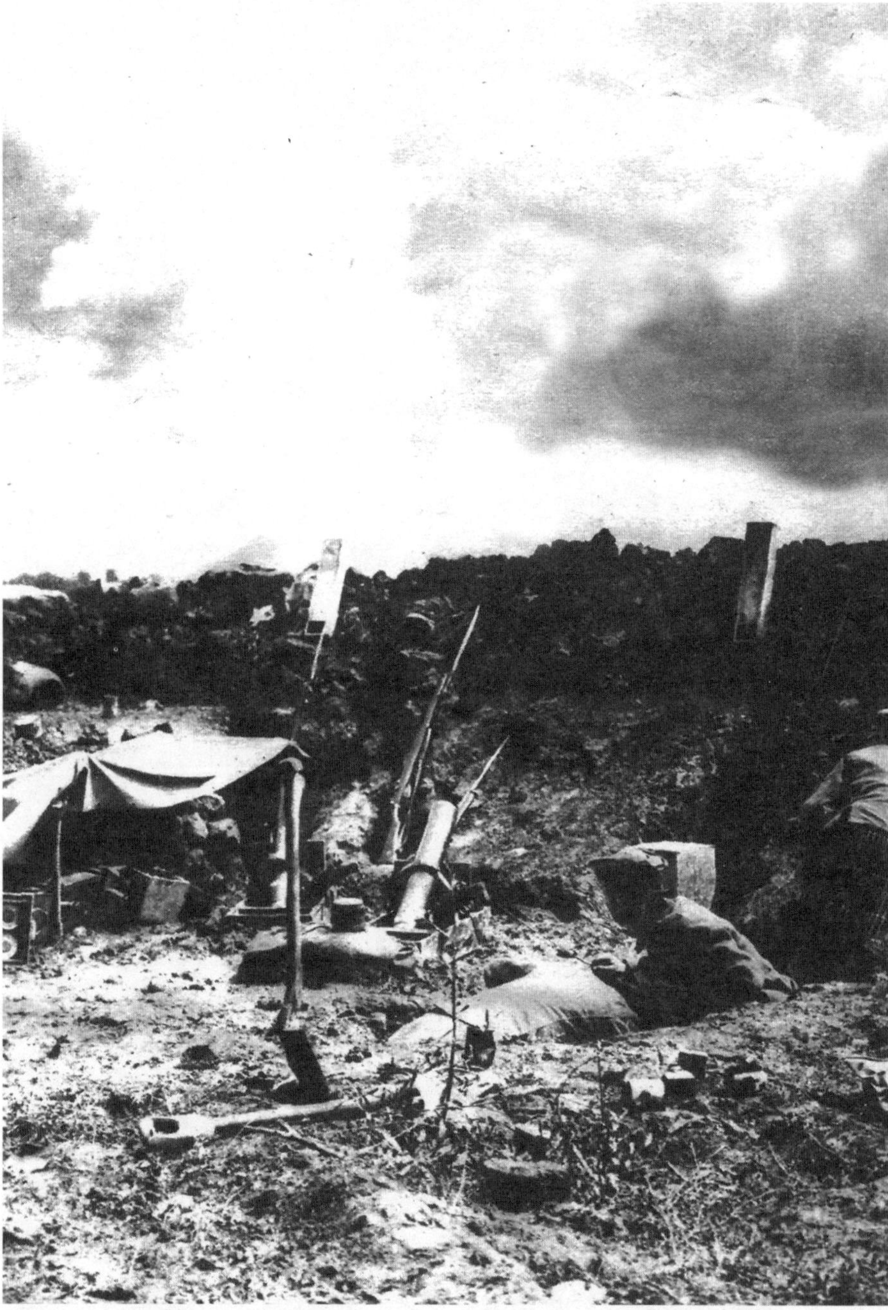

Scotsmen in the front line on the Somme

A German 84mm shell explodes just over the parapet. The Scottish regiments play a leading role in battle, with these three recognisable by their kilts and caps as they duck at the moment a German shell explodes.

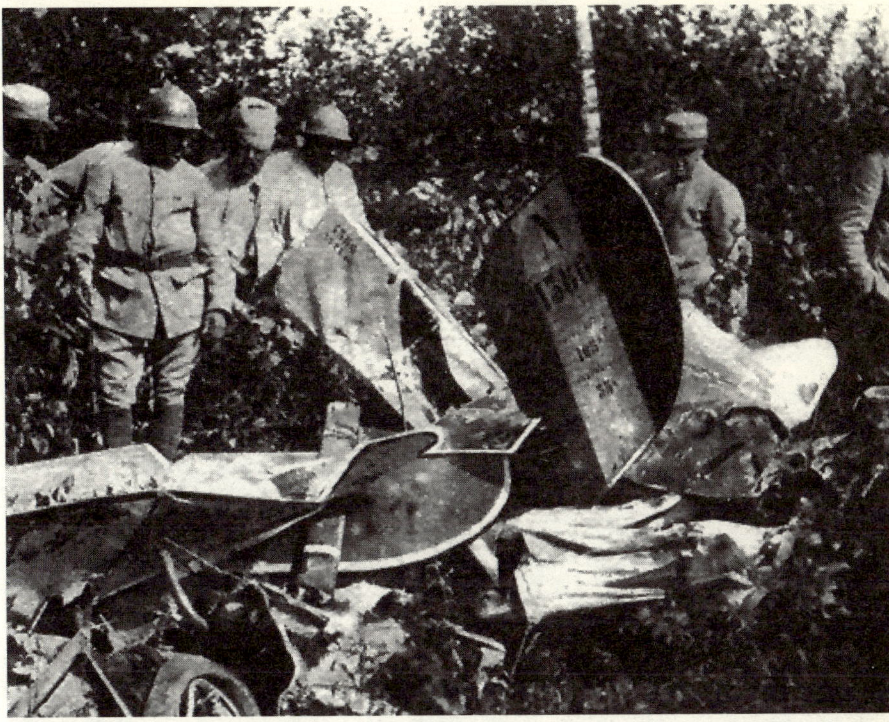

The sublime sacrifice of airmen

July 27th, an Albatross (German aeroplane) - whose pilot was nearly 6' 3" tall and made almost daily visits across allied lines - was shot down near Chalons. The photograph shows the wreckage being examined. Allied aircraft were also destroyed in the aerial fighting.

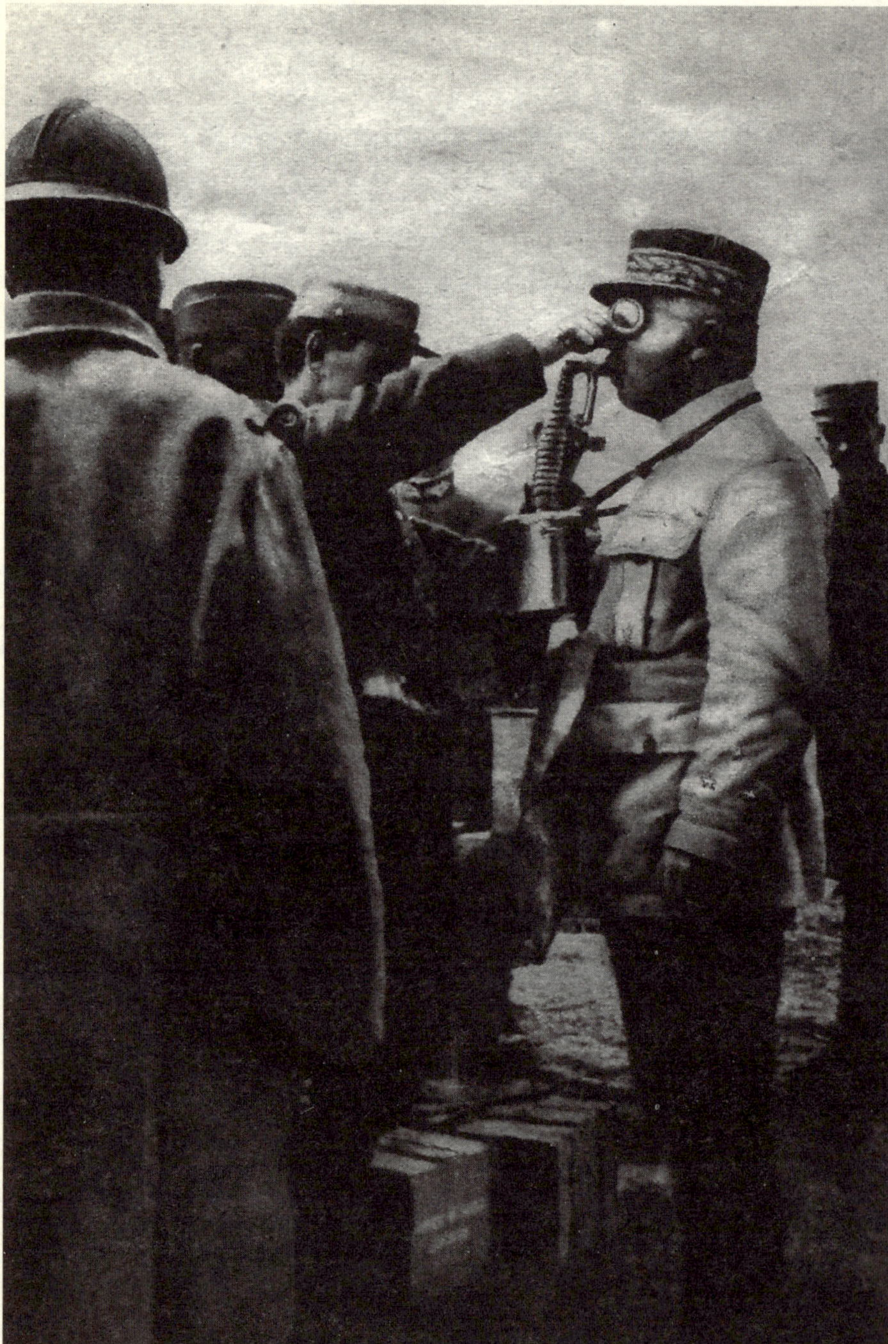

General Franchet (France) tries on a gas mask

The General experiments with a new gas mask, the design having recently been modified to make it easier to use. Similar models are used by all allied troops on the front line.

The valiant British army in the Somme

British successes continue on the Somme. Since July 26th we have controlled the village of Pozieres, which is of major importance and has formed the new front. Since July 1st, the young troops, under Kitchener have proved that their bravery can match the best Prussian and Brandenburg regiments, whose qualities have been praised so much elsewhere.

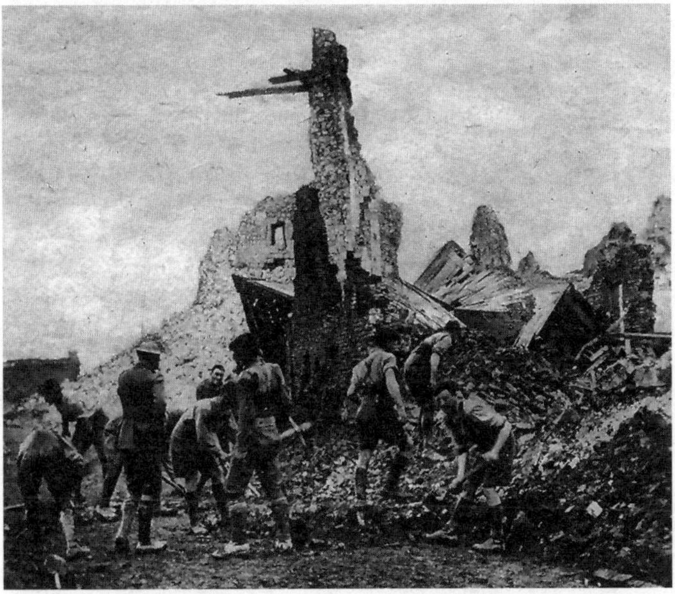

Clearing a route through the village of Contalmaison

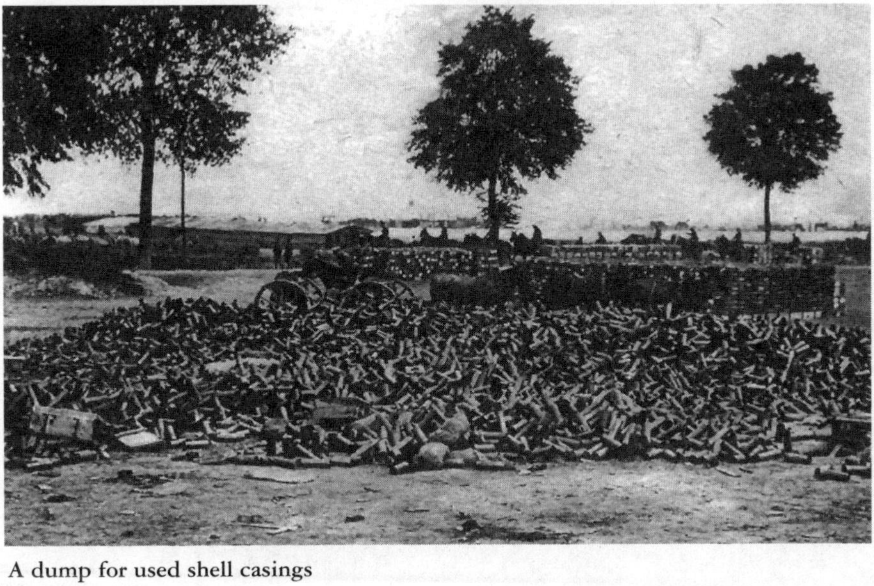

A dump for used shell casings

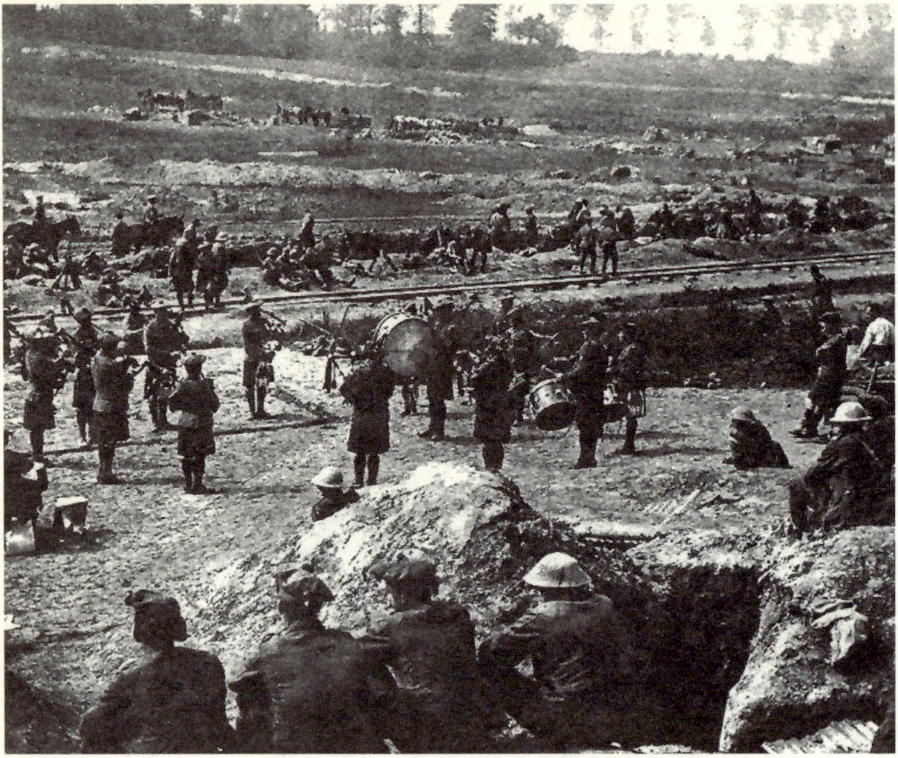

A concert after the battle

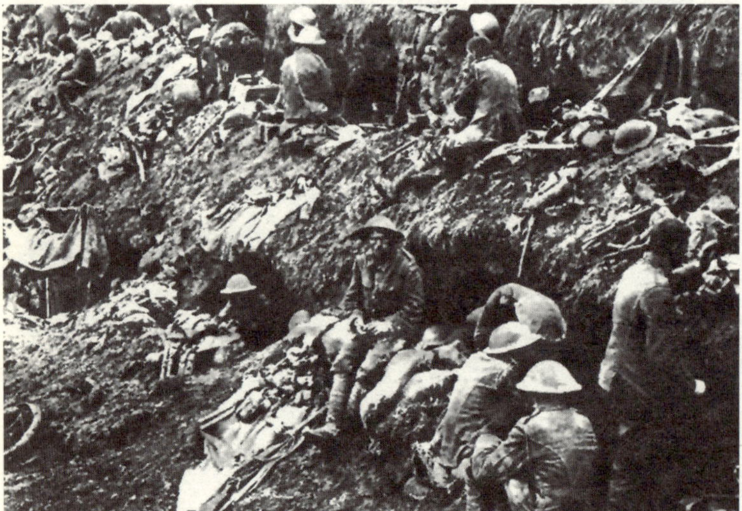

A position taken from the enemy

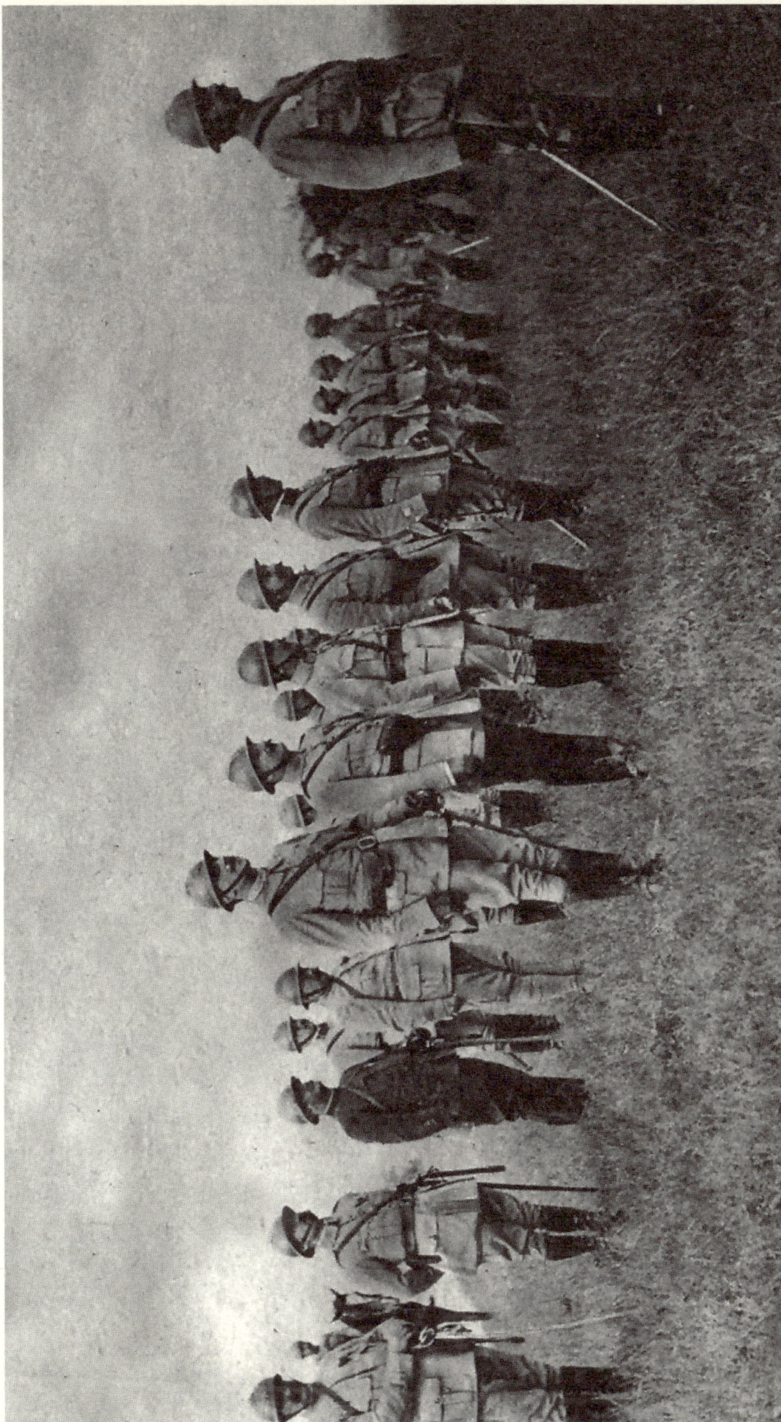

French officers parade in Picardie

A parade before General Marchand in Picardie, during which he decorated a number of officers, paticularly those who were involved in action at a farm in Monacu. Despite some of them having been severely wouded they put on a brave face.

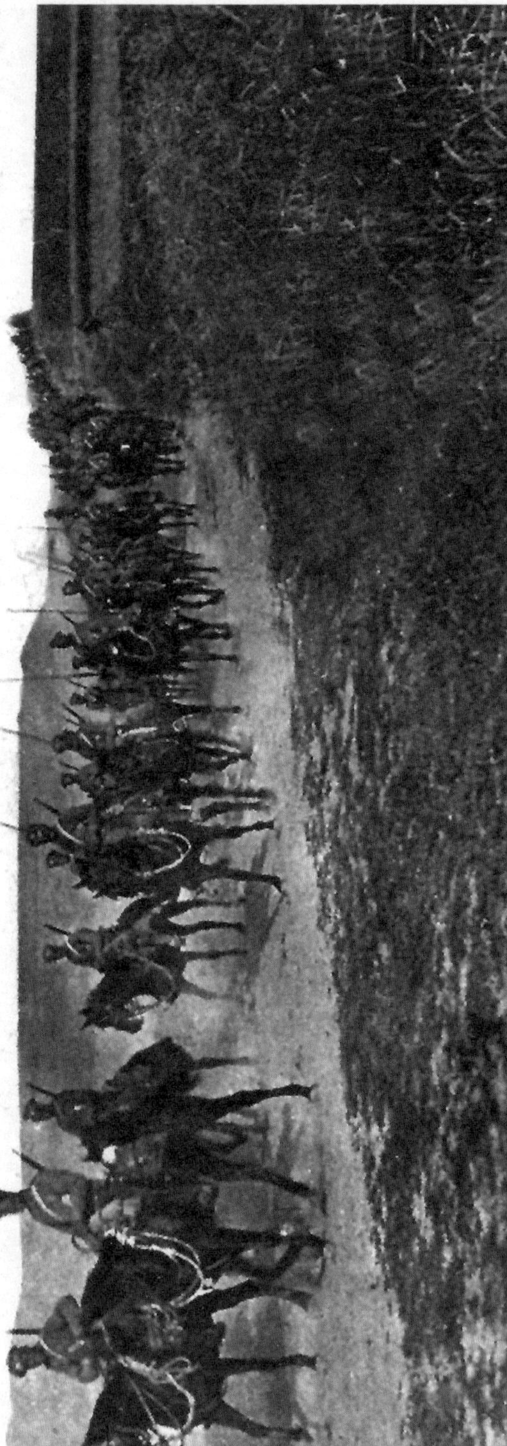

A Russian mounted regiment

There is a great deal of enthusiasm and bravery, spurred on by the successes of the Cossacks in the Bukovine region. In a two month offensive, the Russian troops took about 350,000 prisoners.

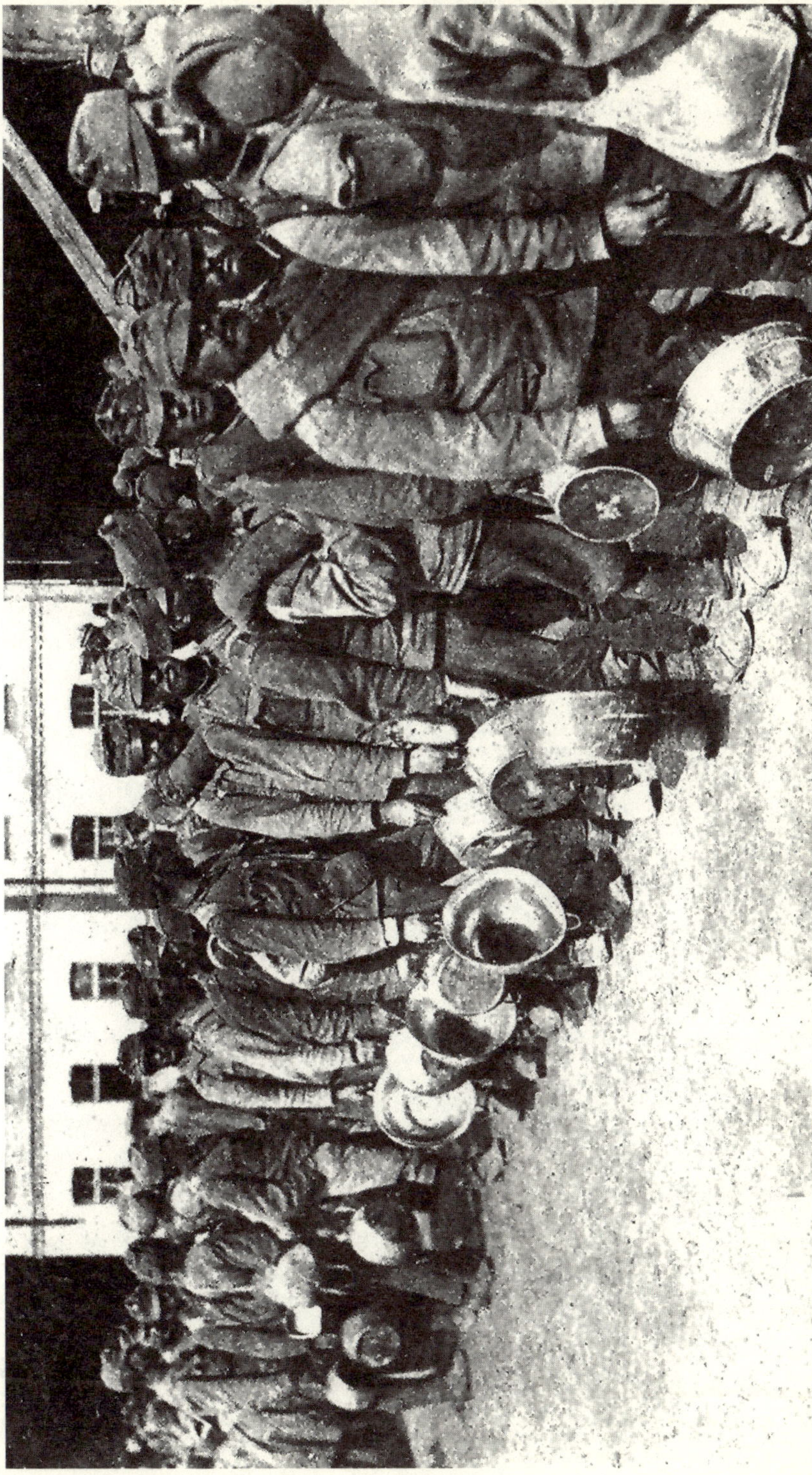

Austrian prisoners waiting for their soup

The defeated Austro-Hungarians are now feeling tired and lost. Here they are waiting for the distribution of food during their long walk back to Russia.

- NEWS REPORTS -

Thursday August 10, 1916

Allied gains to the north of the Somme with enemy detachments dispersed under fire in Champagne. Violent fighting on the right bank of the Meuse in the Fleury sector. The enemy had gained a foothold in some trenches around Thiaumont. Counterattacks have allowed trenches to be retaken near Chapitre-le-Chenois, with 200 prisoners.

The Russians are advancing on the Sereth. To the south of the Dniester, they have progressed on a wide front, taking the city of Thonacz. They say that they have captured 2,000 Germans and several heavy cannons.

The Italians, following the offensive in the Carso, at Monfalcone, have a further success. They have captured the bridgehead of Goritz, in the same region, with 8,000 prisoners, of which 200 are officers.

Friday August 11, 1916

To the north of the Somme allies have completely reoccupied the wood at Hem with 50 prisoners. In the region of Chaulnes, an artillery struggle between Lihons and the railway track at Chaulnes. The Germans defeated everywhere. A French pilot has forced a German plane to land at Lerouville. Six other hostile planes have been shot down in the Somme and further aerial action elsewhere, including the railway tracks at Tergnier and the station of La Fere.

The Italians entered Gorizia, capturing 11,000 prisoners and leaving the enemy in disarray.

The Russians have progressed to the south of the Dniester. They took the town of Tysmenitza and captured several thousand prisoners.

Saturday August 12, 1916

The British pursued the enemy to the northwest of Pozieres; executed a lucky manoeuvre to the south of Arras and defeated a similar attempt by the enemy who were trying to reach Hulluch.

To the south of the Somme, a German patrol approached allied lines with flame throwers to the west of Vermandovillers. On the right bank of the Meuse, intermittent shelling in the region of Fleury and Vaux-Chapitre.

The French shot down a German plane over the Somme and two others were forced to land. Their squadrons dropped some shells along the front at Lassigny-Combles, and on the stations at Digny, Apilly, Bazincourt and Spincourt.

The Russians, after their success at Tysmenitza, continue to advance towards Stanislau.

The Italians are in control of the whole left bank of the Isonzo, between Tolmino and the sea, having used cavalry attacks to storm enemy lines. An estimated 12,500, or more, prisoners continue to gather in their concentration camps.

Sunday August 13, 1916

Allied troops are advancing to the north of Bazentin-le-Petit, defeating all enemy counterattacks and making major progress to the northwest of Pozieres. Over allied lines to the south of Douaumont, an enemy plane was shot down by an American pilot.

To the north of the Somme, a brilliant French infantry attack - several German trenches taken, establishing new lines to the south of Maurepas and along the road that goes towards Hem. To the north of the wood at Hem, a fortified enemy position was taken with 150 prisoners and 10 machine guns.

The Russians have defeated the army of General von Bothmer, commander of the Austro-Hungarian-German South Army on the Eastern Front. On the right bank of the Sereth, they have captured 104 officers and 4,872 soldiers; in the south part of Monasteritza, they took 2,500 men, including a colonel; on the Zlota-Lipa river, their total was 1,000 men.

The Italian army has progressed rapidly along the Carso river, to the East of Monfalcone; on the plains at Doberdo and to the east of Gorizia.

Monday August 14, 1916

British pilots have bombed the hangars used by the Zeppelins based in Brussels, the railway tracks at Mons and Namur, the stations at Busigny and Courtray.

Allies have penetrated the village of Maurepas, with the southern part and the cemetery under allied control. Forward lines have advanced on the south slopes of hill 109 and to the west of Clery. A total of 1,000 prisoners have now been taken, and 50 machine guns captured. All hostile counterattacks have been defeated.

On the Carso, the Italians have passed the Vallone and now occupy Oppachiasella. They took 270 men and 3 cannons. Around Goritz, the Austrians are reinforcing, there is resistance to the east of the city where they are now using heavy artillery. The Italian alpine troops have conquered a new position on the Tofana, in the Dolomites.

The Russians are entering Stanislau having progressed along the river Sereth.

Tuesday August 15, 1916

The British troops have defeated a hand grenade attack to the southwest of Guillemont. They have dispersed enemy positions to the north of Pozieres.

Allied troops strengthened positions on the land to the north of the Somme. A German counterattack on the church and cemetery of Maurepas, under allied occupation, has been halted by machine gun fire. Eighty prisoners were taken. French troops fired 120 large calibre shells on the station at Metz Sablons, the railway workshops, and the barracks at Metz.

The Russians have taken the last sector of the fortified ramparts that the enemy had created near Pripet on the Romanian border. The troops of Generals Tcherbatchef and Sakharof seized several villages on the Strypa. General Letchitsky has occupied the city of Nadvovisagr and crossed the Bistriza river.

The Italian troops have further successes on the lower Isonzo. They have progressed beyond the Vallone and taken 1,565 prisoners on the high ground near Nadligem, and 533 others to the east of Gorizia. Austrian planes have bombed Grandin-Compulto.

Wednesday August 16, 1916

On the British front, success and significant progress to the west of Pozieres.

To the north of the Somme, rapid shellfire in the region of Maurepas. Quiet night on the other sectors. To the south of the Somme, the French widened their positions to the south west of Estrées, taking several lines of enemy trenches.

Reims has been bombed by enemy planes, 6 civilians were killed.

The Russians have defeated the enemy on the western bank of the Stokhod. They have driven back the Austrians along the higher Sereth. They reached the north bank of the Dniester near Mariampol. The total number of prisoners taken is 83,000 since August 4.

The Turkish offensive continues around Hamadan, in Persia. Austrian planes have bombed Monfalcone but there were no victims or damage.

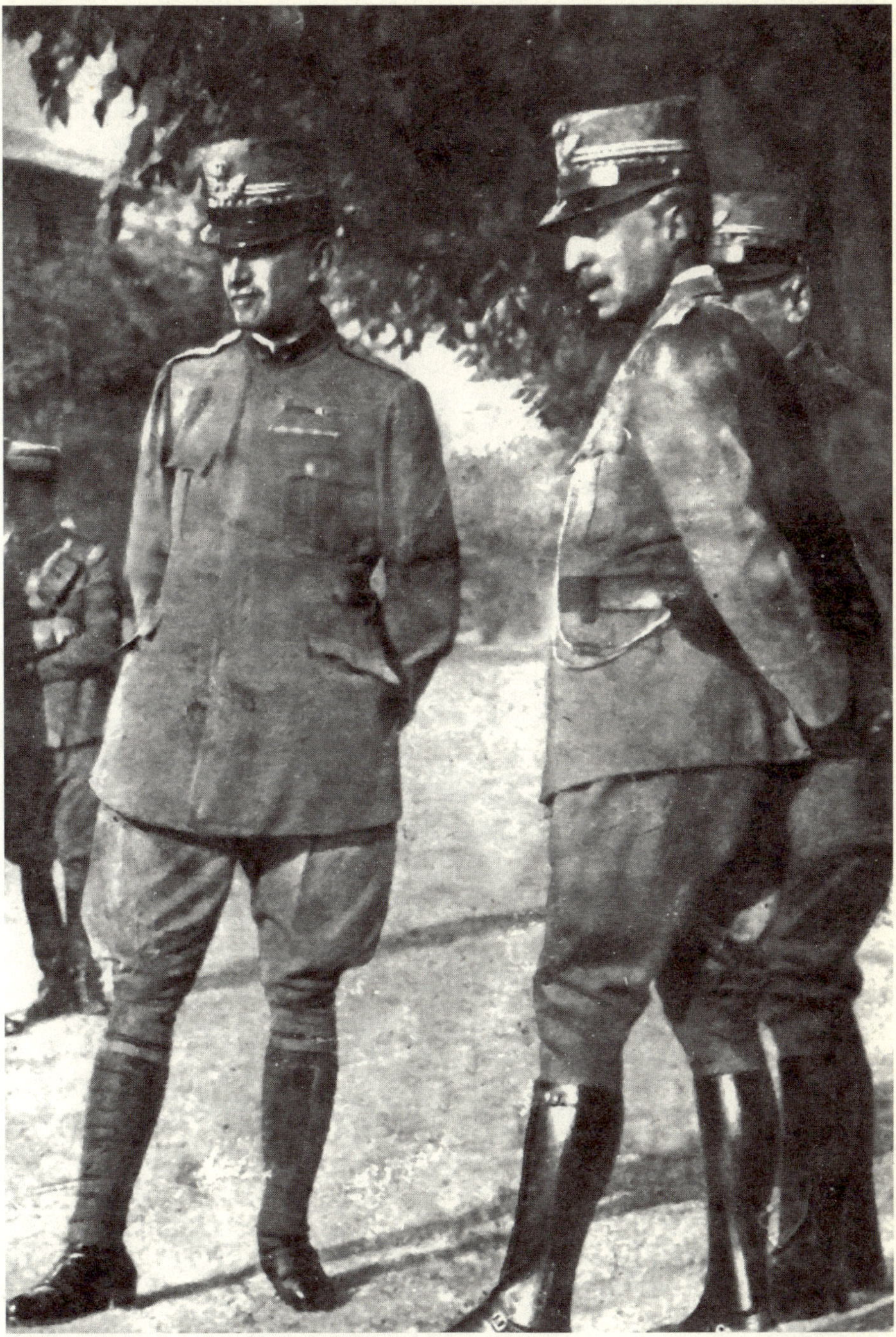

Duke of Aoste, who controls the lower Isonzo.

A major part of the Italian success is credited to the Duke of Aoste, cousin of the king, who commands the army operating in the Lower Isonzo. The Duke is seen here, on the left, with one of his generals in a small town that they have recently conquered.

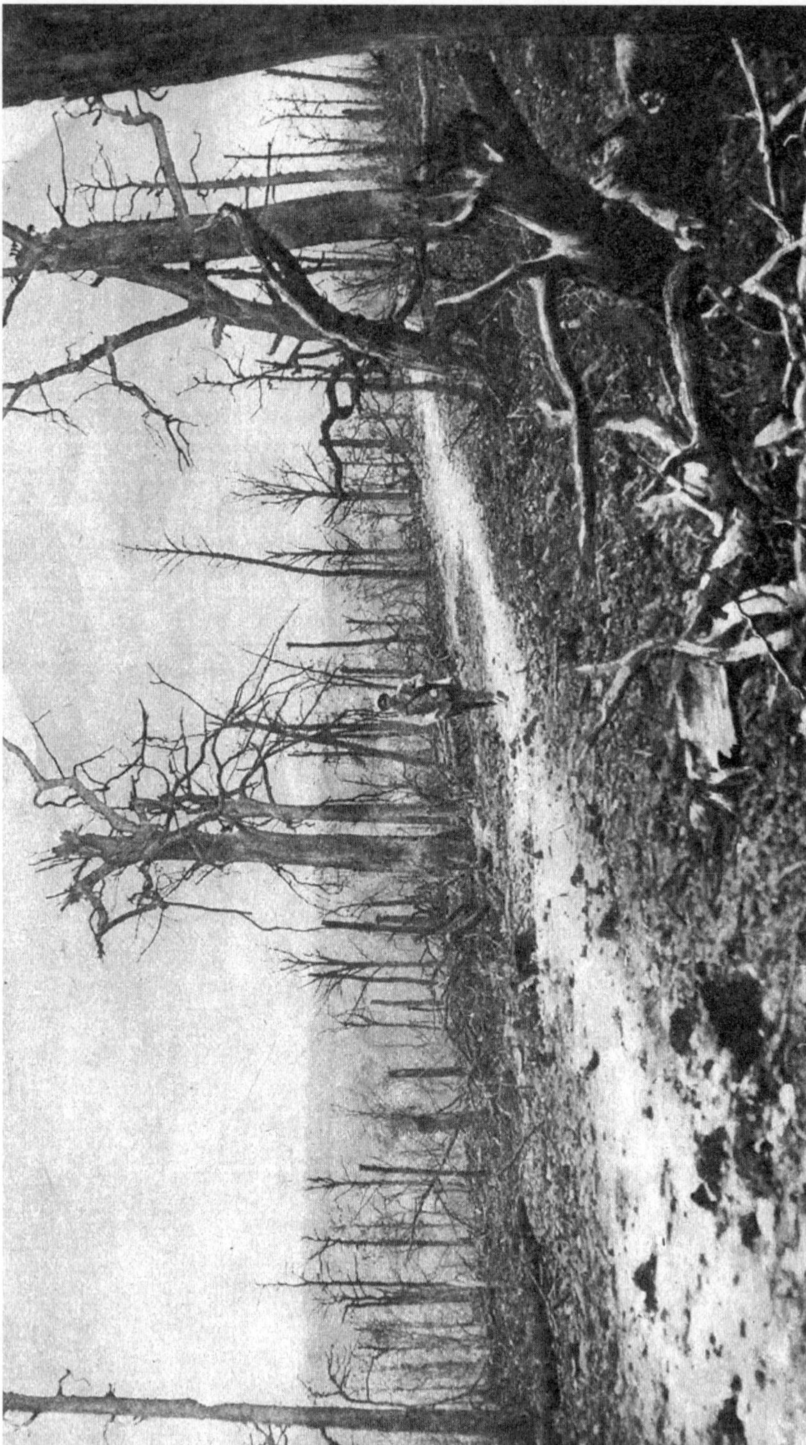

A wooded path outside Souville

This was once a path through the woods between Souville and Belleville, but constant shelling has significantly changed the view.

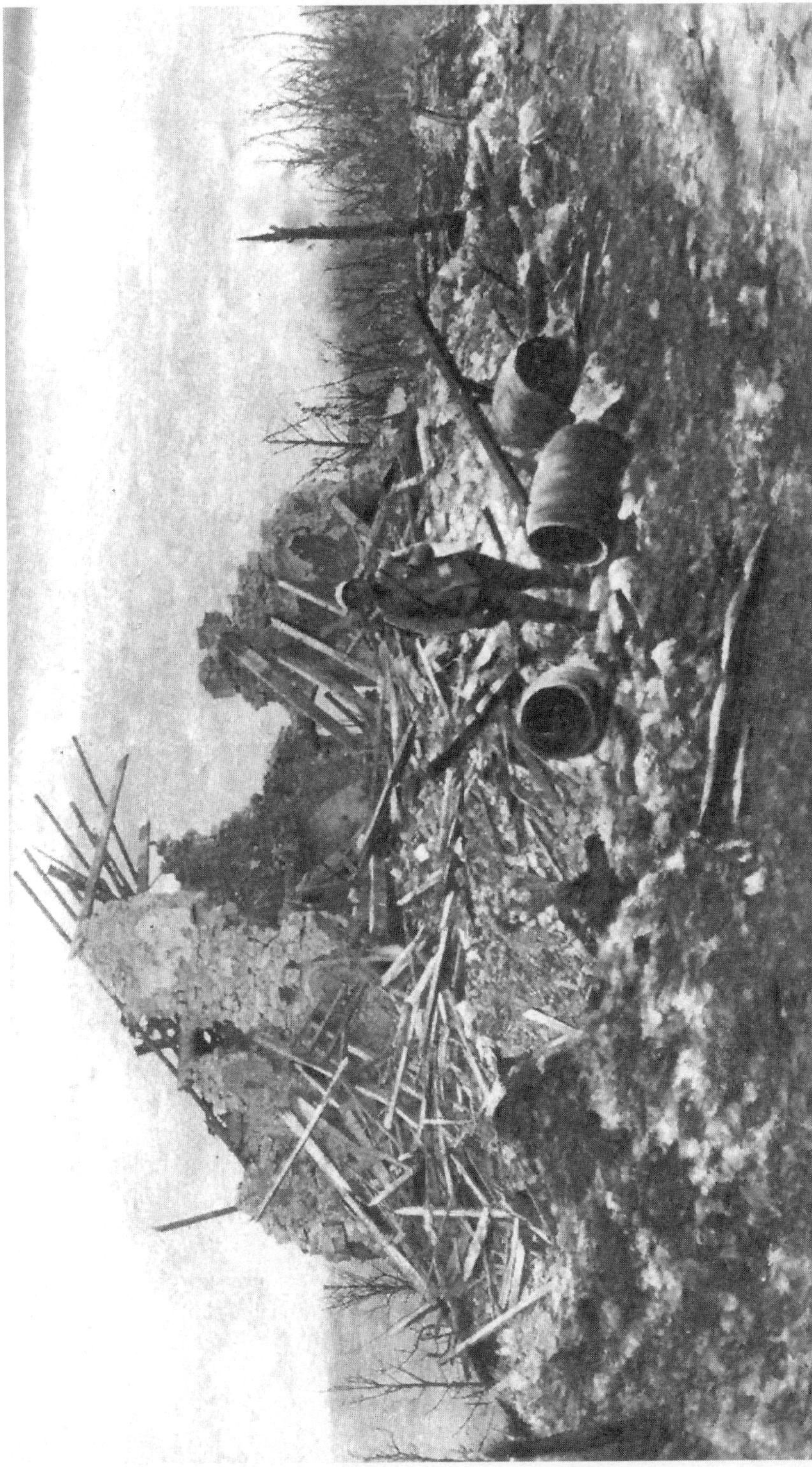

Another view, near Souville

Here we see a ruined building on the outskirts of Souville, which the Germans attacked after they shelled the village of Fleury in France.

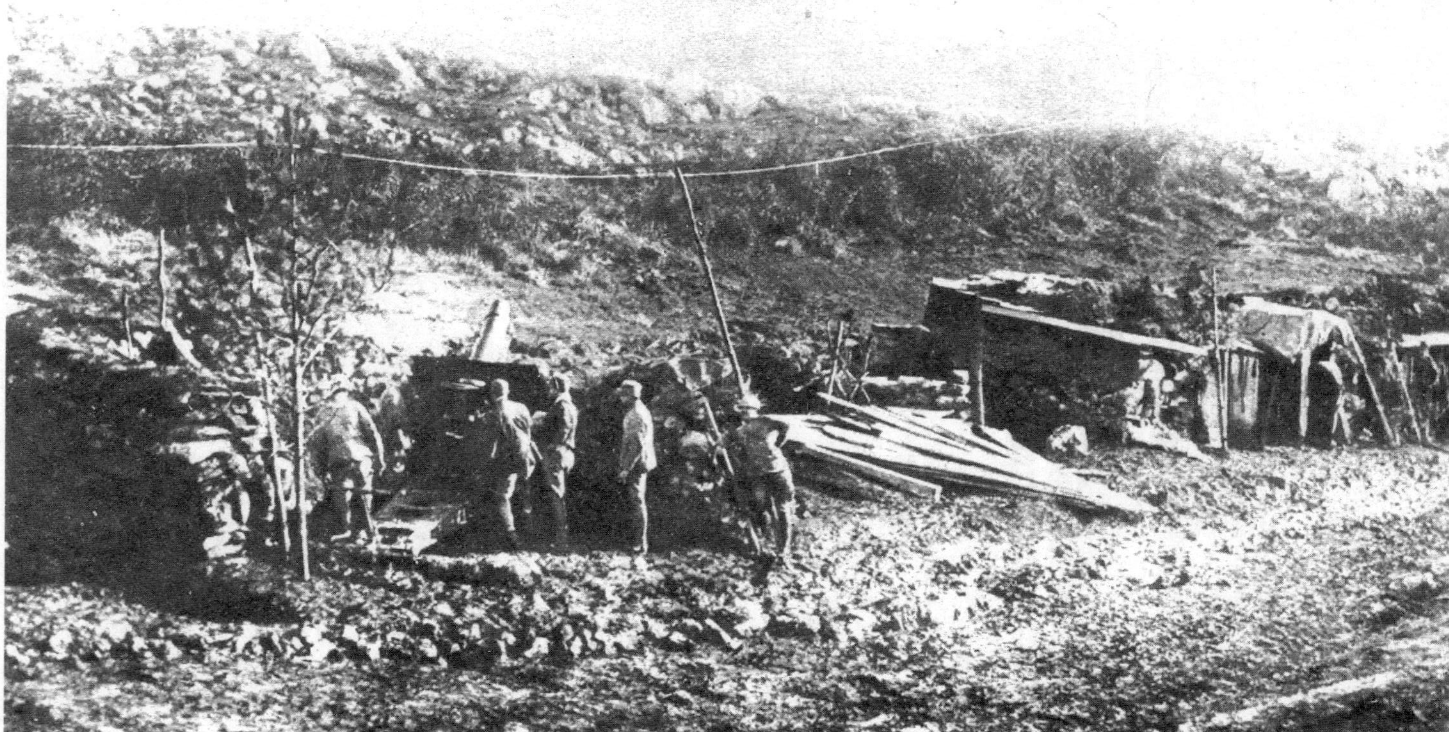

A cannon near Polazzo, Italy.

This photo and that on the next page were taken at the time of the first attack near Montfalcone. This 149mm gun is behind a ridge at Polazzo in the Carso, the heights of which are the key to Gorizia.

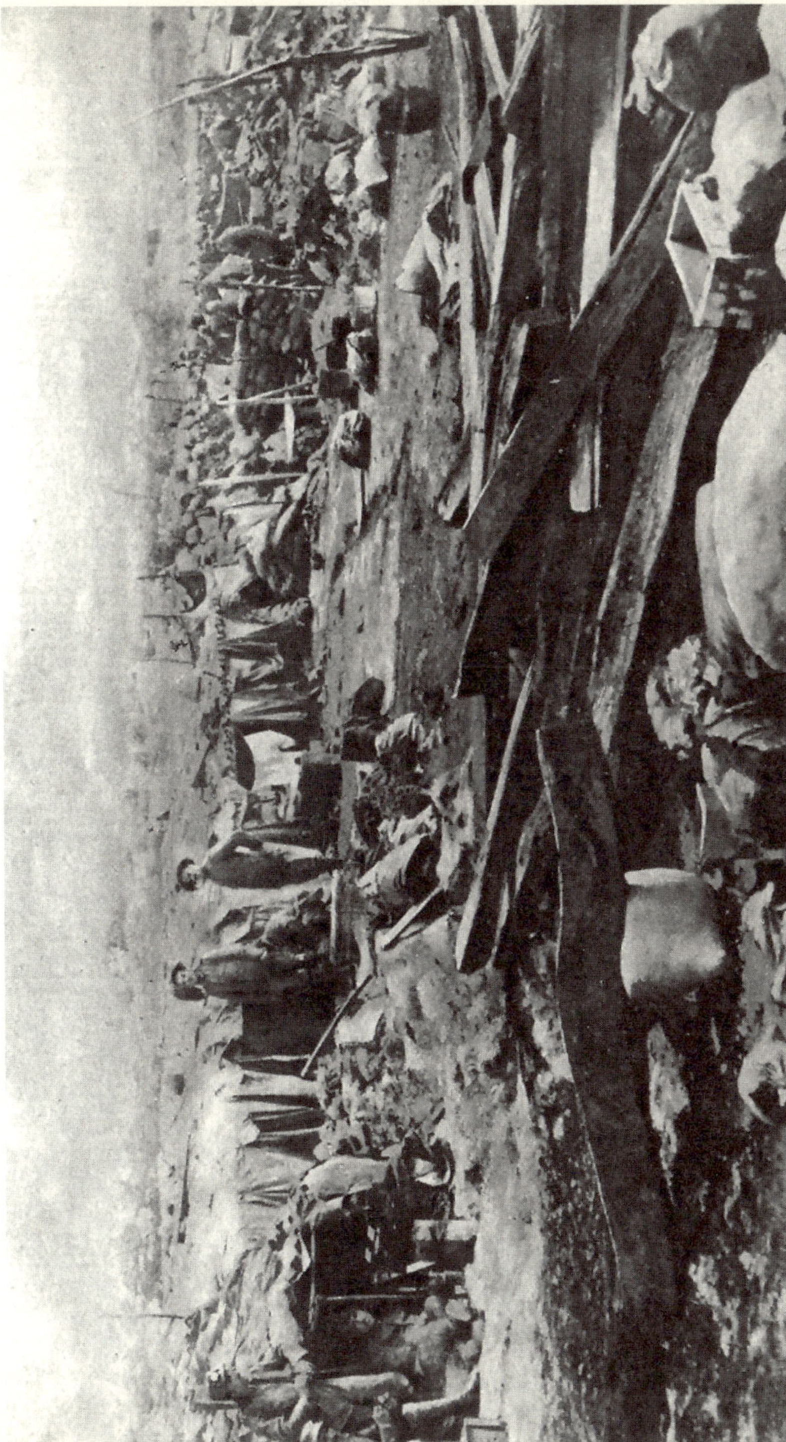

A covered trench near Castelnuovo

A large covered trench or" Trincereronne" above Castelnuovo, provides a base for one of the most important Italian attacks.

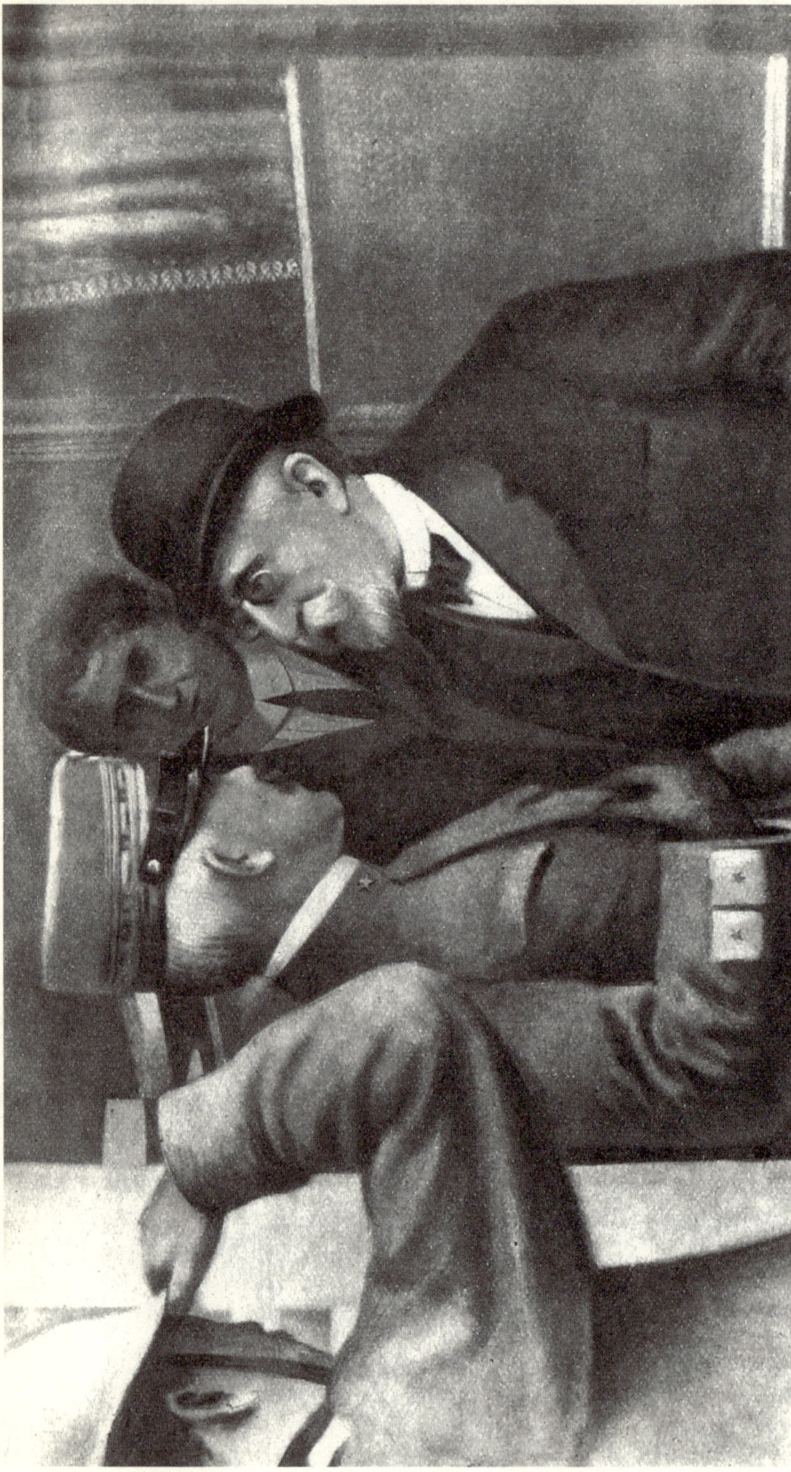

The organisers of the Italian offensive

Mr. Boselli, president of Italy, with General Porro, commander in chief of Italian forces at a meeting near the front.

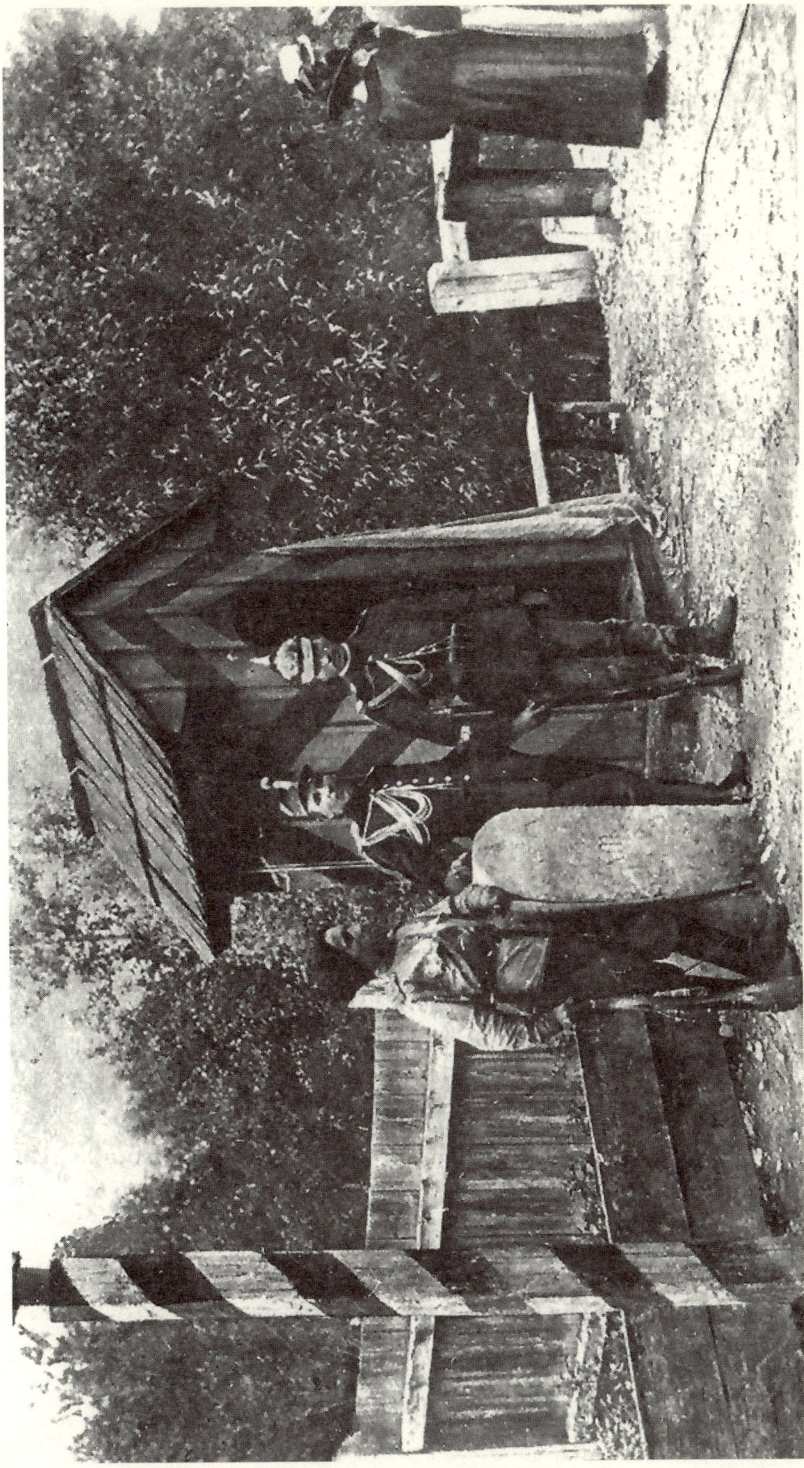

Russian and Romanian border guards at the Bukovine frontier

Following their possession of the Bukovine region, our Russian allies border guards have replaced those of the Austrians. Here is the border at Itcani-Burdujeni with a frontier guard and a Romanian policeman and a Russian Cossack.

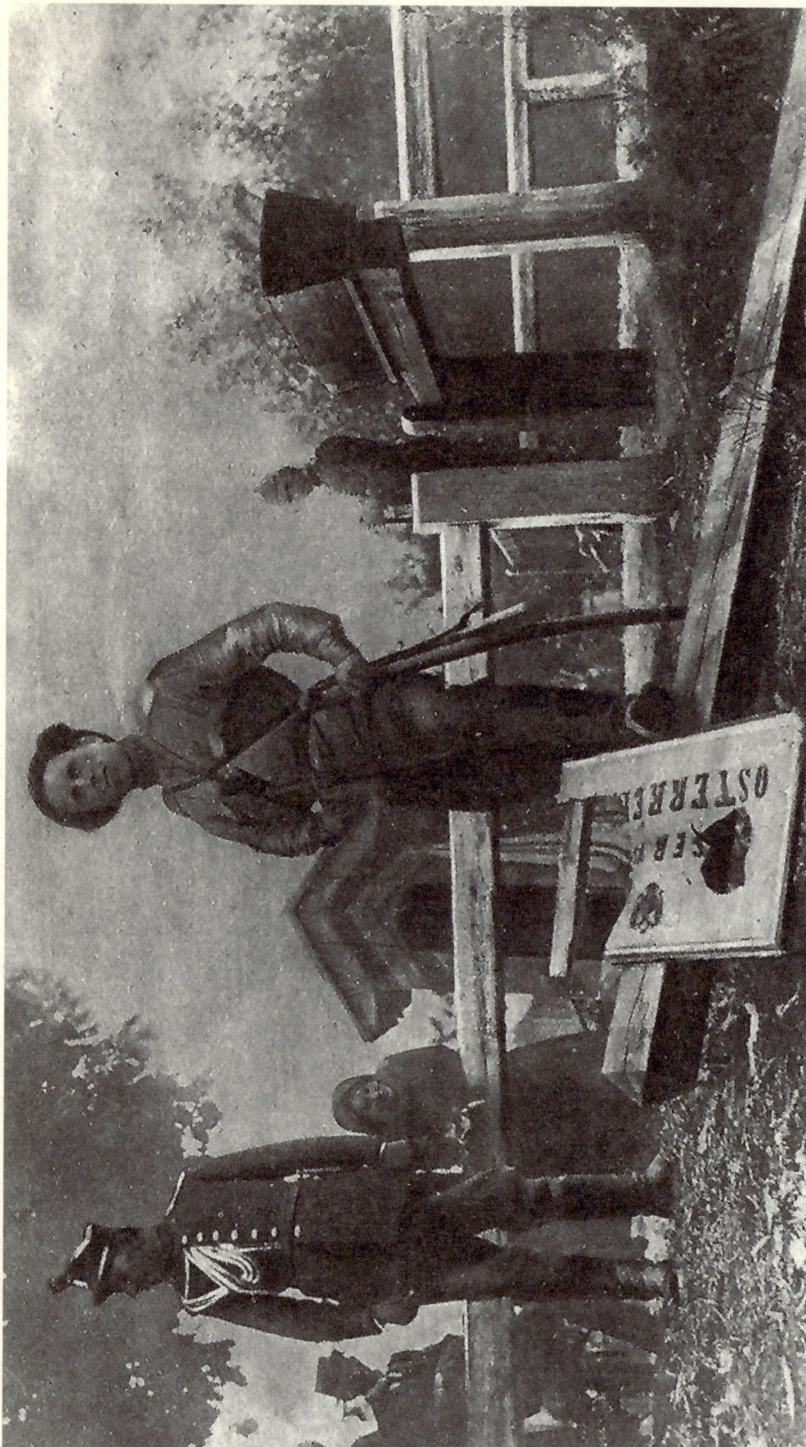

The second photograph shows the same Cossack with his foot on the old signpost that announced Kaiserthum Oesterreich (Austrian Empire)

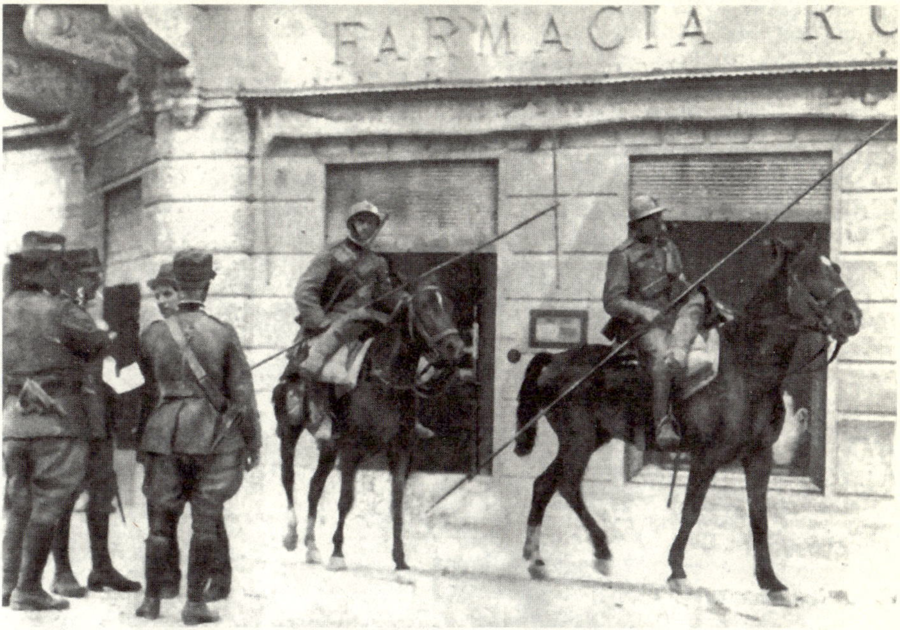

The arrival of Italians in Gorizia after the Austrian evacuation of the city

An Italian cavalry patrol on the streets of the conquered town. After a furious battle on the outskirts of Gorizia, which destroyed many buildings, the centre of the city hardly suffered. The population, who had scattered, returned and immediately hung out Italian flags from windows.

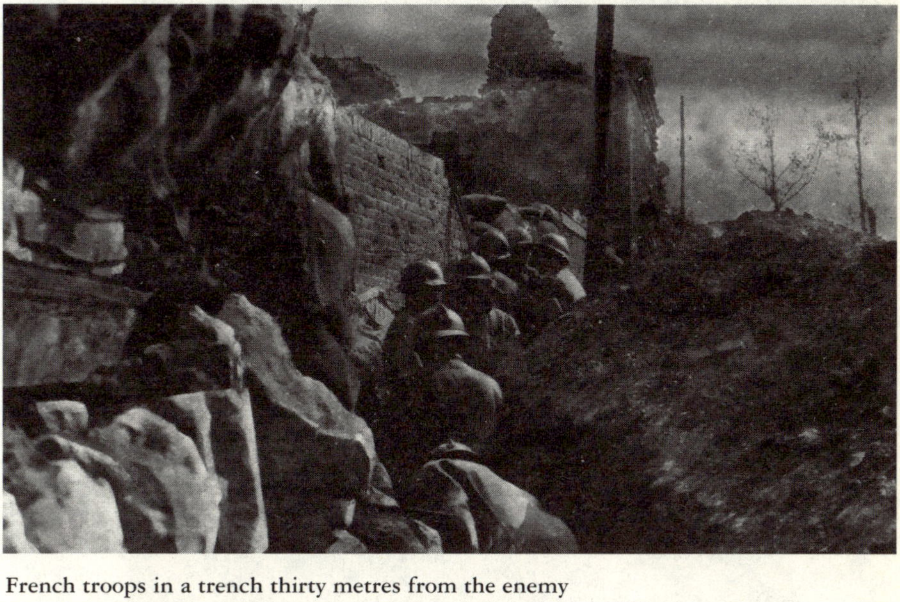

French troops in a trench thirty metres from the enemy

On July 9th (1916) across a four kilometres front to the north of Belloy and Santerre in the Somme, allied troops approach the gates of the town of Péronne, at this point only 30 metres from the enemy.

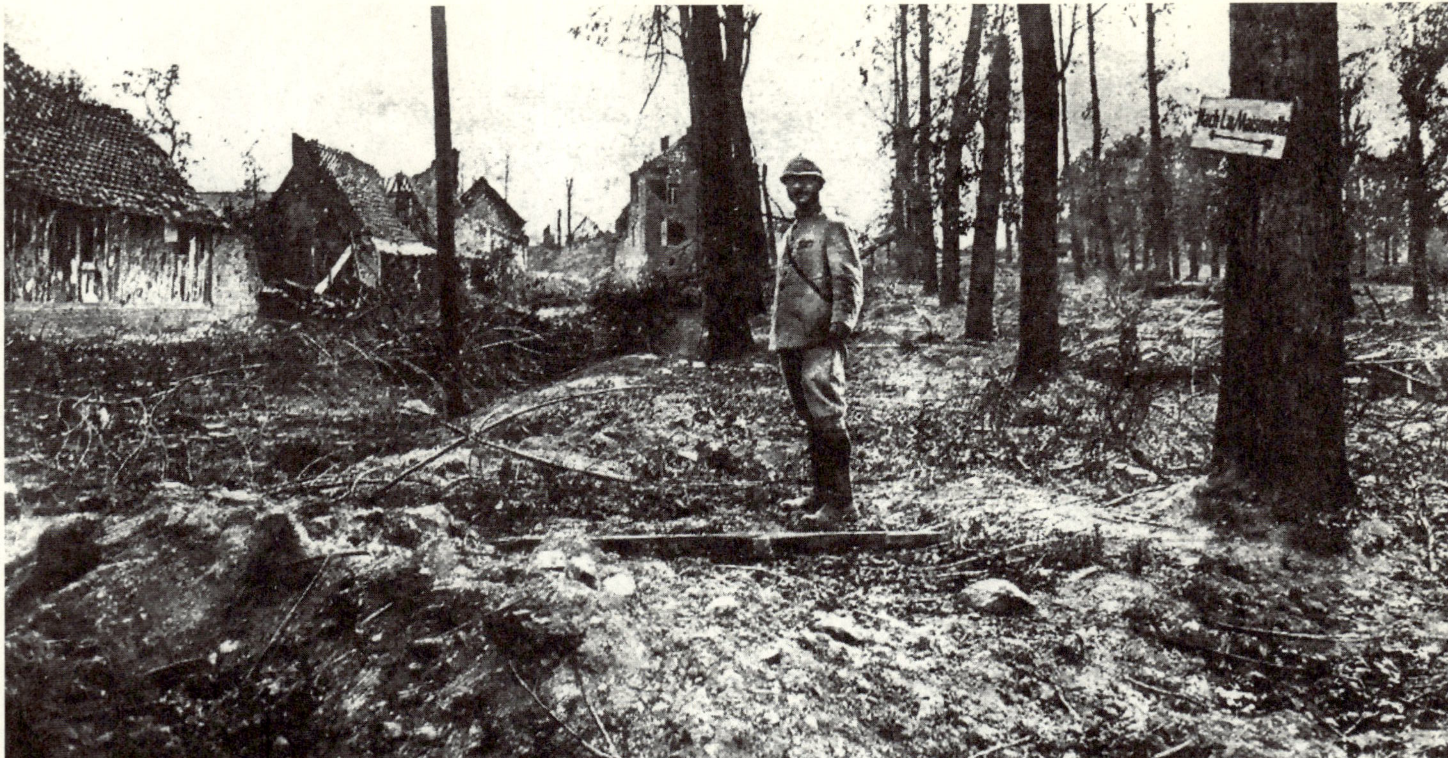

View outside Péronne

Note the destruction of the village and the German sign "Nach La Maisonnette" (to the Maisonette).

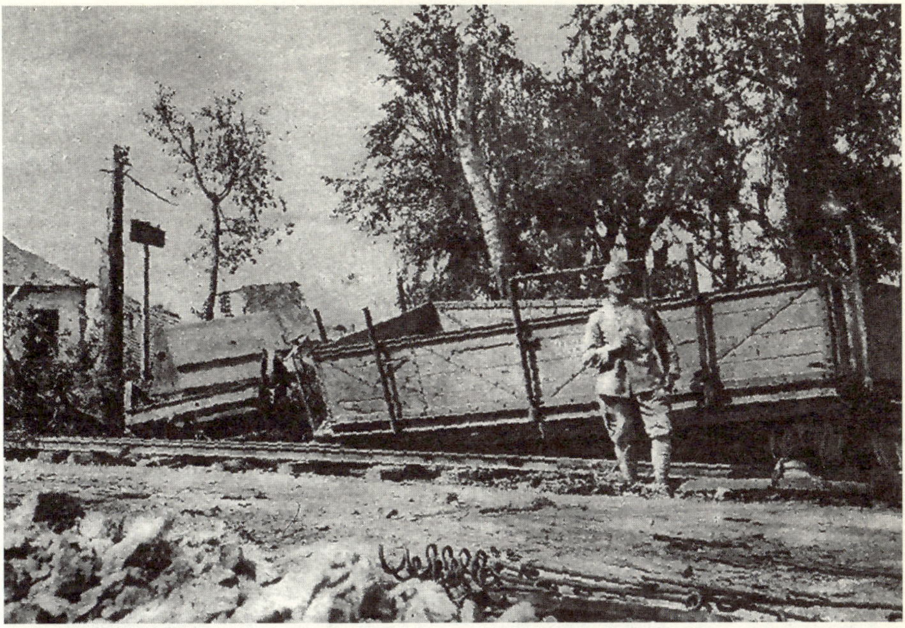

German equipment in the village of Biaches

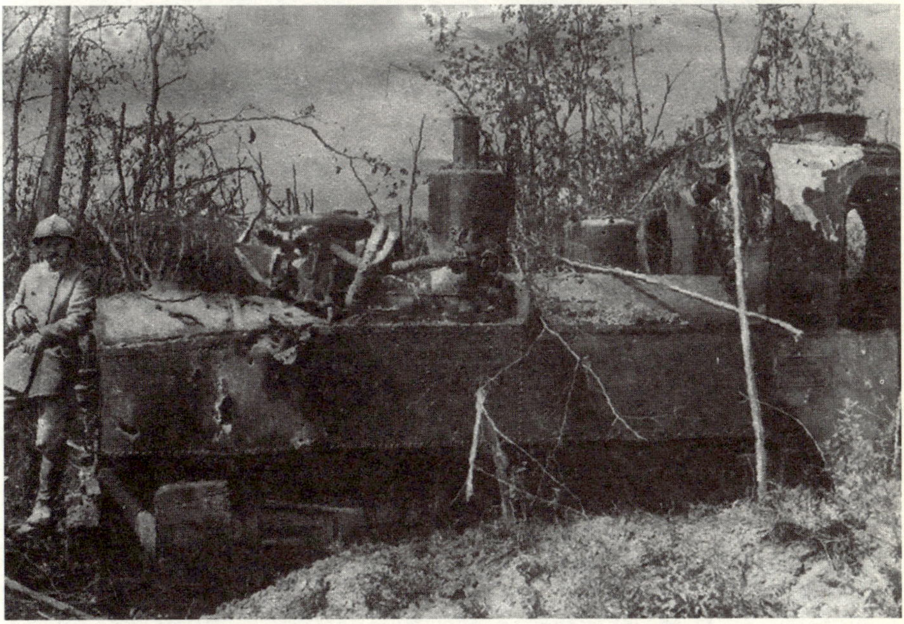

Taken on July 7th, we see a German wagon in the village and a locomotive in the woods near Biaches. When allied troops conquered Biaches, they brought back more than 300 prisoners and a considerable amount of equipment. This railway was a narrow gauge one, specifically installed by the Germans for restocking munitions.

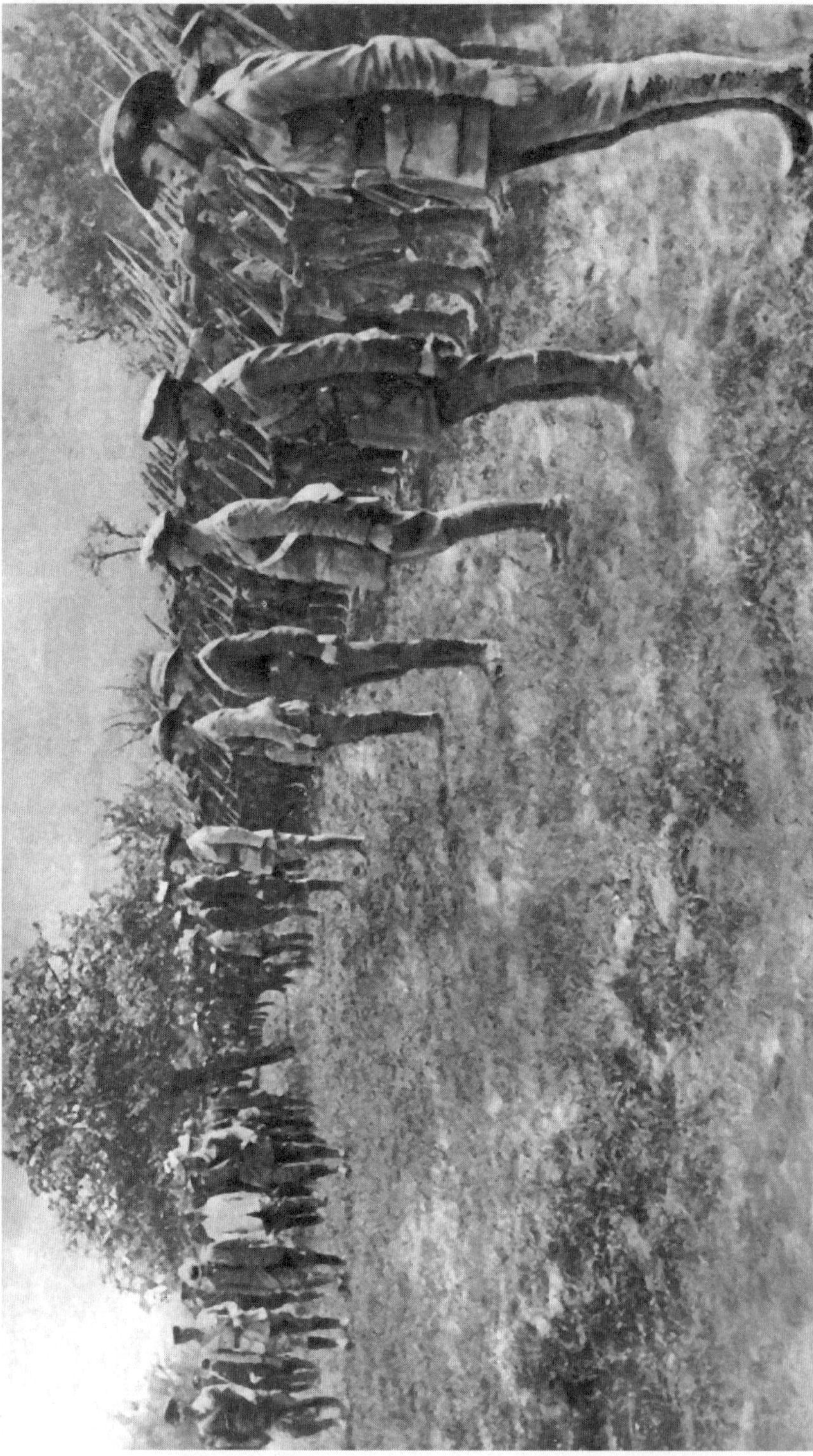

Mr. Hughes, Prime Minister of Australia, inspects "ANZAC" (Australian and New Zealand) troops on a visit to the Somme.

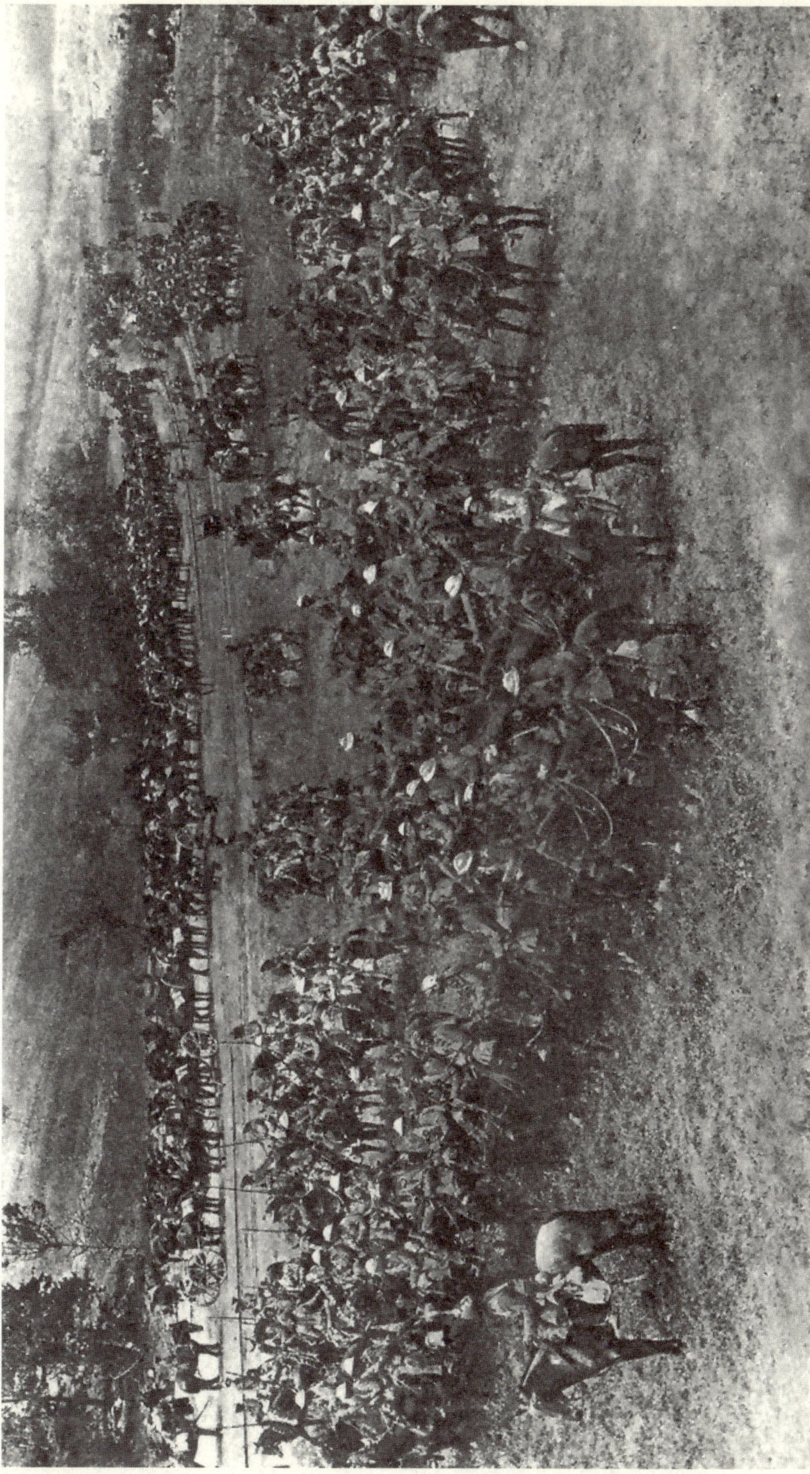

British Colonial regiments in the Somme

A Hindu cavalry regiment and "ANZAC" troops demonstrate the loyalty that they have shown for the past two years along with Canadians and others.

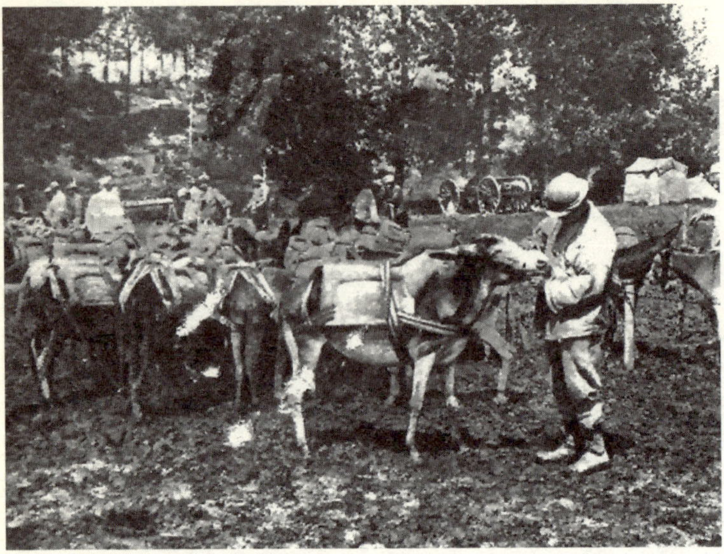

Donkeys used for transportation

Convoys of small donkeys are now used for the transportation of the supplies and munitions on the front.

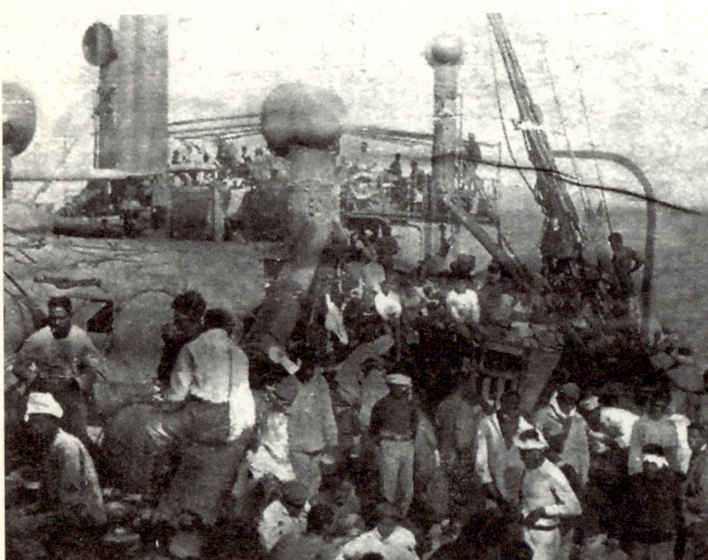

French colonial troops from the Pacific on their way to Europe

The natives of the islands of Societe, Loyalty and New Caledonia have formed a contingent of excellent soldiers.

- NEWS REPORTS -

Thursday August 31, 1916

On the Somme, only an average day for artillery action. Bad weather continues.

In Lorraine, the enemy continues to attack in the sector near Reillon. Artillery fire thunders non-stop on the whole of the Macedonian front. The Italians have taken a number of prisoners.

The Russians have progressed in the wooded region of the Carpathians near the Hungarian border, and taken several hundred prisoners in Asia Minor. The Romanian advance is generally to the west of the Transylvanian Alps and on the low Danube.

Friday September 1, 1916

The British, during an attack on Martinpuich, have captured 2 officers and 124 men. The bombardment of Béthune by the German artillery has provoked a counter attack by allied artillery. On the Somme, the artillery was very active all day.

Near Dixmude, artillery has destroyed German encampments on the right bank of the Yser. The Romanians continue to make progress. A Russian navy flotilla is now off Constantsa.

Saturday September 2, 1916

The Germans have launched counterattacks against the British positions between Foureauxes and Ginchy.

Three German planes were shot down by the French, two on the right bank of the Oise, the third near Douaumont.

Sunday September 3, 1916

Heavy artillery action in all British sectors - especially in the Maurepas sector.

The Germans have directed violent and repeated attacks on the French trenches to the south of Estrées. On the right bank of Meuse, an agitated night.

Allies have asked Greece to take some measures against the German secret agents in Piraeus. Bulgaria has declared war on Romania. Romania announces it has taken 1,800 prisoners in the first three days of war.

Monday September 4, 1916

A raid by 13 Zeppelins took place on England. One of the air ships was shot down close to London. The British army, north of the Somme has attacked and used intense artillery fire on German positions along a 4 mile front, from Maurepas to the river. Sweeping through the enemy's positions, allied troops seized everything in their path and reached Combles.

A strong German counterattack was launched to the south of Forêt, with many deaths under our fire. So far, we have taken 2,000 prisoners. In the Forêt sector, we have captured 12 cannons and 50 machine guns.

The Romanians have announced 1,537 more prisoners taken.

Tuesday September 5, 1916

The British have progressed between Somme and Aisne, along a 2 mile hostile front, and 800 metres deep, including the village of Guillemont. British troops also took Dar-es-Salaam, capital of the German East-Africa.

On the Somme, the battle develops relentlessly on both banks. To the east of Forêt, German counterattacks have been broken by French machine gun fire. The French have also retaken part of Vermandovillers with 2,700 prisoners.

The Romanians have entered Sibiu (Hermannstadt) in Transylvania.

Wednesday September 6, 1916

Allies have progressed to the East of Guillemont, toward Salsemont and Leuze, taking more than 1,000 prisoners. In spite of bad weather, allied troops have progressed on the Somme front, but the enemy has reinforced to the south with counterattacks at many points on French positions, notably to the southwest of Barleux, to the southeast and to the south of Belloy.

Between Vermandovillers and Chilly, German pockets have been taken with allies reaching the borders of Deniecourt. Along the two banks of the river, 6,650 prisoners were taken with 36 cannons, of which 28 were heavy.

Russian progress in the Carpathians. A Romanian statement suggests 645 new prisoners.

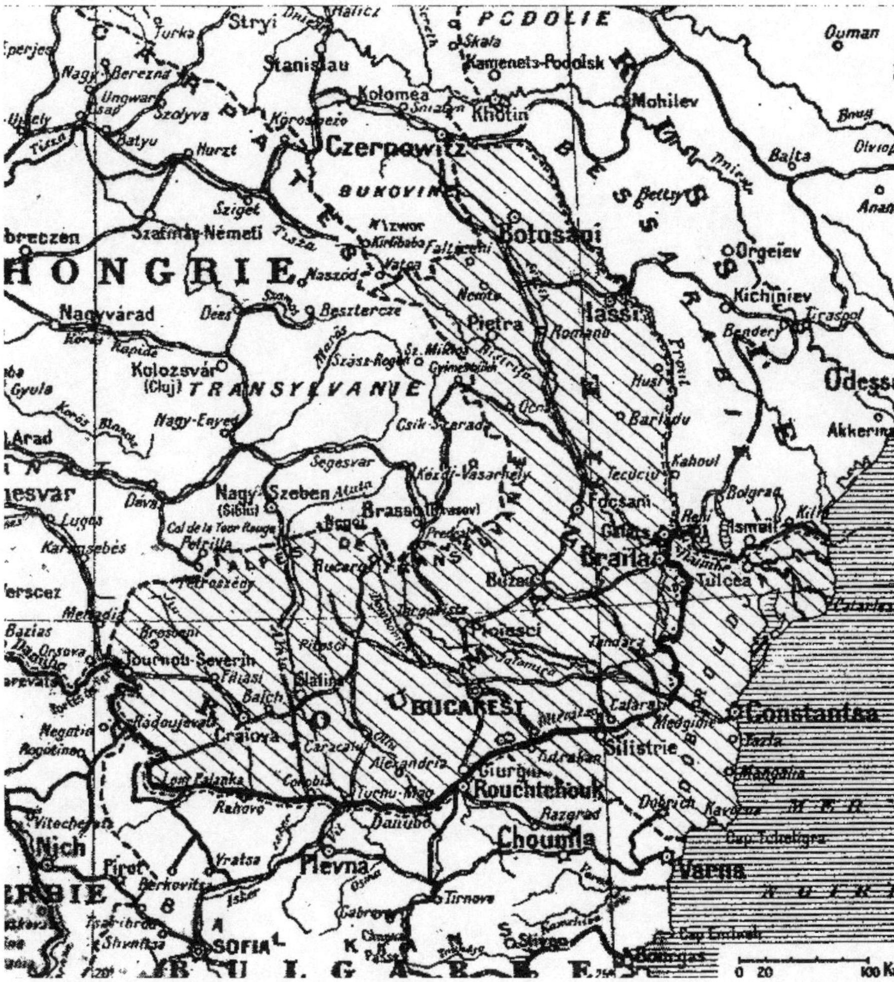

Map of Romania and adjoining countries

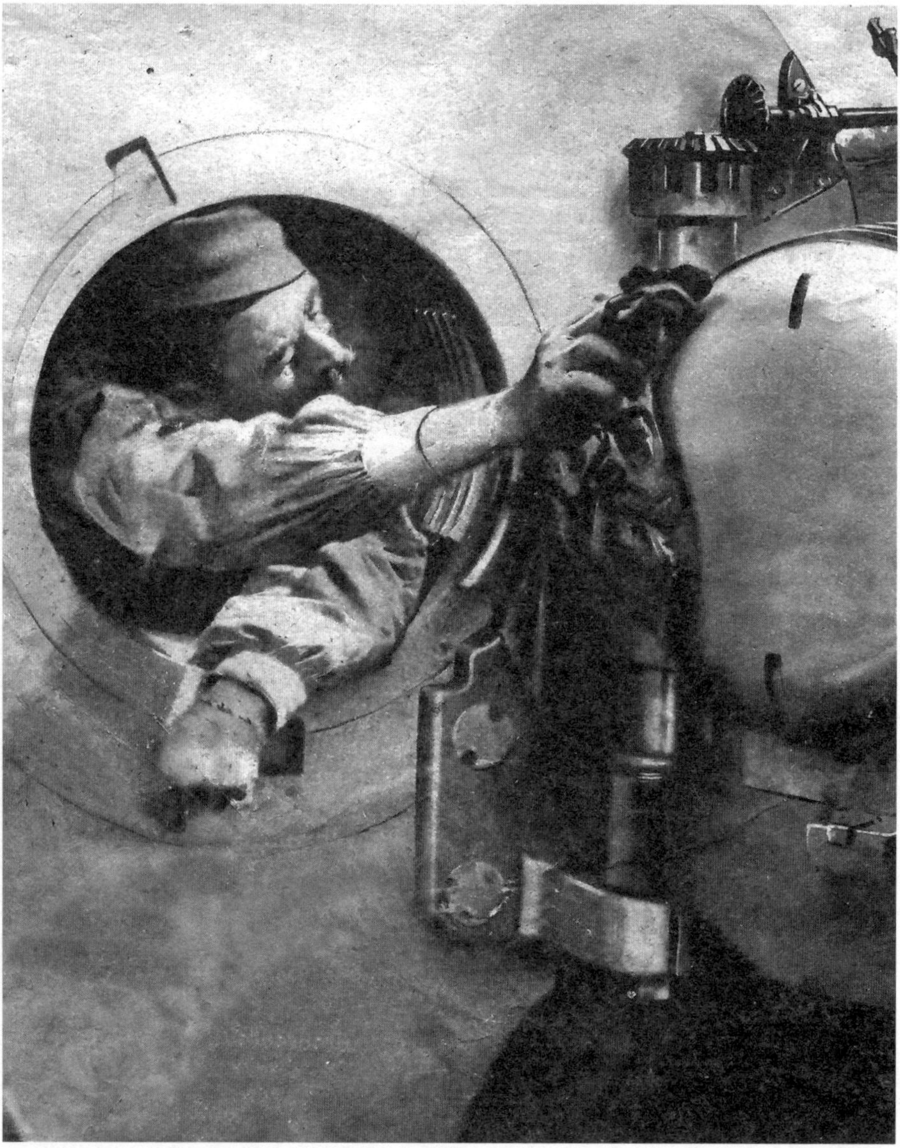

A man's body in the barrel of a cannon

This photograph gives an idea of the power and the dimensions of an 8" gun, where a man can enter the breech just to clean it.

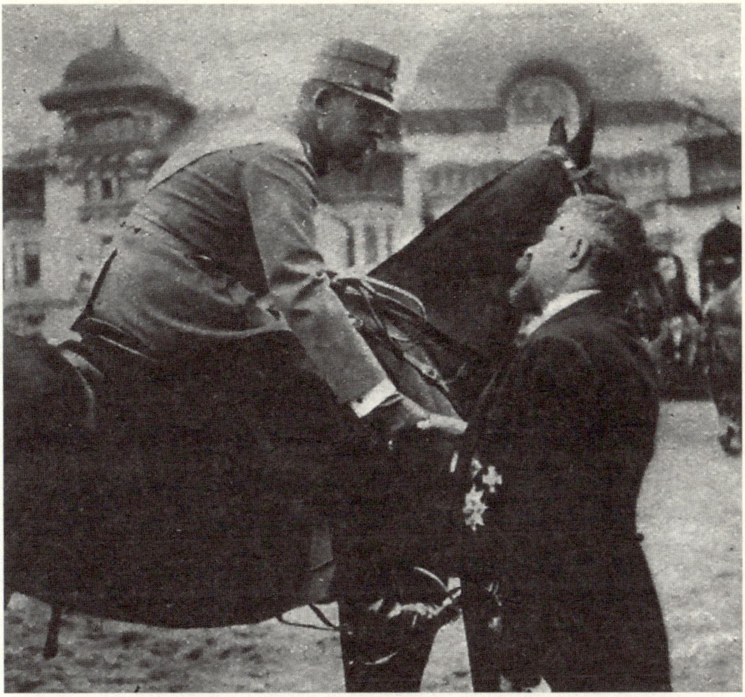

The King of Romania and Mr. Bratiano, Prime Minister of Romania

The King of Romania who has now declared war on Austria, Germany, Turkey and Bulgaria, and is effectively commanding his own armies.

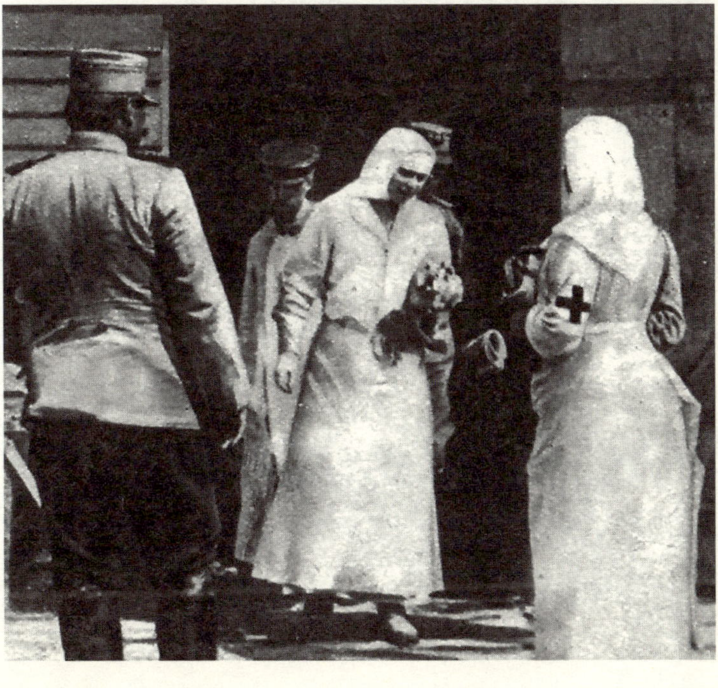

Queen Marie of Romania visiting a hospital

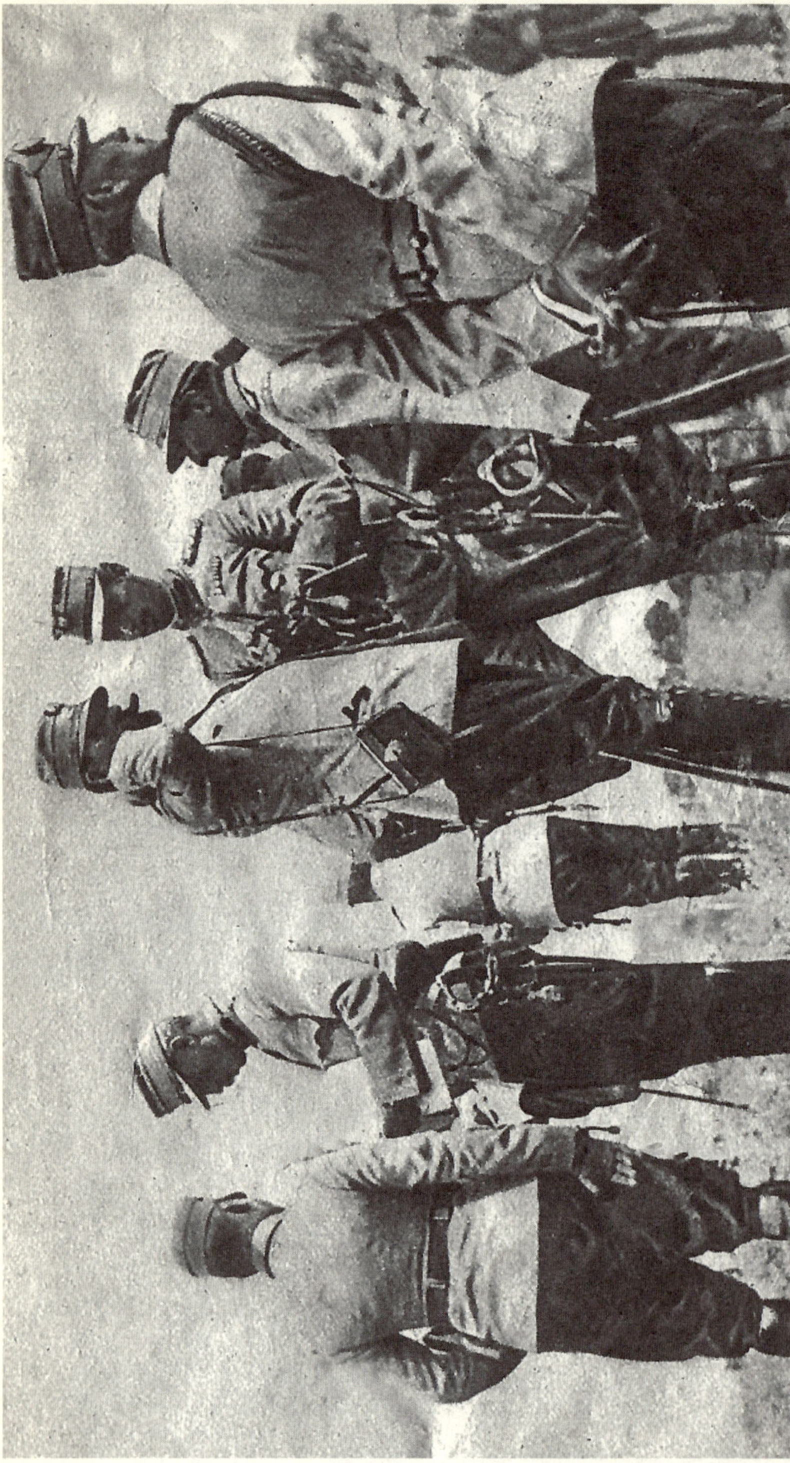

The sovereign of Romania in discussion about the war

King Ferdinand and his heir, Prince Carol in discussion with their generals.

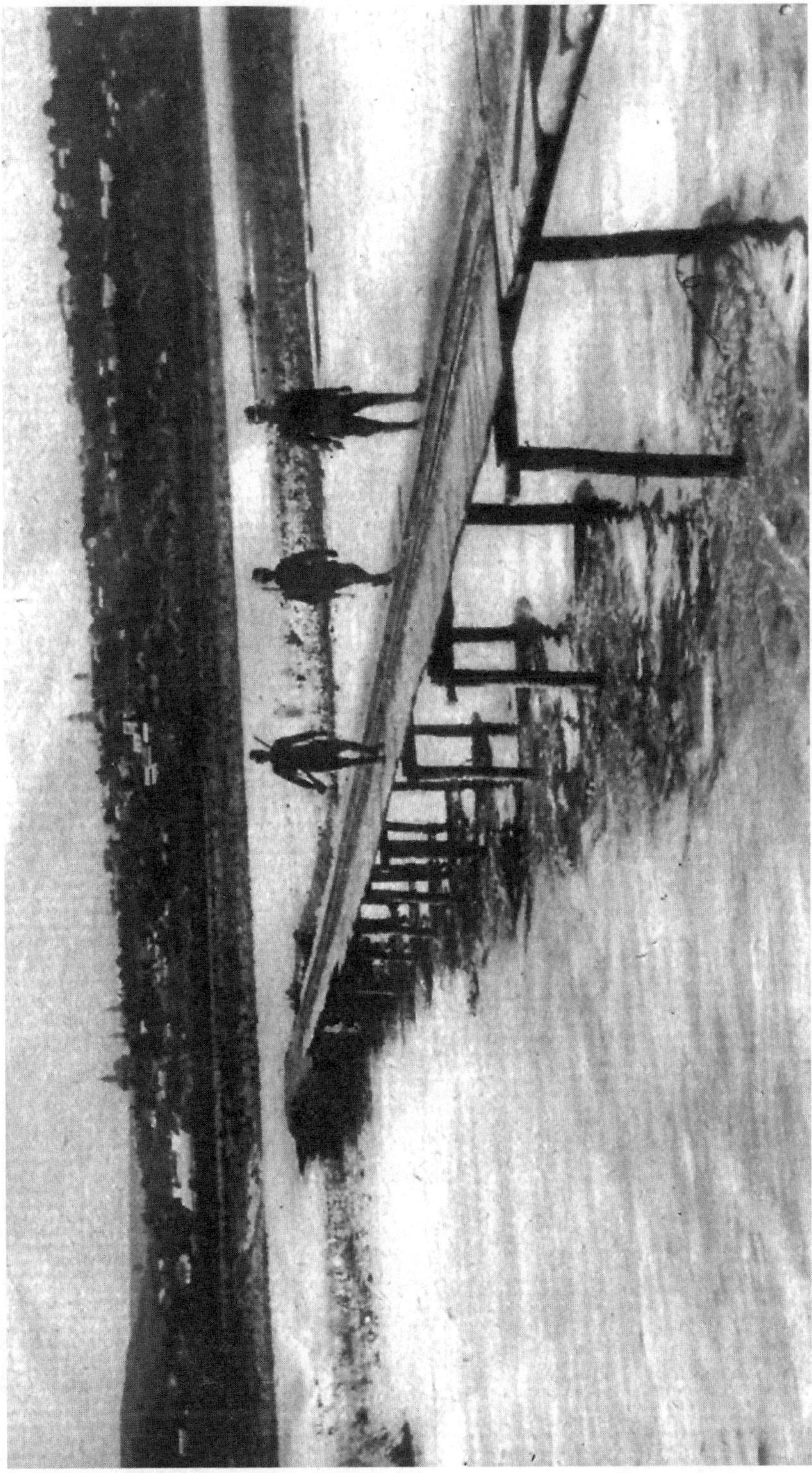

A temporary bridge over the Suceava

A temporary bridge built by the Russians over the Suceava river to Romania, replacing one burnt by Austrians.

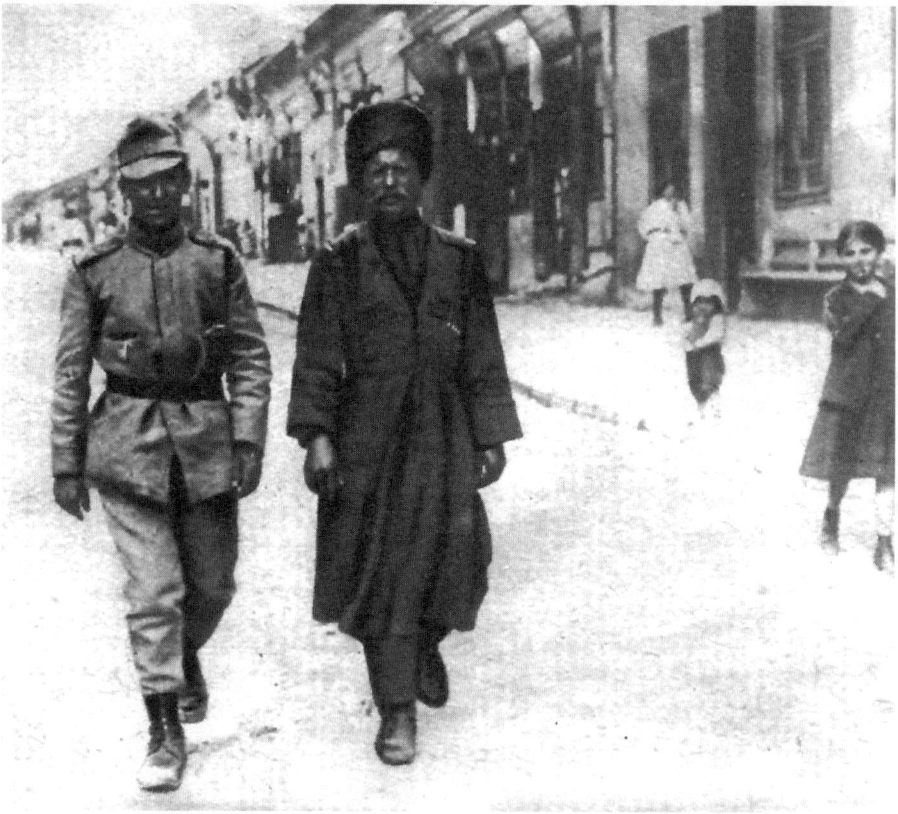

Romanian and Cossack soldiers in the city of Itcani on the border.

At the same time that Romanians cleared the Transylvanian Alps, Russians cleared the Romanian border and joined their new brothers-in-arms as allies.

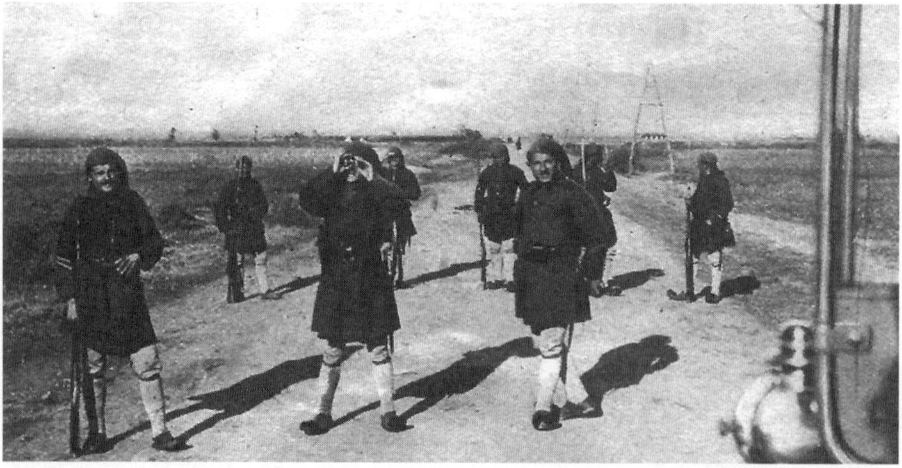

A Greek patrol close to Drama following the Bulgarian attack on Sérès

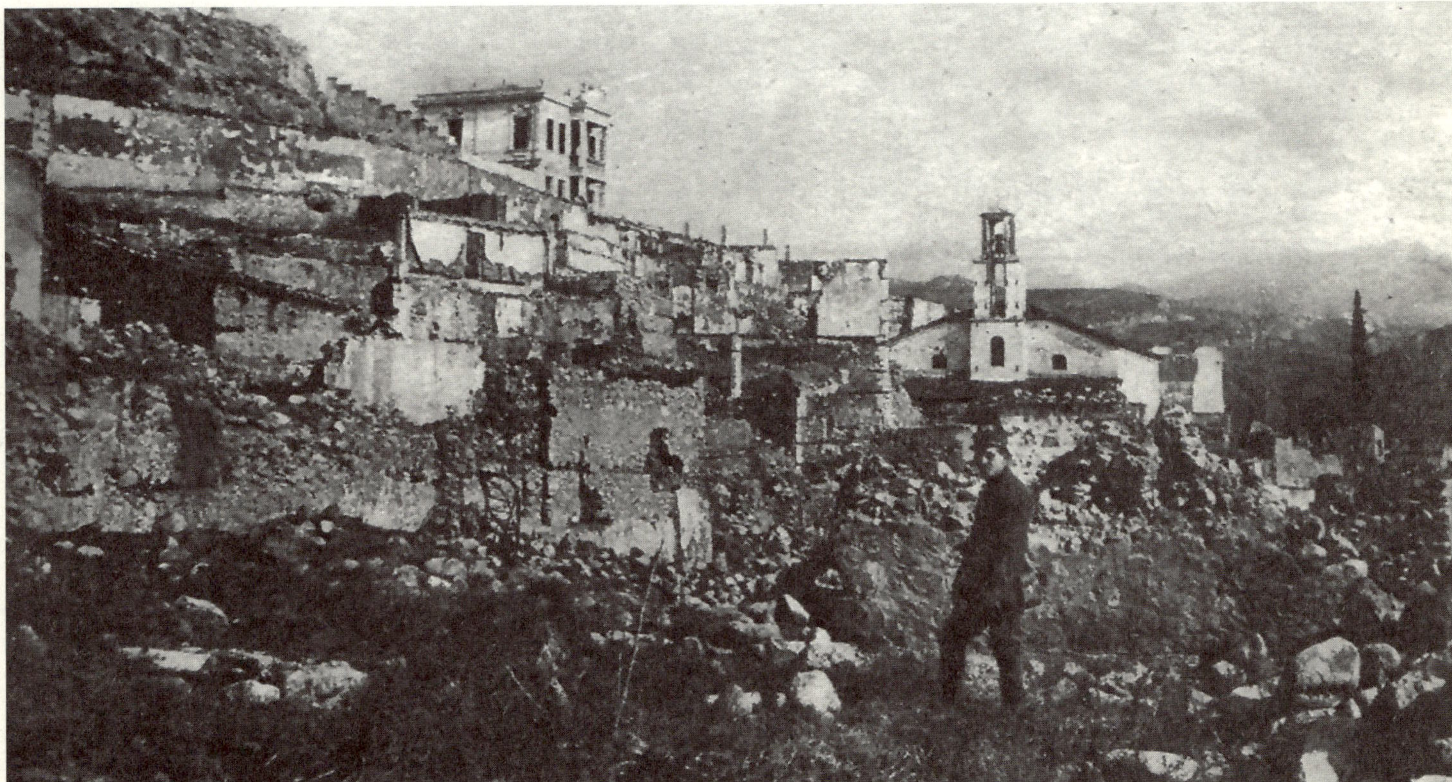

The Greek territory invaded by Bulgarians

Greece has had its territory invaded by the Bulgarian army, seizing Drama and Sérès. Everywhere Bulgarians entered without a fight except at Sérès where, against orders, Colonel Christodoulos defended with a mere handful of men. This photograph is of a district of Sérès.

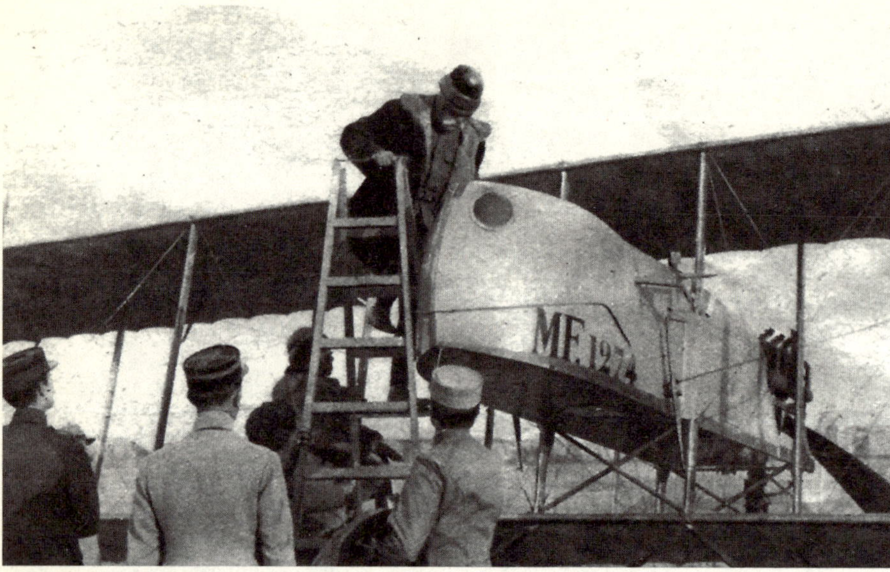

General Sarrail (France) takes his first flight

The chief of occupying forces in Macedonia before and after his first flight.

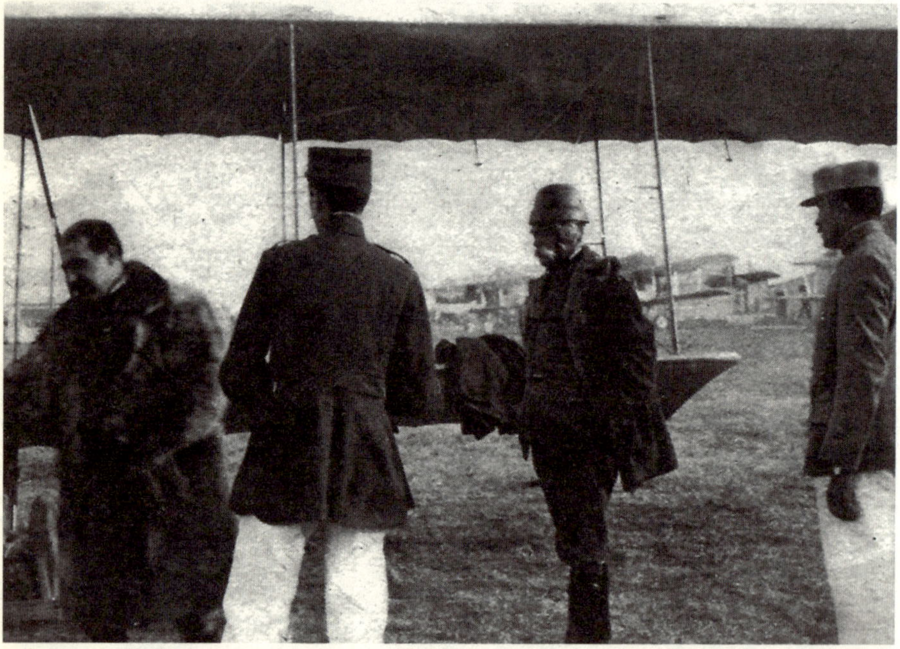

These photographs were taken some days before the Salonika insurrection (during which Greek volunteers asked for the right to fight with the Allies). This was not just a flight of fancy, but to see the region's defences for himself.

The Germanic attitude of the Greek government has created the revolution in Salonika

The Bulgarian advance on Sérès, in Macedonia, provoked such an emotion that on the 31 August a revolutionary uprising exploded in Salonika. A body of volunteers formed itself, claiming the right to act against the invading forces alongside their Allies until a temporary government was formed. The signal for the revolution was given at eleven o'clock in the morning by the state police (crétoise). Lieutenant Tsaconas called on his 300 policemen and urged them to arrange themselves under the orders of colonel Zymbrakakis. By five o'clock, these revolutionary troops had worked their way towards the allied areas.

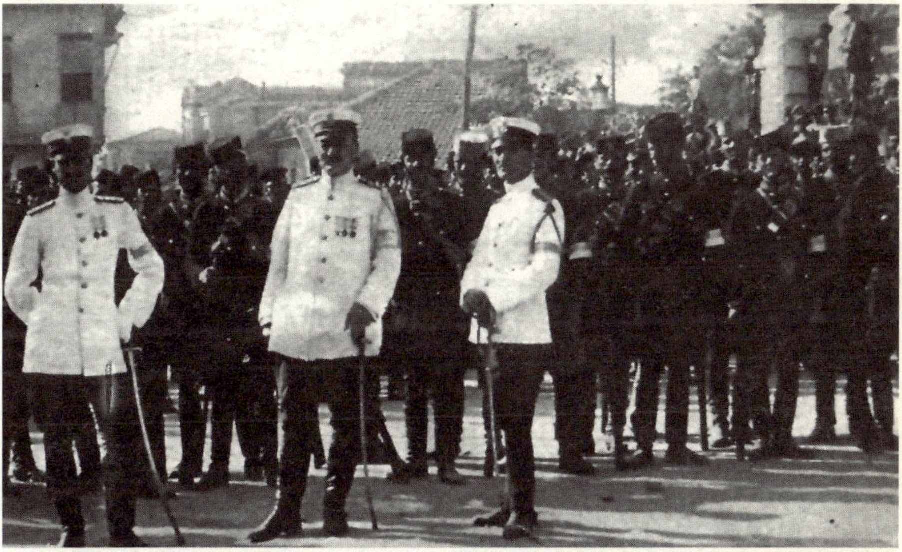

A crétois policeman. In the middle, lieutenant Tsaconas

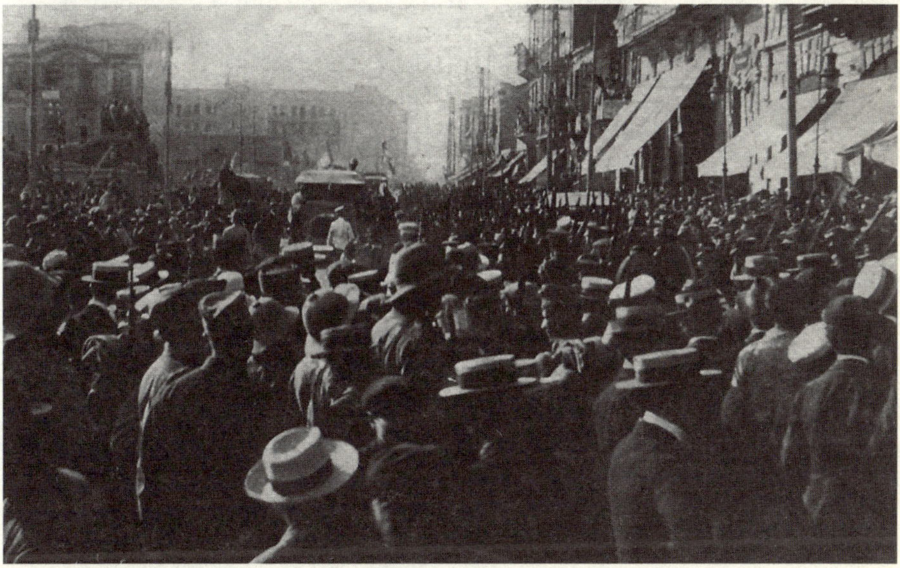

Troops and demonstrators clear Venizelos Street

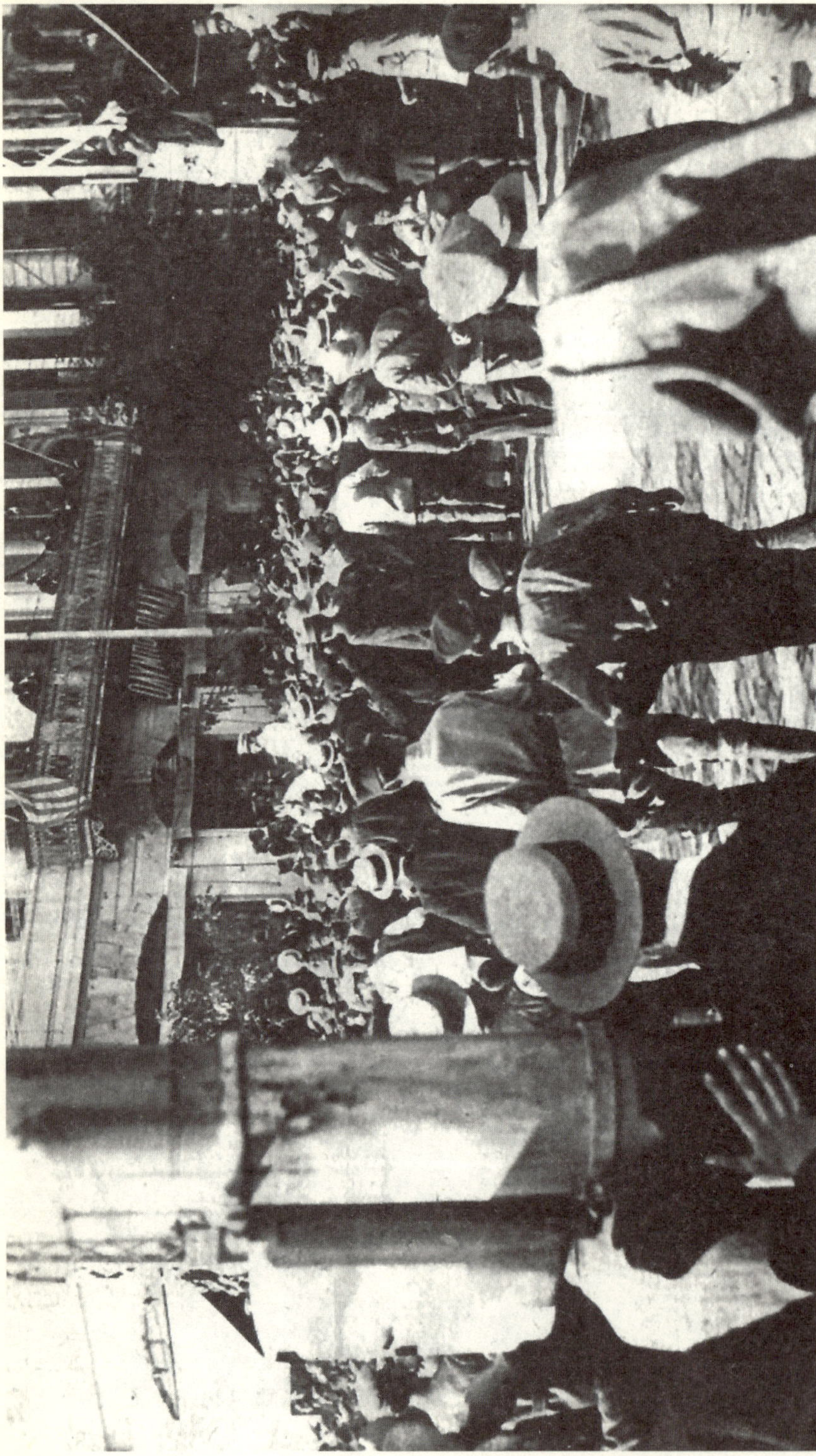

The victory parade

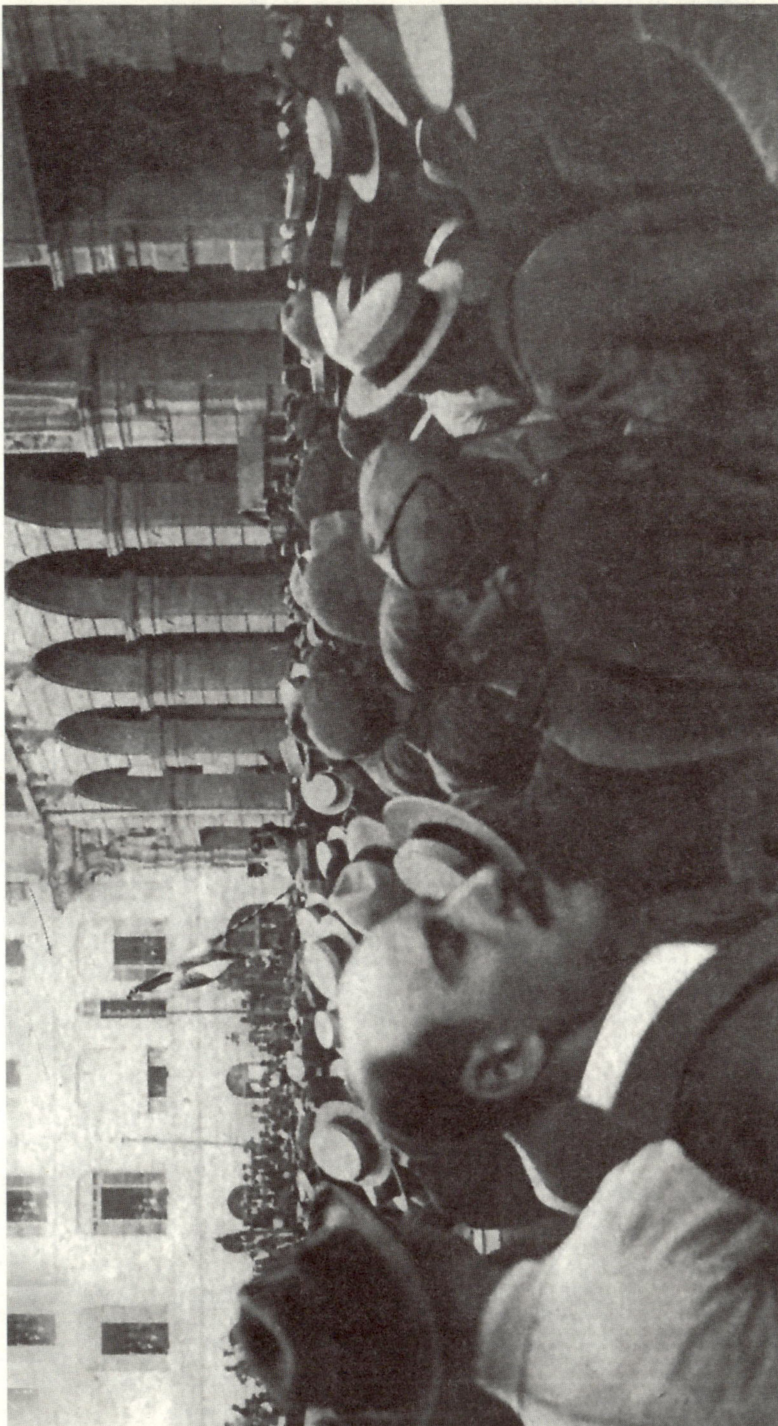

Colonel Zymbrakakis, on horseback,

With lieutenant Tsaconas, being harangued by the crowd in the General District. Officers can be seen in the windows of allied headquarters.

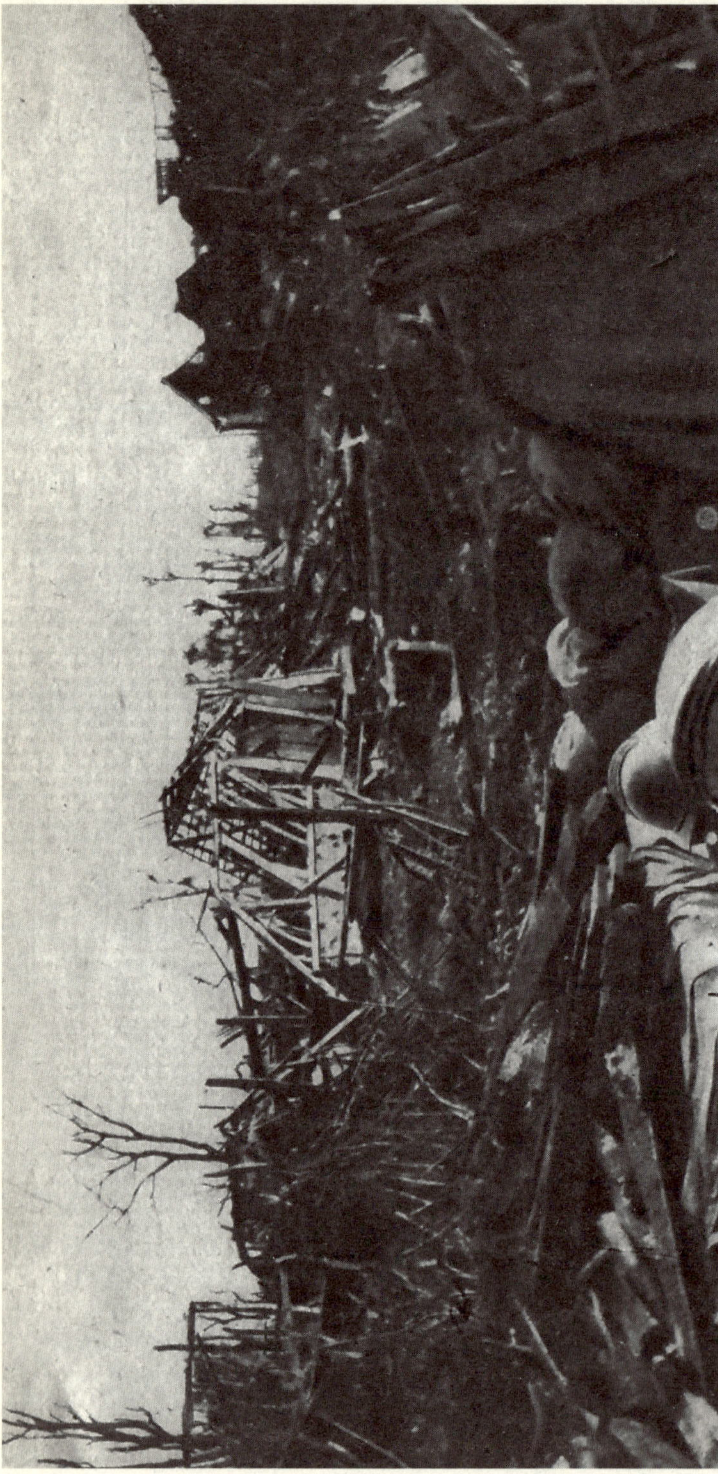

Maurepas (south west of Paris) taken in 12 days

Maurepas was significantly entrenched by the Germans who had earlier made a fortress of nearly every house. The village was taken in three stages, on the 12th, the 18th and the 24th of August, 1916, with the latter two being major battles. The town is now in ruins.

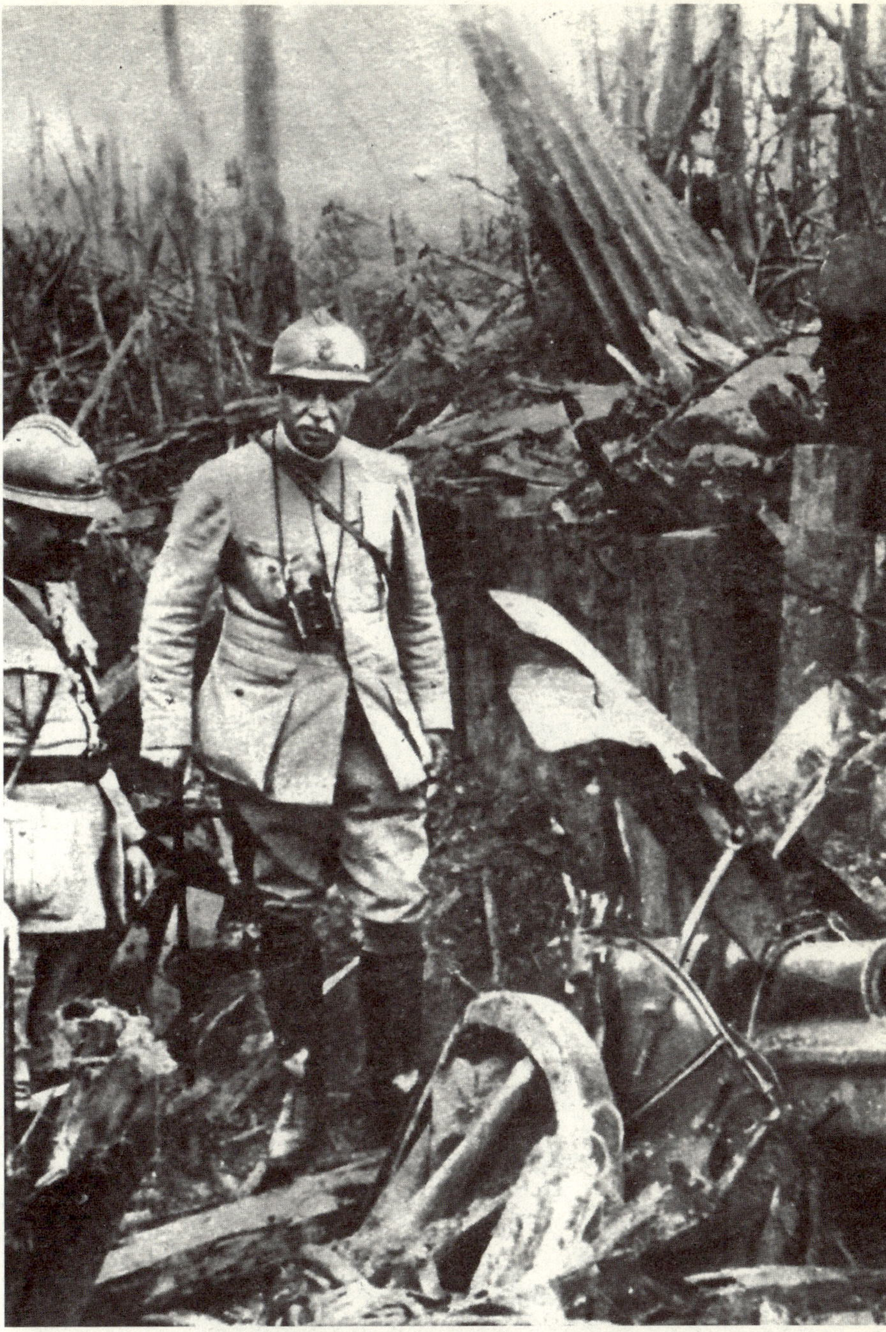

General Fayolle leading his troops into the newly taken areas

Sir Douglas Haig (UK) and General Fayolle (France) have led attacks against the Germans in Picardie. Here we see General Fayolle, in the middle of the photograph, examining the effects of our counter offensive on a hostile battery in a wood – later taken from the German artillery.

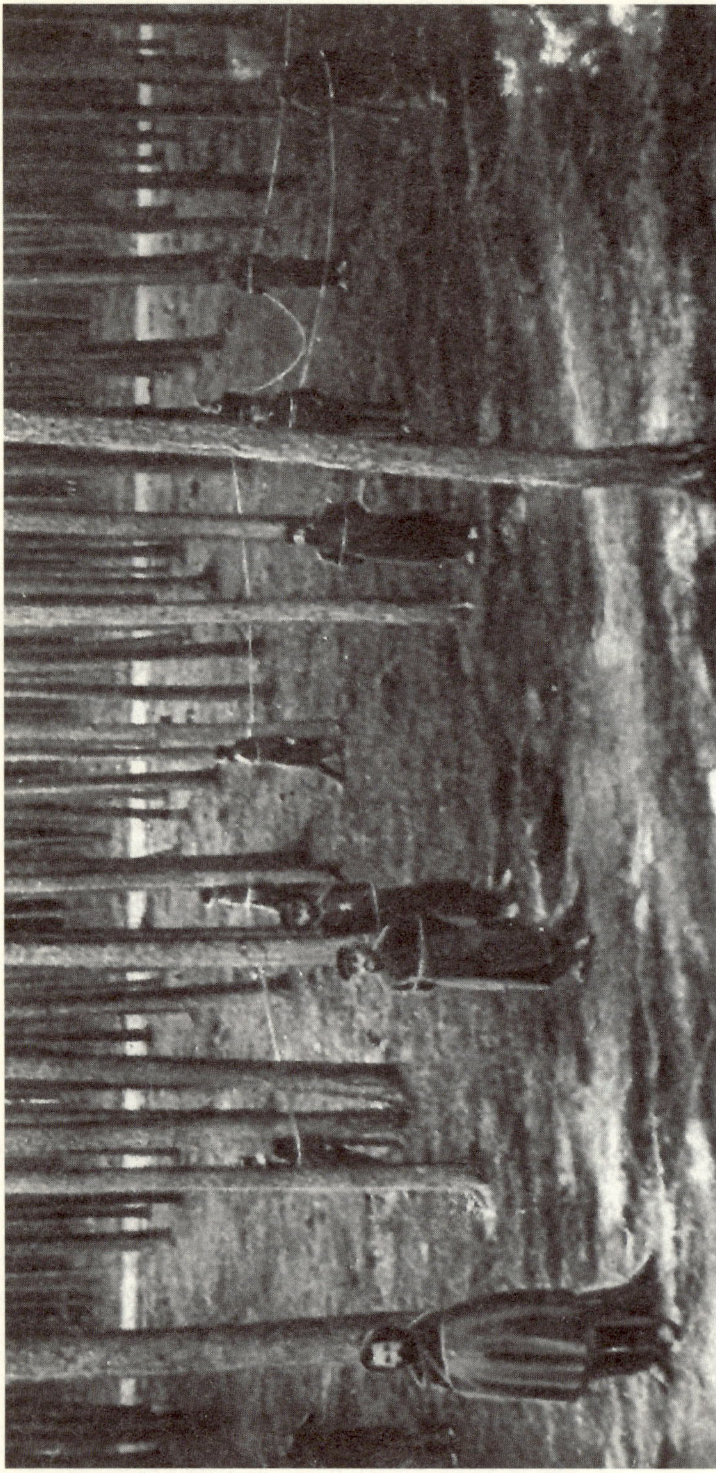

French prisoners in Bavaria

French prisoners tied to trees, in the rain, at a camp in Grafenwoehr (High Bavaria), perhaps for forgetting to salute non-commissioned officers or being a few minutes late for a roll-call. In the winter of 1915 they also kept them like this, half naked in the snow.

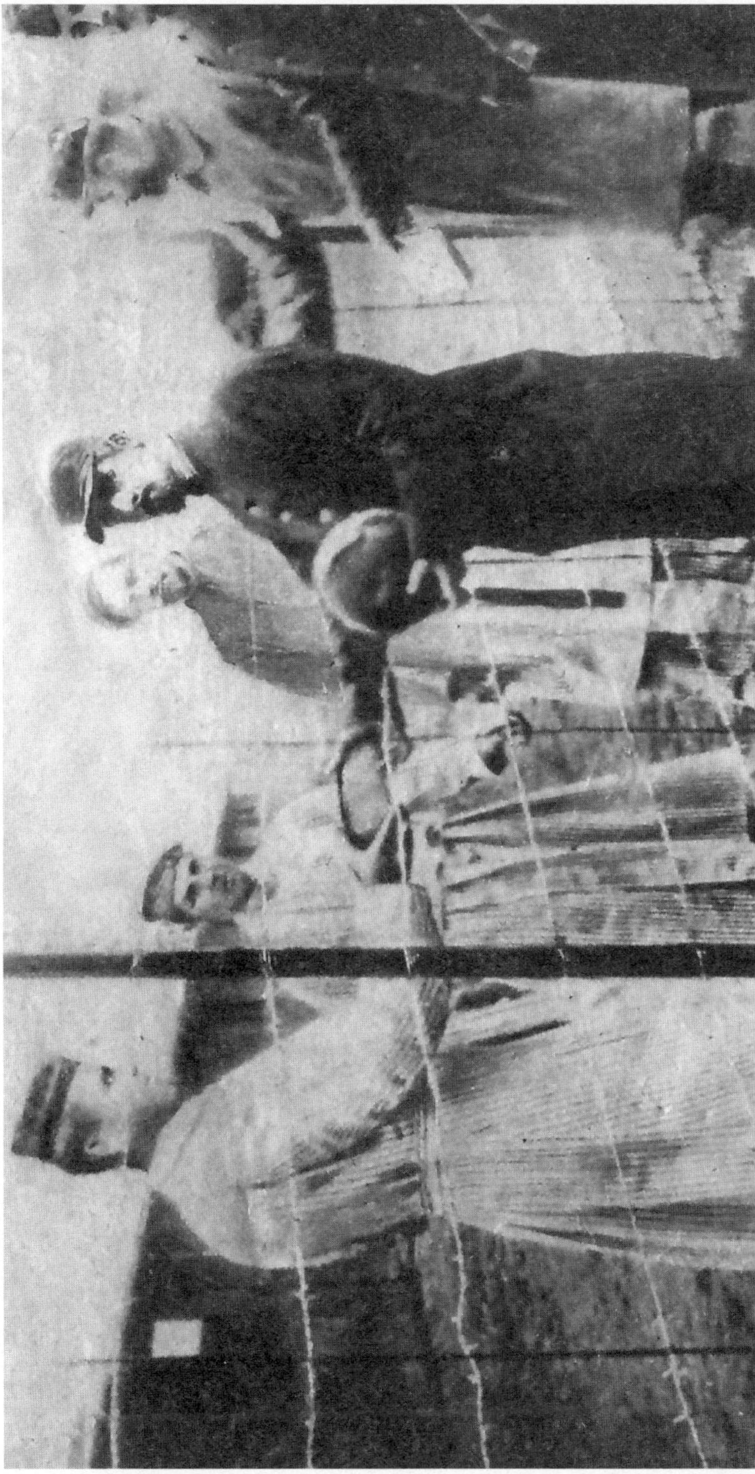

How French prisoners treat the wounded Germans

This photograph shows French prisoners at the same camp, sharing rations with Germans who had been injured near Verdun.

- NEWS REPORTS -

Thursday September 30, 1916

British troops have progressed toward Lens taking more prisoners. The Indian regiment have had success in Mesopotamia and now continue towards Baghdad.

Further Allied success in Champagne region, with 23,000 prisoners taken plus 79 guns. New groups of Germans are still surrendering under the continuous thrust against their positions. French troops have progressed in Artois reaching Vimy, taking 300 prisoners.

A crisis in Sofia, Bulgaria with Ministers Tontchef and Bakalof offering their resignations to the King.

Friday October 1, 1916

In Belgium, heavy French artillery supported the action of the British fleet against coastal batteries.

In Artois, little changes. French planes have bombed Guignicourt, Bazancourt, Warmeriville, Faverger bridge and Saint-Hilaire. Mr. Venizélos, Greek Prime Minister, has made an important speech about the return of their land, declaring that the situation was now serious and that a treaty should bind Greece with Serbia.

Saturday October 2, 1916

Progress in Artois - having defended two German counter attacks in the Givenchy wood and regained some ground, 61 prisoners are taken. A German counter attack has broken through in Champagne.

French guns with a greater range, have been moved forward by train to Vigneulles-les-Hattonchatel. The Germans are using long-range shells on Verdun. The French airship Alsace has bombed Amagne-Lucquy, and the railway stations at Attigny and Vouziers. It has now gone back to its base. On the Belgian front, artillery fighting continues.

The Russians consider that the offensive against them at Hindenburg failed completely. They have advanced their lines in Dwinsk, and the German newspapers acknowledge their progress. The situation has become very serious in the Balkans.

Sunday October 3, 1916

The British have dug in at their positions to the northwest of Hulluch. In Champagne, the German shellfire continues near Vedegrange. They are now using gas shells more frequently. French heavy artillery continually cooperates with the British fleet, shelling the Belgian coast.

Two strong German advances defeated in Lorraine. Sixty-five French planes bombed the railway stations of Vouziers and Challeranges.

The Russians advance along the whole northern front. They have taken back areas south of Dwinsk and have pushed back the Germans beyond the Chara, continually gathering momentum. The Italians are fighting a battle for the possession of Tolmino. The Bulgarians are concentrating on the Serbian and Greek borders.

Monday October 4, 1916

British troops have retaken several trenches in northern France. Heavy shelling continues on both sides south of the Somme, around Beaufort and Bouchoir. The Bulgarian government has published a statement stating that the British-French intervention in Macedonia will precipitate an explosion of the conflict.

In Champagne, a German counterattack against the positions gained to the north of Mesnil, again using gas shells. French artillery has silenced several enemy batteries. Fighting continues in Argonne and the Vosges.

A Russian squadron has bombed Zunguldak in the Black Sea.

Tuesday October 5, 1916

The struggle continues in Artois and everywhere the German positions have been held despite counter attacks. The German use of gas shells continues in the Champagne region. French planes dropped 400 shells on the station at Sablons, Metz.

The Russians strengthened their position on the whole Oriental front, destroying enemy cannons and capturing prisoners. Russia has requested that the cabinet in Sofia recall their foreign diplomats.

Wednesday October 6, 1916

Heavy shelling on both sides along the whole front to the north and east of Arras. The French airship Alsace was captured by the Germans in the meadows at Rethel. French planes are operating from the fields near Péronne, south of Arras.

Mr. Venizélos, although having the majority, has resigned following an interview with King Constantine of Greece.

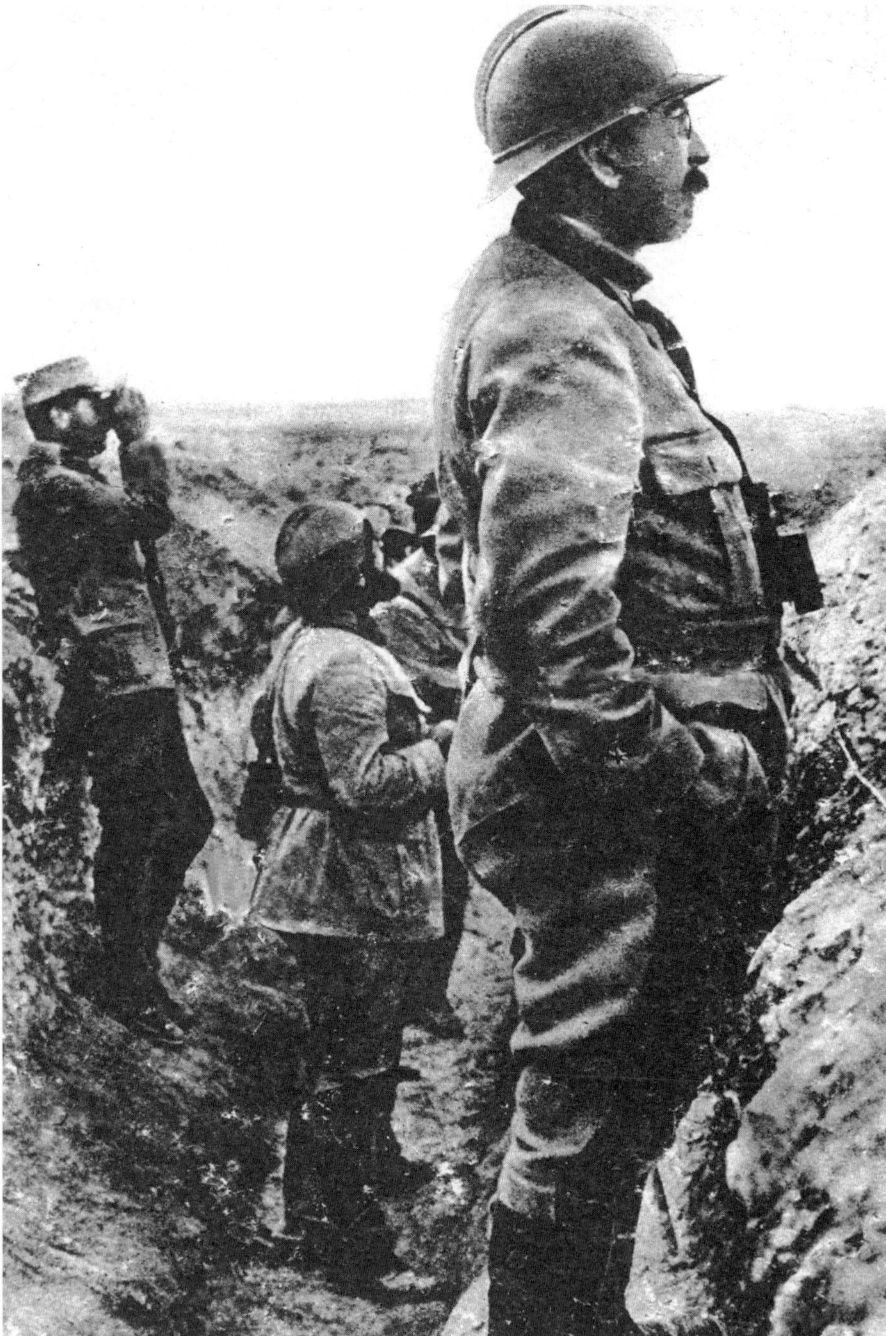

A General Controls artillery action

This photograph was been taken on the morning of 25th September during the assault on Main de Massiges, showing French generals observing the artillery action.

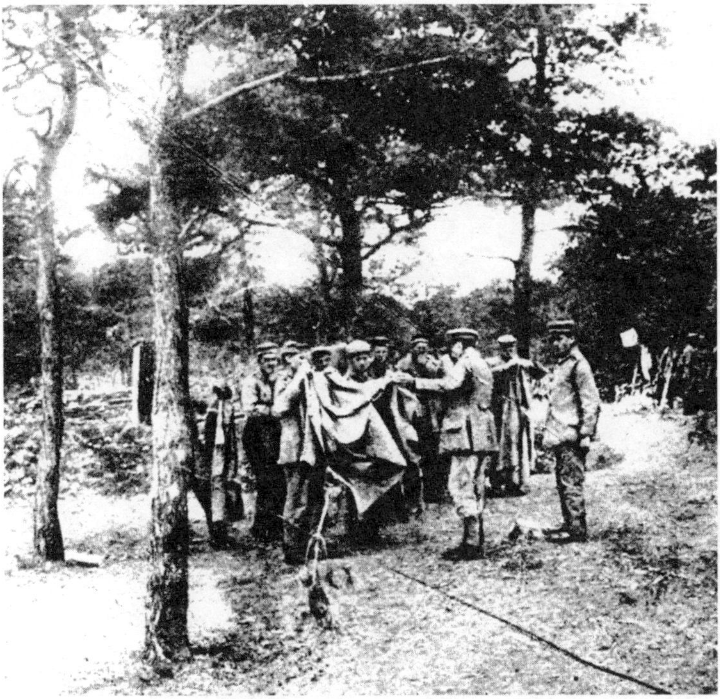

September - behind the German lines in the Champagne region

Distribution of overcoats and winter uniforms near Perthes, Artois.

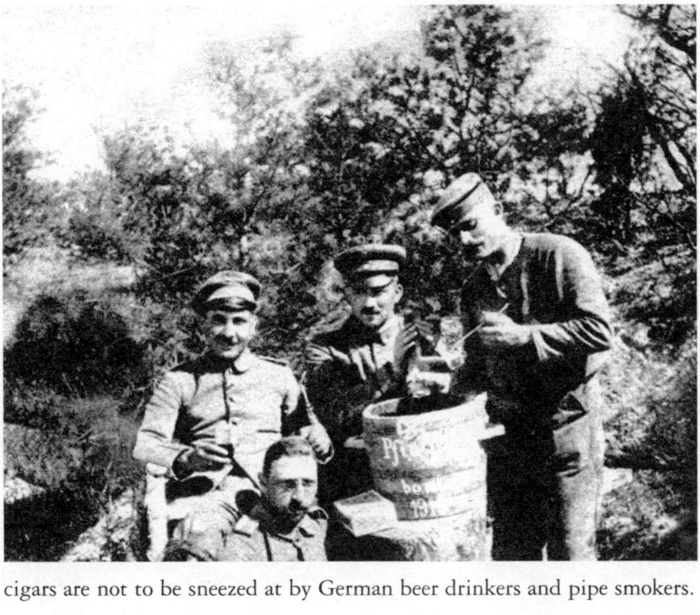

An off duty afternoon

Wine and cigars are not to be sneezed at by German beer drinkers and pipe smokers.

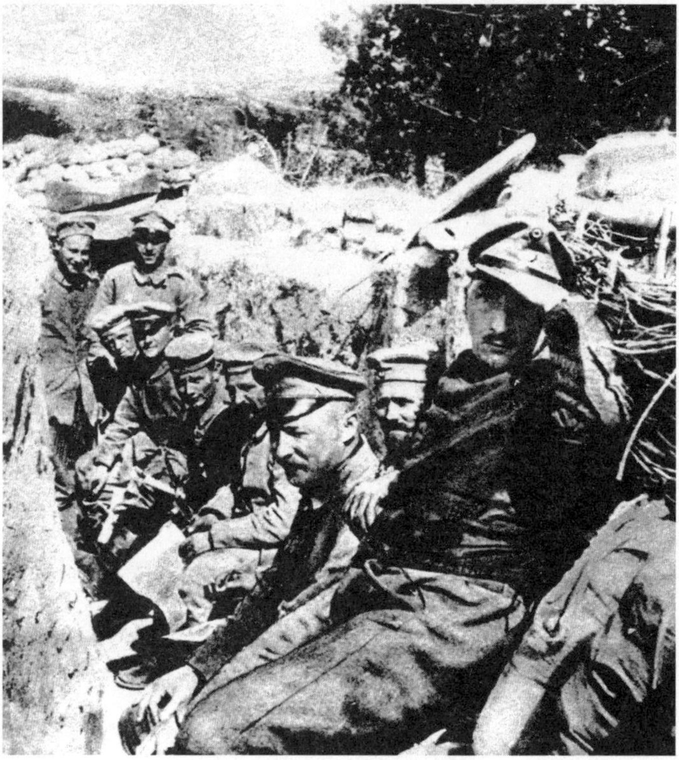

View of the German trenches

A view of conditions behind the German front lines.

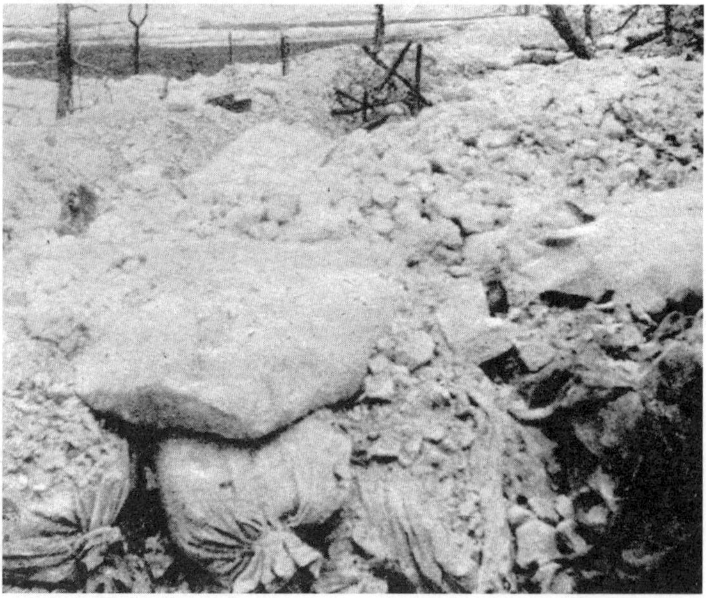

A view towards the French front line in the Perthes region.

Taken from behind the German line in the chalky soil of the Champagne region.

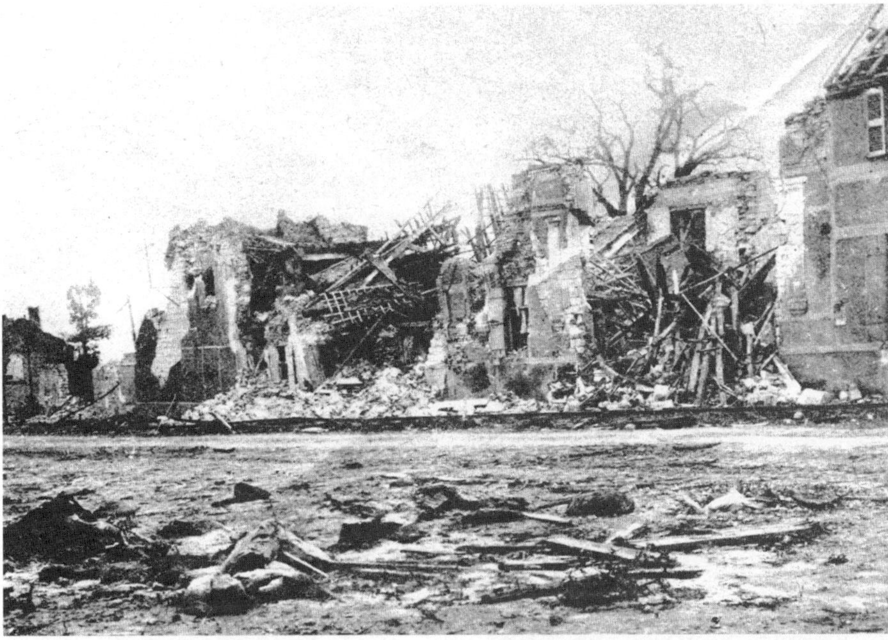

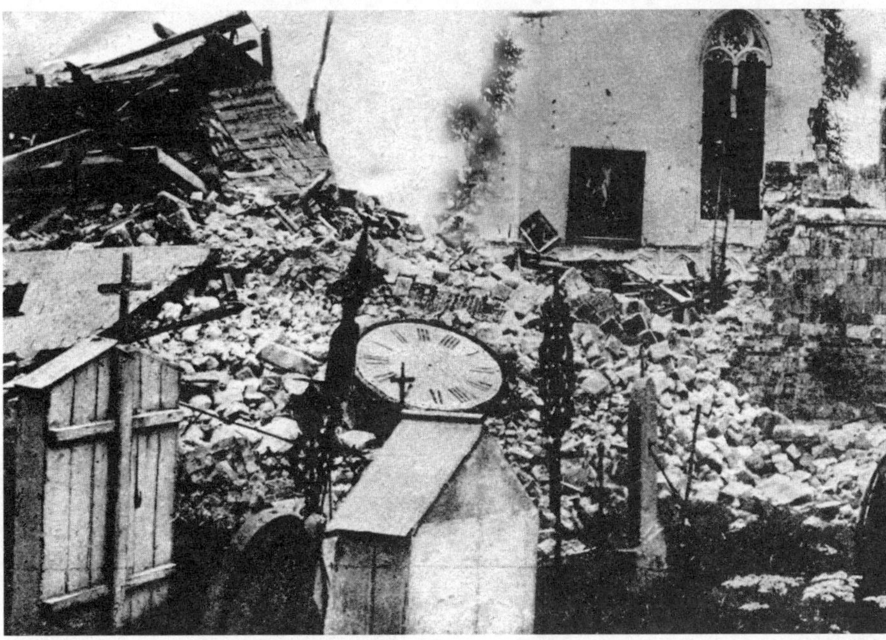

The effect of allied fire on the enemy positions

These German photographs show the effect of allied artillery at Vimy, in Artois. Vimy was an objective in the big offensive of 25th to 30th September and was one of the enemy's strongest positions.

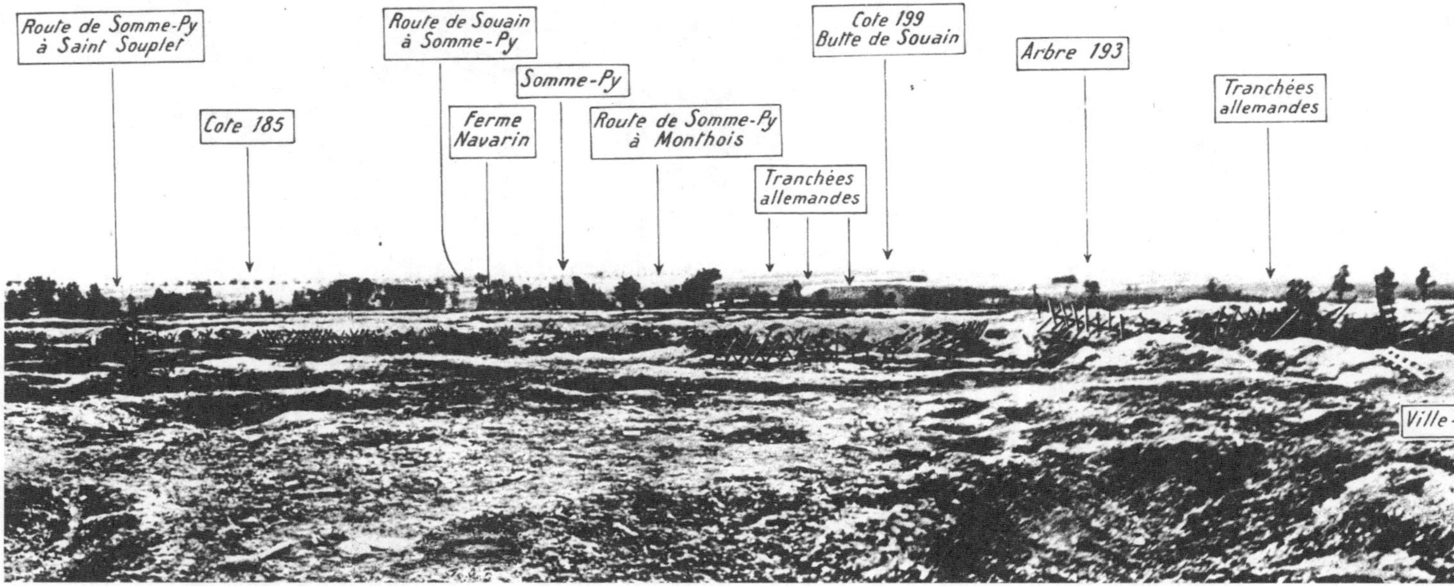

The battlefield for our offensive of September 25th

The ground taken from the Germans in Champagne, in the foreground - shell craters and the new line of trenches.

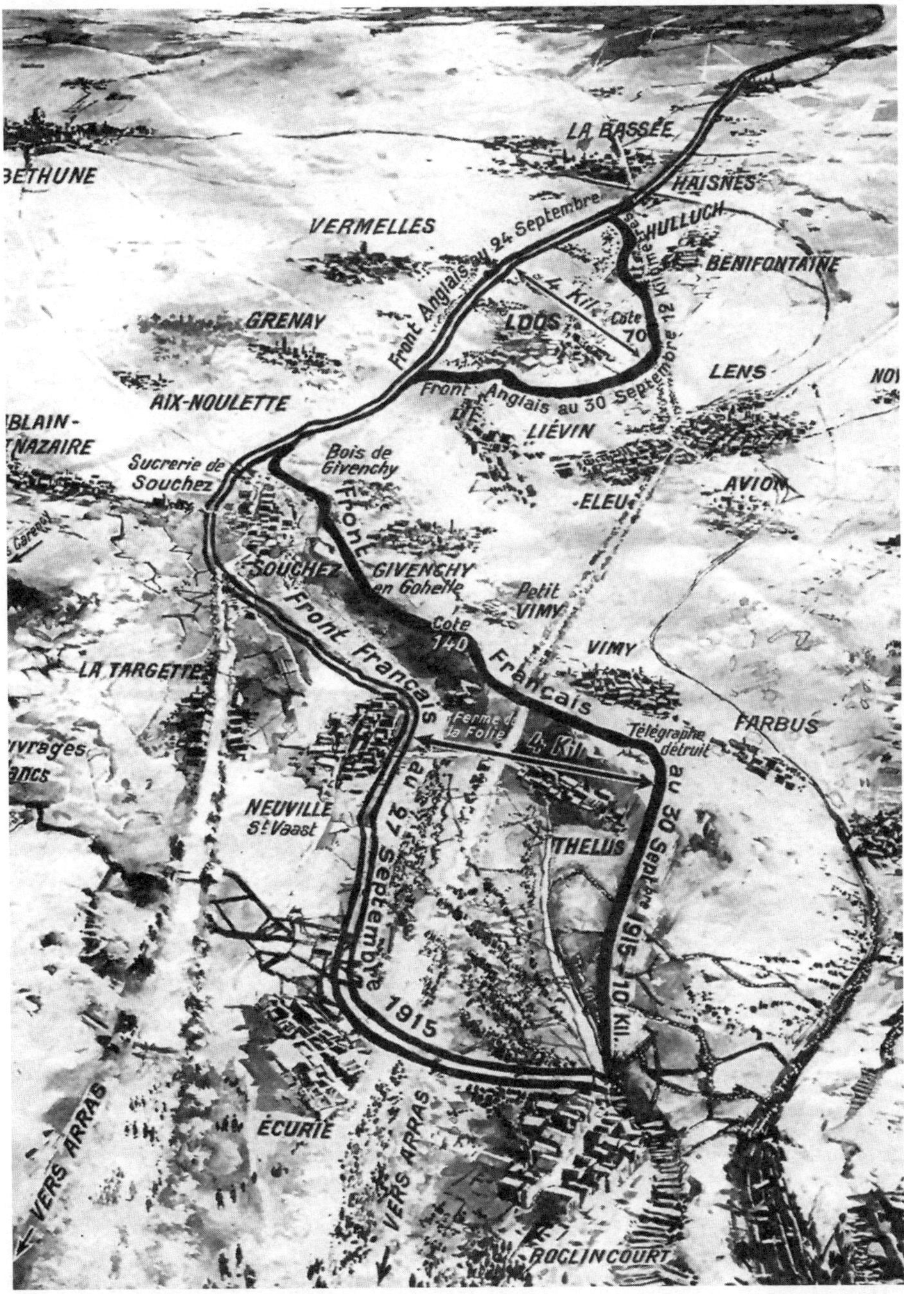

The Allied advance on the Artois front

A map showing the land taken by the British and French troops. In two places, an 11 kilometre front advanced by 4 kilometres, the British near Lens and the French at Vimy.

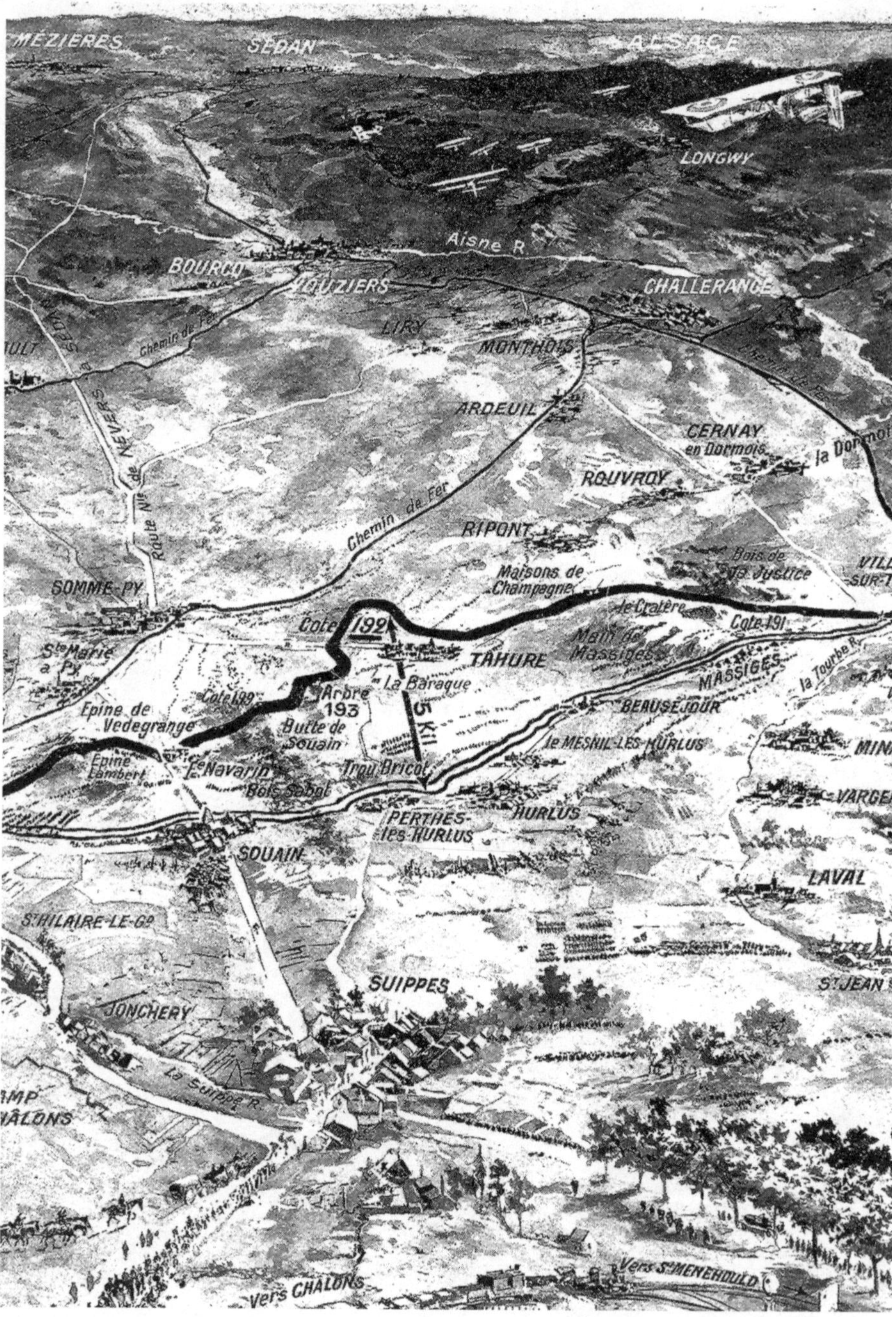

The French advance in the Champagne region

A map showing the advance of 6th October along a 25 kilometre front, gaining, at most, 5 kilometres (3 miles).

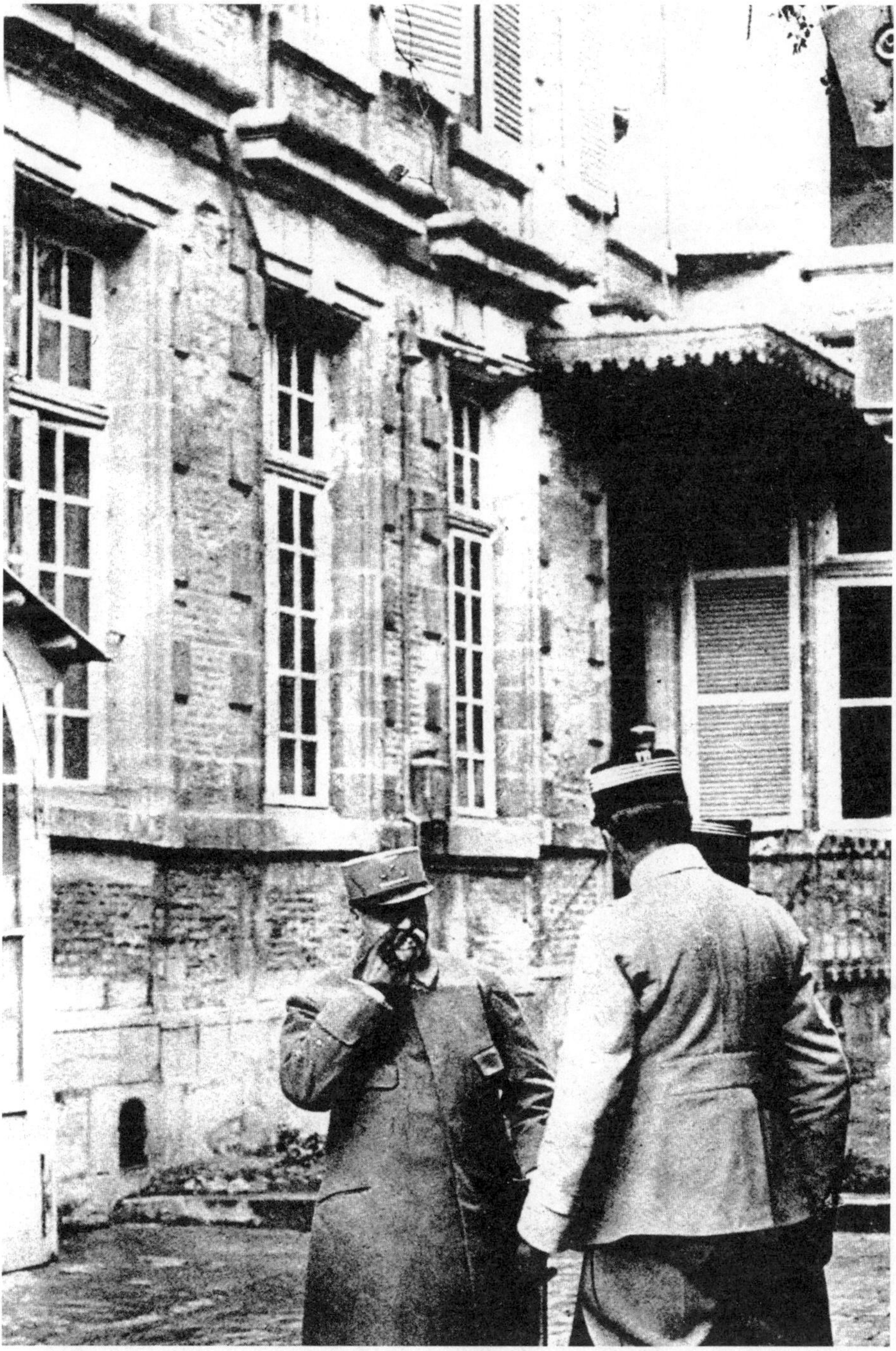

The general who directed the attack in Champagne

General Castelnau with officers on September 24th, in the courtyard of the old hotel that had become their temporary district headquarters prior to the offensive.

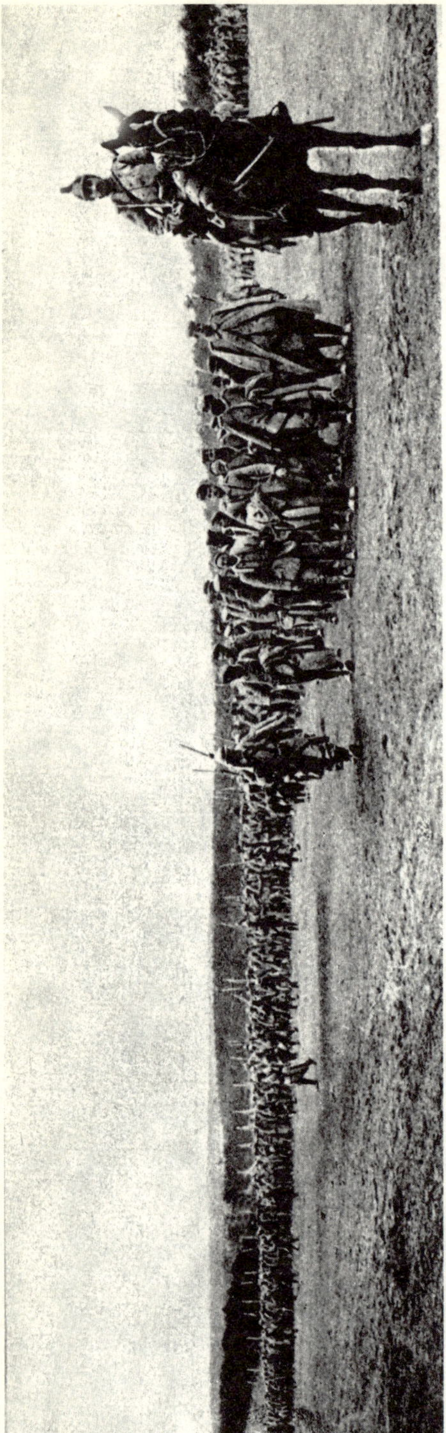

Long lines of German prisoners

There are some 3,000 prisoners in this photograph who have arrived in Auve, from Chalons and Suippes.

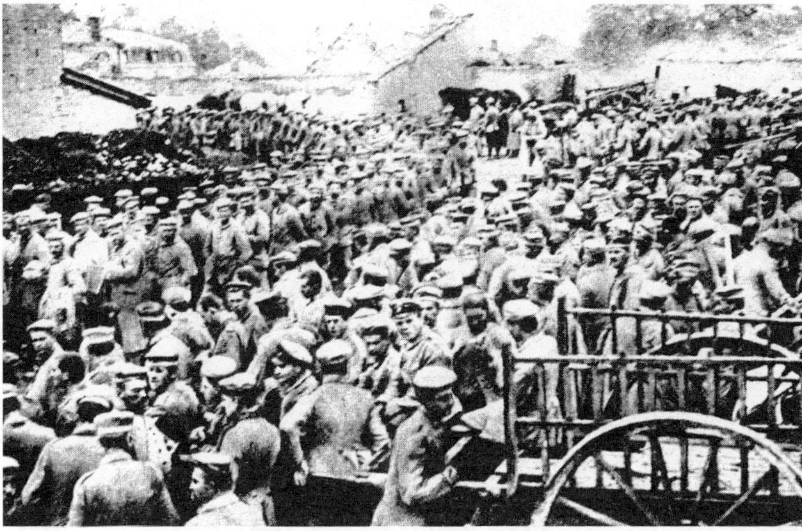

A prisoner of war camp

The camp at St. Etienne-du-Temple, near Chalons, gives an impression of the allied success.

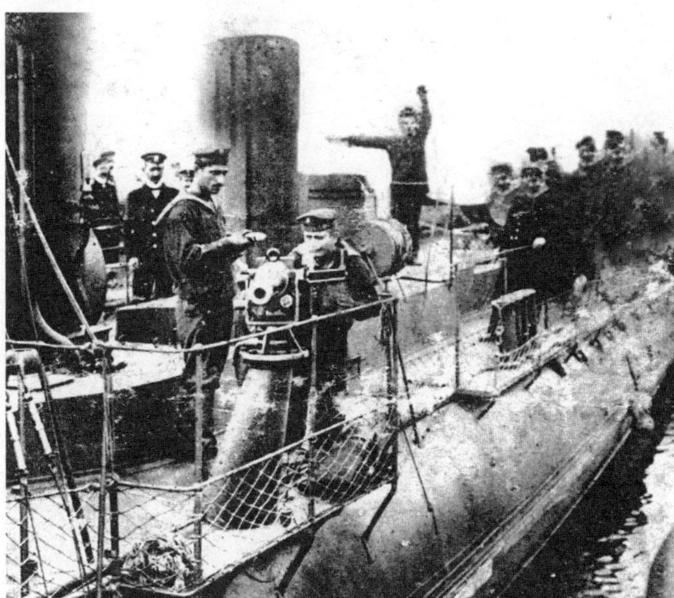

Bulgarian marines on a submarine

The Bulgarian fleet only includes a gunboat and six submarines.

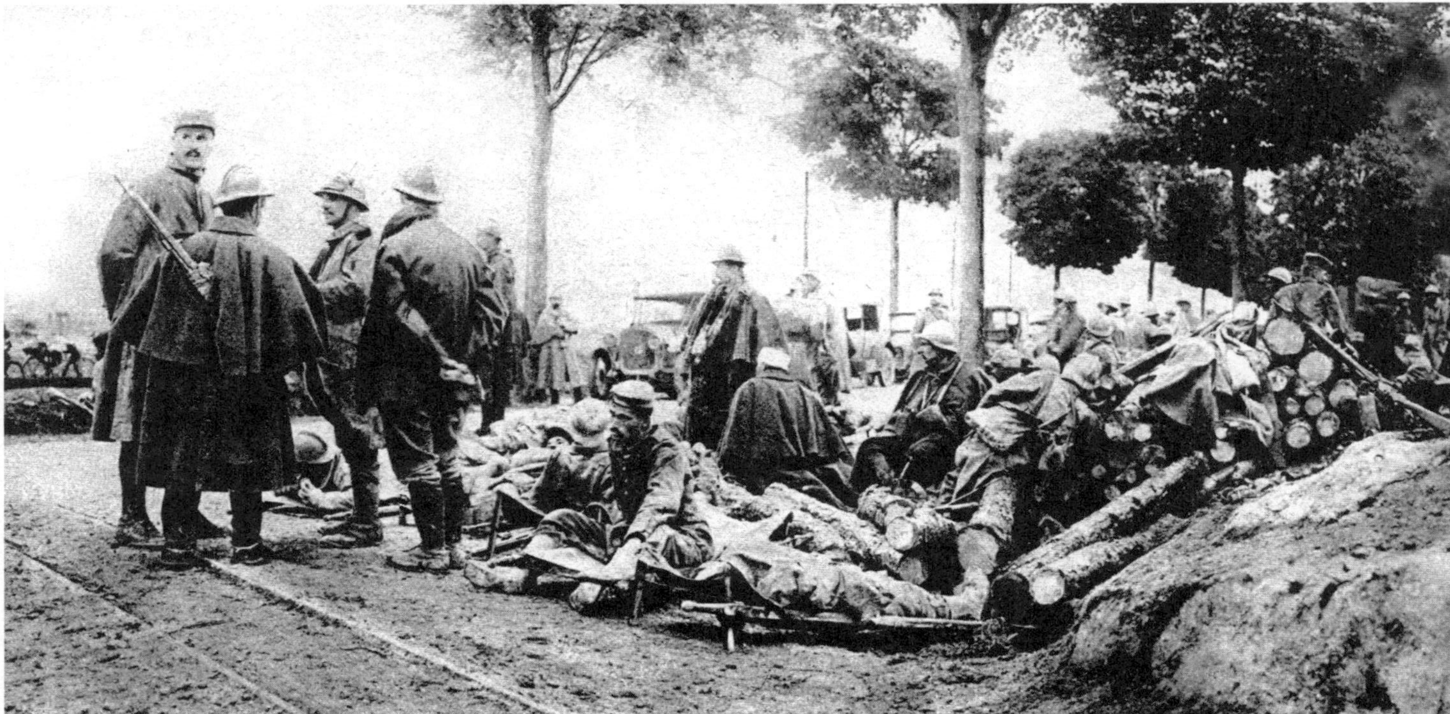

The wounded waiting for transport

Injured French and Germans wait together for ambulances to transport them on the road to Auve.

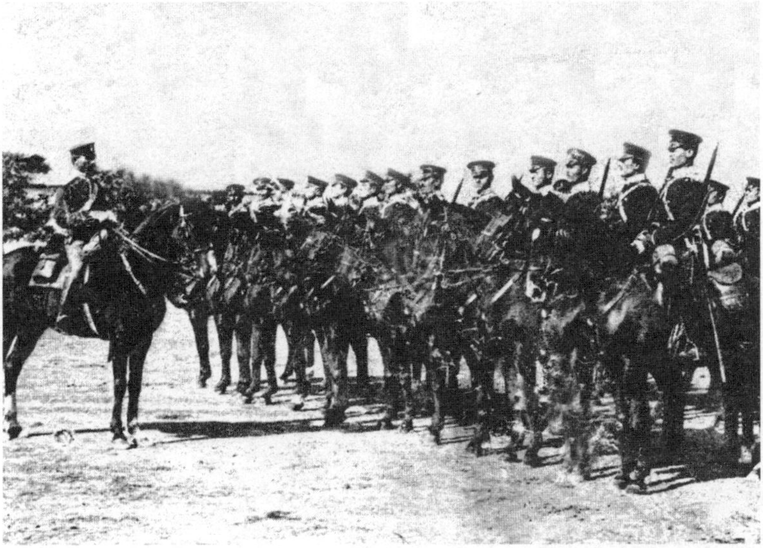

Bulgarian troops

The military draft is obligatory in Bulgaria. It begins at twenty and ends at twenty-six years of age. The army consists of 400,000 men. These photos show members of the Cavalry and Infantry regiments.

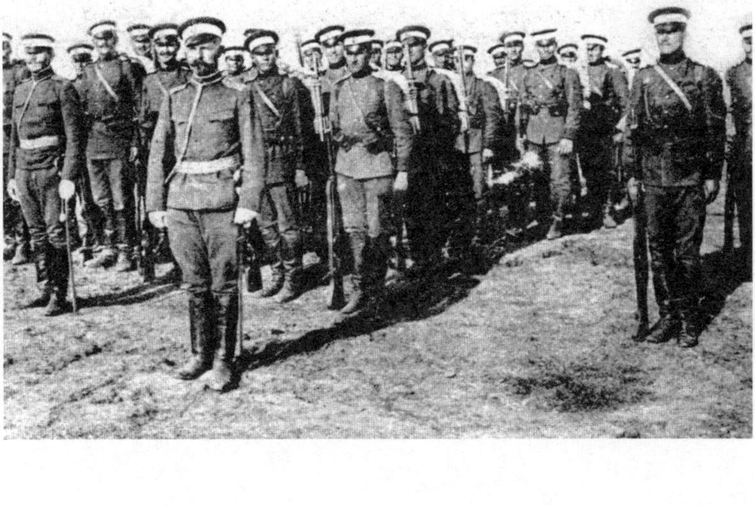

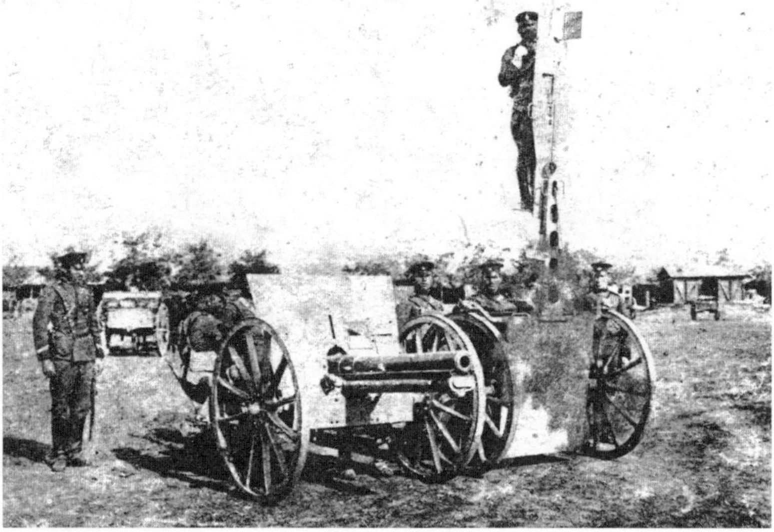

A Bulgarian light artillery company.

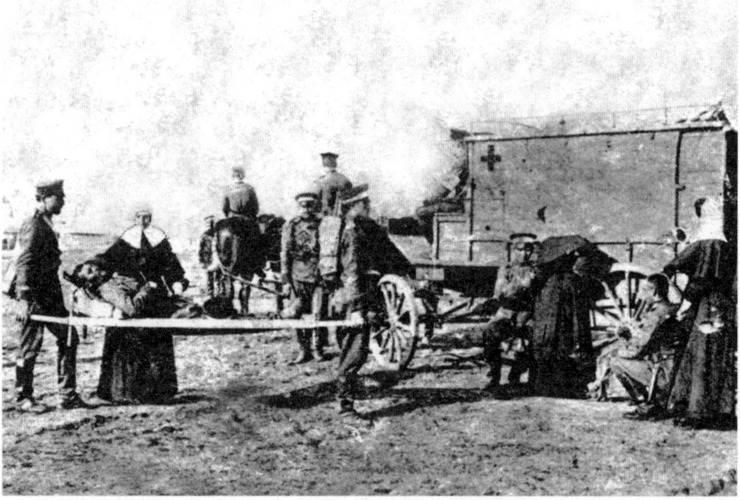

A Bulgarian ambulance with medical staff.

Casualties of the First World War

The First World War lasted for four years and three months. It began on August 4, 1914 and ended on November 11, 1918. It involved sixty sovereign states, overthrew four Empires (German Empire, Hapsburg Empire, Turkish Empire, Russian Empire), gave birth to seven new nations, and took ten million combatant lives. Millions more were wounded or reported missing and the cost was approximately £35,000 million (£769,000 million = 2003).

Country, including overseas protectorates	Known dead	Seriously wounded	Otherwise wounded	Prisoners or missing
Russia	2,762,064	1,000,000	3,950,000	2,500,000
Germany	1,611,104	1,600,000	2,183,143	772,522
France	1,427,800	700,000	2,344,000	453,500
Austria-Hungary	911,000	850,000	2,150,000	443,000
Great Britain	807,451	617,714	1,441,394	64,907
Serbia	707,343	322,000	28,000	100,000
Italy	507,160	500,000	462,196	1,359,000
Turkey	436,924	107,772	300,000	103,731
Romania	339,117	200,000	unknown	116,000
Belgium	267,000	40,000	100,000	10,000
United States	107,284	43,000	148,000	4,912
Bulgaria	101,224	300,000	852,339	10,825
Greece	15,000	10,000	30,000	45,000
Portugal	4,000	5,000	12,000	200
Japan	300	unknown	907	3
Totals	**9,998,771**	**6,295,512**	**14,002,039**	**5,983,600**

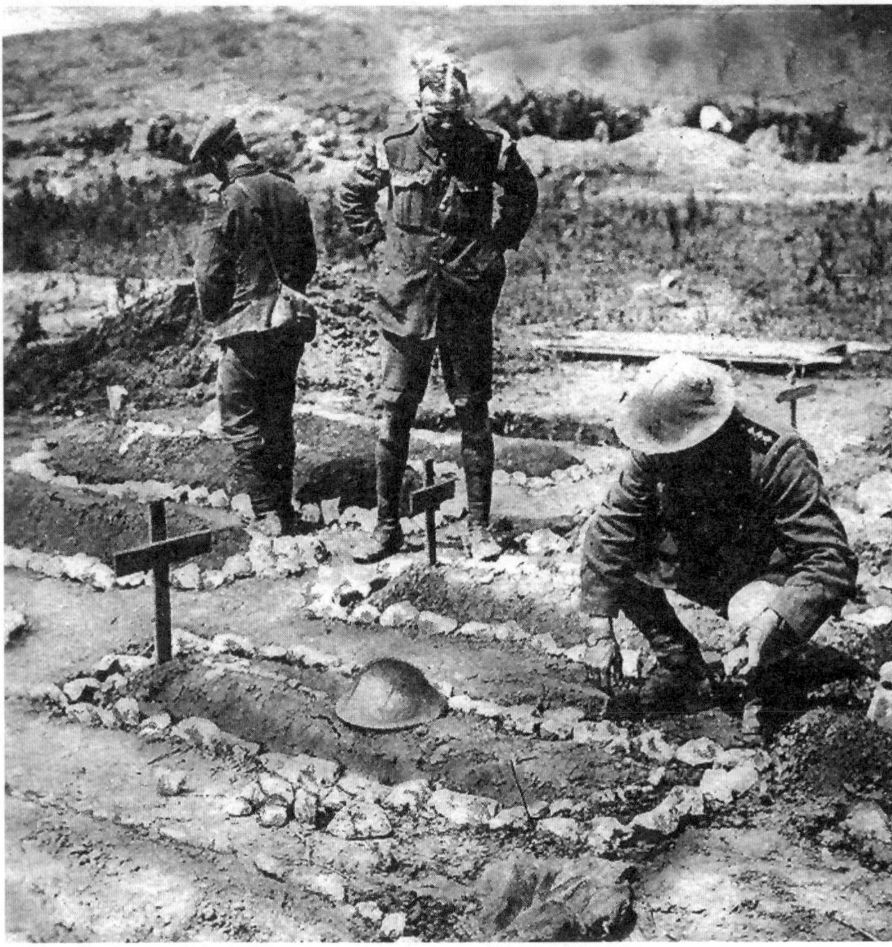

A British chaplain attends to the graves, in honour of those who fell

July, 1916, Longueval, Somme.